CONSCIENCE
& COURAGE

ANCHOR BOOKS
DOUBLEDAY

·

NEW YORK
LONDON
TORONTO
SYDNEY
AUCKLAND

·

CONSCIENCE & COURAGE

~~~~~~~

RESCUERS OF JEWS
·DURING·
THE HOLOCAUST

~~~~~~~

EVA FOGELMAN

AN ANCHOR BOOK

PUBLISHED BY DOUBLEDAY

a division of Bantam Doubleday Dell Publishing Group, Inc.
1540 Broadway, New York, New York 10036

ANCHOR BOOKS, DOUBLEDAY, and the portrayal of an anchor are
trademarks of Doubleday, a division of Bantam
Doubleday Dell Publishing Group, Inc.

Conscience & Courage was originally published in hardcover
by Anchor Books in 1994.

Book Design by Nancy Field

The Library of Congress has cataloged the Anchor hardcover
edition as follows:

Fogelman, Eva.
Conscience and courage : rescuers of Jews during the
Holocaust / Eva Fogelman. — 1st ed.
p.   cm.
Includes bibliographical references and index.
1. Righteous Gentiles in the Holocaust—
Biography.
2. World War, 1939–1945—Jews—Rescue.   I. Title.
D804.3F64   1994
940.53'18'0922—dc20
[B]   93-34021   CIP

ISBN 0-385-42028-5

First Anchor Paperback Edition: February 1995

10 9 8 7 6 5 4 3

To my loving father and mother
For their hope in life

CONTENTS

CONSCIENCE & COURAGE

INTRODUCTION

AT SIX IN THE MORNING on March 20, 1942, Simcha Fagelman was already hard at work in the village bakery of Illya, a Byelorussian town a hundred miles east of Vilna. On this snowy, freezing March morning, he counted himself lucky that he had a warm, indoor job baking bread. Even so, the twenty-six-year-old Jew could not shake a sense of dread. Like a low-lying fog, a sense of doom hovered in the streets, seeped into doorways, and crept into the back of his mind.

Simcha was not a man given to fearful imaginings. He was a soldier, or rather, with the invasion and occupation of this part of Poland by the Russians, an ex-soldier turned baker. Chased away from his Vilna home by Lithuanian locals on a Jew-killing rampage, he lived in this little Jewish village with his aunt and uncle and a crowd of other relatives. Life in Illya under the Russians was harsh, but not unbearable. Simcha got along well with his Russian supervisor and sometimes invited him home for dinner.

But within the past nine months, Illya's fragile peace had been shattered by the Germans. They had rolled their tanks into town and issued an endless stream of restrictions, directives, and orders aimed at Jews. Then one morning after the invasion, the Germans intercepted the Jews on their way to work and marched them all off to the village square. But the soldiers had missed Simcha. He had already left for work.

At 7 A.M. that day, members of the German Gestapo burst into the bakery searching for Jews who had slipped through their roundup. At that moment, Simcha happened to be screened from view by a large oven. "No Jews here," his Russian supervisor told the Germans confidently. The soldiers left.

Without a moment's hesitation, the Russian baker hustled Simcha up to the attic, locked him in, and hid the attic ladder. To divert attention and deter closer inspection, he then turned on the bread ovens full blast so that the place became unbearably hot.

Through cracks in the planks in that cramped, breathlessly hot attic, Simcha looked out into the square. He saw Illyan Jews, including his aunt, uncle, cousins, and friends, crowded into the square, stripped of their clothes, and shot. The whole exercise was completed in less than half a day. Nearly all of Illya's Jewish population—one thousand Jews—were murdered. Of the dozen or so family members who had lived in Illya, only Simcha remained.[1]

That night the Russian returned to his bakery and told Simcha what had happened. They both knew it was only a matter of time before the Nazis would find the attic hiding place. Simcha's best hope was to head to the forest and hide.

Simcha found another Jewish survivor, Shraga Salemyanski, son of the town's flour miller. Together they ran into the forest. They wandered in the woods without food or water for several days, not daring to ask for help lest they be shot or reported to the Nazis by some enterprising peasant hoping for a reward. Eventually they had no choice. They were starving.

Picking a farmhouse at random, they rapped on the window. A stranger's eyes peered out at them and then disappeared from view. Simcha and Shraga waited. Moments later, the face reappeared and a hand shoved a bottle of milk and a loaf of bread out the window. The fugitives grabbed the food and bolted.

Throughout that spring and summer, Simcha and Shraga lived on nerves, luck, and the charity of strangers. Their days were spent in the forest sprawled in a ditch they had dug for themselves and covered with leaves and moss. Their nights were spent scrounging for food. They survived on wild blueberries and walnuts. Every few days one of them ventured to knock on an isolated farmhouse door to beg for something to eat. They turned into seasoned scavengers. A bottle of milk and a half a loaf of bread supplied two or three days' worth of meals.

As they escaped northward, Shraga headed to the houses of two farm families he knew. These families, afraid their neighbors would see them and have them all arrested, shooed the men off their property. That night various family members trekked into the woods to bring the two men food, give them clean clothes, and carry off their dirty lice-infested clothes to be washed. Aware that the fugitives could not survive the freezing winter temperatures in the woods, the farmers arranged for the Jews to meet a Byelorussian partisan group. The two men joined this resistance group and spent the rest of the war waging guerrilla warfare against the Germans.

Simcha Fagelman owes his life to the courage of a Russian baker and the generosity of farmers who shared their own scarce food to help a fellow human being. Simcha never forgot them. Neither did I. Simcha Fagelman is my father.

This book is my tribute to those who risked their lives to save my father and thousands of other Jews. It has been a long time in coming, and the route has been somewhat circuitous, involving as it does my family's history and how I came to view it. My father and mother met after the war, and I was born in a displaced person's camp in Kassel, Germany. A few months later, the family immigrated to Israel, and Simcha Fagelman began life anew as Simcha Fogelman.

In my eyes, Simcha Fogelman was a heroic figure—a partisan fighter and a soldier in the Israeli army. I grew up fascinated by his wartime exploits, and I identified with his and our new homeland's fighting spirit and vitality. It was not until I was in my twenties that I saw him any differently.

At the time, I was in Boston studying family therapy, and an offhand comment by a teacher that my father was a Holocaust survivor led me to view him through a different prism. I saw myself in a whole new light—as a child of a survivor. I began reading about

Jewish young adults whose parents had survived Nazi persecution but who felt haunted by a past they had no part in creating. They felt isolated and alienated even from their Jewish peers. I wanted to bring these children of survivors together so that they would have a forum in which they could share their experiences and break through their sense of isolation. In 1976, I, together with my friend Bella Savran, a social worker whose parents were also saved from death by Polish peasants, formed a support group for children of Holocaust survivors.[2]

Not surprisingly, these group discussions left me with many questions about human behavior and motivation. I needed to know more. In 1979, I enrolled in a doctoral program in social and personality psychology at the Graduate Center of the City University of New York (CUNY). There I was fortunate to study with Stanley Milgram, whose landmark experiments led to his ground-breaking book *Obedience to Authority.* Dr. Milgram's work promulgated the idea that most people surrender personal responsibility for their actions if those actions are dictated by an authority figure. Milgram's was the first psychological explanation of how—and why—good, decent people could carry out horrendous deeds.

What caught my attention, however, were not those who obeyed authority, *but those who did not.* Why didn't they? I remembered my father's war stories. I once again saw the Russian baker and the farm families in Byelorussia who helped my father. What possessed these people? Why had they risked their lives for someone the authorities considered beneath contempt?

John Slawson, executive vice president emeritus of the American Jewish Committee and a social psychologist, was interested in some of these same questions. He wanted to explore altruism as the opposite of authoritarianism. Stephen P. Cohen, one of my professors at CUNY and a professional mentor, and I were also intrigued. We took on Slawson's project but gave the study a different slant; altruism, we felt, was a stable personality characteristic, but altruistic behaviors are jointly determined by the combination of personality and situational features. Opportunity to help, social support for such action, economic resources, nature of living quarters, and characteristics of the person in need of help are all factors which impeded or enhanced the proclivity to rescue. It was a social-psychological approach to understanding human behavior.

As project director, I wanted to explore what traits, if any, rescuers had in common. Were they adventurers with a penchant for living on the edge? Were they people who had an extraordinary capacity to tolerate risk? Were they social misfits indifferent to community pressure? But most important, whatever their individual characteristics, could their moral courage be taught? Could children learn not only to distinguish right from wrong but also to develop moral integrity to act on that distinction? These questions formed our basis of inquiry in Slawson's altruism study, or, as it came to be known, the Rescuer Project.

Conscience and Courage: Rescuers of Jews During the Holocaust grew out of in-depth interviews conducted for the Rescuer Project and my observations based on them. Over the course of the past ten years, I and staff volunteers have interviewed more than 300 rescuers in North America, Israel, and various European and Eastern European countries. I confirmed each rescuer's recollections by interviewing the Jews they saved or, when that was not possible, checking their story against archival material. Time has been of the essence. The events I wanted to investigate occurred nearly fifty years ago. Memories were fading, and the rescuers and those they protected were dying.

Tracking down rescuers proved to be more arduous than I had imagined. I started with the archives of Yad Vashem, Israel's national authority for the commemoration of the Holocaust. Initially, I found only some names in its files whose current whereabouts I could trace. I then placed newspaper and magazine advertisements, passed out questionnaires at Holocaust survivor gatherings, and wrote articles on the topic, hoping that rescuers would respond. My research encouraged survivors to search for their rescuers, and before long, I found myself invited to a number of joyful reunions. Serendipity provided still other names. A friend of mine, a German Holocaust survivor, was purchasing a typewriter ribbon in Manhattan and recognized the store owner's accent as German. In the course of their conversation, the store owner revealed he was a Jew who was saved by a German

Christian woman. That woman was now his wife. My friend passed her name on to me.

Most of those I spoke with were startled to be approached by someone researching rescuers. They had never thought of themselves in the heroic way that the word implies. They were, however, eager to help me in my research despite their reluctance to relive the trauma of those times. I often had to visit them several times before all my questions were answered. In Stefania Podgórska Burzminska's case, for instance, it took nearly seven years of interviewing before I got the complete story of her wartime exploits on tape. Sometimes a complete rescue story only emerged after talking to other people. I discovered, for example, that the boy Martha K. hid in her Berlin apartment for two years was the son of a Jewish man she fell in love with but was prevented from marrying by her family. He had married another woman, and the boy was their child.

No one knows for certain how many non-Jews risked their lives to save Jews during the Holocaust. There were nearly 700 million people in Nazi-occupied territories. Only a tiny fraction of them were involved in rescue activities. Moreover, rescue activity demanded utmost secrecy. Lives depended on it. Many rescuers were discovered and killed. Some sheltered a Jew for a night; others hid several people for years. Some made single, one-time gestures; still others were part of an anonymous network that searched for hiding places, papers, food coupons, and money for Jews. The parting words between some Jews and the Christians who saved them were: "Promise me that you will never tell anyone my name. Don't ever write to me. Good luck."

Most of the rescuers I interviewed were telling their stories for the first time; secrecy about wartime rescue activities was an old habit not easily broken. But even if they had been inclined to talk, the world was not always eager to listen. After liberation, people were anxious to forget the recent horror and get on with rebuilding their lives. In some areas which had fallen under Nazi control, locals were still rabidly hostile to Jews and other minorities. Survivors risked the lives of their rescuers if they openly acknowledged and thanked them. All in all, the wisest course was to say nothing.

The rescuers paid a terrible price for this silence. A vital part of their inner self was muffled, and it left some of them psychically wounded. Often the strong attachments they had formed with the people they had helped were abruptly severed; many never knew if their charges lived or died. They felt cut off and bereft.

Talking brought some of these emotions out and started a much-needed healing process. In the beginning, however, many rescuers did not understand how talking about past events could help. Many of these men and women were of a generation that was unfamiliar with the practices and benefits of sharing their feelings. In hundreds of interviews with rescuers, only a few had sought professional help in overcoming trauma caused by their wartime activities.

Not all Holocaust survivors were so supportive of my work. Since so few non-Jews had helped them, many survivors doubted the rescuers' altruistic motivations. Many worried that by highlighting the courageous acts of a relative handful of individuals I would obscure the essential fact that six million Jews were murdered. Two-thirds of the Jewish population of Eastern Europe was wiped out, and most people had done nothing to stop it.

That, however, is precisely the point of my interest. At a time of worldwide upheaval, when civilized norms were held in suspension, a few individuals held fast to their own standards. They were not saints. Nor were they particularly heroic or often all that outstanding. They were simply ordinary people doing what they felt had to be done at that time. With a few exceptions—such as the highly publicized rescue efforts of Swedish envoy Raoul Wallenberg, who saved more than 30,000 Hungarian Jews—they were people who were easily overlooked.

Conscience and Courage aims to correct this historical oversight. It tells their stories and, in doing so, undertakes to explain why these people became rescuers. When I started, many of the rescuers talked to me under the condition that their names remain anonymous. Many have since changed their minds. For those who have not, I have used only a first name and an initial. When necessary, I have also altered identifying details. In those instances in which I have rescuers' permission to tell their stories for my book, I use their full names, proud to give them, at last, the public recognition they so deserve.

Conscience and Courage traces the psychological making of a rescuer. I argue that the act of rescue for the men, women, and children who undertook it was not aberrant behavior caused by the heinous conditions of World War II. Nor did it stem from an unconscious yearning for death. Rather, as I view it, the act of rescue was an expression of the values and beliefs of the innermost core of a person. It is a core nurtured in childhood, which came to expression during the Holocaust in the act of rescue, and then continued in the postwar years. Saving Jews came from that inner core and became part of it. This rescuer self was and, over the years has continued to be, an integral part of their identity.

In the main, my book is based on my interviews and subsequent relationships with rescuers; but on occasion I use written accounts of well-known rescuers and, where possible, archival verifications. In Part I, I discuss the process of awareness and transformation that turns a bystander into a rescuer and the resulting emergence of a rescuer self. I describe how that self coped on a daily basis with the harrowing routine of rescue, and I show how, over time, relationships between rescuers and their charges developed and changed. In Part II, I discuss five distinct motivational types and demonstrate how motivations grew from an inner core of unshakable values and beliefs. I show how these values were developed in childhood and how patterns of parenting and gender differences contributed to the emergence of a rescuing self. Personality is only part of the story, since each rescue required a set of environmental circumstances that would permit the person to act on his or her beliefs. Finally, I talk about rescuers' painful postwar experiences and discuss how memorialization can both heal their pain and inspire others to undertake morally courageous actions.

The effort to bring rescuers' deeds to public attention have been spearheaded by Harold Schulweis. For more than a quarter of a century this Encino, California, rabbi has encouraged scholars to study rescuers and fought tirelessly for public recognition of their deeds.[3] In 1986, we joined forces and founded the Jewish Foundation for Christian Rescuers. The foundation, which is now part of the Anti-Defamation League, is devoted to finding rescuers, publicly honoring those who have officially been recognized, and tending to their medical, financial, or social needs. Through foundation conferences, rescuers have met one another and are reclaiming their past. They are now speaking out about their experiences, writing their memoirs, and lecturing on the need for tolerance for and acceptance of people who are different.

This ongoing contact with rescuers has enriched me immeasurably and has yielded insights into their postwar lives. I have become connected with many rescuers in a profound and indelible way. At the end of an interview, I would often be asked about my life. "Where were you born?" "Why are you doing this research?" "Do you have a family?" So we talked, and, over time, many became friends.

My interviewees were happy for me when I got my doctorate. They were thrilled when I got married. Jean Kowalyk Berger, a Ukrainian seamstress who hid seven Jews in her small farmhouse, sewed a negligee for my honeymoon. These friendships, along with those of my colleagues and family, kept me going when the subject matter threatened to depress and overwhelm me.

Beyond a personal mission to record individual instances of moral courage during an immoral time, my book has a broader goal. I want to give altruism back its good name. It is not a concept with which people are very comfortable or about which they know very much. Altruistically inclined people are seen as weaklings, as "do-gooders." Psychoanalysts dismiss the act of rescue as narcissism overlaid with rescue fantasies, or they assign it unconscious defenses such as the need for power or the need to be loved. Holocaust scholars relegate rescuers' deeds to a footnote.

But the moral courage of the rescuers and their actions deserve attention. They are as much a part of that era's history as the gas ovens at Auschwitz. My book is designed to fill this historical gap. I show rescuers as they really were—not mythic heroes, but ordinary men, women, and children. The fact that these good deeds were done by imperfect people in no way dilutes their lessons for today. Their stories of compassion and courage, their acts small and large, are exemplary even if the individuals sometimes are not.

People in the 1990s are hungry for role models. They are ready to hear the rescuers' stories and to learn from them. School and university Holocaust courses are inviting rescuers and survivors to bear witness before they die. Children of survivors and their offspring are eager to find out what happened to their parents and grandparents. Moreover, with the collapse of Communist regimes, rescuers are feeling freer to talk. Poles and Russians and the Jews they saved who immigrated to Israel are able to write each other once again, and even to visit each other. But this new freedom has an ominous side too, one which particularly demands that the full story be told. In Eastern Europe, in Russia in particular, there is a movement to rehabilitate war criminals and whitewash their pasts.

Jewish survivors and their families vow to remember and retell instances of Nazis' inhumanity so that such atrocities will never happen again. This book looks at those few who defied authority and put themselves at risk to act humanely. These are their stories. By unearthing them, recording them, and studying them, it is my hope that these acts of compassion, too, will never be forgotten and that they will be repeated again and again and again.

PART I
THE RESCUERS

"The universe exists on the merit of
the righteous among the nations of
the world, and they are privileged
to see the Divine Presence."

.

—The Babylonian Talmud
(Hullin 92a, Berakhot 17a)

· 1 ·

A STILL
SMALL VOICE

GERMAN INDUSTRIALIST Oskar Schindler was a woman-
izer, a manipulator, and a seasoned briber. Swedish envoy Raoul Wallenberg was a habitual liar and a shameless forger. Hungarian police
magistrate Lajos Mihalcsik was a criminal adviser. Henri Reyndeers
was an antisemite. Katrina W. was a tramp. Dutch social work student Marion van Binsbergen Pritchard became a murderer.

I could rattle off the names of dozens of other sneaks, thieves,
smugglers, hijackers, blackmailers, and killers. I interviewed scores of
them. They are individuals, families, networks, and even whole villages, who used their occupational skills and natural cunning to do
whatever was necessary to save Jewish lives during World War II.
They are people who, in many cases, defied the law and risked their
own lives for strangers. They are spiritual heirs to the *Lamed Vav*—the
thirty-six people of Jewish tradition whose sole task it is, in every
generation, unknown to themselves or others, to do good for their
fellow men. In Hebrew these non-Jews are called *Hasidei U'Mot
Ha'Olam*—"righteous among the nations of the world." They are
rescuers.

They are peasants, aristocrats, businessmen, clergy, nannies, doctors, social workers, diplomats, and blacksmiths. They are of no particular nationality, economic class, education level, sex, or age. They are of various temperaments and religious leanings and political persuasions. Some believed fervently in God; for others, the Holocaust confirmed their belief that God did not exist.

Singly and in groups, they saw a need, found an opportunity, and acted. When a stranger knocked on the door of her home in the French village of Le Chambon-sur-Lignon, Magda Trocmé's response was reflexive. This pastor's wife listened to a bedraggled stranger explain that she was in danger. She was a German Jew coming from northern France, and had no place to go. Could she come in? "Naturally, come in, come in," was Trocmé's unhesitating reply.[1] Most others were more guarded and careful. With reservations, Jopie D., a Dutch psychoanalyst, hired an eighteen-year-old Jewish girl as a maid. She warned her, however, that "should the Germans threaten me or my daughters I cannot guarantee my response."

Rescuers' actions, whether they were religious or not, extended beyond the deeds of the Good Samaritan parable in the Bible. In the parable a priest came along and, seeing a bloodied traveler, crossed the road to avoid him. Next came a Levite, who also saw the traveler and avoided him. But then came a Samaritan who saw the traveler and felt compassion. He bound up the man's wounds and carried him to an inn. As he left the next day, he left money for the stranger's care. While this biblical story encouraged some to get involved, rescuers were well aware that their decision to help was far more demanding and dangerous than caring for a wounded roadside stranger.

The German directives were clear and the punishment for defying them equally clear. A Pole caught selling bread to Jews outside the Warsaw ghetto, for example, was automatically sentenced to three months at hard labor. Jean Kowalyk, a nineteen-year-old who would later hide seven Jews in the small farmhouse where she and her mother lived, learned early on that the Germans meant what they said. When the Polish village of Zorotowyci was invaded by the Germans, all food became the property of the Third Reich. The penalty for raising cattle or chickens for home consumption was death. Jean's aunt was caught raising food to feed her nine children. She was arrested and sent to a concentration camp. Sixteen weeks later only her clothes came back home.

The Good Samaritan went on his way after a night; a rescuer could not. No one knew how long the war would last. In some cases, an offer to provide a safe haven for one night stretched into months and sometimes years of nerve-racking tension. The unsettling and terrifying conditions of war added more pressure to an already intense situation. Fear of discovery loomed over the rescuers' every action and haunted their every thought. Some of the rescuers' charges were difficult people who, under the best of circumstances, would have been hard to live with. They complained to their hosts and quarreled among themselves. Sometimes it was the rescuers who were unbearable. Underlying these tensions was the rescuers' awareness that they had voluntarily put themselves and their loved ones in grave danger. They sometimes wondered: Should they continue to place their children's lives in peril? Should they continue to serve their family meager rations so there was enough food for those in hiding? Should they continue to risk their lives when their children were dependent on them?

Rescuers constantly wrestled with these questions, and their answers shifted from moment to moment. Fear often was the deciding factor. Marion van Binsbergen Pritchard, who shot a Dutch Nazi policeman to protect the lives of a father and his three children whom she was hiding, conceded this was the case:

> There were times that the fear got the better of me and I did not do something I could have. I would rationalize . . . that I should not run a risk because what would happen to the three children I was responsible for, if something should happen to me, but I knew when I was rationalizing.[2]

The strain of such a life was nearly unbearable. Some could handle it just so long. Jopie D., who, frightened and hungry near war's end, could harbor her young maid no longer. She told the maid to get on her bicycle and go to her relatives in eastern Holland. Both knew the ride was dangerous. It meant cycling unprotected through territory occupied by weary and desperate German soldiers. Her young charge survived, but Jopie's failure of nerve and purpose occupies her thoughts to this day.

Sometimes, as was the case with Danish rescuer Svend Aage Holm-Sorensen, the strain shows later. "It was almost impossible for me to talk about that time without shaking all over or without getting such a big lump in my throat that I was unable to speak," said this leader of the Danish rescue network when asked why he did not write about his exploits.

These men, women, and children who risked their lives to save others were flesh-and-blood human beings with strengths and faults. Yet they saw people who were different from them and responded, not to these differences, but to their similarities. While most people saw Jews as pariahs, rescuers saw them as human beings. This humanitarian response sprang from a core of firmly held inner values. These values, which included an acceptance of people who were different, were unwavering and immutable. And central to these beliefs was the conviction that what an individual did, or failed to do, mattered. They recognized that for many Jews the choice made by a bystander could mean life or death.

Most rescuers are still bewildered that anyone would make a fuss over what they did. Miep Gies, known in Anne Frank's diary as Miep van Santen, says, "I am not a hero." Yet this warm, intelligent woman risked her life repeatedly to help the Franks when they were in hiding. "I stand at the end of the long, long line of good Dutch people who did what I did or more—much more—during those dark and terrible times years ago, but always like yesterday in the hearts of those of us who bear witness. . . . I have never wanted special attention. I was only willing to do what was asked of me and what seemed necessary at the time."[3]

In different places and in different accents, I heard these same sentiments time and again. It is what a seventeen-year-old Polish girl who hid and fed thirteen Jews in her apartment said. It is what a man who underwent financial ruin and the death of his own son felt. And it is echoed in the sentence "Someone came who needed help, we did not think about the risk" uttered by a Danish fisherman who ferried a boatful of Jews to safety.

Theirs are the quiet voices of conscience and courage. I think of them as the "still small voice" that the biblical prophet Elijah heard as the voice of the Lord.[4] It is the voice of Lajos Mihalcsik, a Hungarian police magistrate, fining Jews for minor infractions and then telephoning them secretly the next day with suggestions of how to get false identification papers or a hiding place. It is the voice of a German girl performing a small act of rebellion by substituting the words *"Drei Liter"* (three liters) for *"Heil Hitler,"* the required salute. Failure to give it was punishable. Perhaps the true measure of rescuers' distinctive qualities was how their behavior and attitude differed from the millions of others in Nazi-occupied countries. In his documentary *Shoah,* Claude Lanzmann interviewed a farmer whose fields were near the Treblinka death camp. Through a translator, Lanzmann and the farmer had the following exchange:

> Does he remember the first convoy of Jews from Warsaw on July 22, 1942?
>
> He recalls the first convoy very well, and when all those Jews were brought here, people wondered, "What's to be done with them?" Clearly, they'd be killed, but no one yet knew how. When people began to understand what was happening, they were appalled, and they commented privately that since the world began, no one had ever murdered so many people that way.
>
> While all this was happening before their eyes, normal life went on? They worked their fields?
>
> Well, he says, it's this way: if I cut my finger, it doesn't hurt him. They knew about the Jews: the convoys came in here and then went to the camp, and the people vanished.[5]

To me this bystander represents the millions of people who looked on indifferently, and in many instances even approvingly, as Hitler systematically murdered six million Jews. However, my rational side knows that in most situations there was little that an individual could have done to stop the massive killings. German rifles permitted no interference. In the cities, Nazi roundups of the Jews for deportation were well organized and thorough. Nazi informers were everywhere and eager to report Jews in hiding to the authorities. In the country, each Jewish community was isolated and unarmed. Jews were terrified by rumors of slaughter, but had no real information. They were easy prey. With lightning speed, the *Einsatzgruppen,* heavily armed killing units drawn from the SS, Waffen SS, Gestapo, State Police, and other groups, moved from town to town from the Baltic to the Black Sea, murdering Jews. In each town, the whole action was often over in a matter of hours. Farmers had no choice but to go on plowing their fields.

Only a handful of individuals managed to find ways to help. At times, the jobs they held determined the kind of help they were able to offer. During a Nazi rampage, a Bulgarian baker was able to hide nine Jews in his oven. In Poland, Jews fleeing the murderous destruction of the Lvov ghetto found refuge in the sewers where their two rescuers worked.

The bigger the job, or business, the more people who could be protected. German factory owner Oskar Schindler sheltered 1,200 Jews by recruiting them as workers and then insisting to Nazi authorities that they were essential industrial workers critical to the German war effort. Raoul Wallenberg used his diplomatic post to save thousands of Hungarian Jews from deportation by forging Swedish passports and then arguing with the authorities that the owners of these passports were protected citizens of his neutral country. It was an arrangement made in desperation and carried out in total seriousness. It worked. Even so, there was a touch of comedy in the whole enterprise. One Jew whom Wallenberg rescued recalled that it seemed "so strange, this country of super-Aryans—the Swedes—taking us under their wing. Often, when an Orthodox Jew went by, in his hat, beard, and sidelocks, we'd say: 'Look, there goes another Swede.' "[6]

While some rescuers' jobs provided the means to help Jews, their personalities shaped the whole enterprise and determined how successful they were. Schindler was a notorious carouser and bon vivant, all of which he used to good advantage. Drinking with Nazi officials kept him well informed and bribing them with black-market brandy and cigarettes ensured their cooperation. Wallenberg used his considerable administrative talent to recruit a network of 400 people to help him prevent the deportation of a quarter of a million Hungarian Jews. On one occasion, Wallenberg and his associates freed a group of Jewish deportees by gambling that the Nazi officer in Budapest would not be able to read Hungarian. They produced an assortment of official-looking, but irrelevant, documents—like driver's licenses and tax receipts—which Wallenberg passed off as evidence to a German officer as identity papers and proof of their protected status.[7]

Heroics came at a price. Danish war resister Harry LaFontaine and the Jews he was ferrying to Sweden were captured by the Nazis. The Jews were sent off to a concentration camp, but LaFontaine was taken to Gestapo headquarters for questioning. "The Gestapo figured that I might have something to tell them," recalled LaFontaine. "They put my hand between two bars and they broke all five bones. From then on all they had to do was pinch it and I would tell them anything." (LaFontaine survived the war and went on to become a special-effects expert for the film industry, working on James Bond movies, among others.)

When I began thinking about the rescuers and altruistic behavior, there was very little psychological literature that could answer my questions. The psychological community's response to the atrocities of World War II was to try to examine those factors that permitted evil to blossom. Two questions occupied everyone's thoughts: How could these atrocities have occurred? Could it happen in the United States? John Slawson of the American Jewish Committee urged a group of social scientists who had fled Nazi Germany in the thirties to study these questions. These scientists attempted to isolate those elements in personality and upbringing that predispose people toward hostile reactions to racial and religious groups. The result was the landmark study *The Authoritarian Personality*. This study found a close correlation between a number of deep-rooted personality traits

—such as lack of independence, submission to authority, rigid moralistic reactions, and overt prejudice—and a hierarchical, authoritarian, parent-child relationship.

Psychology is a field which typically studies the normal behavior of the majority. Aberrations are largely ignored. The scientific community's interest in Stanley Milgram's experiments, for example, centered on how most subjects obeyed authority; there was scant interest in those who refused.

Milgram's obedience-to-authority paradigms, for example, were designed to see under what conditions ordinarily decent people would obey a malevolent authority. In his experiments, subjects were told they were taking part in a study to understand the effect of punishment on learning. They were to be the "teacher" and attempt to teach the "learner" a string of nonsense words. If the learner made a mistake, the teacher administered a somewhat painful electric shock. The intensity of the shock increased with each mistake. The learner in all cases was an actor. There were no shocks, but Milgram wanted to explore the lengths people would go to carry out orders from an authority figure—in this case a scientist clad in a white coat. Milgram found that the majority of his subjects administered severe shocks to learners—some even forcing hands onto the metal shock plate even after being told that these learners had a heart condition. The experiments showed that ordinary people simply doing their jobs, without any particular hostility on their part, can become agents in a terrible destructive process.

Rescuers, like Milgram's subjects who refused to follow the experimenter's instructions, were not part of the norm. They were an oddity and, for a long time, were ignored. Researchers were not even sure what to call these aberrant people. "Righteous Gentiles" lacked the necessary academic objectivity. "Christian rescuers" made the necessary distinction between Jewish and Christian rescuers, but failed to take into account rescuers from other religious groups. Tina Strobos, a Dutch psychiatrist who saved more than a hundred Jews in Amsterdam, remained a steadfast atheist and grows prickly when called a "Christian" rescuer. Most researchers, myself included, call them non-Jewish rescuers.

Other factors also contributed to the rescuers' invisibility. In the wake of the Allied victory, world attention was focused on military exploits and political concerns; the rescuers were forgotten. "Nobody, I mean, *nobody* wanted to hear about what happened in the concentration camps," recalled Svend Aage Holm-Sorensen, a Danish rescuer whose efforts landed him in one of the concentration camps. "The bookstores were filled with books about [military] heroes and saboteurs, living and dead, written by professional writers." A war-weary public was anxious to return to civilian life and busied itself with trying to regain a sense of normalcy. The initial horror and revulsion at the discovery of the concentration camps gave way to an even greater eagerness to forget their existence.

Sixteen years later, the public was jolted into hearing about crimes against humanity. The 1961 war trial of Adolf Eichmann, chief logistician for the Nazis' plan to exterminate the Jews, focused public attention on the concentration camps and brought the first awareness of individual rescuing efforts. At the trial, the written testimony of a German construction engineer named Hermann Graebe was read to the court. While working on assignments for the German railroad, Graebe deliberately recruited Jewish labor for his projects and, using all the authority of his position as chief construction engineer, fiercely protected them from Nazi murder squads. Thanks to his extraordinary effort, the lives of more than 300 Jews in the Ukraine, Poland, and Germany were protected.

Although Graebe was not present at the trial, his words about the mass murders he had witnessed in Rovno echoed loudly in the courtroom. The killing of 800 to 1,000 men, women, and children had so revolted him, he wrote, that he vowed to do what he could to prevent further Jewish deaths.

Harold Schulweis, a young congregational rabbi in Northern California, heard about the testimony of Hermann Graebe at the Eichmann trial and found solace in it. He saw the German engineer's acts as a glimmer of hope in an otherwise bleak portrayal of man. In 1962, Schulweis made a strong plea to acknowledge the moral heroism of the rescuers:

Wisdom, faith, truth urge our search to know, record and hallow
these acts of the righteous. Which code of ethics argues that evil
be allowed to eclipse the good? Which perverse logic holds that
we obliterate the memory of man's nobility so as to preserve the
memory of his degeneracy? In unearthing the crimes of villainy,
the virtues of humanity must not be buried.[8]

Schulweis's eloquent plea shattered the silence that had surrounded
the rescuers as well as the world's reluctance to recognize their deeds.
At the same time Israel's Yad Vashem Holocaust Martyrs and Heroes
Memorial Authority was reminded of its mission to recognize non-
Jews who risked their lives to save Jews.[9] Yad Vashem was founded to
correct what Prime Minister David Ben-Gurion feared was historical
ignorance on the part of the Israeli generation born after the Holocaust. In 1953 the Commission of Martyrs and Heroes Remembrance
Law was passed to recognize individuals worthy of the title "Righteous Among the Nations of the World." This law merely mentioned
"the high-minded Gentiles who risked their lives to save Jews," without defining who they were.[10] However, it was not until 1963, two
years after the Eichmann trial, that the museum began to fulfill its
mandate to honor non-Jewish rescuers.[11]

The delay was understandable. No one wanted to dwell on those
dark times. Those who did look back tended to see the war years in
stark, black-and-white terms: ally or enemy; persecutor or victim.
Like an old-fashioned photograph of stiffly posed figures, the world's
memory froze people in these rigid, absolutist positions, which was
reinforced by military chroniclers' and historians' accounts of the war.

Yad Vashem changed that notion by defining a different kind of
war hero: rescuers. Yad Vashem defined who they were and how the
State of Israel would recognize them. The ceremony honoring them is
a public and solemn occasion. A carob tree is planted along the
Avenue of the Righteous, an avenue that leads up to the museum
itself, and a plaque bearing the rescuer's name and nationality marks
the tree. The story of the rescuer's deed is recounted at the ceremony
and filed in the museum's archives. Israeli officials then present the
rescuer, or in some cases an entire rescuing group, with a medal and a

certificate. The medal bears a Talmudic inscription: "Whoever saves a single soul, it is as if he had saved the whole world." The inscription places the rescuer's act in the important context it deserves. The Talmudic image is that of a global scale, representing the idea that all deeds, good and wicked, are in exact balance. The very next act of any person can tip the scale in either direction. In the rescuers' case, their altruistic deed made a critical difference. Goodness won.

Yad Vashem has honored more than 11,000 rescuers. The criteria used by its awards commission to screen candidates are stringent and controversial. Only non-Jews are eligible. Jews who saved Jews are not recognized by Yad Vashem or anywhere else. To be considered for the honor, a person's deed must be above and beyond the simple offer of a helping hand. The good farmers who gave a bottle of milk and a loaf of bread to my father saved his life, but by Yad Vashem's standards, theirs was an ordinary act of charity.

Yad Vashem's recognition commission also screens out those who saved Jews for personal gain. These include people who were anxious to convert their charges to Christianity, people who wanted to adopt a child, and people who were paid or were promised payment in the future.[12] Candidates must be nominated by the person or persons they rescued, or their candidacy must be supported by other documents or witnesses. Each submission must clearly show that the nominee did not participate in Nazi activities or engage in a rescue effort as a last-minute attempt to fashion a favorable end to their war persona.

My definition of a rescuer generally follows Yad Vashem's guidelines, although I do not classify anybody until after I have talked to the rescuer and, where possible, to the person or people he or she rescued. Cases are not always clear-cut, as Israel's Supreme Court Justice Moshe Bejski, a former Schindler worker and now head of Yad Vashem's Commission on Righteous Among the Nations of the World, is the first to admit: "It is the spirit of the law rather than the word of the law that makes a difference in whether one is deemed a Righteous Among the Nations."

Take the case of the two sewer workers, Leopold Socha and Stefak Wróblweski. Originally, they agreed to help twenty-one Lvov

Jews for money. Six days a week for thirteen months the workers came to the dank, dark hideout to visit their charges. They brought food, news, and Sabbath candles. Every Friday, the workers took out the dirty laundry and every Monday they brought it back freshly washed and ironed by their wives.

But then the Jews ran out of money. Among themselves they decided that the fair thing was to pool what resources they had left and save the person who had contributed the most money. The sewer workers had other ideas: "As long as you are under our jurisdiction and we are responsible for you, you are equal," Socha told them. "Either you all survive, or nobody."

Out of the original twenty-one Jews, ten survived. They explained the circumstances of their miraculous survival to the commission at Yad Vashem, and the commission bestowed the title of Righteous Among the Nations of the World on the two sewer workers and their wives.

Yad Vashem judges have given themselves a nearly superhuman job. They must look beyond the superficial circumstances and see into rescuers' hearts and minds.

On the face of it, Hungarian army officer Barna Kiss would not be high on anyone's list for honors. Kiss was the army officer in charge of a forced-labor battalion that marched from Budapest to the Russian border. These late-war forced marches of concentration camp inmates were so notorious for their brutality that they were called "death marches." Prisoners, half starved and barely able to shuffle their feet, were bludgeoned and bullied into moving along. Those who could not keep up were shot or left beside the road to die. Very few Jews survived these death marches. Barna Kiss's Jewish battalion was different. When his marchers looked as if they were about to pass out, Kiss gave them water. When they stumbled and fell, he helped them walk. Thanks to his efforts 214 Jews—an extraordinary number considering the length of the march and the condition of the prisoners—survived. He was honored at Yad Vashem.

Inevitably, when assessing such subjective matters as intent and motivation, mistakes are made. Survivors point angrily to awards that are undeserved. In one instance, a German family was honored for rescuing a Jewish woman by hiring her as a nanny for their son. At the urging of the son and on the testimony of the nanny and her daughter, the German father and mother were honored. As it turned out, the father was a Nazi. When he and his wife hired the nanny, they did not know she was Jewish. It was only after the war that they learned she was Jewish.

However, beside the thousands who deserve Yad Vashem's honors but won't ever be recognized, these errors seem small. Miep Gies estimated that she was one of 20,000 Dutch men and women who helped shelter Jews. Some acted alone; others were part of an organized network effort whose work and safety depended on secrecy and anonymity. These nameless forgers, businessmen, and homeowners provided false identity papers, food coupons, money, and shelter. Caution dictated that people should know as little as possible about one another. Families who opened their homes to people the resistance sent avoided introductions. Over a three- or four-year period, Jews might stay in as many as forty different places. Some of these unknown rescuers were caught and killed. No tree marks their heroism.

Purposeful anonymity, combined with the rescuers' reluctance to discuss their wartime activities, wrapped them in a cloak of invisibility that initially made them difficult to find. I discovered just how difficult when, in the summer of 1981, I flew to Israel to attend a worldwide gathering of 10,000 Holocaust survivors and their children. I thought that through the survivors I should find the names of some rescuers. Amid tearful first reunions of survivors and those from their hometown, ghetto, or concentration camp, I handed out questionnaires. I did not return home with hundreds of names. For survivors, it was too emotional a time to be bothered with a researcher's questions. After the conference was over, a few did fill out my questionnaire and send it on to me.

Years later, I realized why a gathering of Holocaust survivors is not the best place to look for rescuers. Survivors have their own hierarchy of suffering, and they feel that those who survived by hiding did not undergo the same degradation and humiliation as those who survived the camps. The stench of the death camps still hovers over them; the camp numbers tattooed on their arms mark them as walking reminders of a nightmare no one wants to remember. Israelis referred to the Holocaust victims as *sabonim,* or soaps—a callous allusion to the eventual fate of those who were gassed. Thus concentration camp survivors were doubly degraded. Their gatherings are devoted to mending their psyches and boosting their trampled sense of self.

Academics and health professionals also defined a Holocaust survivor as someone who survived concentration camps and/or ghettos. It is only within the last few years that historians and psychologists have acknowledged an array of experiences in surviving Nazi persecution: hiding, escaping, disguising oneself as an Aryan, fighting in a resistance unit. My research was among the early attempts to broaden the definition of a survivor.

Nevertheless, such an inauspicious beginning did yield the name of a person who would become my first rescuer interview. Ilse Lowenberg, a German survivor, wrote that her life was saved by a German seamstress who hid her in her studio apartment in Berlin. Lowenberg, an Orthodox Jew, described her rescuer as a "beloved sister." Each year, she traveled from her home in Queens, New York, to New Jersey, and they celebrated Christmas together.

On a cold December day, I took a bus to Somerville, New Jersey, to interview this rescuer, Elizabeth Bornstein. I was eager and thought I was prepared. I had read memoirs, consulted with historians, reviewed research on altruistic behavior and moral development. Still I was not ready for this unprepossessing woman whose bold actions had saved the life of her Jewish husband as well as that of her Queens friend. Elizabeth Bornstein was also somewhat surprised. She had been concerned that her memory would fail her and that she would not have much to tell me. She made notes of names, dates, and times. But her memory did not fail her. Wartime terror, the fear of discovery, the pressures of daily life came back to her in a rush. It was as if it had happened yesterday. Six hours later, she still had more to tell me.

The next time I saw her was at a ceremony at the Israeli consulate in New York honoring her as one of the Righteous Among the Nations of the World. My interviews had started the public recognition process.

Whenever possible, I encouraged survivors to write a testimony so their rescuer might be recognized by Yad Vashem, if only to pay public tribute to a courageous individual and fill in a historical gap. For many rescuers the recognition process healed psychic war wounds. Some rescuers, who never knew if their charges lived after they left their care, discovered that there was a happy ending to the story they helped to write. They reunited with the people they had saved for the first time since the war. For others, the testimony validated and integrated a part of their selves that they had stifled long ago.

It was not always easy to convince survivors to write a Yad Vashem testimony. They had memories of their own behavior they considered shameful and wanted at all costs to conceal it from their loved ones. For example, when Rivkah H. was in hiding in Francesca M.'s farmhouse, she had an affair with another man who was also in hiding with them. At the time, she was a married woman with a five-year-old son. After the war, she left her husband and immigrated to Palestine with her son and her lover. They married and had another child. Rivkah H. ordered her son never to tell anyone, including his half–brother, he had a different father. Rivkah H. lived in terror that her past life would be revealed. Finally acceding to pressure to honor Francesca M.'s courage and sacrifice, she wrote her testimony. Forty years later at the Yad Vashem ceremony, Francesca M. was reunited at last with those she had risked her life to save.

In 1985 my search for rescuers was given a boost. An Israeli television show reported on the dire living conditions of some of the rescuers living in Israel. The television camera showed rescuers, many of whom had married their charges and immigrated to Israel, living in poverty. Many were widowed and isolated. Neighbors snubbed them for not being Jewish, and they were not eligible for a full Israeli pension for the same reason. The show caused an uproar. There was an immediate outpouring of concern. The Israeli Parliament met in special session to investigate the situation and Yad Vashem's Department of the Righteous Among Nations arranged for social services and special events. A search to identify and help rescuers in Israel began.

A year later, Harold Schulweis founded the Foundation to Sustain Righteous Christians, later renamed the Jewish Foundation for Christian Rescuers, and I became its director. The organization's mission is, in Schulweis's term, *hakarat hatov,* recognition of goodness. The aim is to find rescuers, provide financial and social support when necessary, and publicly acknowledge their moral courage. Thanks to the foundation, more than 1,200 rescuers in eighteen different countries are currently receiving financial, medical, and social service help.

With the publicity generated by the Israeli television show, as well as by articles on rescuers, they were no longer invisible. Where once I had trouble finding their names, I now had so many leads I could not follow them all. A number of volunteers from the foundation helped me with my interviews, and also helped survivors write their testimony. Later, with the opening up of Eastern Europe and the breakup of the Soviet Union, I was inundated with names of still more rescuers.

As fascinating as the rescuers' stories were, I also noticed that they had a disquieting effect on many listeners. Rescuers' altruistic behavior throws people off balance by calling into question their own vision of themselves as good people. As they listen, they cannot help but wonder: What would I have done? Would I have had the courage to defy authority? Would I have risked my life? My family's lives?

General audiences listened, they wondered, and they doubted their own capacity for selfless action. This discomfort, in turn, led to a disbelief that anyone could engage in altruistic behavior. People looked for ulterior motives. This was especially evident in responses received from young people who are nurtured in large measure by electronic media. "What's the angle?" they want to know. Many young people simply do not believe that there were then, or are today, individuals who do not put their own concerns first.

In the spring of 1986, a Polish rescuer, the Jews she saved, and I led a workshop on rescuers at the Diaspora Museum in Tel Aviv. The rescued and the rescuer shared memories of that rescue as well as its aftermath. The Israelis who attended the workshop had never met a rescuer. They were incredulous. They grilled the survivors about the rescuer's motivation. Were the survivors sure that their rescuer did not expect a payoff when the war was over? Did she acquire their possessions when they were in hiding? They were openly disbelieving that anyone would respond from a deeply felt sense of morality or personal integrity.

Jews whose families were dispossessed of their homes, rounded up, and then murdered without so much as a murmur of protest simply did not believe in selfless acts. They figured Katrina W., who distracted a German border guard by having sex with him so a Jewish family could slip across the Swiss border to safety, must have been paid. They dismissed Henri Reyndeers's conversion from antisemite to Belgian network rescuer as too improbable to be believed.[13]

Yet even in those dark times, there were a few morally courageous individuals who felt that what they did and how they behaved mattered. Their motive was altruistic. They saw a need and wanted to help. Ona Simaite ate only potatoes and cabbage in order to have food to give to Jews. Elizabeth Heims, a German Quaker from Munich, died in a concentration camp trying to protect the Jewish orphans she was hiding. The citizens of a dozen villages in the south-central French regions of Vivarais-Lignon and the Cévennes conspired to hide approximately 5,000 Jewish children and hundreds of families from the Nazis. In Assisi, Italy, Franciscan monks cared for 200 Jewish fugitives.

An incident in Wankheim, Germany, summarized the spirit of many of the rescuers. It was known around those parts that Parson Richard Goelz offered sanctuary to enemies of the Third Reich. One day Nazis burst into his parsonage searching for the fugitive mayor of Leipzig. They demanded to know if the parson's latest visitor was their man. Replied the parson: "It would have been a great honor, but it is not he."

· 2 ·

THE WAR AGAINST
THE JEWS

MANY RESCUERS FOUND it impossible to explain to any-
one who did not live through those times why they acted as they did.
In war, there were no rules. The familiar seemed strange, and the
bizarre seemed normal. In retrospect, rescuers' behavior, in some instances, was not understandable even to them. How could they have
endangered their families? How could they have done what they did
or said what they said? History has taken little note of them, and the
little that has been written about them gives no insight into their
psychology or motivations. Historians are content to leave the answers
to such matters to others. Their interest lies in explaining the context
in which rescuers' actions took place.[1] Nevertheless, a historical over-
view of this particular period provides the necessary background for a
true appreciation of the deeds of the rescuers. While it may be difficult—perhaps impossible—for those who were not present at these
events to understand their true nature, it is useful nonetheless to
develop some historic background in order to gain a perspective on
the events and on the period.

In 1932, the prospects of most German workers were decidedly
grim. The small financial and psychological improvement Germany

achieved after World War I was wiped out by a world economic depression. German industries were reeling and sinking into debt. Jobs were scarce. Laid-off factory workers milled about in the streets and jammed the beer halls.

In the midst of this financially troubled time, Adolf Hitler and his National Socialist German Workers' Party rose to power. To the unemployed, Hitler offered jobs in his storm trooper (SA) corps and the vision of full employment in the factories and businesses. To industrialists and businessmen, he and his party offered a refuge from the growing power of the Communist Party. To those still stinging from World War I's humiliating defeat and the terms of the surrender, he promised to restore Germany to its status as a world power and to make it the most powerful nation on earth. To this dizzying vision of Aryan grandeur, Hitler added one more element: an abiding hatred of Jews.

Hitler's rabid antisemitism was not a sideshow designed to attract believers and distract others from the main event—his insatiable desire for power and world dominance. On the contrary, racism was at the heart of Nazi ideology. The supremacy of the Aryan race went hand in hand with the restoration of Germany to world power. Hitler railed against the Jews. To him, they were vile, subhuman, filth, vermin, "a cancer on the body of the nation." He called on the populace to wage war against them.[2]

Prewar Germany listened. In January 1933, Hitler was appointed Chancellor of Germany. He then moved quickly to consolidate his power and stifle any opposition. Using the pretense that he was protecting the nation from an imminent Communist menace, Hitler rammed through a series of emergency decrees. These decrees suspended all fundamental freedoms of speech, press, and assembly and gave the government the power to search without a warrant and generally take whatever measures were needed to restore public security.

Strong-armed squads of brown-shirted storm troopers roamed the streets with official impunity. They viciously beat Jews grabbed at random off the streets, claiming that they were rounding up "subversive elements." Those who initially fell into this category were not only Jews, but also political opponents (Communists and Social Democrats) and anyone—journalists, writers, dissenting clergy—protesting the new regime. By March 1933, a scant two months after Hitler's appointment as Chancellor, the prisons could no longer hold the thousands arrested for "preventive" safety measures. That same month the first concentration camp at Dachau, a town not far from Munich, was set up. Others followed quickly. By the summer of 1933, there were ten or more camps and detention centers housing over 25,000 people.[3]

Religious institutions, business groups, and social organizations scrambled to curry favor with the new regime. Early on, the Vatican, eager to protect its priests and preserve its religious foothold in Germany, recognized the new National Socialist state. On July 8, 1933, the Vatican signed a concordat with Nazi Germany, which gave the new regime respectability and legitimacy. The German Federation of Judges pledged their allegiance. It was a sad omen of what would be played out again and again throughout the war and across the continent: a general institutional failure to repudiate Hitler's racist policies. The decision of whether to agree to those policies or to defy them was left to the individual. On the one hand lay authority, safety, and institutional neutrality, if not approval. On the other hand lay human decency. Each person made his or her choice. It was a personal, and sometimes lonesome, decision.

Luitgard Wundheiler remembered how her father, a judge in Marburg, Germany, weighed the matter. In 1936, her father had just received the letter sent to all German civil servants asking him to join the Nazi Party by signing a loyalty oath. He discussed it with his wife and then called the fourteen-year-old Wundheiler into his study. He gave her the letter to read and asked her if she thought he should sign. To her, his choice was clear: he should not sign it because to do so would be a lie and he never lied. Fifty-seven years later, Wundheiler still remembered the judicial clarity with which her father presented exactly what was at stake:

> Before you say yes or no so clearly and so spontaneously, I also want you to know what the possible consequences are. I don't

know what the consequences will be definitely, but there will be some consequences. Under the best of circumstances, I will lose my job. Under the worst of circumstances, you will never see me again in your whole life because they will do away with me. There are a number of possibilities in between. Maybe they will put me in a concentration camp and sometime later release me, but there will be some consequences, and I want you to know that.

As it happened, her father, who was stubbornly honest and passionately committed to justice, refused to join the Nazi Party. He was summarily dismissed from the judiciary but managed to land a job as a court messenger. For the remaining years of Nazi rule, he and his family existed barely above the poverty level.

For most Germans the choice between personal beliefs and national policies actually came earlier. In April 1933, the Nazis called for a boycott of Jewish businesses. It was the first instance of state-sponsored antisemitism, an organized and official attempt to stamp Jews as "other." Guards stood outside stores and doctors' and lawyers' offices owned by Jews to intimidate callers. This was a key moment. Would it work? Would Germans refuse to be bullied into singling out their neighbors and friends?

A few individuals defied the boycott, but most stayed away. Significantly, "the universities were silent, the courts were silent; the President of the Reich, who had taken the oath on the Constitution, was silent," Leo Baeck, Berlin's preeminent leader of the liberal Jewish community, wrote. To Rabbi Baeck, this was "the day of the greatest cowardice. Without that cowardice, all that followed would not have happened."[4]

In very short order what followed were a series of laws that increasingly isolated Jews and circumscribed their rights. Jews were kicked out of the civil service and barred from practicing law. They were thrown out of the universities and secular schools. They were forced to sell their businesses. Finally, on September 15, 1935, the notorious Nuremberg Laws were passed. The Nuremberg Laws, named after the city where the National Socialist Party had its convention that year, translated Nazi racial ideology into political reality. Jews were defined as anyone who had at least one Jewish grandparent. A Jew who had converted to Christianity, or children of mixed marriages, who were called *Mischlinge,* were also included. All were stripped of their citizenship. Marriage and extramarital relations between Germans and Jews were forbidden and made punishable by imprisonment.[5] What had begun as a small action, a boycott, to pry open a crack between German Jews and the rest of the citizenry, was now a yawning chasm. People crossed that chasm at their peril.

Punishment for defying these racist laws was immediate. There was no warning, no appeal, no second chance. A teacher who was reported to be kind to a Jewish student lost his job. A storekeeper acting as a front for a Jewish owner was arrested. Anyone could be a target of police action, not just political dissidents. Those not following the Nazi Party line were declared insane by psychiatrists friendly to the Third Reich and sent to concentration camps.

Concentration camps struck terror into the heart of the civilian population. Even before the establishment of the death camps and the gas chambers, vast numbers of people died or were killed in these camps. Camp inmates succumbed to exhaustion or illness as a result of malnutrition, backbreaking labor, and sadistic guards. Some were shot while supposedly attempting to escape.

Word got around fast. In Berlin, Elizabeth Bornstein, a Protestant seamstress, was frantic to win the freedom of her Jewish husband, who had been sent to the Buchenwald concentration camp. In desperation she wrote a personal letter to Hermann Göring, the Interior Minister of Prussia and later the chief of the air force. She based her slim hope on the fact that Göring also had a five-year-old daughter and her family plight might touch him. To her amazement, her letter was answered. Bornstein was told to bring proof that her parents were Aryan and her daughter was baptized.

In fact, her daughter had not been baptized. She had not bothered because she felt her pastor would have refused to baptize a baby with a Jewish last name. Now she had no choice. Fearful her pastor might reject her request and report her to the authorities, she approached him nervously and told him her story. The pastor understood the situation immediately. He had just been released from a concentration camp and knew its horrors firsthand. "Come to church on Sunday, and after church I will baptize the girl," he told her.

Nine months after he was arrested, Elizabeth Bornstein's husband was released from Buchenwald. He was ill with typhus and limped on a smashed leg. But for the moment at least, he and his wife were safe.

From the beginning, Hitler's totalitarian aims and compulsion to drive the Jews out of the Third Reich were obvious. Genocide came only after this failed. His modus operandi never changed. To subdue the local population and crush any opposition, he employed three strikingly effective tools: the subversion of laws by issuing new ones (especially ones rescinding the rights of Jews and isolating them); an endless flow of propaganda; and energetic terror (the trademark of the Nazi regime). At first, many Germans did not bother to challenge such a crude and comic figure, and as time passed it became increasingly more difficult and dangerous to do so. The historian Lucy Dawidowicz put it this way:

> Hitler came to power legally, exploiting the letter of the law to subvert the law. Sensible people were sure that Hitler could not last long, that decency, rationality, and political order would—must—reassert themselves. No civilized nation, no rational people, it was held, could endure mass hysteria as a substitute for parliamentarianism, the rule of terror instead of the rule of law. But the Germans had entered upon a macabre era in which evil and irrationality would reign for twelve endless years, in which the whole nation would be suborned.[6]

In the aftermath of the Evian Conference, the unsuccessful attempt to find havens for German Jews, the shooting of a minor German Foreign Office official in Paris by a Polish Jew whose father had been ousted from Germany was used as an excuse for the nights of November 9 and 10, 1938—*Kristallnacht*—which ended any hope that rationality would soon reassert itself or that any political body would intervene on behalf of the Jews. Under orders from Berlin, storm troopers went on a countrywide rampage against the Jews. Synagogues were burned to the ground. More than 7,000 Jewish businesses were looted and destroyed. Nearly 100 Jews were killed and thousands more were beaten and injured. Approximately 30,000 Jewish men were arrested and shipped off to Dachau, Buchenwald, and Sachsenhausen. Whoever spoke out on behalf of the Jews risked being rounded up with them. The Jewish community was fined a billion reichs-marks for damages.

No German organizational voice condemned the barbarity. Individuals, such as Monsignor Bernhard Lichtenberg, Berlin's head of the bishops' relief program, spoke out against the mayhem. Other people helped. Cardinal Michael Faulhaben provided a truck for the Chief Rabbi of Munich to save religious objects from the synagogue before it was destroyed. Hundreds of Germans hid Jewish friends, neighbors, and colleagues. Even visitors helped. While the mob raged outside his Berlin hotel, recently deposed heavyweight boxing champion Max Schmeling hid the two sons of a friend, a Jewish clothing store owner, in his suite. Feigning illness, the former champ stayed in his hotel room for four days until he got word that it was safe to move the boys.

In 1933 when Hitler came to power, there were a half million Jews living in Germany. Sixty thousand emigrated during the first two years of the National Socialist Party's regime. Germans urged their Jewish friends to leave, as did some Jewish leaders like Berlin's Rabbi Baeck. Those with inside glimpses into the new regime were particularly adamant. Frieda Suss repeatedly urged her mother's Jewish neighbors in Bavaria to leave. Suss was married to an official with the French embassy in Berlin and knew that Jews were in terrible danger. Her mother's neighbors, the Kissinger family, did not want to leave. Louis Kissinger, a math teacher, was a World War I veteran and believed "they will not touch German officers," Frieda Suss recalls. His son Henry loved football and did not want to leave either. The Susses were insistent. Suss opened a bank account in Holland with his own paycheck and money given him by Kissinger. Eventually, the Kissinger family escaped to Holland, where, thanks to Mr. and Mrs. Suss, they had money enough for passage to the United States.

After *Kristallnacht,* Jews did not have to be convinced, they were desperate to leave. In late 1938 and early 1939, 50,000 Jews left Germany. When, in March 1938, Hitler's troops marched into Austria and annexed it, 85,000 more Jews fled. A year later, still more escaped when Hitler rolled into Czechoslovakia. As the tide of Jews flowing out of Germany and Austria grew into a flood, countries began to shut their borders to Jewish refugees. The Evian Conference, called by Franklin Roosevelt on July 6, 1938, to deal with the mass exodus of refugees, ended in failure. It was clear no country wanted them. Without help, Jews were trapped.

Once again, individuals rushed into the void. They risked arrest and concentration camp imprisonment to help. They provided Jews with the forged documents, passports, and money necessary to leave Germany. The nature of the problem, however, demanded a less individual and more organized approach. In Germany, as well as in other European nations, underground organizations formed. In Stuttgart, for instance, nineteen-year-old Marion Fuerst worked for a network financed by sympathetic businessmen. The tall, blond, and blue-eyed Fuerst worked as a department-store cashier. Confident that her Aryan looks put her beyond suspicion, she stuffed forged documents, train tickets, and money into her clothes. During the day she slipped these items into packages of Jewish customers who whispered that day's code word—a Latin word or a name of a plant.

On September 1, 1939, Germany invaded Poland. Two days later, Britain and France declared war on Germany. Hitler was finally able to pursue his military and ideological aims wholeheartedly. He lost little time doing so. Within a month Poland fell. The spoils were divided between Germany and its peace partner, Russia. Russia took over Lithuania, Latvia, and Estonia while the Nazis ran the western portion of the country. Those Jews who could fled from the oncoming Germans. In Wishkow, a small town near Warsaw, my mother's father persuaded a man with a horse and buggy to give his family a ride out of town. They kept moving east into Russia, one step ahead of the bombs, and later the invading Germans. When they had stopped running, the Germans were far behind and they and some

250,000 other Polish Jews were deep inside Russia in such unfamiliar places as Uzbekistan, Siberia, and the Ural Mountains.

Hitler regarded Poland's Slavs as a race only slightly less subhuman than Jews. He and his troops saw no reason for tactical refinement. Their methods were crude and murderous. Hitler seized total control of the Polish government and immediately began to slaughter a portion of its populace. In the village of Szalas, all 300 males over the age of fifteen were seized, many machine-gunned and the rest locked in a school which was then set on fire.[7]

Although Polish Jews were already singled out for special torment and death, at this stage the killing was random. Deportations and gas chambers were still in the future. For the moment, Hitler was content to strip the Jews of their homes and businesses and move them into ghettos. Jews from the surrounding villages were uprooted from their homes and were packed into the ghettos. Faced with crowded and filthy living conditions, Jews paid neighbors or friends to shelter their children. In some other instances, neighbors asked Jews to leave their newborn babies and infants with them for protection. By December 1940 most of the major cities in German-occupied Poland included ghettos.

Initially these ghettos were "open," and people could come and go in relative freedom. During those days, neighbors brought food, medicine, false documents, money, and information. Eventually movements in and out of the ghettos became rigidly controlled. The Gestapo, Polish guards, and Jews coerced into acting as policemen monitored everyone's comings and goings. Papers and permits were checked, and individuals were searched for contraband.

The Warsaw ghetto was the largest ghetto. There a population of half a million was crammed into a hundred-block section of the city. In all the ghettos, space was tight, food scarce, and disease rampant, but the sheer size of the Warsaw ghetto made conditions there all the more horrendous. Among those confined there was Emmanuel Ringelblum, a historian whose extraordinary diary described ghetto life. On November 16, 1940, the day the Warsaw ghetto was closed off from the rest of the city by brick walls and guarded gates, "many

Christians brought bread for their Jewish acquaintances and friends," Ringelblum wrote. "This was a mass phenomenon." A few days later, his entry was more somber: "A Christian was killed . . . for throwing a sack of bread over the wall."[8]

War had upped the ante. To be sure, threats of imprisonment in a concentration camp or the newly built labor camps continued to be effective deterrents. But now the Nazis murdered civilians for both major offenses and minor infractions. At the Polish town of Torun, for example, twelve young boys aged eleven to sixteen were shot as a reprisal for the breaking of a window in the local police station.[9] Such senseless killing served its purpose. People were frightened into compliance.

The German authorities employed additional methods to ensure local cooperation. When they took over a town, they rounded up all the prominent citizens and held them hostage. The message to the town's people was clear: comply with our orders or punishment will be meted out not only to the guilty parties but to local leaders and perhaps the entire village as well. (One of the most notable examples of this principle of collective responsibility occurred later in the war. The Germans wiped out the entire village of Lidice, Czechoslovakia, and killed 2,000 Czechs in Prague in retaliation for the assassination of Gestapo chief Reinhard Heydrich on May 27, 1942.)

On October 15, 1941, the German authorities passed a law requiring the death penalty for all Jews who left the ghettos without permission. The same punishment applied to "persons who knowingly provide hiding places for Jews." Any Christian who learned that a Jew was breaking this law had an obligation to report the crime or be subject to the *same* punishment.

This law was widely publicized and determinedly implemented. In the town square of Lodz, a Christian mother and father and their children were hanged next to the Jews they had harbored. These public executions sent the Nazi message to villagers even in remote areas. Every Polish farmer was aware that if he helped a Jew he risked his life as well as the lives of his wife and children.

Yet, remarkably, thousands of people continued to hide Jews. Attics, cellars, sewers, ditches, pigsties, haystacks, brothels, closets, pantries, space behind double walls, monasteries, convents, orphanages, schools, and hospital quarantine rooms were converted into temporary shelters and long-term hideouts.

In April 1940, the Germans invaded Denmark and Norway. In May, German troops took over Holland, Belgium, and Luxembourg. A month later, France fell. Again, Hitler spread his new laws and directives, propaganda, and terror. Just how effective these tactics were in preventing resistance depended on a host of factors: the terrain of the occupied country; the closeness to a neutral country or free zone; the level of antisemitism present before the war (high in Eastern Europe, lower in Western Europe); the severity of Nazi control; and the stage of the war. For example, Holland is a small, but densely populated country cut off from Britain by the North Sea. Its terrain is virtually flat. There was no space or natural feature—thick forests or inaccessible mountains—where Jews could escape or armed resistance could hide. However, Poland, Czechoslovakia, France, Yugoslavia, Italy, Greece, and those parts of Russia occupied by the Germans all had terrain that supported greater resistance.

The presence of a resistance group, however, did not necessarily mean Jews would be rescued. Russian and Polish resistance groups were devoted to one goal: ridding their countries of the Germans. Anything else was a distraction. My father was reminded of this one day when he found a group of Jews hiding in a wood near the camp of his Byelorussian resistance group. They were near starvation. My father, knowing all too well what life hiding in the woods was like, stole bread from his group's rations and brought it to them. He was caught, and brought before a tribunal for judgment, which ordered his execution. At the last minute, however, the order was reversed by the group's commander, who thought my father was too good a soldier to lose.

The resistance groups in France, Denmark, Belgium, and Holland, however, tried to help Jews. Despite the disadvantages of their flat terrain, the Dutch found ways to resist the anti-Jewish directives. Workers went on strike to protest the dismissal of Jews from their civil service jobs. In retaliation for the killing of a Nazi and an attack on a German police patrol by a small Jewish resistance group, the Nazis brutally and viciously rounded up 400 Jewish men and boys and sent them to Buchenwald. The Dutch were horrified. On February 25, 1941, workers in Amsterdam and a few other cities in the area went on strike. The strike continued for two days until the Germans broke it by force.

The Nazi occupation of Holland spurred two very different reactions. Many citizens gravitated toward the newly forming resistance networks, while the number of collaborators also increased. The Nazis had bombed their beautiful city of Rotterdam, turning it to rubble, and had chased their government into exile. The occupiers of Holland were Nazis who were fanatically devoted to the Führer. These ideological thugs were "anti-Jewish and anti-anybody who helped the Jews," Dutch rescuer Johtje Vos recalled.

France and Belgium, on the other hand, were occupied by the German military. Many were career army officers and not necessarily devoted to Hitler or particularly in tune with his antisemitic ideology. In France these military occupiers did not have the manpower or the enthusiasm to rule with an iron fist. The French police were left on their own to carry out German orders.

France was initially divided into two zones: the German occupied zone to the north and the unoccupied or free zone in the south. The unoccupied zone was run from Vichy by Marshal Henri Pétain and Pierre Laval, who made good on their pledge of cooperation with the Germans by rescinding the rights of Jews and promulgating a series of anti-Jewish laws. Even so, southern France offered Jews relatively more freedom and a chance to escape deportation. Among Frenchmen it was whispered that in the mountainous region of Vivarais-Lignon, descendants of the once persecuted Huguenots lived and in their quiet way offered shelter to other persecuted people. The village of Le Chambon-sur-Lignon, where Magda Trocmé opened her door to all comers, was in the center of this region. It was surrounded by a dozen other villages that, when combined, formed an informal rescue network that hid Jews and managed their escapes to Switzerland. Jewish families from Paris and elsewhere procured false identification papers and headed to this mountainous region of south-central

France and the neighboring region of the Cévennes. If that proved to be impossible, they put their trust in the villagers and just sent their children.

As Hitler's juggernaut rolled on, the Germans needed an ever-increasing amount of manpower, supplies, and war matériel to keep pace with its war effort. To meet those needs, special labor camps were set up adjacent to or near concentration camps and run by the same sadistic staff. Yet even the forced-labor effort of Jewish males between the ages of fourteen and sixty and others who ran afoul of the Third Reich was not enough. More manpower was required. Hitler's High Command solved the problem by pulling young adults off the streets of occupied countries and shipping them to Germany to work. No permission was asked. Everyone was fair game. To avoid these random roundups, Polish, French, and Dutch families hid their older children.

Vichy France, Finland, and Denmark were allowed to keep their own governments as long as they did not fight the Germans. The Danish government, for example, stayed in power, running the country's internal affairs without German interference. This democratic nation with a history of religious tolerance did not countenance Nazi persecution of their Jews. Danish officials refused to comply with Nazi demands to make Jews wear yellow stars or to herd them into a ghetto. Danish political leaders simply dismissed the question of special treatment for the Jews with "There's no Jewish problem in Denmark." The Germans eased their pressure in enforcing anti-Jewish restrictions; they did not want to disturb the cooperative stance of the Danes and lose what they were after—namely, food.

According to popular legend, the king donned a yellow star during his morning ride down the main street of Copenhagen and 50,000 Danes wearing Jewish stars marched in the streets in protest. The fact that neither King Christian X nor the Danes did any such thing has not tarnished the legend's popularity or its credibility.

In April 1941, German armies took over Yugoslavia and Greece. Two months later Hitler broke his nonaggression pact with Russia and sent troops over its borders. Just behind his foot soldiers came special units called *Einsatzgruppen*. These were Nazi killing squads whose mission was to root out all undesirables—political commissars, active Communists, and above all Jews—and murder them. In the Ukraine, Latvia, Estonia, and Byelorussia, soldiers invaded a town, rounded up all the Jews in the square or marched them to a nearby grave site, and shot them. Villagers might be woken up in the middle of the night by a knock on the door—by Jews who crawled out from a heap of corpses or somehow evaded the death squads. They had no time to think about their response. They had to decide instantaneously whether to save the person's life or turn him away. Some reported the knock to the local Gestapo in the morning for a reward.

In fact, many locals were all too happy to help the *Einsatzgruppen* in their work. Romanians cleared a path for the oncoming Germans by murdering thousands of Jews. Ukrainian nationals, rabid antisemites, hunted Jews like rabbits and shot them. In Lithuania, 200,000 of a total of 250,000 Jews were wiped out without so much as a murmur from any political or religious leader or institution. But certain individuals, ordinary citizens, helped. A librarian at the Vilna University in Lithuania, Ona Simaite, and two other women founded the Committee to Rescue Jews. They found hiding places, provided forged documents, and raised funds for hundreds of Jews.

Other Jews fled to nearby woods. Their story is very much like my father's. Life in the woods was a harsh, chancy affair. Every day brought a desperate search for food and every moment the fear that a farmer would report their whereabouts to the authorities. Often villagers refused to give food to those in hiding because they were also hungry and scared. But a few helped. Those too afraid to have Jewish families stay in their houses brought information and food to Jews hiding in the woods. They washed their clothes, discarded their waste, and stood watch for Nazis.

On January 20, 1942, in the Berlin suburb of Wannsee, representatives of the Nazi party were told that Hitler had given the go-ahead for the "Final Solution to the Jewish question." The Final Solution was the code name assigned by the German bureaucracy to the annihilation of the Jews. The killing squads were deemed too inefficient and too expensive a solution. From then on the answer to the Jewish problem lay in the mass deportation of Jews to concentration camps for extermination by gassing. As Dutch historian Louis de Jong stressed, such a solution took the civilized world unaware:

> Here we approach an aspect of the Holocaust which is of cardinal importance and which can never be sufficiently underlined. That the Holocaust, when it took place, was beyond the belief and the comprehension of almost all people living at the time, Jews included. Everyone knew that human history had been scarred by endless cruelties. But that thousands, nay millions of human beings—men, women, and children, the old and the young, the healthy and the infirm—would be killed, finished off, mechanically, industrially so to speak, would be exterminated like vermin—that was a notion so alien to the human mind, an event so gruesome, so *new,* that the instinctive, indeed the natural, reaction of most people was: it can't be true.[10]

While the *Einsatzgruppen* continued their special tasks in the East, Nazi energies were now devoted to deporting Jews to six death camps: Auschwitz, Belzec, Treblinka, Sobibor, Chelmno, and Majdanek. To accomplish this, the Germans used deception and terror. "Resettlement in the East," and, even later, labor camps, were part of the fundamental lie used to deceive Jews concerning their fate. The Germans went to extraordinary lengths to give credence to their lies. Jews about to be deported were permitted to take along personal belongings. Railroad and building signs were changed to disguise the nature of the final destination. Those not immediately sent to the gas chambers were ordered to send postcards and letters home informing their families of their safe arrival. To fortify the belief that those deported were still alive, the Germans encouraged those Jews still remaining to write to their "resettled" relatives. Tens of thousands of such letters were handed over to the Germans. Of course, not a single one was ever delivered.[11] How easily both Jews and non-Jews believed the lies, went for the feints, or chose to be fooled differed from country to country, from town to town, even from family member to family member.

In Denmark at the moment of mass deportation, Danes

launched a daring rescue that transported by fishing boats more than 7,200 (out of 7,800) Danish Jews, half Jews and Jewish refugees to safety in Sweden. In the Netherlands and in Belgium, some from the local population protested Jewish deportations. In Belgium, the rescue of the Jews was seen as an integral part of the resistance movement. The resistance set up a special branch, Comité de Défense des Juifs (CDJ), that alerted Jews to deportations and provided money, documents, and hiding places. Jews and non-Jews, with the crucial support of the Belgium Catholic Church, worked together to save lives, particularly those of children.[12]

Even those governments aligned with the Nazis balked at mass deportations. Italy, Germany's principal ally, declined to let Jews be deported from either Italian soil or from those parts of France and Greece that Italy occupied. To curry favor with Germany, Italian leader Benito Mussolini enacted a flurry of anti-Jewish laws, but the Italians refused to do much about them. Italian troops who occupied parts of southern France, Croatia, Yugoslavia, and Greece aided Jews in all these areas. In the summer of 1941, Italian soldiers stationed in southern Croatia intervened to save Jews and Serbs from being massacred by the Croatian police. Once again, individuals took the initiative. Weeks later the heads of the Italian Foreign Ministry and the army made it official policy that Croatian Jews were to be protected.

Romania's leader, Marshal Ion Antonescu, after initially condoning the unrestrained murder of Jews by his militia, reversed direction and ignored the Nazis' request for deportation. Instead, he let it be known that Jews could buy their way out and immigrate to Palestine. Similarly, Bulgaria stubbornly resisted mass deportation of its Jews. The government had already bowed to the demand that 12,000 Jews under Bulgarian occupation in Thrace and Macedonia be deported, and it was determined not to give in to any more deportation demands. In general, Nazi ideology and anti-Jewish laws were not accepted by Bulgarians because they were not tinged by an antisemitic tradition. Angelo Giuseppe Roncalli, who later became Pope John XXIII, interceded with King Boris III on behalf of the Bulgarian Jews, with the Turkish government on behalf of the Jews who reached that country, and he did his utmost to prevent the deportation of Greek Jews.

In Greece, little could be done to stop mass deportations. Most of the 76,000 Greek Jews lived in the port city of Salonika, a Sephardic settlement that dated back to the fifteenth century. Quickly and efficiently, the Nazis shipped these Jews to Auschwitz. Those Jews who lived in various places in southern Greece, however, were more fortunate. Despite a Nazi directive that any non-Jew caught providing shelter would be shot without a trial, Archbishop Papandreou Damaskinos, on his own initiative, instructed the Greek monasteries and convents to shelter any Jew who knocked on their door. Athens's chief of police, Anghelos Evert, provided Jews with false identification papers, enabling them to pass as non-Jews while on the run.

In March 1944, Germany invaded Hungary, and in quick order anti-Jewish decrees were issued and deportations to Auschwitz began. Jews in the countryside were deported immediately, but those in Budapest were herded into special houses. By this time, escapees' accounts of the gas chambers at Auschwitz had reached the West, and at last the voices of protest were heard. The International Red Cross, the Pope, the king of Sweden, and Allied leaders all protested the deportations. The effect was immediate, if not permanent. Deportations were suspended for three months. When they resumed, it was left to the ingenuity of individuals on the scene, like Raoul Wallenberg and Spanish legation representative Angel Sanz-Briz, among others, to save as many Jews as possible from certain death. Diplomats claimed sovereignty over as many of these Jewish houses as they could and declared the people inside their protected citizens.

The more reverses Hitler's military war suffered, the more determinedly and frantically he pursued his racial war. The pace of killing at the death camps quickened. In the face of the advancing Russians to the east, the Nazis evacuated labor camp prisoners westward. Some were shunted into cattle cars; others marched. Starvation, disease, and Nazi brutality took their toll. Tens of thousands died.

Allied troops were marching steadily and inexorably toward Berlin. The defeat of the Third Reich was a foregone conclusion. On

April 30, 1945, Hitler committed suicide and eight days later the Germans surrendered. Hitler's twelve-year reign of murder and coercion came to an end. It was a reign which, nearly half a century later, still challenges our understanding. Evil was rewarded and good acts were punished. Bullies were aggrandized and the meek trampled. In this mad world, most people lost their bearings. Fear disoriented them, and self-protection blinded them. A few, however, did not lose their way. A few took their direction from their own moral compass. Why? Did they see the world as it was or through some other lens? When they looked around, what did they see?

· 3 ·

AWARENESS

"SHE WAS A PECULIAR and passionate person, my mother. She never lacked for opinions on the political scene. Though this merely embarrassed us children, it often made Father downright angry." This is how Wendelgard von Staden describes her mother, Irmgard.[1]

Father was Baron Ernst von Neurath, and his brother was none other than Hitler's first Foreign Minister, Konstantin von Neurath. Protected as she was by an aristocratic and influential family name, Irmgard von Neurath could afford a certain outspokenness. Yet, as her daughter made clear in her conversations with me and in her moving memoir of the war years, *Darkness Over the Valley,* Irmgard von Neurath was more than just an independent-minded wife. She was a woman attentive to her surroundings and, above all, curious about them.

So in July 1944, when von Neurath heard about strangers who came from a newly built barrack in the nearby Vaihingen meadows to beg for food in the village, she took her daughter to investigate. Through persistent inquiries, she discovered that famished Hungarian laborers were building an underground aircraft factory by day and foraging for food in the village at night. The Hungarians told her that the Germans did not mind them leaving the site in the evening, but they did not want Germans from the surrounding villages coming in —"and I don't believe that any, apart from Mother and myself, ever tried to," commented Wendelgard von Staden.[2]

Later, the Nazis expropriated a grove and little valley of the von Neuraths' property to build "a special camp" to imprison "dangerous criminals"—Camp Wiesengrund. Just who these dangerous criminals were became apparent when one day the von Neuraths received an order from the rationing office demanding that they deliver beans to the camp. Wendelgard's mother, overworked as she and her helpers were, told officials if they wanted beans, they'd better send someone to pick them.

Soon thereafter, Wendelgard and her mother heard a strange sound, the sound of wooden clogs shuffling along a dirt road, and looking out the window, they saw a procession of thin, staggering figures with shaved heads and greenish faces coming toward them. The procession stopped at the von Neuraths' door, and a guard announced that the work detachment from Camp Wiesengrund was here to gather the beans. Irmgard von Neurath thought these supposedly "dangerous criminals" looked like madmen and asked the guard what sort of prisoners they were. Jews, she was told, come to collect the food.

Von Neurath decided that before these scrawny prisoners picked anything, they needed to eat. So she boiled up a kettle of potatoes. Just as she lifted the lid to pronounce the potatoes ready, the prisoners rushed for the food, knocking over the kettle in the process. Hot potatoes spilled to the ground and a melee ensued as prisoners fought for the soiled, hot potatoes while guards cursed and struck them with their rifle butts. "What kind of people are these anyway?" von Neurath asked, horror-struck at the sight. "They're no longer human beings." They are Jews, the guard shrugged in reply, subhuman.

> I was standing next to Mother, when suddenly we heard a man's voice behind us. The voice itself was low and soft, speaking in good, clear German, but there was an undertone of almost menacing fury. "It's you who've made us into animals, and you'll pay for what you've done to us."[3]

The prisoner's words, spoken near that upturned potato kettle, suddenly gave Irmgard von Neurath a heightened awareness that those people were not madmen or subhuman. She realized with a new clarity that these were human beings crazed and reduced to atavistic behavior by hunger. Most importantly, she understood that these people needed help.

Later that evening Wendelgard described her mother pacing the floor, agitated by her new awareness. "Do you realize what it is, that so-called special camp?" she asked her husband. "It is a concentration camp, it can only be a concentration camp. And do you know what that means? It means that if the front comes any closer, they'll kill those people—that is, if they haven't already died of starvation."[4]

That night von Neurath concocted a plan to help these prisoners. She would ask the camp commandant to send the same group of prisoners to her farm each day to help her with the work. In that way, she could see they got enough to eat, protect them for a while from the Nazi guards, and find out what was going on inside the camp.

In their work on bystander intervention, social psychologists Bib Latané and John Darley have delineated a five-stage process by which observers turn into active participants. Their stages are: noticing that something is amiss; interpreting the situation as one in which people need help; assuming responsibility to offer that help; choosing a form of help; and, finally, implementing that help. Latané and Darley's first two stages—noticing and interpreting—are what I call awareness.

The awareness of the imminent danger and probable death of Jews was an essential first step toward becoming a rescuer. It was a clear-eyed view that saw what most others did not. In some cases, rescuers' awareness of the Jews' plight became so evident that they could not trace it to one particular incident. In other cases, the sights, smells, and sounds of that moment of critical realization are etched forever in the rescuer's memory. Even today, for example, Wendelgard von Staden's head reverberates with the sound of the concentration camp inmates' clogs shuffling toward the farmhouse.[5]

It took a determined effort to penetrate the propaganda, to be aware. Those who became rescuers made that effort. Their heightened sense of empathy overrode Nazi propaganda and their own instinct for self-preservation. They saw these victims of Nazi persecution as people, different from themselves perhaps, but still part of the same human community.

The plight of the Jews and other victims of the Nazis touched a deeply personal chord. In some cases, rescuers had been made more sensitive by an earlier near-fatal illness or the death of a family member or dear friend. In other cases, their empathic response was heightened by a deep religious or moral conviction that "there but for the grace of God go I." In 1984, when I talked with Dutch rescuer Theresa Weerstra, her close identification with the Jews and empathy for what they suffered were still painfully close to the surface:

In Amsterdam they rounded up Jews, opened the bridges and drove them into the channels to drown. I saw with my own eyes one hundred and twenty Jews killed. . . . I was with my sister on an open field. We saw the Jews forced to kneel and put their hands up. As one by one they lost their balance—ping—they were shot. One gone, two gone, three gone, one hundred and twenty gone. And they left them there . . . And mothers cried for their babies . . . It brings tears to my eyes . . . I was a mother; I had children.

A person's ability to assimilate death imagery and empathize with the suffering of others is an essential ingredient in awareness. No one acts unless he is aware of the need to help. Often a specific incident brought that need into the forefront of a person's consciousness. For Irmgard von Neurath, seeing those prisoners claw each other for scalding potatoes made her aware of the inmates' desperate condition. For German industrialist Oskar Schindler, who took over a bankrupt enamelware factory outside of Cracow, where he kept Jews from deportation to death camps by employing, housing, and feeding them, a trip to the Prokocim train depot, where acts of dehumanization were directed against the Jews, showed him just how precarious and dangerous was the position of the Jews.

On June 3, 1942, Schindler was home drinking coffee when one of his secretaries called to tell him that his office manager, Abraham

Bankier, had not come to work. The secretary reported that she had seen Nazis marching Bankier out of the ghetto to the railroad depot. A dozen of Oskar's other workers were with him.

Oskar called for his car and drove to the train depot. The station was crowded with Jews—Jews standing in orderly lines and Jews already jammed into cattle cars. The sight brought Schindler to a standstill. "It was the first time Oskar had seen this juxtaposition of humans and cattle cars," wrote Thomas Keneally in his extraordinary book *Schindler's List,* "and it was a greater shock than hearing of it; it made him pause on the edge of the platform."[6]

Schindler moved along the line of more than twenty cattle cars, calling Bankier's name. After artfully dropping the names of Third Reich higher-ups and hinting broadly that unless his industrial workers were released the German officer would find himself in southern Russia, Schindler got his workers back.

Bankier later admitted that none of them had picked up blue stickers to identify them as essential workers, without which they had been rounded up for deportation. Suddenly testy, Schindler told him to get the stickers immediately. "What his curtness covered," wrote Keneally, "was dismay at those crowds at Prokocim who for want of a blue sticker stood waiting for the new and decisive symbol of their status, the cattle car."[7]

People became aware of Hitler's intentions at different times and in different ways, depending on their exposure to Nazism: what they saw or heard and what they experienced personally. Some of those who read Hitler's diatribes against the Jews in *Mein Kampf* when it was published in 1925 took him at his word and dedicated themselves to fighting him. The book—a mixture of autobiography, ideology, and political game plan—made it clear that Hitler believed that it was his sacred mission in life to destroy the Jews and break their supposed international political stranglehold. Others saw enough or sensed enough early on to be alarmed. When Hitler came to power, for example, Aart Vos, a Dutch businessman, went to Germany to visit a family with whom he had been friendly over the years. The family had two sons, but Vos hardly ever got to see one of them. He was out every night. Vos asked his hostess where her son went, but she only replied that it was better that he not ask. Vos persisted and was told that the son belonged to a secret club. (This club shed its clandestine origins and became known as the Hitler Youth.) The mother explained that her son's evenings were taken up with special training: catching animals—rabbits, pigs, mice, or rats—and killing them. They were acclimating themselves to killing and to the sight of blood.

This incident made an enormous impression on Vos. "That for me was a warning," said Vos, who with his wife, Johtje, hid thirty-six Jews during the war. "I talked to several friends about it. When the war started in Holland in 1940, I knew the cruelty of what they had done in Germany."

Despite the Nazis' virulent antisemitism and their murderous forays into the Jewish quarter in Amsterdam, the awareness that Jews were in mortal danger was not self-evident. In wartime, civilian upheaval and brushes with death are commonplace. Food and housing shortages, air raids, and gunfire are normal events. People's energies and attention are focused primarily on one thing and one thing only: survival for themselves and their families. All other concerns are pushed aside. While local citizens were aware that Jews were losing their civil liberties, most interpreted this change as temporary, not fatal and not necessarily warranting intervention.

Moreover, the Nazis' explanation that Jews were to be resettled in the East to work for the German war effort seemed plausible enough. As the German war machine rolled across Europe, through Poland and Russia, every hand was needed to keep it moving and in prime condition. It was not unreasonable to assume that as long as Jews could work, they were of value to the Third Reich and, therefore, safe.

To buttress this fiction, the Nazis ordered Jews who were not yet selected for the gas chambers to write postcards or letters to their families telling them that they were safe and that their living and working conditions were tolerable. This Nazi ruse was particularly cruel in contrast to actual conditions. A letter dispatched from the slave-labor camp of Buna, also known as Auschwitz III (where 25,000 of 35,000 prisoners perished), read: "I have now been here four weeks and I am well. I am in good health. Work is not particularly heavy.

We start at seven in the morning and we work till four in the afternoon. Food is good: at noon we have a warm meal and in the evening we get bread with butter, sausages, cheese, or marmalade. We have central heating here and we sleep under two covers. We have magnificent showers with warm and cold water."[8]

Some Dutch Jews managed to slip in the truth on their postcards home. At the end of a card sent from one of the camps a Dutchman might say, "Give my regards to Ellen de Groot." As this was a common Dutch name, the Germans did not censor it. What they did not know was that in Dutch *ellende* meant misery and *groot* meant terrible. So the message managed to tell of "terrible misery."[9]

The Nazis' determination to murder all Jews was never a matter of public knowledge, much less of public record. On July 31, 1941, Hermann Göring gave Gestapo chief Reinhard Heydrich an order in the form of a cryptic letter to rid all territories under German control of Jews. The message was clear: Eliminate the Jews quickly and quietly.[10]

Concentration camps were carefully screened from public view. The camp on the von Neuraths' farm, for example, was tucked in a valley and was so hidden that at the war's end liberating French forces had to be told of its existence.

Behind their campaign to exterminate the Jews, the Nazis created a blizzard of antisemitic propaganda. Since the twenties, many German veterans from the first war, for instance, were convinced that Jewish "treachery" was behind their humiliating defeat. The Jews provided a convenient scapegoat for any number of ills and frustrations. The Jews, they felt, had shirked their duty. Those in the army had held safe jobs behind the front. Others had grown rich supplying goods for the war effort. In Poland, Latvia, Estonia, Byelorussia, and the Ukraine, Nazi repetition of centuries-old antisemitic slurs that the Jews had killed Jesus and had sprinkled the blood of Christian children into their Passover matzos were regarded as home truths, not heavy-handed smears. Most Eastern Europeans were cooperative, if not eager, participants in the Nazi campaign to rid their towns of Jews.

Even in countries with a history of religious tolerance and liberalism, the crude Nazi propaganda was surprisingly effective. Marion van Binsbergen Pritchard, a social work student in Amsterdam at the time of the Nazi invasion, remembered the Germans showing the film *The Eternal Jew* at school:

> We sat through it, laughed out loud and thought it was ridiculous. But what impressed me in retrospect was that one of the students said to me the next day, "You know, that was an awful movie, scurrilous, and I don't believe a word of it, but what it has done is divide us into 'them' and 'us.' I wish it didn't, but now I look at people and say, 'Aha, you're Jewish.'"

It is only a small step from a belief that Jews are different to a conviction that they merit different treatment. Moreover, the Nazi social hierarchy placed Aryans, the superior race, at the top, with everyone else several rungs below. Jews occupied the lowest rung. Those wishing to climb the ladder, or simply hang on to their place on it, stepped on the Jews first.

This elitist construction of social hierarchy stifled people's natural empathy. Compassion for others rests on the recognition that the one asking for help differs little from the one offering it. By making empathy with Jews difficult, Nazi propaganda became an integral part of the Final Solution. "It is all right as long as it is only Jews," the populace was encouraged to believe. "They don't respond as we do."[11]

Other psychological principles kept awareness of the Jews' plight at bay. Self-preservation did not allow the reality of the Jews' fate to become conscious; it would have been too painful, too dangerous, too terrifying.

In his insightful work *Vital Lies, Simple Truths,* psychologist Daniel Goleman discusses this psychic obtuseness. He calls the things we notice our "frame." Everything else, especially those things that may cause us anxiety or pain, is kept from conscious view. Our mental pictures are cropped, eliminating clues that anything is amiss. It is a primitive response to the threat of danger that characterized many people under Nazi occupation.

Looking back, it is hard to understand how people in the midst of the Holocaust could have been unaware of it. Several years ago German rescuer Gitta Bauer spoke in Essen about her rescue experience. Her contemporaries in the audience "didn't know," they told her.

Bauer was enraged. Not know? The local park benches had signs that read: "No Jews allowed!" Jews were paraded through the streets carrying the message: "I am a Jewish pig." Jews were booted from their jobs, jeered on the streets, and thrown out of their homes. Not know? The murderous marauding of *Kristallnacht* was carefully orchestrated by the Nazis to be a nationwide event. Synagogues were set on fire, store windows smashed, and Jewish burial grounds desecrated. How was it possible that here in Essen, which had a Jewish synagogue and cemetery, people did not know the Nazis' intentions? "Even if you did not see it with your own eyes," she castigated her listeners, "you had to be aware."

In fact, most people were not aware. Although it is difficult for rescuers to understand, other people saw the situation differently. They did not see the world the rescuers did. Like a horse shielded from sights to the left or the right, most bystanders were equipped with blinders. To the right of them were Gestapo agents in the dead of night knocking on doors to arrest a relative or a friend. To the left of them were high walls of a concentration camp or a letter announcing a loved one's death "from a sudden illness." They kept their vision narrow to protect themselves and allow themselves to focus on surviving in this new, terror-filled Nazi world. Mistreatment of the Jews became background noise.

The Western Allies were not any less blind. Despite Polish diplomat Jan Karski's direct report of what he witnessed in the Warsaw ghetto and the Belzec death camp, U.S. Supreme Court Justice Felix Frankfurter was incredulous. Although he made arrangements for President Franklin Roosevelt to hear Karski's report, Frankfurter remained skeptical of the account. "I did not say that he was lying," Justice Frankfurter explained later. "I said that I cannot believe him. There is a difference."[12]

On one end of the awareness spectrum were those who sensed

from the beginning what Hitler had in mind. On the other end were those who became aware only when they saw the slaughter of the Jews firsthand. For example, it was not until the Germans built a labor camp in front of her house that Ukrainian Jean Kowalyk began to fathom the Nazis' grand scheme. One of Kowalyk's dearest childhood friends was a Jewish elementary school classmate, Blumka Friedman. Kowalyk had not seen her around the village recently. One day, as Kowalyk was passing by the newly built labor camp, she saw Blumka. "What are you doing there!" Kowalyk shouted to her from behind the camp's barbed-wire fence. The question died on her lips as she looked about at the ragged, emaciated forms huddled inside. Kowalyk's father had died in the past year and her two brothers had just been dragged off to the Russian army. The misery she saw in that labor camp resonated within her. Without thinking, and ignoring a nearby Gestapo guard, Kowalyk reached into her handbag and threw her lunch sandwich over the fence to Blumka. From then on, whenever she could, she sneaked food to Blumka and other camp inmates. Even a leg wound, received when a camp guard saw Kowalyk throwing bread and shot at her, did not stop her.

Like Kowalyk, Irene Gut Opdyke had a keen, empathic nature that gave her a will to see what others ignored. In Gut Opdyke's case, she saw more than most and remembered it all. I first met this still-beautiful, energetic woman in 1986 soon after she had been honored by Yad Vashem. She had been a nineteen-year-old nursing student living away from her Polish upper-class Catholic family in a dormitory in Radom when Germany invaded Poland. She was on the way to her hospital shift when Nazi bombers screeched overhead. Suddenly, a building nearby exploded, and someone pulled her into a ditch. As screams pierced the smoke-filled air, Opdyke raced to the hospital and worked round the clock with little time to think about the mayhem outside.

As the Germans and Russians marched through Poland, Irene Gut and some of the senior nurses decided to join the Polish resistance. Just before Christmas, at the height of the frigid winter, Gut's group arrived in a small village. Gut was assigned guard duty as the others went into town to barter tobacco and coffee for food. Russians entered the town and captured her and her friends. Gut was raped and beaten, then left for dead in the forest outside the village. Fortunately, she was found and taken to a hospital where a woman doctor helped her overcome her physical and emotional trauma.

Once she had recovered, Gut worked as a nurse in the infectious disease unit of a POW camp. In 1941, she decided to take advantage of an exchange of Polish prisoners between Russia and Germany and find her family. She made her way back to Radom, where she was briefly and joyfully reunited with her family. But soon the Germans sent her father to another town to work, and her mother followed him. Gut and a sister were left to fend for themselves in Radom.

Gut was assigned to work as a waitress at the town's hotel, which now served as a Nazi officers' club. Her first day on the job, she noticed a group of Gestapo guards surrounding a barbed-wire fence behind the hotel. She thought no more about it until several weeks later, when from behind the hotel she heard gunfire and cries for help. She ran to the window, wrenched the drapes apart, and watched in disbelief and horror as men, women, and children tried in vain to dodge bullets and bolt to safety. At that moment, her boss, a Nazi major, Ruegemer, strode into the room and put his hand over her mouth, warning her to be quiet and shut the curtains. He explained that the barbed-wire fence enclosed a ghetto for vermin, and the Gestapo was cleaning out a few. It was not her business, he warned her.

Gut said nothing, but several days later, after a Nazi ball, she asked her boss if she could take home some leftover food. Major Ruegemer assented, and after work, she and her sister, who also worked as a waitress at the officers' club, went around to the back. They pried open a loose spot in the barbed-wire fence and left the food there. This became their daily ritual. Each day after work, the two sisters brought food to the ghetto.

One day, while coming to work, Gut and her sister watched helplessly from across the street as the Gestapo closed down the ghetto behind the officers' club and marched the Jews out of town.

Like the scene she had witnessed earlier from the curtained window, the death march of the old, the lame, and the helpless seared her memory and scorched her heart:

> If I close my eyes I can still see them. It was a horror. I saw a beautiful blond woman very heavy in her ninth month of pregnancy, and another woman with a wounded leg. She walked slowly, a little girl holding her skirt, and there were many crippled men, hobbling on crutches. There were young boys too, like from the yeshiva with payos, pale, tall, like walking skeletons. One of the women I saw was married to a Polish man and he came running from the street calling her name, and when he reached the line of marchers, he was shot and fell to the ground.
>
> Then I saw another woman with a crying baby in her arms. One of the Gestapo was yelling at the baby, "Shut up! Quiet! Stop yelling!" The mother tried to quiet the baby. She opened her blouse and tried to breast-feed, but her baby was scared, or cold, or in pain, because it was just crying. Then with one movement of his arm, the Gestapo officer pulled the baby from its mother's arms, took it by the feet, and threw it with the head to the ground. The baby was instantly quiet. I will never forget the inhuman, shrill scream that the mother let out as she jumped to reach her child.

Who would have dreamed that such things were possible? Who could have imagined such horrors? Certainly, Jews could not. "Men," the French philosopher François La Rochefoucauld has said, "cannot look directly at either the sun or death." Many victims, such as Treblinka death camp survivor Richard Glazar, suspected nothing. As he recounted for filmmaker Claude Lanzmann, Glazar and an older fellow passenger on a German deportation train were leaning out the train window trying to figure out where they were headed. Their train had turned off the main track and was rolling through a wood at a walking pace. The old man in Glazar's compartment saw a young Polish farmhand nearby and asked him by hand signs, "Where are we?" In response, the boy made a gesture that both men thought was peculiar. He drew a finger across his throat. "We didn't really pay much attention to him," Glazar recalled. "We couldn't figure out what he meant."[13]

Friends of the Jews often had a hard time trying to convince them that, for safety's sake, they needed to leave their homes. Many German Jews, who felt themselves to be more German than Jewish, could not believe their lives were threatened. (Frieda Suss pleaded for a long time before the Kissingers were convinced that her information from the French embassy in Berlin was believable.) Jews in other countries had similar reactions. On Saturday, July 11, 1942, Janny Blom saw an announcement in the Dutch paper ordering all Jews to report to their local synagogues. The Jews were being shipped to Westerbork, a way-station on the way to resettlement in the East. They could take only one suitcase, the announcement said. Starting the next day, the Germans would be rounding up Jewish boys sixteen years or older in alphabetical order.

Janny Blom read the announcement with dismay. She was worried about her former boss, Samuel Vreedenburg, a dentist in whose office she had worked as an assistant until her marriage. She was very fond of her boss and his family, as was her husband, Willem, and their three-year-old son. She was very worried about the nephew of Marianne Vreedenburg, Johnny Veeth, who was sixteen years old. That day Janny and Willem rushed over to the Vreedenburgs' home to ask them what their nephew planned to do. Marianne told the Bloms that her nephew had nothing planned. He would probably comply with the order. "My brother-in-law says maybe it will be just work camps," Janny remembered Marianne Vreedenburg saying. "Maybe it will be good for the boy." Janny Blom could not believe her ears. "How stupid can he get!" she blurted out furiously. "We heard several people say that they are destroying them!"

The Bloms offered to hide the Vreedenburgs in their home when their turn for deportation came, and their offer was quickly accepted. Their spontaneous act of compassion and kindness was repeated in thousands of homes throughout Holland. In his 1990 Harvard lecture, Dutch historian Louis de Jong, who had escaped to England earlier in the war, offered the following poignant footnote to this Dutch outpouring of compassion and concern:

It may be true that over a hundred thousand Jews were deported, but it is equally true that the Dutch underground tried to save 25,000 Jews. I would like to add that many Jews, my own parents among them, refused the help that was offered them because they believed that deportation gave them a better chance to survive than going into hiding.[14]

As it turned out, it was a poor calculation. De Jong's parents, as well as the rest of his immediate family, perished.

Tragically enough, such miscalculations were common. Despite friends' warnings and pleas for them to flee, Jews refused to believe that the Nazis planned to murder them. It was very difficult to change the minds of Jews because the Nazi plan to deceive them was very convincing. Dutch rescuer Arnold Douwes, who pried over 3,000 Jews from their Amsterdam homes and hid them in homes in Nieuwlande, found a simple way to get around this problem: he lied. He exaggerated the comforts of farm life and poetically described Nieuwlande's pastoral attractions. He told Jewish families that the schools were first-rate and that they would be placed with supportive farm families. On the other side, he told reluctant Nieuwlande farmers that it was just one Jew who needed shelter for only a single night. When Douwes showed up later with several Jews, he shamed farmers into hiding them and bullied them into extending their stay.[15]

A few citizens in occupied Europe were jarred into the awareness of the Nazi plan to annihilate the Jews. In psychological parlance, these bystanders underwent a "transforming encounter," an incident of such jolting power that the person who experiences it is forever changed. Unlike a moment of awareness, rescuers' transforming encounters involved more than simply a realization that Jews were being slaughtered.

Certainly there were others in Budapest that October day in 1944 who saw what Italian Giorgio Perlasca saw. Perlasca was the Budapest representative of a Rome-based company that supplied meat to the Italian navy. As a soldier in the Italian army, Perlasca had fought in the Spanish Civil War, in which General Francisco Franco had given all those who fought with him documents that promised them Spanish protection. Having decided that this was as good a time as any to take Franco up on his promise, Perlasca was headed to the Spanish legation in Budapest to seek protection.

On the way, Perlasca saw a gang of Hungarian Nazis chasing a ten-year-old boy. They caught up with him, and one of them took his gun and bashed in the child's head. Perlasca could not believe his eyes. "I asked people there why, and they answered, 'Because he was a Jewish child,'" Perlasca remembered.

Perlasca pressed on to the Spanish legation in Budapest. There the Spanish minister, Angel Sanz-Briz, issued him a regular diplomatic passport. While the paperwork was being processed, Perlasca noticed that hundreds of people were lined up outside the Spanish legation. Some of them were fighting to get inside. They were Jews seeking protection from deportation. Like Raoul Wallenberg, Sanz-Briz was issuing phony papers—in this instance letters of protection —that certified the bearer as a Spanish citizen who was entitled to the protection of the Spanish government. His hope was that the Nazi government of Hungary, which valued its relations with Madrid, would respect the documents and leave their bearers alone. Sanz-Briz gave a letter of protection to anyone who could get to his office and ask for one.

The incident of the Jewish boy and the mob was fresh in Perlasca's mind. The Nazis' intentions toward the Jews were clear, and Perlasca felt that unless he did something, more children would be murdered. He instantly volunteered his services to help save Jewish lives. Perlasca came face to face with death, and the impact of that meeting was electric and its effects immediate. It transformed an Italian fascist into a man determined to do whatever he could to save Jewish lives. Similarly, the spilled potatoes galvanized Irmgard von Neurath into action. "What that prisoner had said alongside the upturned potato kettle had set my mother thinking," Wendelgard von Staden recalled. "It was as if his words had suddenly brought home to her what was really happening to these people."[16]

For Oskar Schindler, seeing Jews put on trains made him realize, in a way that had not penetrated his conscience before, that Nazis regarded Jews as cattle. But it was an incident the next day that transformed him from a sympathetic onlooker into a rescuer. The morning after the cattle-car episode, Schindler went horseback riding with his German mistress. The two rode in the hilly parkland overlooking the Jewish ghetto where a line of women and children was being led away. At the rear of this column, dawdling, was a little girl dressed in a small scarlet coat and cap. Right behind this line came SS teams with dogs to sniff out those who had evaded them the first time. The SS squad did not even wait for the column ahead to turn the corner. They pulled Jews from their hiding places and shot them on the street. While the girl in scarlet turned her head to watch, one soldier shot a woman in the neck; when her son slid down a wall whimpering, another SS jammed a boot down on his head and fired. This sickening spectacle transformed Schindler. He realized that the Germans' lack of shame meant that their acts were officially sanctioned. They tolerated witnesses, such as the little girl in scarlet, because they believed all the witnesses would also perish. "Beyond this day," Schindler claimed, "no thinking person could fail to see what would happen. I was now resolved to do everything in my power to defeat the system."[17]

Dramatic, transforming encounters were the exception rather than the rule. Some rescuers were victims of Nazi mistreatment, arrested on the suspicion of being Jewish and dealt with accordingly. Others were relatives of mental patients, the elderly, or the infirm, murdered in the Nazis' euthanasia program. Still others were parents whose children were kidnapped for Third Reich labor. Such personal suffering at the hands of the Nazis increased the likelihood of becoming aware that Jews were also victims.

Other rescuers with whom I talked said that their awareness came from accumulated influences and events. Such was Gitta Bauer's experience, for example. Bauer traced her first awareness of the Nazi Party to 1929 when she and her father watched a group of young men in brown uniforms sporting the storm troopers' insignia, the *Hakenkreuz*, or swastika, march down the street. Ten-year-old Bauer looked up at her father and asked him who these people were. Her father, a proud World War I veteran, surprised her by his contemptuous reply: "These are people who *want* another war."

Four years later, Bauer recalled that one day her father came home shaken. He had found a young man—a Communist and therefore deemed a Nazi enemy—stabbed in the street. The incident confirmed the Bauers' darkest forebodings about the rise of Hitler and his minions.

But Hitler's power to fire the German imagination was such that Bauer found herself drawn to his National Socialist Party, despite living in a vehemently anti-Hitler family. In 1936, the sixteen-year-old Bauer took part in the opening ceremonies of the Berlin Olympic Games. Its theatricality stirred her nationalism. "The Olympic stadium seems to me the effigy in stone of National Socialism," she remembered writing in her diary. When she told a young priest what she had written, he was appalled. Hitler was hell-bent on destroying the Church and all of Germany, he admonished her.[18] The priest's words nipped her nascent patriotic enthusiasm in the bud. Even so, it was not until *Kristallnacht* two years later that she realized what Hitler's nationalism entailed. She saw the beatings, the arrests, and the killings. Before, all this had been in her peripheral vision; now she really saw it:

> We walked the streets and saw the flames shooting out of the synagogue. When we came home we heard that the rabbi had been beaten up and was found in the streets. He was a very gentle man, not very tall, on the slim side, so it was very easy for these hoodlums to overpower him. They tore his beard—it was terrible.

The ability to see clearly, to strip away the gauze of Nazi euphemisms and recognize that innocents were being murdered, is at the heart of what distinguishes rescuers from bystanders. It was the necessary first step that made the ensuing rescue activity possible and, in some cases, inevitable. Unlike others who heard about the Nazis' gassing and mass-murder techniques, when a friend miraculously escaped a death camp and returned home to tell Dutch woman

Theresa Weerstra about the gas chambers, Weerstra believed this preposterous account readily enough. She had witnessed Nazi inhumanity. She was aware. She believed them capable of any barbarity. Like those who would be rescuers, she was prepared for action.

· 4 ·

ACTION

"The hand of compassion was faster
than the calculus of reason."

—Otto Springer, rescuer

BYSTANDERS WITH A BROADENED "frame of aware-
ness" could see the need for action; they still, however, needed opportunity, and they did not always have that opportunity. Some circumstances were too dangerous or uncertain for bystanders to be of any
help. One day in 1942, in Amsterdam, social work student Marion
van Binsbergen Pritchard was riding her bicycle to class. In front of a
Jewish children's home there were Nazis loading children onto trucks.
She stopped abruptly. The children, who ranged in age from babies to
eight-year-olds, were frightened and crying. "When they didn't move
fast enough, a Nazi would pick them up by an arm or a leg or even
hair and throw them into the truck," Pritchard remembered. She was
so shocked by what she saw that she found herself crying in rage.
Then two women came along the street and tried to stop the loading.
The Germans heaved them into a truck also.

   The two Dutch women did not act thoughtlessly. They made
the same kind of instantaneous calculations made by all bystanders.
Their decision was to challenge the Nazis directly. However, they
misread the situation, misjudged their capabilities, and paid dearly for
this mistake. This lesson was not lost on van Binsbergen. To challenge

the Nazis directly was suicidal, she decided. To have any chance of success, one's actions had to be clandestine.

The incident at the Jewish children's home took only minutes. Those minutes, however, changed the course of Marion van Binsbergen Pritchard's life. She was transformed into a determined rescuer. When van Binsbergen was asked to hide three children, she surreptitiously transported them to her family's country house and sheltered them until liberation.

Marion van Binsbergen's story illustrates the link between awareness and action. Rescuing behavior resulted from a combination of elements of the situation (such as the number of bystanders present) and of the person (the willingness to take responsibility, a personal sense of competency, and empathy).[1] Even though there are certain characteristics that differentiate helpers from nonhelpers, most social psychologists agree that there is no single set of attributes that will predict helping behavior. Once a "helping" type of person becomes aware of the need for help, often subtle elements of the situation play predominant roles in determining whether the individual will intervene in a specific situation.

In 1970, Bib Latané and John Darley's experiments placed their subjects in apparently dangerous situations that called for action. In one, students were in a room taking a "test" when pungent smoke entered the room. When a student was alone, he called for help; however, the presence of others made it much less likely that anyone would do anything. The social psychologists called this the principle of "diffusion of responsibility": that a person is much less likely to take responsibility and intervene in a situation requiring help if he is one among many.[2]

In the terms of Latané and Darley's experiment, rescuers were the subjects who took action about the smoke. They did not think that someone else would take care of it; they took responsibility. Despite the fact that others saw what was happening to the Jews, it was the rescuers who felt that unless they, personally, did something, another person would die.

Assuming responsibility is the third stage in Latané and Darley's bystander intervention model. It is the stage from which the final two, choosing a form of help and implementing it, flow logically. Psychologist Elizabeth Midlarsky feels that the willingness to take responsibility involves competency—the confidence that you can alter events to bring about the desired outcome. Midlarsky sees competency as a necessary precursor to helping—whether or not one can actually alter the situation is less important, as long as the person feels capable.[3] Other psychologists called this belief in one's ability to influence events "internal locus of control." Samuel and Pearl Oliner's findings in the Altruistic Personality Study support Midlarsky's view that rescuers strongly believed they could influence events that made them feel that what they did, or failed to do, mattered a great deal.[4]

Rescuers were no fools; nor were they suicidal. They were not about to offer help unless they felt there was a very good chance that they could pull it off. They needed to have faith in their capacity to assess situations and find solutions, not just in their ability to outsmart the Nazis. There was seldom time for measured thought. There was only time for a quick assessment of self and situation.

It was very difficult. There were scores of unknowns. No one knew how long the war would last or, until the end, who would win. How long would the commitment be? Several weeks? A couple of months? Janny Blom's offer to shelter the Vreedenburgs was a spur-of-the-moment decision based on listening to Winston Churchill's speeches on her illegal radio. She guessed that the Vreedenburgs would have to hide out with her for six weeks until the war was over; they stayed for three years.

To shelter a Jew was an illegal act. An offer to help immediately pitted the bystander against his or her law-abiding family, friends, and neighbors. It ruined any chance of preserving a normal life. Moreover, it meant being totally responsible for the survival of another person. Unlike a parent, who ordinarily has months to adjust to the role, rescuers had little time physically or psychologically to prepare. In most cases, they were thrust into the middle of a desperate situation with little time to agonize over issues. The nature of the request was clear and, as Dutch rescuer Wilto Schortinghuis (among others) recalled, the consequences of granting that request were equally clear: "The rule was: if you help Jews, you will be treated as one and sent directly to a concentration camp." (The rules of the game were different in Poland. There, anyone caught harboring a Jew was shot or hanged.)

Most social psychologists use a rewards-costs approach for helping to predict the nature of assistance that a bystander will choose to provide. The rewards for helping, as perceived by the bystander, must outweigh the costs if helping is to occur.[5] The reward for most rescuers was the personal satisfaction of doing the right thing and remaining faithful to their consciences.

Milgram's obedience studies give modern-day researchers a hint at just how difficult it must have been for most people to help others by disobeying authority. His studies found that while the majority of people, when asked, are certain that they would not actively harm another, few (in the experiments) were able to follow through with action. On the contrary, audiences who hear about the rescuers during the Holocaust hesitate to claim they would risk their own lives to save a stranger, acquaintance, or even a friend. Accustomed to thinking of themselves as good people, honesty compels them to admit that when push comes to shove they are not sure they would risk their lives for someone else.

Rescuers framed the question in other terms: "Can I live with myself if I say no?" Once they decided they could not, situational factors enhanced or impeded their action. Wilto Schortinghuis still feels guilty for those Jews he turned away because sheltering more people would have imperiled the lives of those he was already harboring. Although he and his wife successfully hid twenty Jews on their farm near the Belgian border, this Dutch pacifist was haunted by the ghosts of those who were killed after he refused to shelter any more.

The social psychologist Kurt Lewin called conditions that impede or enhance certain behavior "channel factors"—"stimulus or response pathways that serve to elicit or sustain behavioral intentions with particular intensity or stability."[6] If an opportunity to help is presented, various channels increase the likelihood that a bystander will undertake a rescue. Examples include: direct requests for help and availability of resources—e.g., existence of a reasonably safe hideout (a cellar, an attic, a ditch in the woods, a double wall, a tunnel), access to food, a disguise for a Jew to pass as a non-Jew, information, or an escape route to safety. Even when the opportunity presents itself to help, a channel is narrowed if one does not have the resources to be of any assistance.

Another situational factor that increased or decreased the likelihood of a bystander's decision to undertake a rescue was the physical characteristics of the person asking for help. A Jewish woman who could pass as an Aryan, with blond hair and blue eyes, was more likely to be offered shelter than a Jewish man with identifying traits— accented speech with Yiddish intonations, dark curly hair, a hooked nose, dark eyes, big ears, a beard, and a circumcised penis. Another was the existence and attitudes of other family members. If a potential rescuer's social support system was hostile, it could deter a potential rescuer from taking action.

Studies comparing rescuers and bystanders show that there were people who wanted to help but the fear of endangering their own children or themselves immobilized them. Other bystanders who were asked for help were inhibited because of lack of resources—limited space and no access to extra food. While it is true that there were rescuers who converted their one-room Berlin apartments to shelter people in need and found ways to obtain food-ration cards, the odds of succeeding under such conditions with limited resources generally impeded those with even the best of intentions.[7]

Most rescuers did not initiate the rescue. A friend, an acquaintance, a friend of a friend came and asked for help. This was the main channel to action. A direct, personal request provided an opportunity to act on individual intentions. Those who took responsibility were not hindered by how that help would endanger them and their family. All they thought about was that someone was in trouble. Of course they would help.[8]

This was Gitta Bauer's response when, on July 21, 1944, the day after the attempted assassination of Hitler, she was approached by a friend of her aunt. The woman needed a hideout for her daughter, Ilse Baumgart, a twenty-one-year-old half-Jew, or *Mischling,* who had been living unobtrusively in Berlin, but now was in deep trouble and running for her life. Baumgart had managed to forge documents that certified she was an Aryan. Soon afterward, she was drafted into the female corps of the German air force, the Luftwaffe. She worked a night shift as a teletype operator. The previous night she had been dozing at her desk when her supervisor shook her awake with the news that someone had tried to assassinate the Führer. Still half asleep, Baumgart mumbled, "Is the pig dead?" And she added, "If the attempt is successful the war would finally be over." There was no retracting what she had thoughtlessly said. Her supervisor immediately denounced her to the commanding officer. But it was late in the war, and the commanding officer did not have the heart to arrest her. Instead the officer told her pointedly: "I will give you fifteen minutes to think about what you have done. Alone. And then I will come back and you know what I have to do. You will be arrested."

Baumgart took the hint and ran. But she knew of nowhere safe to stay. Her mother appealed to Bauer. Like other rescuers, Bauer instantly assessed the situation and her capabilities. She knew that unless she helped, Baumgart would be caught and deported, which, for Jews, meant death. On the other hand, Bauer was alone. There was no one to help her make the decision, or help her with the day-to-day responsibility of rescuing. Her parents had moved to a safer place in southwestern Germany and so she was staying in their Berlin apartment by herself. In the end, her decision came down to whether or not to help a family friend in need. "What else could I say but 'I'll take her into my home'?" Bauer asked me. Bauer hid the girl in her apartment for nine months, an experience she likened to "giving birth." She and her "baby" made it through.

Bauer, like many other rescuers, had a sense of self that did not allow her to say no, along with a personal assurance, developed and nourished in childhood, which enabled her to see clearly that to do nothing meant certain death for the victim. In addition, she had a more or less secure place to hide Ilse Baumgart, had no family whose lives would be threatened, had no other responsibility that would interfere with her decision, and had the emotional and intellectual ability to solve problems in day-to-day life, such as finding food. It was, in Lewin's terms, the "state of both person and environment"[9] which led to Bauer's statement: "What else could I say but 'I'll take her into my home'?"

A last-minute, desperate plea was the channel. It was how Jean Kowalyk and her mother and other family members were transformed into full-fledged, if reluctant, rescuers with a houseful of Jews who escaped from the local labor camp. Each day, Kowalyk and her mother saw skeletal prisoners march in and out of the labor camp next door. There was little they could do but watch. On a few occasions they managed to sneak a piece of bread to one or two who were brave enough to jump out of line and quick enough to jump back in. One day, Kowalyk's mother became ill. Rather than transport her to a town miles away where medical help was available, Kowalyk's brother asked the commander of the labor camp to allow a Jewish doctor to see his mother. Dr. Solomon Berger came and was allowed to come daily until Kowalyk's mother was better. During the course of one of his visits, he asked Kowalyk's brother if he would help if things got worse. Kowalyk's brother, who had four small children, was reluctant to agree. But Kowalyk and her mother said they would help.

One night not long afterward, Kowalyk answered a knock at her door. There stood Dr. Berger. "He came into the room and grabbed my mother and started to kiss her and cry," Kowalyk remembered. " 'Please help!' he kept saying. 'Please save my life.' " Kowalyk agreed and told him to return the following night. She then ran to her brother's house and told him the situation. He, in turn, called on their sister's husband, and the two of them built a double wall to escape from the attic which was to be his hiding place. The next night, a grateful Dr. Berger arrived. Jean and her mother had his hiding place ready. A few minutes later, however, they heard a knock on the window. To Kowalyk's horror, there stood nineteen other lice-infested Jews seeking shelter. Dr. Berger had mentioned their offer to a few friends. Kowalyk pulled them indoors and then dashed to her brother and sister for help. Between the three of them, they found hiding places for all nineteen.

Kowalyk was not alone in undertaking more than she had planned. Other rescuers, especially those who were part of underground groups, talk about how wartime circumstances forced them into deeper anti-Nazi commitments than they had intended. Danish rescuer Harry LaFontaine, for example, started almost innocently enough by publishing an anti-Nazi newspaper. His paper, which began publication soon after the German takeover of Denmark in 1940, printed the unofficial version of events taking place in the country and listed the names of people who the editors thought were working too closely with the Germans. From there things just snowballed, LaFontaine recalled:

> I don't think anybody who begins a protest thinks that one day it's going to come to a point where they would use explosives and guns. You start out showing your disappointment by writing and distributing a few newspapers. Then you find that the enemy believes there is no such thing as "passive resistance" and if you are caught you have absolutely no protection. If you take up a fight against any government, you are a criminal; you are not protected by the Geneva Convention; you are not under the protection of the people you like to work with because they can do nothing for you. You are absolutely and completely on your own. And one day you find out that just because you wrote about being dissatisfied with the situation, you can be shot. So then you take the explosives in your hand and say, "If I have to die anyway, I might as well do something in the meantime."

Most commonly, one thing led to another, and when the opportunity presented itself, LaFontaine assisted in transporting Jews to safety in Sweden.

Aart Vos distrusted the Nazis from the start. The nocturnal adventures of his German friends' son was a warning. When Vos's dear musician friends, Alice Heksch and Nap de Klijn, were scheduled to move into the ghetto, Vos and his wife, Johtje, were afraid for them. The musicians had a very valuable grand piano that they were not allowed to take along, so Vos obtained false ownership papers. Their friends also asked the Voses if they would keep a suitcase of valuable papers. When the summons finally came for them to enter the ghetto, their friends grew fearful. Heksch and de Klijn did not want their three-year-old son to share their uncertain future. Vos volunteered to keep him too. "It is very difficult to say how we started [rescuing activities]," said Johtje Vos, who joined her husband in converting their Laren, Holland, home into a haven used by the Dutch underground. "You don't get up one morning and say, 'Now I'm going to hide Jewish people.' It's something that grows. You start with a suitcase and a child and a piano."

John Stenekes's rescuing, too, was a gradual process of increased commitment. Who could say why he started? John and Berta Stenekes were a young married couple who owned a bakery in Friesland, Holland, the same farm community northeast of Amsterdam where Theresa Weerstra and her husband lived. John Stenekes's only knowledge of Jews came from Bible stories. Yet he knew about the concentration camps from reading an underground newspaper and through his contacts with resistance workers. At first, Stenekes performed small tasks, as needed, for the underground. From time to time, he housed boys from the city who were escaping from the Germans' forced-labor roundups or were sent to him because food was more plentiful in the country. He also sent a weekly supply of extra food to his aunt and uncle in Amsterdam. They needed the extra food because they were hiding two Jewish girls in their attic.

Stenekes, who was one of sixteen children, had a sister living a few blocks away who was hiding two Jewish children, a twelve-year-old boy named Jacques and a nine-year-old girl named Anna. These children would come over every day to take the Stenekes's baby girl Rosie for a ride in her carriage. Berta Stenekes, who was seven months pregnant, never knew these neighborhood babysitters were Jewish.

Finally, the anxiety involved in hiding two Jewish children became too much for Stenekes's sister. She told him she was going to move them into a hotel. Such a move would be extremely dangerous since any hotel or pension management would demand identification, and they would discover right away that the children were Jewish. Stenekes wanted them to stay at his house, but first he needed to consult with his wife. He told Berta that Jacques and Anna were Jewish and what their situation was. His wife did a quick calculation.

They were already housing three people. Two more bodies to feed and house was too much, she thought. But Stenekes told her that unless they took the children in they would be killed. Neither spouse's moral conscience would permit that. "We didn't know where else they could go," Stenekes said. "So we took them." They hid them for over two years.

To take rescuing actions, people had to be in situations where action was possible, where channel factors like the availability of food, the physical features of the Jews, the presence of supportive others, and characteristics of the request linked intentions to behavior. Without resources, support, and stamina one could not act—no matter how much one saw and how responsible one felt. This is the essence of why a personality test can never accurately predict who will or will not become a rescuer. Action may come from the core of the self, but it is inhibited or reinforced by situational factors. Our case studies illustrate that only when an aware person, with feelings of responsibility, was in a situation that provided necessary resources was it possible for that person to act.

· 5 ·

THE RESCUER
SELF

"IT IS AMAZING HOW MUCH noble, unselfish work these people are doing, risking their own lives to help and save others," Anne Frank wrote in her diary. "Our helpers are a very good example. . . . Never had we heard one word of the burden which we certainly must be to them, never had one of them complained of all the trouble we give."

As the world knows, Anne Frank's family was betrayed by an informer and sent to concentration camps. Anne died two months before the end of the war at Bergen Belsen. So the last word on Anne's rescuers goes to one of them, Miep Gies: "I willingly did what I could to help. My husband did too. It was not enough."[1]

This tragic result long obscured the personal sacrifice and commitment that Miep Gies and others like her made to save Jews. That sacrifice was enormous. When bystanders transformed themselves into rescuers, they put concern for their own survival in the background and took responsibility for the well-being of others. They became outlaws in a Nazi no-man's-land. Their ideas of right and wrong were out of fashion. This was new for them, since before the war they had been very much part of their communities. Most rescuers were not loners or people who felt alienated from society.[2] But the secret of rescue effectively isolated them from everyone else. Neighbors viewed people who harbored Jews as selfish and dangerous because they risked their lives and the lives of those around them.

A rescuer's life was intricate and terrifying. A careless word, a forgotten detail, or one wrong move could lead to death. Dutch rescuer Louisa Steenstra recalled that German soldiers arrested the sixteen-year-old daughter of a friend for merely saying hello to a resistance man who was in their custody. She was sent to a concentration camp, where one hour later a guard shot her for insolence.

At home the strains were often just as great. Overnight, relationships changed, as families adjusted to a new member being sheltered. The home atmosphere could become poisonous if one spouse did not support the other's rescuing efforts. Comfortable routines were upset and new patterns had to be developed. Husbands and wives gave up their privacy. Children found themselves sleeping with strangers whom they had to learn to call brother, sister, aunt, uncle—whatever the situation or the occasion required. "Sibling" rivalries and jealousies developed.

A core confidence, a strong sense of self, and a supportive situation had allowed bystanders to undertake the rescue. But once the decision to help had been reached and the rescue had begun, a different self—a *rescuer self*—emerged, to do what had to be done and to keep rescuers from becoming overwhelmed by new responsibilities and pressures.

A "transformation" had taken place. It was not simply their behavior that changed. Successful rescuers became, in effect, different people. Psychohistorian Robert Jay Lifton explains the psychological process: When people find themselves in a world that no longer makes sense, their identities—the ways they behave, even notions of right and wrong—no longer seem to fit. They become "de-centered." In an effort to reestablish psychological equilibrium, they try hard to find new centers, to create new selves.[3] This new self, in the case of the rescuers, was built on strong moral foundations. It allowed them to do what was necessary—including plotting, stealing, lying, taking risks, enduring hardships, putting loved ones in jeopardy, and living in fear—all in the service of setting the world (and their place within it) on solid ground.

The act of rescue often entailed anxiety and great risk; rescue acts could also unleash strong feelings of guilt (at not being able to do more, at risking one's family in the service of others), rage (at the oppressors), terror and sadness (at witnessing atrocities and dehumanization), all of which ostensibly could induce inner chaos. But it is apparent from my interviews that rescuers have a strong equilibrium. They were able to withstand intense de-centering experiences and the accompanying pain and confusion. As Robert Jay Lifton points out, such experiences can help to *re-center* people, allowing them to achieve a new mode of flexible psychological coping.

The rescuer self kept the fear of death and the knowledge of Hitler's Final Solution at bay. French pastor and underground leader Marc Donadille summed it up:

> On some level we knew [the gassings] were true, incredible as it seemed—but we pushed it to the back of our minds and got on with the daily work of rescuing. It didn't make sense to say to the Jews we were rescuing, living side by side with, in our houses, 'Hitler is going to kill you all.' What haunted us was to save the Jews that were there. We had enough to do to keep them hidden, safe and fed.[4]

The rescuer self had to be competent, resourceful, and practical in order to get through each day safely. Their charges had to eat, and food shopping was a major problem. To avoid arousing suspicion by buying too much food at once, rescuers wandered far afield. In large cities such as Amsterdam this was not a problem at first. Janny Blom, who was feeding an extended family of five, and Miep Gies, who was buying groceries for seven people in hiding as well as for herself and her husband, distributed their purchases among several stores. These ruses were not foolproof. One day Gies's local vegetable man noticed that she was buying large amounts of vegetables. Without saying anything, he began putting vegetables aside for her shopping visits.

Months later when she stopped by to shop as usual, he was not there. He had been arrested for hiding two Jews.[5]

In rural villages, the daily chore of finding food and other basic necessities for those in hiding was nearly a full-time job. Jean Kowalyk had to go to a neighboring town to buy extra bars of soap so that the local merchant would not become suspicious. Toward the end of the war, even rescuers in large cities had to spend more and more time scavenging for groceries. It was not unusual to wait in a long line at a shop, finally get to the counter, and find that there was nothing to buy but a few potatoes. In Holland, those who prepared meals devised creative cooking methods for preparing tulip bulbs.

People in hiding got sick and it sometimes required what seemed like crazy actions to get them well. You could not call in a doctor to help a sick Jew. And you could not bury one who died; that person was not supposed to exist. In 1942, Wladyslaw Misiuna, a teenager from Radom, Poland, was recruited by the Germans to help inmates at the Fila Majdanek concentration camp start a rabbit farm to supply furs for soldiers at the Russian front. Misiuna felt responsible for the thirty young women he supervised. He stuffed his coat pockets with bread, milk, carrots, and pilfered potatoes and smuggled the food to them. But one day one of his workers, Devora Salzberg, contracted a mysterious infection. Misiuna was beside himself. He knew if the Germans discovered the open lesions on her arms they would kill her. He had to cure her, but how? He took the simplest route. He infected himself with her blood and went to a doctor in town. The doctor prescribed a medication, which Misiuna then shared with Salzberg. Both were cured, and both survived the war.

Jews had to be kept well hidden, so the rescuer self planned, plotted, and improvised. Hideouts were secured and contingencies anticipated on the assumption that sooner or later the Germans would search the house. The entrance to the Franks' secret annex was camouflaged by a bookcase. Jean Kowalyk's double wall allowed just enough space to hide her seven charges if they stood and squeezed together. The Voses built a tunnel between their two-story home in Laren and a nature preserve several hundred yards away. The entrance to the tunnel was hidden beneath a false bottom in the coal chute.

Despite the suspicious fact that the coal chute always had coal in it, a rare occurrence in the middle of the war and almost an unheard-of one at the end, the Nazis never found the tunnel.

Each combination of rescuer, victim, and situation created a peculiar alchemy. Whatever its distinctive traits, the rescuer self that emerged never strayed from the person's basic humanitarian values, which were solid and unchanging. They were democratic and humane in nature. It was easier, of course, to harbor a person who was likable than someone who was unpleasant or demanding. But once a rescuing relationship began, it was not easily terminated because of personality differences. Took Heroma and her husband, a doctor, had taken in a single Jewish woman in her twenties who happened to be pretty dull. Shortly afterward, Heroma heard of a famous professor who was looking for a hiding place. She felt very guilty for wishing she could have exchanged this boring woman for an interesting professor. Her rescuer self was not comfortable with the idea that these people were not equal.

The rescuer self was vigilant, inventive, and quick to take the unexpected in stride, holding together when the stress of living in confined quarters unhinged others. During a Nazi raid, while soldiers were busy elsewhere, the Voses had to restrain one Jewish man from a suicidal leap from a window. On another occasion, a Jewish woman staying with the Voses threw a kettle of boiling water at her husband, attacked the Voses, and ran from the house claiming she was going to turn herself in to the Gestapo. Fortunately, she did not. She came to her senses and returned to the house. She survived the war, staying with the Voses for three years, and remained a dear friend. But Johtje Vos recalled her friend's moment of temporary insanity as one of the most dangerous times for them during the war.

To operate effectively, the rescuer self was secret and rescue activities clandestine. The Nazis offered rewards for information that led to the capture of Jews. Informers were everywhere. In Poland, professional confidence men, informers, and blackmailers, called *szmalcowniks,* extorted money and valuables by threatening to denounce their victims to the occupying authorities. As was the case with the Germans, they were alert to any telltale signs of illegal activity. Laundry that was not recognizable as belonging to the homeowner (the wrong-size brassiere on a clothesline, for example) might arouse the suspicions of a neighbor. For rescuers like Jean Kowalyk, who was washing and ironing for seven fugitives, this presented a problem. She solved it by drying the clothes inside the house at night. As it was, Kowalyk's neighbors suspected she was up to something when they observed her chimney smoking at all hours of the day and night. They called the authorities, and Kowalyk's house was searched. Fortunately, the double wall in the attic, behind which the fugitives hid, was not discovered.

Holland was full of Nazi collaborators. While the number of Dutch rescue efforts appears to have been high, the number of people actually rescued represented only 11 percent of the Jewish population.[6] Betrayal was commonplace. In Amsterdam, the Bloms dared not trust their three-year-old son Hubert with the secret of who their guests were, lest in his innocence he blurt out a wrong word. During the day, the Vreedenburgs stayed out of sight in a bedroom on the second floor. Their feet were covered in crocheted slippers so their footsteps would be muffled. At night, they wandered about the house more freely. One evening, Hubert saw them. Janny Blom shooed him into bed and convinced him that he had been sleepwalking. This gave her an excuse to lock him in his room at night.

Rescuers constantly grappled with the question of who could be trusted with their secret. Six-year-old Annie P.'s stepfather told her to let certain strangers into her Bussum, Holland, house after curfew. Her stepfather, noted in this suburb of Amsterdam for his black roses, was a horticulturist who was hiding twenty-five Jews on various parts of his nursery property. Annie was never directly told that her family was sheltering Jews, but she figured it out. So did her stepfather's pro-Nazi neighbors. They noticed that the huge amount of garbage Annie's family threw out was too much, even for a family with twelve children. The neighbors reported their suspicions to the Germans, who raided Annie's house regularly.

On one of these occasions, the officer in charge was particularly frustrated by still another fruitless foray by his troops. He questioned Annie: Did she know where the Jews were hiding? Annie said nothing. The German threw her down and kicked her again and again. Still Annie said nothing. She kept the secret. The Jews survived the war, but the vicious kicking Annie received damaged her spine. Years and a number of unsuccessful operations later, she lost the use of her left leg and required a brace.

The general rule of thumb was: the fewer people who knew, the better. Willem Blom, for example, operated according to this principle. Although he was part of the Dutch underground, he never told fellow members he was sheltering Jews. "If you knew things like that, then you knew too much," said Blom, whose work in the underground involved instructing members on how to operate new weaponry like the Sten gun and the bazooka. Miep Gies's husband worked for the Dutch resistance for six months before he told her of his secret life. ("I didn't want to worry you," he said when she asked him why he had not told her sooner.[7]) Gitta Bauer entrusted her secret to her sisters and a couple of friends whose help she needed. At the very end of the war, when she and Baumgart were desperately hungry, Bauer took a chance and told a German soldier. He did not betray her and in fact gave her food. No one else, including her parents, knew. "We knew they would not abandon her or even denounce her," Bauer told me. "But we knew it would be a terrible burden for them. They would be afraid."

Secrecy became a habit and a way of life. Because the Bloms' house was attached to another house on each side, they whispered constantly. One day Janny Blom found, to her chagrin, that she was ordering meat from the butcher in her now-usual voice—a whisper. As time went on, she picked up the Vreedenburgs' speech inflections. She began answering questions with a question. Years later, she dismissed this as an amusing anecdote, but at the time such slips were often fatal.

Many rescuers retained the habit of secrecy even after secrecy was no longer necessary. Rescuers repressed painful memories of that time and so kept quiet. (It was not until quite recently, for instance, that, through psychoanalysis, Annie P. remembered that German soldiers had sexually molested her.) Some feared for their lives and dared not say anything. Others were somewhat ashamed of the things they did in order to keep their charges safe, and therefore said little. Katrina W., who distracted a border guard by having sex with him, had a daughter from that encounter. Her daughter was raised believing that her father had been killed at the Russian front. When asked about the war, her mother was proud but circumspect in describing her rescue activities. It was not until after Katrina W.'s death that her daughter matched up dates and times and figured out the truth.

Many kept their activities secret because they were afraid to acknowledge how they had risked their families' lives without their knowledge or consent. One Polish rescuer, for example, shielded his wife from the fact that he hid Jews in another apartment across town. During the war, he was afraid the knowledge would have been too frightening for her to bear. After the war, he was afraid that she would be angry to learn how he had gambled with her life.

The rescuer self had to be an actor, changing roles—and even changing plays—with the situation. John Weidner, head of the Dutch-Paris underground network, used eleven different aliases to evade the Nazis. One moment he was acting the part of John Cartier; the next he was Paul Rey. Weidner, who helped 800 Jews and more than 100 Allied airmen cross the borders into Switzerland and Spain, rehearsed his roles. First he memorized the details of each new identity and then he practiced answers to interrogation with another network member. Similarly, rescuers drilled Jewish children on their assumed baptismal names, catechism, religious hymns, and Christmas carols. Christians taught their Jewish charges the proper way to kneel and cross themselves in church. If the Nazis should stop them and ask for a demonstration, which was often the case, Jews would give a convincing performance.

Dutch housewife Theresa Weerstra lived the part of a pregnant woman to conceal the real pregnancy of one of her charges. Weerstra padded her underclothes with progressively fatter wads of clothing and then at the proper time "gave birth" so she could harbor a newborn without arousing suspicion. German Quaker rescuer Olga Halle leaped into the role of "dear relative" when Nazi guards searched the train on which she and an elderly Jewess were traveling. Halle chatted with the guards, but her companion was speechless.

Thinking quickly, Halle told the guards she was taking her deaf relative to Berlin. The guards wished her a pleasant journey. She and her companion escaped.

Other roles were improvised. A knock on the door late one winter night in 1943 thrust Maria Byrczek, a Polish Catholic mother of four small children, into a role for which she had no preparation. Standing at the door of her home in the small village of Jaworzno-Borj on the outskirts of Cracow was an elderly neighbor holding a five-month-old baby girl. The neighbor explained that the child's mother had been taken to a concentration camp and begged the elderly woman to find someone to care for her daughter, Marysia. Could Byrczek possibly take care of her? Byrczek looked at the infant and thought of a mother so desperate that her last hope for survival for her only child lay in entrusting her to a stranger. Byrczek took the baby.

But almost immediately the reality of her own situation sunk in and set her trembling. She realized that if she were caught sheltering a Jewish child, she and her own children would be killed. There was nobody else at home to help her. Her husband was dead, killed by the occupying forces. One sister, who lived in Warsaw, was in a concentration camp. She was crazed with fear. To calm herself and ease her mind, Byrczek created a fictional story. She told villagers that the baby was her sister's. Some unknown people had given her the child because her sister was in a concentration camp and there was no one else to care for the baby. The story was plausible enough, and the role of aunt gave Byrczek the courage and ease necessary to get through each day. Byrczek obtained a birth certificate for Marysia with her sister's last name on it. Her children welcomed their "cousin" and helped raise her. "Thanks to the story, my fear and anxiety were somewhat reduced," said Byrczek, a rescuer I found when her granddaughter replied to my letter published in a Polish newspaper requesting rescuers' names. "But I still could not sleep well, especially during roundups, searches, and night shootings."

Desperate times called for both creative solutions and constant vigilance. The rescuer self always had to be alert. A warning telephone call, a sound of a truck rumbling down the road at night, sent those in hiding scurrying for concealment. Rescuers never knew if an informer had given the Gestapo intelligence about their whereabouts or if the Gestapo was just pursuing a hunch. Whatever the case, rescuers had to give the performance of their lives. On one occasion, the Nazis burst in unexpectedly at the Kowalyks' residence. Jean Kowalyk, who lived with her mother, had practically no warning. Her charges had barely enough time to hide before the soldiers climbed the stairs to the attic. There in plain view was a table littered with cigarette butts and cards. Cigarette smoke still lingered in the air. At this dangerous moment, Kowalyk's nine-year-old nephew spoke up. He confessed that he and his friends had been secretly playing cards and smoking. He pleaded with the soldiers not to tell his mother, as she would beat him if she knew. The Germans promised to keep his secret and left.

From day to day the rescuer self played the part of innocent bystander concerned solely with getting by in these difficult times. It minded its own business and kept out of people's way. This role, of course, concealed the daily scramble to meet the various needs of a hidden household. In a two-room home barely big enough for herself and her mother, Jean Kowalyk housed a pack of strangers in her attic. For eighteen months, she fed them, carried their waste to the outhouse, washed and ironed their clothes, and refereed their fights. Acting the role of a dutiful daughter who gave sewing lessons to make ends meet gave her a necessary cover from suspecting neighbors. Having students come to the house made it seem like business as usual. It also gave her an essential psychological distance from her actions. She need not dwell on the fears and risks. She could escape into her role and almost believe it herself.

Rescuers had to be ready on a moment's notice to shift smoothly from one role to another. One day when John Stenekes and Jacques, his Jewish charge, were returning from Haarlem, a German soldier stopped them and asked for identity papers. Luckily their papers were in order, but the German asked Stenekes if the boy was his son. Without missing a beat, Stenekes became a proud, protective father and said that yes, this fine lad was his son. Then he waited. The German looked Jacques up and down and said, "He is a fine-looking boy. He's got a real Aryan look." Stenekes agreed, and the two went on their way.

Stenekes grew more adept with practice. He felt he "could drop from one person to another at the right moment." His Friesland home and bakery now supported three Jews: Jack, nine-year-old Anna, and a Jewish woman. Their cover story was that the three guests were the surviving members of a Rotterdam family whose home had been bombed. From time to time, others on the run from the Germans stayed with Stenekes too. In October 1944, Stenekes's situation became even more complicated. Seven German soldiers moved into his house. The soldiers were in charge of feeding the 150 soldiers in the area. The Stenekes's home became the local mess tent.

Keeping up their roles of local baker and wife minding their own business took iron nerves. Once Stenekes and his wife were sitting at their dining table with an SS man and the Jewish woman, whose looks and false papers gave her an air of legitimacy. Suddenly, Anna came running in bleeding from a fall and dripping blood all over everybody and everything. The SS man leaped out of the way, sputtering at her, "You damn little Jew!" Everybody in the room froze. Anna and those sitting around the table turned white. "We were shaking on the inside," said Stenekes, until it became obvious that the SS man meant nothing in particular by the remark. It was just an offhand expletive.

In the case of those Germans who were ardently anti-Hitler, playing the role of stolid Third Reich citizen was a twelve-year engagement. Oskar Schindler acted out the part of a German *bon ami* so convincingly that Amon Goeth, the brutally sadistic labor camp commandant with whom Schindler socialized, considered calling him as a character witness at his war trial.[8] Other Germans led similar double lives. Gitta Bauer and Hiltgunt Zassenhaus were two young women who served the Nazi bureaucracy while at the same time trying to undermine it. Bauer was drafted into the army headquarters' training division. Zassenhaus was assigned to be an interpreter for Norwegian and Danish political prisoners held in Germany. While mumbling *Heil Hitler,* Bauer hid a Jew and Zassenhaus, on her translation missions, supplied prisoners with vitamins, medicines, and words of encouragement. "It was a continuous game," said Zassenhaus, who like many other rescuers drew pleasure and courage from outwitting the Nazis. "I was like an actor playing a part. The part included saying, *'Heil Hitler!'* to every Nazi official I encountered. So I would raise my hand and mumble a similar-sounding phrase, *'Drei liter!'*—in English: 'Three liters!' An insignificant point, but at the time it made me feel better."[9]

Rescuers were all too aware that simply playing a part was not enough to fool the authorities. Rescuers constantly scanned their homes for any details that might be out of character. Minor items were sources of worry. Christians who hid Jewish books and valuables made sure they were well concealed. People whose homes functioned as underground shelters needed to ensure that objects and evidence of activity conformed to those of a normal household. Identification cards could not be stashed in drawers lest a search find ones with a "J," for *Jude* (Jew), stamped on them. Family members shared their beds with their charges so that a night raid would not reveal too many unmade beds. In apartment houses, the sounds of the toilet being used had to be carefully coordinated to conform with the number of people supposedly living there.

In the case of Romualda Ciesielska, having the proper props on the stage saved her own life and those of twenty-three Jews. Romualda and Felix Ciesielska were working as Christian relief workers in Cracow. Their office functioned as a forgery operation, providing false identification papers for the Christian underground movement, Ruch Oporu. In December 1940, the Gestapo cut off the Jewish section of the city and began rooting out and murdering the inhabitants. Jews piled into the Ciesielskas' office to escape. As the Gestapo approached their building, Romualda Ciesielska set the stage for the cover-up. She grabbed a Catholic prayer book in the corner of the room and tore it up. With a paste made of flour, she glued holy pictures on the wall outside their offices. The Gestapo entered the building and tore through each apartment in search of Jews. When they saw the holy pictures outside the Ciesielskas' door, they did not bother to go in, thinking it was a Christian outpost.

A few days later, Ciesielska created a new role. She was bringing food to a woman and her eleven-year-old daughter hidden with a peasant family. When Ciesielska arrived in the town, she found Nazis rounding up Jews in the square, providing them with spades to dig their own graves in the forest. Ciesielska first walked away casually, then ran straight to the Jews in hiding to warn them. There was no time to flee, and the Jewish woman looked too Semitic to slip past. Ciesielska ordered the Jewish woman into bed and told her to pretend she was dying. She placed a towel over the woman's head, a cross in her hands, and candles at her sides. Ciesielska grabbed the peasant's apron and tied it on the daughter, who was commanded to kneel at the bed and start weeping. She ordered the peasant women outside to feed the chickens. When the Gestapo arrived Ciesielska told them in German, "Please be quiet, there is a dying woman here." The Germans took one look and left.

Roles played by rescuers were tougher than mere stage acting. They lived their parts day and night. Their roles had to contain a kernel of truth, part of their real experience, or else the Germans and their sympathizers would see them for what they were. When Helena Orchon, a Polish actress and a daughter of a noted director, was asked by a friend to take in a Jewish child and act as if the child were hers, she refused. She felt she could not act the part convincingly. In real life, Orchon did not have any children, and she felt that she would be unable to live the part day after day.

The development of a rescuer self helped these rescuers keep their fear under control. The ego gratification and self-satisfaction gained from successfully outwitting the authorities and protecting others encouraged rescuers to keep up and, in some instances, to expand their activities. Maria Byrczek, who had taken in a baby, later befriended two young women who had escaped from the ghetto. The fugitives hid in the barn, where their presence was kept a secret from Byrczek's children. When Byrczek fed the animals, she left food for the two women. In the winter, she brought them hot water, and late at night when the children were asleep, she allowed them to warm themselves in her house. Only her sisters, who lived nearby, and the village doctor, who provided her with food ration tickets and warm clothes, were privy to her secret life.

There was also a rational calculation which supported doing more. As LaFontaine and other rescuers point out, the punishment was the same for small and large illegal acts. Some rescuers figured that as long as they were going to be shot for hiding one Jew, they might as well hide more. Dutch rescuer Wilto Schortinghuis and his wife began by agreeing to a request from a friend that they hide a Jewish doctor and his wife. Soon, a Jewish nurse from the psychiatric hospital where Schortinghuis's wife worked asked if they would harbor her and her two brothers. " 'If we could have two,' Wilto said, 'we could have four or six,' " Marie Schortinghuis recalled. "The risks were the same."

Rescuers basked in the appreciation of their wards. In the eyes of those they rescued, they saw their own inner goodness and they strove to live up to that reflection. Schindler's workers, for example, believed him to be a humane and unusually compassionate man. Living up to that image of himself spurred him on to further humanitarian acts. Schindler stepped up his efforts to recruit workers from the most brutal labor camps. At his relocated factory in Brunnlitz, he made a deal with the local police to send Jewish escapees to him rather than turn them over to the German authorities.[10]

Rescuers were able to play various roles and take required actions because, at the deepest level of their beings, it was who they were and what they believed that really mattered. They were certain that singling out a group of people, vilifying them, and hounding them to death was wrong. Their neighbors, friends, and co-workers could think and do as they liked, but they knew better; the laws were wrong. Unlike the Nazi doctors studied by Robert Jay Lifton, the actions of rescuers were consistent with their moral beliefs, identities, feelings, and attitudes.[11] They felt good about what they were doing. Many rescuers told me that this time of terror and mayhem was one of the most satisfying periods of their lives. Nothing they did afterward ever seemed so important or so vital.

The rescuer self allowed them to do what was needed to save lives. If the role called for lying, stealing, even killing, they did it. Under other circumstances, they would not have dreamed of behaving in such ways. But these were not normal times.

There were limits. When certain actions went against rescuers' personal sense of values, they refused to do them. Pacifists did not shoot other human beings. Religious rescuers were not about to exact revenge on their persecutors. Tina Strobos, a medical student living in Amsterdam, for example, was asked by the Dutch underground to play the role of a double agent. Strobos felt the degree of duplicity required for that part violated her core sense of who she was. She refused to do it. She agreed readily, however, to steal identification cards for the underground. Without the least compunction, she attended a funeral and waited until all the mourners were in the chapel. She then sneaked into the coatroom, went through their coats, and stole all their identification cards. Another time she invited classmates to her house for a party. When a guest went to the bathroom, she found his or her coat and lifted the card.

They sometimes had doubts. "We had to teach our children to lie," said Johtje Vos, stepmother to a nine-year-old boy and mother to three-year-old and one-year-old girls. "It was one of the greatest problems in that period of our lives. On the one hand, we had to punish them or reprimand them when they lied for other purposes. We had to make them understand the difference between the lies. Our children all knew—even the little ones—what they could say and what they couldn't say."

Rescuers sometimes did things they later regretted. Some, like Jopie D., tossed their fugitives out when food became scarce or neighbors threatened to denounce them. Others took unbelievable, foolish risks. To this day, Johtje Vos is horrified by what she did. It was at a time when a member of their rescue network had been arrested. Everyone's life was in danger. The Voses sat down with their fugitives to decide what to do. In preparation for a move to another hiding place, Johtje Vos had retrieved their real papers. Without warning, the Germans arrived. Aart Vos and the Jews ran for the tunnel. With the children upstairs napping, Johtje Vos realized she could not leave. She scooped up the papers and, desperate for a place to hide them, stuffed them into the pocket of the sweater her son was wearing. "Quietly try to get out of here and disappear with the papers," she ordered him. He did as he was told. As it happened, no one was arrested, but it was the narrowest of escapes. Afterward, Johtje Vos was appalled that she risked her son's life that way.

Harvard social scientist Kenneth Keniston, when studying Vietnam protesters, found that their antiwar acts were part of a longer series of concerned stances, not unique, one-time, one-cause involvements. Similarly, when social psychologist David Rosenhan of Stanford University interviewed committed civil rights workers he discovered a continuity in their moral values.[12] These are consistent with my own observations, that the basic compassion and moral integrity that triggered rescuing activity was repeated over and over during the rescuers' lifetimes. At the end of the war, for example, German soldiers in Friesland were starving. They came to the Stenekes's home bearing suitcases of stolen goods, ready to barter items for something to eat. Berta Stenekes told them to keep their stolen goods. If she had a piece of bread, however, she would give it to them. "In a way, I felt sorry for them too," she said. "They were so hungry."

Similarly, Aart Vos's values would not allow him to turn his back on the wounded German soldier he found in the road. Without giving it much thought, Vos picked up the young soldier, put him on his bicycle, and rode with him to get medical help. Vos was lambasted by a friend for showing such charity. An enemy was an enemy, the friend told him. They gave no quarter, so no mercy was due them. Vos saw it differently. He did not see a generic enemy. He saw a bleeding, young man, and he responded.

The rescuer self enabled people to do things that—in retrospect —seem unbelievable, even (perhaps especially) to them. To this day, John Stenekes is amazed at some of the things he did. "You grew into [these roles] and you don't even realize how intense it got," said Stenekes recalling his young rescuer self. "If someone wanted to give me a million dollars today [to do what I did then], I could not do it. But then it was life and death, and you started to get used to it. It seemed like half the time you did not even get scared anymore. And then it got so you were seldom scared. But if you got scared, then you were really scared."

The rescuer self emerged from the essential nature of the individual, very much a natural development of temperament and experience. Doctors and other professionals carried out their rescues with their professional, concerned, but detached airs. Adventurers such as LaFontaine continued to be adventurers. Before the war, for example, John Weidner was a successful textile executive and an avid skier. During the war, he used his business acumen to assess the factors involved in setting up and running a new enterprise, an escape network: Who needed help? Who would help out? Which guards were open to bribes? Which ones were sympathetic? Like an executive laying out his business plan, Weidner refined his product and assessed the competition. He combined his businessman's instincts and his love for skiing to create an enterprise in which he and others skied Jews and other Nazi fugitives across the borders to safety.

Having listened to so many stories—of quick wits and remarkable bravery—I remain most impressed by each rescuer's perseverance. Day after day they grappled with the pedestrian problems of feeding their hidden households, caring for their charges when they were ill, alleviating their boredom when they could. They risked their lives to bury a dead Jew, to console a crazy one, or to comfort a scared one. In the main, rescuing was not glamorous or filled with dramatic moments of valor. Rather, it was a tedious, enervating job, more like an assembly-line worker's duties than a movie star's. They did not know how it would end. Many rescuers described their weariness from endless days of deception and anxiety. Yet most did not abandon their charges. Most were tenacious in their determination to help. Wilto Schortinghuis spelled it out: "Our whole life changed. We could not have our friends visit . . . even our parents did not know, yet we could not stop them from visiting for three years' time. Whenever someone came to the door, a scare went through the house. We lived under constant pressure, day and night, three hundred sixty-five days a year."

Some rescuers thrived under the pressure. Others are amazed to this day at how they somehow managed. It was not until much later that the effects of their experience would haunt some of them.

· 6 ·

FEAR AND RESCUING

"Courage is not the absence of fear
but the control of fear."

—Dick Chapel, war correspondent

SURVIVORS OF AUSCHWITZ remember feeling removed
from what was happening around them: "I couldn't feel or cry; I tried
to tell myself, this wasn't really happening." Those feelings protected
the inmates from recognizing the full extent of the damage being
done to them.

No one suggests that the rescuers were worse off—or felt greater
fear—than the Auschwitz inmates. But the rescuers were forced to
cope, on a daily basis, with the simple problems of getting food to the
Jews, disposing of human waste, arranging for whatever small comforts were available, over weeks, months, or years of concealment—
while at the same time maintaining a normal front under the watchful
eyes of suspicious neighbors.

When this fear was accompanied by the knowledge that one was
endangering loved ones, the resulting conflict was all but unbearable.
Considered psychologically, the rescuer's position is not unlike that of
someone held hostage by terrorists or tortured by the secret police of a
dictatorial government. Suddenly, the person finds himself in a situation where the rules have been turned upside down. One is rewarded

for acts previously considered bad and punished for being good. The main difference in their conditions is the aspect of helplessness, which is the overriding feature of the prisoner experience. Conversely, the weight of total responsibility for one's own life and those of others was among the exigencies of the rescuer situation. The loneliness of this position was unrelenting because of its voluntary nature: every rescuer made a conscious decision to place himself or herself in harm's way. Because the decision could be rescinded at any time, one's life was entirely in one's own hands. The degree to which rescuers were able to cope with this enormous existential responsibility was remarkable.

Rescuers developed their own strategies for coping with the extreme stresses of both the physical and emotional sides of rescuing. Some had the ability to simply override their fear and focus on whatever action or duty was required of them—how to get an extra ration card, what could be bartered for a loaf of bread, and so on. By concentrating on the daily chores of sustaining a person under conditions of strict surveillance, some managed—at least temporarily—to block out the overwhelming dangers of their rescue activities.

Some rescuers who were adolescents and young adults during the war attribute their ability to withstand fear to the strength or naïveté of their youth. Young people often ignore danger, either through a deliberate, if unconscious, misjudgment of its seriousness or by making light of it or by denying the potential of evil forces in authority to harm them. Their youthful sense of personal immortality, which enabled them to enjoy the adventure without giving a thought to an unhappy ending, undoubtedly helped them cope with the trauma of their rescuing activity.

Some rescuers were involved in networks or enlisted their spouses' active support. These rescuers were able to manage their fears, isolation, and responsibilities by sharing them with others. Emotional support was equally vital. Very few people would have been able to endure the strain of rescuing for such extended periods of time without someone close by to remind them that they were not alone.

In moments of extreme danger, turning to God often alleviated their fear. Spiritual transcendence of the terrifying present made it possible to withstand regular brushes with death. Miracles were reported by believers and nonbelievers alike who turned to a spiritual being not only for guidance but for divine action. For many rescuers, praying for deliverance was a last resort when there was nothing they could do to get themselves out of danger.

Finally, there were those for whom the fear was tolerable because their acts of rescue were fueled by rage against the Third Reich itself. Some of these rescuers reported witnessing or being the target of grossly unfair treatment by Nazism in a way that is different from the encounters others suggest. Good Aryans were arrested on suspicion of being Jewish, perhaps, or German parents of "euthanized" mental hospital patients were denied an explanation of their children's disappearance. But although anger is often a successful way to release the tension of a stressful situation, it is not, generally speaking, a good solution if the stress is stretched out over many months or years. Anger fades with time, and then the trauma of the rescuing experience sets in with a vengeance.

The rescue stories of Stefania Podgórska, teenager, Alexander Roslan, businessman, and Louisa Steenstra, secretary and wife, show different means through which people kept fear at bay when facing the near-certainty of death.

Stefania Podgórska Burzminska: Poland
Strength of Youth and Spiritual Transcendence

Stefania Podgórska was not a very religious person when she began rescuing. Her rescuing activity was initiated through a personal relationship with a young Jewish man—the son of the owner of the grocery in which she worked. But during two of the numerous episodes of terror in her wartime experiences, she had an overwhelming spiritual revelation that allowed her to continue functioning. She committed her soul to God's care, and, to her mind, God responded with miracles.

Brought up with a social respect for her religion—family get-togethers and "Sunday best"—Stefania remains a devout Catholic to this day. Born the fifth of six sisters and three brothers, one of whom died in childhood, to a wealthy farming family, Stefania remembers being pampered as a child. Her grandfather had been a favorite of Polish officialdom—"for some heroic things he did, I think"—and had received a generous estate complete with animal stock and a large plantation house. The Podgórskas owned half a dozen horses, a small herd of cattle, and many chickens, and employed several villagers in running the farm. Stefania rode the horses and played with her siblings in the fields.

But the idyllic country life was not Stefania's style. "I hated the chickens," she says. "And the rooster—I felt that at exactly twelve o'clock midnight, he would start to crow. The chickens would start their cock-cock-cock-cock early in the morning. It made me nervous."

There were Jewish children in the village, but their parents were rather standoffish and would not allow them to play with the Gentiles. "Don't play with the *shikse,* don't touch the *shaygetz,*" Stefania mimics. The boys and girls managed to play together anyway.

In 1938, a year before the war began, Stefania's father died. Stefania and her mother went to visit several older sisters who had moved to Przemysl, a nearby city in southeastern Poland that had a Jewish population of 20,000 and which, in 1939, had the German-Soviet borderline running through it. Stefania, who was almost thirteen and utterly bored with life in the tiny farming village, was ready for wider horizons, and in Przemysl she was instantly enchanted. Cobbled streets, apartment buildings made of plaster and brick, clothing shops, chocolatiers, and, best of all, no chickens! The city was "quiet and peaceful" compared with her country home.

Stefania begged her mother to be allowed to stay. When that did not work, she refused to leave. One of her elder sisters eventually interceded for her with their mother. By the following week Stefania had found a job helping out in a local grocery.

The elderly owner of the grocery was Lea Adler Diamant, a Jewish woman with four sons, a hospitalized daughter, and an ailing husband. Mrs. Diamant was by nature a quiet, collected woman; but after a long lifetime of struggle and little to show for it, she had become habitually morose. Nothing cheered her more than watching Stefania hop around the store, flirting with the young men who came in and singing to herself when there were no customers. Stefania came quickly to seem like a daughter to the burdened Mrs. Diamant.

She was good for business too. Boys would come to the shop to buy chocolates from Stefania; they would purchase two and give her one. "How many chocolates could I eat?" Stefania says with a laugh. "I put the ones they gave me back on the shelf, and Mrs. Diamant complimented me for selling all her chocolates twice over."

After about a year of working for the Diamants, Stefania moved in with them and became a sort of girl Friday for the family. She shopped and cooked for them, sleeping on a couple of blankets laid out in a corner of the two-room apartment over the store.

The war had started, but it initially did not alter Stefania's daily routine, except for a while when the shops were closed. Later they opened again, with German soldiers standing around outside with guns. Then the Germans went away and Russian soldiers appeared. Then the Russians left and the Germans came back in 1941. Stefania learned a couple of words in each language: *da* and *do svidanya, auf Wiedersehen* and *bitte*.

But when the Germans occupied the town for the second time, Stefania began noticing differences. A ghetto was created under her nose, right behind the Diamants' shop, with barbed wire around a run-down neighborhood of apartment buildings. Notices began appearing in the streets: Jews had to wear the Star, Jews could not own businesses. Native Poles would avoid meeting the eyes of their Jewish neighbors.

Stefania's reaction, at the age of sixteen, was pure perplexity. What was behind this? Was there something wrong with the Jewish people that she, in her inexperience, had never known? Or were the Germans just being unfair?

Most sixteen-year-olds are old enough to realize that they need not obey their parents' wishes, but are not yet sufficiently knowledgeable about themselves and the world around them to have determined their own needs. Stefania was already an independent agent. She was so young, however, that helping Jews in defiance of the law was not the kind of natural and instantaneous decision many older rescuers made. Before she helped, she had to make up her mind about who was good and who was bad. Once she chose, she devoted herself completely to her decision.

With a mix of sadness, fear, and confusion, Stefania helped the Diamant family to pack their belongings and move into the ghetto. They begged her to get a permit to continue living in the apartment over their shop, so that she could look after it while they were gone. Stefania soon became the proud occupant of an entire floor in the now empty building. Within a few days another young woman rented the second floor, and the two of them had the run of the place. It was exciting, but eerie. Several families had lived in the building, and at night they still seemed to be breathing.

Stefania soon realized that the Diamants were starving in the ghetto. She began buying food for them and then slipping it under a hole in the barbed-wire fence. A friendly Polish policeman stood by the gap in the fence once in a while, but she convinced him she had a childhood playmate inside and soon she became a regular visitor to the ghetto.

Stefania began to hear screams from the ghetto late at night; when she asked the German soldier at the entrance to the ghetto what was happening, he told her it was just an *Aktion*.[1] One day Mrs. Diamant, pale and shaken, told her that hundreds of people in the ghetto had been taken away.

A few nights later, Stefania was again awakened by screams from down the block. It was another *Aktion*—but this time she could hear Mrs. Diamant's voice among those who were shrieking in terror. "I can't leave my children," Stefania heard her cry. "What will happen to my children?"

The next morning she slipped under the fence to learn that Mr. and Mrs. Diamant had been deported to Auschwitz.

The Diamants had a daughter and four sons, one of whom, Isaac, was soon sent to the Lvov labor camp—populated by a potpourri of Jews, Russians, Gypsies, and Ukrainians. Stefania went to visit Isaac three times in Lvov, bringing food and clothing on the trolley with her. On the third occasion, she managed to work out an escape plan with him: he would dress in the street clothes she had given him, along with a pair of old glasses and shoes. The moment Isaac saw her approach the camp he would bolt and they would both run for their lives.

As was true of many rescuers, Stefania did not start with a huge risk, but built up to it gradually. Emboldened by her ability to sneak food into the ghetto, she grew accustomed to the stress of committing illegal acts for the sake of her friends. Even so, the planned escape from the Lvov camp was much more dangerous than her previous activities. But at the time, there seemed to be no alternative. An escape plan—even a harebrained one—seemed preferable to Isaac's certain death.

On the day of the arranged escape, Stefania's trolley was held up for two hours by a passing German battalion. When she finally arrived at the Lvov camp, she was told that Isaac was dead. He had seen another woman, who looked like her, appear at the appointed hour. He ran to her but she refused to help him. The police caught and shot him.

Stefania returned to town to tell Isaac's brothers of his death. When she arrived at the Lvov ghetto, she was stunned to find only a few families left. Almost the entire Jewish community had been deported or murdered, and two of Isaac's brothers—Joseph and Henek—were scheduled to leave on the next train. Frantic with grief and overcome with helplessness, the two brothers made a suicide pact. They planned to jump off the speeding train before it reached Auschwitz.

Joseph had a loaf of bread that Stefania had given him stuffed inside his shirt. As he jumped from the car he saw a telegraph pole, with a spike sticking out, rush toward him. He lost consciousness as he felt the spike hammer his chest.

When Joseph came to, the loaf of bread had a big hole down the middle and he had merely broken his clavicle. His brother was nowhere to be seen. Jews whose suicide attempt failed when they jumped from the train helped Joseph to the home of an ex-girlfriend, who agreed to put him up for the night.

Joseph spent the next day searching for Polish friends who would hide him from the Nazis. All of them, fearing for their lives, turned him away. At last he went back to the building that had once been his home, and knocked on Stefania's door.

"Who is it?" Stefania asked in surprise at the lateness of this visitor.

"Uh, it's Joseph," he said.

"Joseph who?"

"Well, you remember Joseph. You worked for my mother."

Stefania opened the door. "I saw Joseph," she remembers, "but it was not Joseph. It was like three disasters together. He was dirty, wounded, with blood all over his face and hands."

Joseph begged to be allowed to stay the night, and Stefania agreed instantly. She cleaned and dressed his wounds with the help of her six-year-old sister, Helena, who had come to stay with her in her roomy new apartment. Helena laughed when Stefania dressed Joseph in one of her own nightgowns. "Now I see two Stefanias!" she exclaimed.

That night Joseph became sick. Stefania nursed him for several days, hiding him under the bed whenever the other young woman who lived in the building came by. Gradually she grew accustomed to the danger of harboring a Jew in her home.

Their first crisis occurred when Joseph returned from a trip to the ghetto with Danuta, a young Jewish woman who was engaged to his youngest brother. Danuta was discovered in Stefania's room by the other occupant of the building. With an aplomb that surprised her, Stefania told the other woman that Danuta had come to her for advice about an abortion.

"No problem," said the worldly Polish girl. "Just take a very hot bath and then run up and down these stairs twenty times. That will take care of everything."

Caring for the Jews left in the ghetto became a full-time job for Danuta and Joseph; Stefania worked in a local factory, but continued to do what she could. She began exchanging her dresses for food to smuggle under the barbed-wire fence, sometimes walking thirteen miles to a village where she knew she could get milk and butter in exchange for various articles of clothing. But the situation in the ghetto was growing ever more precarious, and the Jews knew it would not be long before the ghetto itself was liquidated.

The three held a strategy meeting late one night. Joseph's youngest brother, Henek, whom he had not seen since they jumped from the train, was back in the ghetto—he could not survive on the streets, and he had nowhere else to go—and there were other friends there who had heard about the kind Polish girl and her little sister who had taken in Joseph and Danuta. But they could not possibly hide all these Jews from the other occupant of the building. Stefania had to find a new place to live, and Joseph suggested she look in the now deserted Jewish neighborhoods.

The next day Stefania ventured into what seemed like a ghost town. The empty buildings, some without windows and some without doors, frightened her. She knew she had to have at least one window looking out on the street, and a door to hide behind in case she was raided, but there was nothing that suited her needs.

I went out and I stood on the street and I thought: "Where do I go?" I didn't know where to go. Everything was empty, and I was scared. It was so ghostly. And then—you will laugh when I say this, really—then I heard a voice. I heard a voice. While I stood there thinking, asking, "Dear God, where am I supposed to go now to look for an apartment? Where?" I looked around and I was frightened, because nobody was there. And then I heard the voice. Some voice told me, "Don't be afraid. Go a little farther. After this corner, two women are standing, women who clean the street. They are supporting themselves on their brooms. Ask them for an apartment. They will tell you."

So I listened to the voice, and then asked, "How will ordinary women who clean the street know about an apartment?" And the voice said to me, "Go and ask. They will know. They will tell you." So I still thought: "Well, what would *they* know." And this voice again told me, "Go, please go." And I felt like a little push, and the voice said, "Go and ask for a janitor there." And I said, "All right, all right, what can I lose?"

So I went exactly that way, just like this voice told me. After the corner, I saw the two women. There they are, talking together and supporting themselves on their brooms. Okay. I approached them and asked, "Ladies, I am looking for an apartment. Maybe you know something? There's nothing here— maybe you're familiar with this area?"

They said, "Oh, right, we know of an apartment. There's a little small cottage, a one-family, that has a woman janitor. Just ask for this woman janitor and she will show you the apartment."

The cottage was perfect. It had two rooms with both front and rear entrances, complete with a huge attic approachable only from the back, and an outhouse.

As for Stefania's supernatural experience, I can only say that she would not have been able to save anyone without it. Perhaps Stefania had actually walked past those two women and had not consciously registered their presence, but in her anguished uncertainty their image rose to the level of awareness. Or maybe, to give equal time to those who are intrigued by studies of extrasensory perception, Stefania was precognitive and is attributing her own abilities to divine intervention. But regardless of how skeptical outsiders may view the situation (and Stefania, as you will note in her testimony, is quite sensitive to their possible reactions), Stefania experienced the moment as a direct and unmistakable answer to her prayers. It was, in a word, a miracle.

Little Helena rolled around the floor for joy when she saw the size of the place, and Joseph and Danuta danced in the attic. They quickly pulled Henek, a neighbor, and two children out of the ghetto —and all of a sudden, seventeen-year-old Stefania and seven-year-old Helena were hiding five Jews with two more on the way.

The two were wealthy Jewish businessmen, the fathers of the children Joseph and Danuta had brought. The plan was that they would bribe the Polish postman, who came every day to the ghetto, to take them in his mail cart to Stefania's neighborhood. If they encountered anyone on the street once the postman had dropped them off, they were to pretend to be Stefania's supervisors from work checking up on why she had not been at the factory that day.

Stefania and Joseph waited by the window at the appointed hour. After about ten minutes they saw not the postman, but two Polish policemen and two German soldiers patrolling the street in front of the house. They looked at each other, their blood freezing. What would happen when the postman arrived?

After almost three hours of waiting, Stefania could no longer stand the suspense. Ignoring the entreaties of Joseph and the other Jews in the house, she strolled up to one of the Polish officers.

"What's going on?" she asked casually. "Was somebody killed or something?"

"No," said the policeman mysteriously, "but maybe someone *will* be."

"So you're protecting us maybe. Maybe Hitler and Stalin are coming to this very street to fight it out between themselves and you're going to protect me and my little sister?"

The policeman laughed. "Well, if they come and fight, maybe we'll help you kill them both and end the war."

At that moment one of the German soldiers came up and said something harsh to the Polish officer, which made him stand at attention. Stefania's hopes sank.

"Well, goodbye," she said gaily, starting down the street.

"No, wait, stay and talk," the policeman said.

"Only if you tell me why you're standing here," she said, smiling.

The other Pole, who had sidled up to her after the German spoke to the first policeman, replied, "Why not."

The first man shrugged. "Why not. Yesterday the Germans received a note saying that two rich Jews are leaving the ghetto today, coming to this street. They ordered us to catch the Jews, but they don't trust us. We don't believe any Jews are coming. So they're watching us watching them. That's it."

Stefania's heart sank when she heard him say they were waiting for two rich Jews from the ghetto. "I said to myself, 'Oh, God, what will happen today?' " she remembers. " 'Will I be killed today or not?' "

But in spite of her anxiety, she managed to smile. "I can't imagine these Jews would risk their lives to get out of the ghetto," she said. "They know they'll be killed if they try. I don't think they'd do it."

"Well, I agree with you," said the first Pole. "But orders are orders, and we have to stand here."

Stefania left them and walked straight into a nearby church. She kneeled and prayed fervently: "Please, God, get these Germans and those policemen away from here before the postman comes. Please help me, so these two fathers aren't caught and killed, and their children don't grow up as orphans."

When she got back home, the policemen were gone and the Jews had just arrived. The postman, it turned out, had gotten lost on his way to Stefania's and had taken the two Jews all over town before finding the right street. The children were crying and hugging their fathers. Once again, Stefania was certain that her prayers had been effective.

But the operation had not been without its danger. When the postman had let the Jews out, another Pole had discovered them. He told them he knew who they were and where they were staying, and would reveal all to the Gestapo down the street unless they gave him 10,000 zlotys. Terrified, they handed him all the money they had and waited in agonizing suspense for him to turn them in anyway.

He gazed evenly at them. "I'm a thief, not a murderer," he said. "I have what I want. I'll tell you when the Germans are out of sight, don't worry. Maybe we'll meet again after the war is over."

But the blackmailing was not over. One day Stefania received a letter delivered by two street urchins, who demanded that Stefania read it, sign it, and return it to them so they could be paid. The letter was from a Jewish woman in the ghetto; it named all the people she had in hiding and threatened to tell the Gestapo everything unless Stefania took in the author of the letter and her children.

Stefania was shaking. What if the letter was actually from a Gestapo agent, who was just waiting for her signature to raid the house and murder everyone in it?

She talked it over with Joseph. He said the Gestapo did not need an excuse to raid the house—and anyway, he knew the writer of the letter. She had a reputation throughout the entire community as a snooty and manipulative person. Stefania signed the letter, and she and Joseph sneaked into the ghetto that night to confront the woman.

When faced with Stefania's fury, Hanna Z. began sobbing. "It was the only way I knew to save my family," she cried. "Please forgive me."

"You're a blackmailer," Stefania whispered viciously. "You didn't have to do that. Now those stupid boys know where I live, they know I have people in hiding. You're a killer. I'm trying to help people, and you go writing down the names of everyone."

Hanna Z. fell to the floor and kissed Stefania's knees. "I don't know how to behave, it's true," she said. "I thought this was the best way. But I just wanted to be alive. I wanted to save my children. I wanted to live to hear you tell me I did a bad thing, nothing more." She embraced Stefania's legs and kissed her hand. "Please, I beg you. I didn't know any other way."

With a huge sigh, Stefania said it was all right. "Three people more don't make a difference to me," she told the older woman. "They can only kill me once for hiding Jews, not ten times."

She told Hanna Z. to wait for a message about a time and a place for them to escape. The next morning, she sent Helena to play near the ghetto with a note for Hanna Z.

Seven-year-old Helena had grown quite adept at passing slips of paper through the barbed-wire fence unnoticed, but this time she was unlucky. A gang of teenage boys saw Helena take a note from inside the ghetto, and began to chase her.

Frightened, Helena started to run away. Although she could not read or write, Stefania had told her never to let anyone see the little pieces of paper she took from the ghetto. As she ran, she tore up her message and ate the pieces. When the boys caught up to her and found nothing in her hand or pockets, they beat and kicked her so badly she could barely make it home.

For four years after the war was over, Helena was mute. Now in her fifties, she still stutters. The need for secrecy had been impressed on her so deeply, and the trauma of discovery had been so shocking, she could not escape from her habit of silence. Hanna Z. and her children finally were smuggled into Stefania's home, and three more

Jews came after the ghetto was liquidated. With a grand total of thirteen Jews and one little Polish girl to feed and take care of, Stefania was forced to shoulder responsibilities beyond her seventeen years.

Joseph and some of the others built a false wall in the attic, which cost Stefania a good deal of effort just finding the wood. The man who sold her the hammer she needed asked her what it was for. "I'll give it to you free if you're burying Germans with it," he said, grinning.

"No," she replied airily. "I just have to fix the floor in my bedroom."

Helena managed to buy food for them all by telling the shop-keepers that she was selling the extra loaves of bread and sacks of potatoes on the black market. She had to manage on her own most of the day, because Stefania was working in the factory.

As the months wore on, a handsome young Polish boy at the factory where Stefania worked fell in love with her. If she had allowed herself, she could have easily loved him back. But her rescuer self prevented her from trusting this handsome man. Her safety and those of her charges depended on her discretion.

"If I hadn't had these thirteen, my deadly business," she remembers, "I really wouldn't have hesitated, because that was a good boy and a handsome boy. But I couldn't sleep all night, worrying whether he would come and discover my secret. How could I scare him off?"

She went to a photography studio where a girlfriend of hers worked and asked her for a portrait of a handsome Nazi officer. Her friend was puzzled, but when she heard that Stefania wanted to get rid of a Polish boyfriend, she laughed and gave her a photo.

The next day Stefania's suitor called on her, and immediately noticed the picture of the SS officer hanging over her bed.

"What is that?" he asked in astonishment.

"You mean *who* is that," she replied archly. "That is my new boyfriend."

His jaw fell open. "You? And him?"

She nodded.

"I don't believe it."

"Don't," she said curtly, "but it's true. He's my man and I'm going to stay with him."

This boy looked at that picture, then at me. I saw he was like paralyzed. He looked at that picture and then at me, and he became an older man. He couldn't move. For a few minutes he stood and he looked, and he wanted to say something. He couldn't.

Now, my heart was broken. I wanted to cry, really. Because I loved him, but I did this thing to repel him, because my mind knew that I cannot love. But I wanted to cry. There was a moment when I wanted to tell him everything. I wanted to tell him: Listen, I have thirteen Jews. I have to save them. I have to help them. I wanted to tell him. But you know, my mind told me: No, don't tell him. One second I wanted to tell him and the next second it was no, don't tell. But inside my heart, my heart was broken, I wanted to cry but I kept my tears, I wanted to embrace him and tell him everything but I couldn't. I couldn't. I thought: "God, I have to help these people. If I tell him, I don't know what his reaction will be."

Then he moved and he looked at me and said, "You. You and the SS. You." I said, "Yes, me and the SS. Me and an SS man. Look how handsome he is."

And he turned, still looking at me, and went out. I watched him at the window, and he walked like an old man. I can't tell you how much I wanted to cry. I wanted to run after him and cry but I said no, no.

Perhaps in part because of the difficult process of self-definition which had been forced on her by the confrontation with Nazism, Stefania was in touch with a core level of her being. She would go into a sort of trance when her fear was at its greatest, and that state of concentration would make it possible for her to overcome her fear of death.

The source of that strength may be psychological, spiritual, or truly divine, depending on one's frame of reference. One could say it was Stefania's soul acknowledging its immortality or her youth refusing to imagine its own demise. In any case, operating at this level of consciousness both prompted her to take further action when it was required and warned her to hold still when that strategy was necessary. Both times, it probably saved her life; it certainly saved the lives of the Jews she harbored.

In the concluding months of the war, as the Russians advanced from the east inflicting heavy casualties on the German side, an empty building across the street from Stefania's cottage was converted into a field hospital. The formerly deserted street was suddenly swarming with Nazi soldiers, ambulances, wounded, doctors, and nurses. Many of the hospital personnel lived on the grounds—which had been a college campus—and Stefania realized that her situation was now much more precarious.

One afternoon, two SS soldiers knocked on her door. "You have been ordered to vacate the premises within two hours," they read to her from an official-looking sheet of paper. "This residence has been commandeered by the Third Reich. The penalty for noncompliance is death."

"Two hours! How will I find a place for my sister and me in just two hours?" she cried, but they merely repeated the orders and left.

For the next hour and a half Stefania ran through every street in town—but she could find nothing that would shelter all fifteen of them. After three years of looting and deprivation, the buildings were in worse shape than ever. There were doorways but no doors; houses without ceilings; rooms filled with the rubble of loose masonry and roofing material.

Just ruins, nothing more. Almost two hours had gone already. So I came home. I started to cry. I said, "How can I leave thirteen people to certain death? I can run out, but these people will be dead. . . . There was nothing available, nothing. Only twenty minutes left. I came home. I said nothing. All my thirteen came down to me, with the three children. They pressed against me, so tightly, they looked at me. My decision. Will I leave? My decision. Will I leave them or not?

All thirteen of them said to me, "Run away. You don't have to die with us. We have to, but you don't have to die with us. You cannot help us anymore. Save your life and your little sister and run away, because you still have ten minutes." Joseph pushed me. They said, "Run away. Don't die with us. You cannot help us anymore. What you could do you did, but not now. Save your life and Helena. Go. Run away."

And all these people watched me, the children pressed so close I could hear their breathing, my sister too. So I really, I didn't know what to do. I said to them, "Well, first of all, come on. We will pray. We will ask God." You see, I had a picture which I bought as a little girl, of Jesus and his mother, and it always hung on my wall. And I said, "Come on—we will pray. We will ask God."

First I knelt, then my sister and all the thirteen after, behind me. And I prayed, and I turned to look. All thirteen were in deep, deep prayer. And I asked God not to let us be killed. Help, somehow. I cannot leave this apartment. I cannot leave thirteen people for a certain death. I will be alive if I go, but thirteen lives will be finished—children too, and young people. I asked God, "Help, somehow."

And again I heard a voice, a woman's voice. It was so beautiful, so nice, so quiet. She said to me, "Don't worry. Everything will be all right. You will not leave your apartment. You will stay here, and they will take only one room. Everything will be all right. I am with you." And she told me, "Be quiet. I'll tell you what to do." She said, "Send your people to the bunker. Open the door. Open the windows. Clean your apartment and sing."

I was like hypnotized. My head was bent down, and I was listening, I was listening and the voice said again, "Everything will be all right." Then it disappeared. I listened a few minutes more, but nothing more came.

So I got up and said to my people, "Go to the attic," exactly like the lady told me. I said, "I will not move from my apartment. I will stay here, so go to the attic and be quiet, very quiet."

And you see, I was completely different. My people looked at me, all my thirteen, and they thought something was wrong with my mind. But I said, "Okay now, go out, go to the bunker. Everything will be all right if you stay quiet over there."

And I opened the window and the doors, and I cleaned. I started to sing. I don't know how I became so happy. And all the neighbors came, and they said, "Miss Podgórska, what happened? Why haven't you moved? The Gestapo, the SS will come. They will kill you. This is war, this is the military. They have no mercy for an enemy—and they are our enemy. Go out. We don't want to see you killed. You're too nice, too young to be dead."

I said, "I have no place to go." They said, "Don't you have a friend? Go stay with her." I said, "No, I will not leave my apartment." And they also thought something was wrong with me.

The janitor's husband came, and he said, "Miss Podgórska, I will throw you out. Go out. I don't want to see you be killed—I have no place to bury you." And he was serious. . . . I said, "No, I am sorry. I will not move from my apartment." And he said, "Something is wrong with you," but he left.

I kept singing and cleaning my apartment, and exactly ten minutes past the two hours an SS man came. He was so friendly. He was laughing to me from a few yards away. He came closer to the window and he said—he spoke a little Polish, very broken but he spoke—and he said it was good that I hadn't moved from my apartment because they would take only one room. This last room, they would take. He said, "Very well, you can stay."

Thirteen Jewish people had been saved once again by Stefania's inner voice. As inexplicable as this miracle was, the greater wonder by far was that two nurses from the hospital, along with their German soldier boyfriends, slept every night for eight months directly underneath the attic and never discovered the Jews hiding there. Every morning Stefania would watch the Germans collect their rifles and wonder if today would be the day they would shoot her.

Joseph and the others could not stand silently in the attic twenty-four hours a day, so they had a guard posted to watch for movement up the back stairway. At one point one of the nurses actually did suspect that something was going on upstairs. She decided to inspect the attic. Stefania tried to stop her, but was held back by one of the German soldiers.

For several moments Stefania was white with panic—would the woman think to knock on the false wall? But the nurse found nothing but storage and signaled her boyfriend to release Stefania as she came back down the stairs. Luckily, the nurses and Germans were not present during the day; Stefania was therefore able to feed the Jews and remove their wastes. A few weeks before the end of the war, the hospital closed down and the nurses were moved to a town farther behind the front lines.

Stefania remembers her liberation well. Two Russian soldiers came by to ask if she had any vodka in exchange for chocolate, and she invited them in.

They asked her what it had been like living with the Nazis; she told them she had hated it. Then she began questioning them. Where are the Germans? Where is the front?

"You sound like a spy, asking all these questions," one of the Russians joked.

"You asked me questions, now I'm asking you," Stefania retorted. "So, where are the Germans? Are they coming back?"

"Oh, no, no," said the other soldier. "We've already chased them close to Germany. They're never coming back."

The thirteen Jews were standing behind the bedroom door, listening. When they heard the Germans were gone for good they could not restrain themselves and burst, weeping, into the room. The startled Russian soldiers reached for their rifles, but Stefania calmed them down.

"Don't worry, these are friends, Jewish friends," she said. "I and my sister saved them, and they are quiet people, good people. You can put away your guns."

The Jews began kissing the Russians, in expression of gratefulness for the wonderful news brought by them. The soldiers gazed in disbelief at Stefania and Helena.

"Two girls," they said to each other. "Not even two—a girl and a half."

Thirteen people, and their children and grandchildren, are alive today because a teenager ignored the fact that she would be killed for harboring Jews; thirteen men, women, and children are alive today because a teenager believed in miracles.

·

Alexander Roslan: Poland
Transcendence of Fear Through Emotional Numbing

·

For many rescuers simply preserving Jewish lives was not enough; they went to extraordinary lengths to maintain their charges' health—physical and otherwise—devoting themselves to the quality of life, as well as to its preservation.

An outstanding example of this commitment was that displayed by Alexander Roslan. He conducted a rescue that was striking both for its misfortunes and for the amazingly resourceful way he handled them. Born in 1909 in a small village called Retniki about twelve kilometers from Bialystok, Alex was five when his father died in World War I.

Alex was the second of five brothers—but, as he put it, he was "always the leader," and made sure that his siblings were not taken advantage of after his father's death. Alex saw to it that the family property was divided among the siblings. He and his brothers worked the farm his grandfather had owned, milking the cows, planting and harvesting a variety of vegetables and tending the apple and pear orchards. The whole family lived in a three-room wooden house—bedroom, living room, kitchen—exactly like the hundred or so other houses in the unpaved village. The Roslans' farm was bordered by a forest, and Alex remembers playing soldier there with his brothers and his next-door neighbor, the village shoemaker's daughter Mela—whom he later married.

Alex's childhood provided him with models of altruism: his mother and grandmother often sheltered and fed wandering Gypsies. His grandparents' religious faith did not make much of an impression on him, nor does he consider either his mother or himself particularly religious.

Five years or so before the war, Alex began to worry that the Russians would take over Retniki and deprive them all of their livelihood. He split the farm up five ways and sold his portion, opening a fabric shop in Bialystok with the proceeds of the sale. By this time Alex and Mela had two children, Jurek and Mary. Alex remembers doing a great deal of business with the Jews of Bialystok.

When the Russians moved into Poland in 1939, Alex fled with his family to Warsaw. There he began dealing on the black market. The family lived in a two-room apartment in the center of town; the children slept on a couch and their parents on a bed a few feet away.

The Warsaw ghetto was only two blocks from Alex's home. He was moved, mostly by simple curiosity, to see the ghetto in spite of the strict injunction against civilian visitors. One of his brothers, a member of the Polish underground, sneaked him in.

Alex was overcome with horror by what he witnessed. It was early in the morning, before the cart came to pick up the dead bodies of children lying on the street. The parents of these young unfortunates, he was told, had long since died or been deported. Corpses of toddlers and teenagers alike swarmed with flies. Alex remembers the flies, vividly.

Alex gave some bread to the desperate children who came pleadingly toward him, but he was overwhelmed by the futility of the act. He came back to the ghetto several times, to engrave the images of dying children on his psyche and to reinspire himself with a feeling that something had to be done. At last he told an old friend from Retniki, a chauffeur who had worked for a Jewish family now living in the ghetto, that he would take in a Jewish child.

Alex characterizes the liquidation of the ghetto as the most difficult period of time for him during the war. "You can't eat," he says. "You can't sleep. If you see things like that, you can get sick." Yet he was only a bystander at the time of the mass deportations, not a rescuer. From an objective point of view, his rescuing experience was infinitely more stressful—because of the intimate losses he suffered while living with the constant fear of his own and his family's danger. He was able to block out the terror and sorrow of his rescuing experience by focusing on his empathic feelings for the dying children in the ghetto, and all his repressed grief and fear have heightened the indelibility of those images in his mind.

Although his remembrance of the mass deportations from Warsaw may be tinged with the emotions of later years, the event certainly had a tremendous impact on Alex at the time. He had two children of his own, and was feeding two Catholic children as well—one of them severely crippled. He was willing to take in a girl, he said, because girls were less dangerous than boys. They were not immediately identifiable as Jews upon genital inspection. But the child whom Alex's friend had found was a male, a thirteen-year-old.

Jacob Gutgelt had a large, well-shaped nose, a sensitive mouth, and big brown eyes aided by thick glasses (which made it very difficult for him to disguise his Jewishness). Alex was stunned by the obviousness of the child's genetic heritage. In his general ignorance about Jews, he had believed that "only grown-ups looked Jewish."

For a crucial moment, Alex feared the risk to his own children. He hesitated; then reached a decision, saying simply, "Okay, I'll take him." In the same breath he instructed Jacob never to look out the window, because someone outside might see his face.

We can assume that during this moment of hesitation, every experience relevant to Alex's moral training kicked in: the repeated trips into the ghetto, the example of Alex's mother helping Gypsies in defiance of her neighbors, the voice of his grandmother insisting that "we are all God's children." Alex wanted to help because of who he was and he was *able* to help because he could cope with fear by numbing his normal responses. He turned from the issue of whether he should help and moved instantly to the practical question of how he could keep everyone safe—therefore his warning to Jacob never to look out the window. In those few seconds of uncertainty, it was as much Alex's ability to cope with fear as it was his moral strength that saved Jacob's life.

Interestingly enough, Alex hinted during the interview that the root of his confidence lay in the fact that he was "somebody no one recognizes," hence he could ignore the danger. He seemed most pleased to make this claim of unnoticeability, a reaction I found interesting. Behind this statement was surely a sad time during his adolescence when Alex had considered himself not very attractive;

everyone recognizes a good-looking person. Alex seems to make a virtue of something most of us would feel was a drawback.

Some research has shown that people get involved in helping others when they are happy and content; an emotional threshold is reached where the proposed sacrifice seems less important than the rewards of doing good. But the idea of feeling better about oneself probably serves as an enticement to be altruistic, even when one is basically happy. Thus, Alex could be glad not to be especially good-looking, since it made him feel safe when he wanted very much to do something risky. He had accepted his looks at an earlier stage in his life, but now there was reason to feel lucky about them. Later, he was able to use that sense of well-being in order to transcend his fear.

Alex instructed his children in their new roles. He informed them exactly what the family was doing and why, being quite clear about the danger. Thus, he hoped, no innocent tongue-wagging would attract trouble.

But trouble surrounded the Roslans, as it did most rescuers. Because of an unlucky encounter with a neighbor in the hallway, Alex was inspected twice by Gestapo agents.

The first inspection was on Easter Sunday. Alex got ten minutes' warning from his brother in the underground. He had put a false wall into a cupboard and hidden it with dishes; it was there that Jacob was secreted when the Gestapo arrived with Alex's brother-in-law, who had tried unsuccessfully to head them off. His own children went into the kitchen and made noise so that Jacob could shift position in the cupboard without being heard.

Alex wined and dined the Germans for seven hours, getting them all drunk so they would forget why they had come. It was a risky strategy because Alex was uncertain whether his brother-in-law, in alcohol-induced loquaciousness, would say something to alert the Nazis.

A few weeks later the same agents arrived again—this time clearly expecting to be entertained in the same grand style. Again Alex hid Jacob in the cupboard and plied the Gestapo with drink; again they neglected to carefully inspect his apartment.

After the second visit Alex was frantic. "Now what do I do? Millions of things went through my mind. I had to survive. I could take the boy and go to the ghetto. No. It was too late. I would not give up."

Alex decided he had to get away from the city; it was too crowded, too difficult to keep a secret from one's neighbors. He found a house in a suburb of Warsaw and hid Jacob in a hollowed-out couch when the family moved there. Claiming it was the best seat in the house, Alex insisted on sitting on the sofa for the whole truck ride.

Everyone liked the new home, which was situated on a tree-lined street and had a pretty garden. But the house was still terribly risky. It was a two-family home; how could he keep a secret from the couple next door?

In addition, the black-market customers and suppliers who knew Alex best were much harder to reach. He could not simply disappear all day to go to market, or he might never see his family again. Much of the merchandise, being clandestine, arrived after curfew, when Alex could not possibly be far from home. Alex had severely limited his business opportunities by moving to the suburbs.

In his interview, Alex did not say whether he had considered the possibility of dire poverty when he decided to keep Jacob and move his family away from the center of town. Probably he chose to trust in his own proven ability to make money. A very important ingredient for coping with stress through the numbing of fear is a sense of personal competence and self-esteem, and Alex had financial self-confidence.

He set his entire family—Protestants, Catholics, and Jew—to making candy under his wife's supervision. This he sold on the black market at an extraordinary profit, thanks to the scarcity of such luxuries during wartime occupation. Soon the Roslan clan was doing as well as most of the others in the neighborhood.

Jacob grew comfortable as a member of the family, tutoring Alex's daughter in math and reading. He read to Mary from Heinrich Graetz, the great Jewish historian. Life settled down to what passed for normalcy in wartime Poland: Jurek and Jacob slept on the couch, and Mary slept in the bed with her parents.

It had been so for only a matter of weeks when a member of the underground came to beg Alex to take in Jacob's brother, Sholom.

This was too much for Mela, Alex's wife. When she had agreed to hide Jacob, she had not known it would mean the unbearable suspense of two Gestapo inspections and a complete uprooting for her family. Now she realized there was a price to pay for rescuing that was below the ultimate punishment—but dear nonetheless.

"You're playing it very dangerously," she said to him that night.

"What's the difference?" Alex pleaded. "It's the same danger to hide two Jews as for one."

Alex could see his wife's determination cracking. He overcame the fear of losing her and the worry about hurting her by deciding to maintain confidence in her intelligence and internal strength. Perhaps, too, his faith in her helped her to stick with her initial decision and not leave him. The next day, Alex accepted Sholom into his growing household.

Sholom, who was nine years old, had been kept for several months on a rooftop. Exposed to wind and rain as well as the neighbors' prying eyes, he had been unable to so much as sit up while there was still light out. From dawn to dusk he had been forced to lie silently on the roof.

When he came to Alex's house, he was pathetically skinny and a nervous wreck, starting in terror at the slightest unexpected sound. Alex had nothing to give him but hot soup.

Two months later Sholom came down with scarlet fever, and infected Alex's own son, Jurek. Luckily, the local doctor could be trusted enough to visit both patients—but Sholom was too sick to be cured at home.

Mela was frantic. She had known taking Sholom would bring nothing but misfortune. Jurek was sent to the hospital, and Sholom remained wasting away at home.

But when Jurek went into the hospital, he did something extraordinary. Jurek took only half of his medication and hid the rest. He took notes, in his fever, on what the doctors and nurses did to cure him. When his mother came to visit, he gave her the medicine and the notes and told her to use them to help Sholom.

Much has been written about teaching moral values, of the need for parents to make an effort to impress the importance of these values beyond the implied instruction of serving as role models. Thus, merely saying you shouldn't hurt another human being, and refraining from threatening your own neighbors, is quite different from actually punishing your child for fighting. In Jurek's case, his father's willingness to make supreme efforts on behalf of others made it impossible for the son to do less. Alex's decision to incorporate his children into the rescuing activity, and the shared anxiety that that life involved, indicated the weight of these values to his son.

Jurek's effort was to no avail, however. In spite of his medicine and expertly guided care, Sholom grew thinner and weaker. One morning, Alex came in to ask him how he felt. "Fine," he replied, adding that he wanted to go to the bathroom.

"He talked with me," Alex remembers. "Then he died."

Note the lack of emotion in Alex's testimony. He does not remember how Jacob reacted to his younger brother's death, or how his own son felt after the sacrifices that he had made. In order to make it through the grief Alex brought into his life by agreeing to help, he has utterly suppressed it.

Sholom's death, a tragedy and a failure after heroic effort, left little time for mourning. Sholom's dying presented Alex with a terrifying problem: Where could he bury the corpse?

"I was afraid just to dig a hole," Alex recalls. He had to choose his moment carefully, or the people with whom he shared his house would wonder what was going on.

In the middle of the night he went with the crippled Catholic boy into the earthen basement of the suburban house, wrapped Sholom's body in a sheet, and put it into a laundry basket to bury it.

Both Poles hesitated over the meager grave, unsure of how to bury a Jew. "I think Jews go like they're sitting," said the boy, "so when Judgment comes they can jump out of the grave quickly."

Alex found this difficult to believe, but he had no better information himself. They sat Sholom up in the laundry basket and buried him in the basement.

Then Jacob became seriously ill. For lack of medicine, a slight ear infection developed into a raging fever. The infection threatened to spread to Jacob's brain. The good doctor who had kept quiet about Sholom earlier could do nothing for Jacob at home. He voiced a hope that the Russians would open up the front so Jacob could be put into a hospital. But this was 1943 and the Russians were two years away.

Finally Alex's brother in the Polish underground suggested a doctor with a private clinic—hospitals were too dangerous, and Jacob was on the verge of death.

"What if I go to the doctor and the doctor goes to the Gestapo?" Alex asked. "Then we'll kill him!" said his brother. This, of course, was slender comfort to a family man. But Alex's brother trusted this doctor, so Alex decided to take the chance.

> I went there. Maybe the doctor would be there, I thought, maybe the clinic would be there—maybe not. The war has destroyed a lot. Maybe the building has been destroyed. But I went to this address. The building was okay, the clinic was there. I knocked on the door. A man opened the door. I said, "I'd like to talk with Dr. Stepanovicz," and he said, "I am Dr. Stepanovicz." I showed him the card [from the first doctor, describing Jacob's symptoms]. He said, "Right away—get to the hospital! The boy must be put into a hospital!" I say, "Doctor, I don't know. Maybe it will be better in the clinic." He says, "No. I won't have an empty bed for another week. I have no place right now." But I said, "Doctor, the boy is a Jewish boy."
>
> I watched his eyes for a reaction. I was scared. He said, "Go home. I will send a doctor to check the boy. The doctor will be safe, no danger."

Alex's careful enumeration of each step he took—walking to the clinic, knocking on the door, greeting the doctor—reveals the depth of his fear. Every instant of this errand is permanently imprinted on his memory. Yet he tells the tale dully, with only a raised eyebrow and listless gestures to communicate his emotion. Alex could not feel his fear forty years later.

The doctor that Stepanovicz sent for was already examining Jacob when Alex got home. He told the Roslans that he would operate for free, but needed 10,000 zlotys to bribe the nurses who would assist him.

"But I had no money at all," remembers Alex. "I didn't have any opportunities to make money in the country. The doctor went. I waited for a miracle."

At the time, it probably seemed to Alex that this was the greatest moral juncture of his life. He could have rested easy with the knowledge that he had tried to save two Jews and circumstances had taken them from him; he could have decided that the risk to his own children was too great to trust outsiders with Jacob's difficulties.

But Alex considered Jacob a member of his family, and the transforming visions of dead and dying children in the Warsaw ghetto still haunted him. Also, he was stubborn and determined not to give up, as well as supremely self-assured about his ability to raise money eventually. Sholom's death had energized rather than sapped Alex's strength; he had given up so much and lost one already, he'd be damned if he would just let the other one go.

All he needed was money, and that was usually obtained easily enough. While Mela cried and begged him to just let Jacob go, pleading that it was too dangerous, Alex schemed. He realized he had one asset: his home.

The next day he sold it.

On his way to the real estate agency in Warsaw, he encountered a young man who was willing to give him 16,000 zlotys on the spot for the place and the furniture. "I was young, I was strong," Alex says. "All the time I believed that if I had one chance I would get the money."

Mela was hysterical when he came home and told her they had to move again. "Sholom died, Jacob will die," she cried. "We are homeless. Two or three days, Jacob will die!"

But the deal was done. Alex bought a one-room apartment for 6,000 zlotys. It was a fifth-floor walk-up, with nothing but a stove in one corner and a toilet in the other, in the heart of Warsaw. "I didn't care," he says. "Maybe tomorrow, I figured, something would bring me luck."

The next morning he wrapped Jacob's face in bandages like a

burn victim and took him to the clinic. Within a few days the boy was well enough to come home—to sleep on the floor of a single room bereft of furniture, shared with Alex, Mela, and both of their children.

Financially, the family's situation had become so precarious Alex felt he could not reveal the truth to his wife. He told her he had a few thousand zlotys left from the sale of the apartment; he had exactly one sack of potatoes.

At least the Roslans were back in Warsaw, where Alex still had contacts. He went to a friend who bought German furs to sell on the black market. After joking around with him for a while about the old days, he asked if he could sell a fur on commission. The man gave him a coat to sell. Half an hour later Alex came back for another coat —with fifty zlotys in his pocket. Within three days all the coats were gone, and Alex looked around for another business.

He heard about a woman who was selling German army blankets out of her basement. He bargained her down to almost half her asking price and sold the lot of them to slipper manufacturers, who used the material to make cheap night shoes. Through the woman with the blankets, Alex connected with the underground saboteurs who were stealing German army goods by the truckload. Soon he was selling flannel and other items and turning huge profits.

Alex bought a three-bedroom apartment in the center of town, which went a long way toward soothing his wife's anxieties. A few months later, flush with his new black-market businesses, he bought a second apartment to keep his wife and children safe.

Just as things started going well for the family, Jacob's uncle approached Alex a third time—to ask him to hide Jacob's youngest brother, David. David was seven years old. Because their resources were greater, both Alex and Mela agreed much more easily to this proposal than they had to Sholom.

But Alex was a little too successful as a businessman. Nobody wanted to attract the notice of the occupation forces, and the mysterious appearance of wealth was a sure way to get jealous neighbors to alert the Gestapo.

One day Alex got a phone call from his suppliers. They had a truckload of shoe leather for him. "It's too heavy," Alex said. "I don't want this." But they insisted. They had to get rid of it; it was too dangerous for them to try to hide the goods.

A few hours later, Alex received a phone call from an anonymous member of the underground. "Get out of the house!" the caller said, and hung up.

Alex was arrested for selling government property on the black market. He was not beaten, but the boys from whom he had bought his goods were tortured for their refusal to identify him. The entire experience was so terrifying Alex has almost entirely blocked it out. He was afraid of what he would say under torture, whether he would reveal the presence of a Jew in his household and so doom his entire family.

Although some of the guards were members of the underground, they could not manage to get him out. After six weeks Alex's wife finagled his release by bribing someone to steal his prison records. The bribe was in American dollars and once he no longer existed officially at the jail, it was merely a matter of a few more payments to free him.

"I was in shock," he says, "I felt like I was blind. The corridors were open. We went to the office and I signed a phony card. We went to the gate. He opened the gate. I saw my wife. We left."

Alex insisted that his wife try to raise funds for the boys who were still in the jail, suffering on his behalf. The day after his release, he asked her to go around the neighborhood to collect money from the underground.

But when Mela went out the next day, she found downtown Warsaw utterly empty. There were no streetcars, no traders—not so much as a beggar on the sidewalk. Frightened, she came home.

Surprised by her quick reappearance, Alex went to the window. He saw what looked like a German motorcycle coming down the street—but then realized that it was not a swastika but the Polish flag flying from the rear of the vehicle. Just as the motorcycle passed by the front of Alex's building, there was a tremendous explosion and the window blew out of its frame.

It was the beginning of the Polish Uprising. Alex and his family had a front-row seat to almost two solid months of guerrilla warfare. They lived in basements, trying always to stay near the front lines of the battle because the Germans were less likely to shell close by their own quarters.

They shared their basements with hundreds of other Poles, whose buildings had also been destroyed by relentless gunfire and bombings. Everyone could see that Jacob was Jewish, but now there was no one to whom to complain. "We were all Jews during that time," Alex jokes darkly.

It was at this point in the war that Alex's personal tragedy occurred. Jurek, the boy who had halved his own medicine to try to cure Sholom's scarlet fever, was killed by a stray bullet when he went outside to fetch water for the family.

In the interview, Alex related this event simply—"I lost my son" —and required gentle pressure to go into detail. Jurek was fifteen years old. Alex never found out whether the bullet that killed his son was fired by a Nazi or a fellow Pole.

After the Uprising was suppressed, the Nazis emptied Warsaw. The Roslan family began to drift from village to village.

The war was almost over, but the danger to Alex had magnified. Poland was in a state of chaos. He had nowhere to hide. In addition, he was grieving over the loss of his son, but he also had to figure out how to feed his family (he still had money earned from the black market) and avoid the Nazis.

Throughout the years of subterfuge, of possible betrayal and tragedy, Alex had maintained his confidence. He had buried his anxiety deeply, in an effort to shield his family from the trauma they would endure if they had known how frightened he was.

But now the strain was too much. He was vulnerable as they walked like beggars through the towns and fields with the very Jewish-looking Jacob. He had no means of earning a living; the root of his self-assurance, which lay in his ability to make money, was cut off. The Roslans would settle in a town for a few weeks, then pack up and flee in the middle of the night when Alex or Mela heard the neighbors whispering that they were Jews.

At last Alex left his wife and daughter with David in one village and kept on the move with Jacob, wandering ever closer to the Russian front. Alex describes the effect these final months had on him:

> I was different. I don't know how to put this feeling into words. I just felt mentally and physically different. I was scared all the time. I was never scared before. Before, it was different. When I spoke to people I thought I was smart. Now I felt I was not as clever as I was before. I was shy.

Alex reports that he has been unable to cry since the war. Mela often has nightmares and goes on long crying jags afterward. Alex claims that these post-traumatic reactions are the result of the unbelievable stresses of life after the Uprising—as if six weeks in jail, three Gestapo raids, Jurek's and Sholom's deaths, and Jacob's near-fatal illness would not have affected him this way without the strain of those final months of wandering. Again, Alex has burdened one set of incidents with the emotions attendant upon many. This is clearly part of his unconscious strategy for coping with the past.

However, Alex certainly had reason to be terrified as he meandered aimlessly through the countryside with Jacob, constantly looking over his shoulder and yet knowing he would be helpless to save them should something go wrong. His new neighbors, all temporary, all strangers, would inevitably see Jacob—he could not keep the boy hidden twenty-four hours a day. And when the neighbors caught a glimpse of Jacob's face, they would begin to comment.

Several weeks before the end of the war, Alex finally decided that he and Jacob would stay where they were no matter what. He could not take the strain of wandering anymore. After only a few weeks, they were kicked out of their apartment; Alex's landlady accused him of being a Jew.

Alex heaved a huge sigh of relief—thank goodness no one suspected the truth! He invited his landlady to accompany him to the doctor for a genital inspection, which proved his racial status—much to his landlady's chagrin. Then he asked that the doctor give him a certificate, to obviate any future accusations.

But in the end, the official paper was unnecessary. Russian tanks entered the village soon after this incident. The Roslans were safe, and Jacob and David were free.

Alex's rescuing activity was fraught with peril at both extremes—when he failed to save Sholom as well as when he became too successful financially. Jurek might have died even if the Roslans had not protected Jacob. After all, Alex could have remained in the center of Warsaw, and would still have been living there when the Uprising took place. But the fact remains that the rescue engendered years of terrible anxiety and several episodes to which the only possible response was unadulterated terror.

Alex's response to that fear was to deny it and to rely on his sense of invisibility as well as his salesmanship. Although he talks of "miracles," he does not mention God and refers several times to luck. He seemed impervious to both his wife's nerves and his brother-in-law's weaknesses, maintaining a rigorous faith in them as "good" or "smart" people. And he was very careful to keep his fears to himself, knowing that the family needed to feel unquestioning confidence in him or else they would be traumatized by their insecurity. But in the end, it was Alex who was emotionally damaged, who no longer has the confidence or capacity for enjoying life that he once had.

Alex says he has heart trouble whenever he reminisces about the past. But he would, he says, do it again:

> I took in Jacob, and the aunt [of all three boys] said, "Please, tell me I can trust you, because we do not know you." I said, "Trust me." And they trusted me, like we had become one family. When Sholom died, when Jacob was sick, my wife thought we would not survive. I said, "Mela, if I lost everything, I will not break my promise."

Louisa Steenstra: Holland
Supportive Network and Anti-Nazi Rage

Louisa Steenstra, former secretary at a furniture factory owned by Dutch Jews, had become a full-time "professional" rescuer by the time her home was raided by the Gestapo. The Dutch, as we have seen, saved Jews by acting quickly and in unison following the Nazi invasion. Louisa's parents, brother, and sister all harbored Jews in their houses; her husband, Albert, was an active member of the de Groot underground. Together the Steenstras formed a solid wall of protection around a total of five Jews and their own infant daughter, Beatrice.

Louisa remembers Groningen as a lovely, cobblestone-paved town crisscrossed by canals and bordered by a pleasant lake. As a child she would skate on the canals in the winter, and her neighbors would bring the church organ out on the street to provide music throughout the night.

The Jewish community in Groningen dates from 1573. By 1931 there were about 2,500 Jews—about 2.5 percent of the population, concentrated in traditional Jewish fields of employment like the garment industry and finance. Louisa says that she worked for or with Jews all her life.

Louisa's rage, which sustained her throughout the war but has left her bereft and shaking to this day, was born on May 10, 1940. She turned on her radio to learn that 30,000 people had been killed that day by German bombers over Rotterdam.

The Dutch government, threatened with the bombing of all of Holland's major cities, capitulated within four days. "Thirty thousand people," Louisa says, still in shock. "When you hear that, how can you feel? I hated them. I couldn't stand the Germans. I couldn't stand it."

Shortly after they conquered Holland, the Germans immediately enacted laws disallowing employment of or ownership of property by

Jews. Louisa was manifestly disgusted by the new regime, and refused to go to work in the main office of her formerly Jewish-owned sleep-wear factory, now run by Nazi sympathizers.

Unlike the situations faced by Stefania Podgórska and Alex Roslan in Poland, Louisa had more support. Many Dutch tacitly encouraged defiant acts against the Third Reich. The factory in which Louisa Steenstra worked employed more than a hundred people, six in the front office. Of those, only two continued their jobs under Nazi management—and Louisa clearly has no patience with them even now.

Louisa told her husband, "I am not going to work for the Germans. I will kill myself first." When the Germans came to her door to order her back to the factory, she told them she was pregnant. She was not.

It was not only Louisa's anger but her open, flamboyant personality that gave her strength. She coped by engaging in dramatic acts of defiance from the very beginning—acts that were only slightly modulated by caution.

Louisa did get pregnant, in 1941, and gave birth to a little girl. She recalls sitting in the hospital with her husband, Albert, and her mother-in-law discussing her daughter's name.

"Beatrice Irene," said Louisa determinedly, drawing a gasp from Albert's mother. This was the name of the Dutch queen's grand-daughter in exile. Louisa wanted the Nazis to know right from the start whose side she was on.

"Please, not that," her mother-in-law begged, in tears. "She needs to have another name. It's too dangerous, Louisa."

Louisa shared a long look with Albert, who had already become involved in the underground. He gave a slight shrug, indicating that they might as well soothe the old woman's fears.

"All right. We'll call her Beatrice Wilhelmina, or Trixie for short," said Louisa, thinking: But my daughter's name is Beatrice Irene!

A few hours later, when Albert's mother had left, a nurse who had overheard the conversation picked up Beatrice and showed her to the couple next to them. Louisa and the other mother had given birth around the same time, both to girls—but the other woman's husband had come to visit his wife in the slick black uniform of a member of the Nazi Party.

"This is Beatrice Irene," the nurse said to the Nazi with a sly smile. "Our little princess."

Louisa's heart leaped at this show of defiance, and she noted with pleasure the stiffness of the other couple when they heard her daughter's name. But then she sobered. "It could have been worse—you have to be careful," she remembers now. "Many people got killed by those people on the other side. They betrayed their own people."

Louisa says, "We saw it every day." Only her confidence in the support of her family and Dutch society in general allowed her to openly declare herself anti-Nazi—even in front of a member of the party itself—in spite of the risk that all knew she flouted.

Louisa was arrested even before she began sheltering Jews—just for doing a few favors for a Jewish woman, the sister-in-law of someone Albert had met at work. "She had two children," Louisa explains. "She couldn't go to parks anymore. She couldn't go to restaurants anymore. You could not do the wash at the laundry. No books from the library. All that work, I did for her. She would make up a list."

One night her Jewish friend was raided while Louisa was in the house. The police officers ordered her to dress the children and go with them to Westerbork, the main transit point leading to Auschwitz, which was situated outside Groningen. The Jewish woman's husband had already been deported to a Dutch labor camp, and she had not heard from him; she began weeping uncontrollably and collapsed in front of the policeman. Louisa, shaken, took the children upstairs to dress them.

One of the officers, who knew Albert, followed her up.

"What are you doing here?" he whispered. "Is this woman a friend of yours?"

"I'm just helping," Louisa whispered back.

"Don't tell the other officer anything," he warned her. "That guy's a Nazi, a sympathizer. He'll try to arrest you. Be careful."

Louisa could barely manage to close the buttons on the children's shirts, her hands were trembling so badly. When she brought them back downstairs, the hard-faced policeman was waiting for her.

He took her to Gestapo headquarters simply for being in the house of a Jew.

Louisa was expected home any minute. Beatrice was breast-feeding, and it was time for her meal. Louisa was taken to the station and told to sit outside an office, where she remained for several hours.

Finally a German officer called her in and began to interrogate her. Did she know any other Jews? What had she been doing there? Why was she helping these Jews?

"They've been friends for years," Louisa lied.

Did she know any others? Was she part of a network?

"No, no, no. I worked for a Jewish company, and I knew these people. I brought them a few books. Please, let me go. I just want to see my baby," Louisa pleaded.

Louisa was kept in jail, incommunicado, for two days and two nights. The strain must have been unbelievable: Albert had underground contacts, Louisa herself had already joined a network to help Jews, and she had no idea how much the Nazis knew or what she would say if tortured. She was not told how long she would be incarcerated.

She got a message to her husband through the sympathetic police officer, and Albert managed to get her out of jail. Her reaction was not precisely what the Nazis might have hoped.

"When they put you down like that," she says, "you feel you have to do more to fight against them."

Louisa began sabotaging Nazi plans in earnest. She arranged to contact the good police officer, who eventually became a close family friend. He would let her know when a raid was being planned, and she would run to all the Jews she knew to warn them.

But even this was not enough to satisfy Louisa's need for action against the Nazis. "Inside I was so mad," she remembers. She spent a few days in a constant state of nervous excitement—longing for vengeance, concerned for her Jewish friends, fearful of repercussions. She wandered around the house, pacing, too distracted to so much as pick up a broom and sweep out the kitchen. Finally, she decided to bring clothes for her Jewish friend's children in Westerbork.

In order to carry out her plan, she had first to go to Gestapo headquarters in Groningen. It was tantamount to entering the lion's den. Louisa wanted to ask permission to go to a Jewish house and bring a suitcase into Westerbork—after being arrested merely for her presence in the same house the week before.

"Don't go in there," said the people in the waiting room outside the office of the appropriate Gestapo bureaucrat. "The guy in there is a monster, a sadist."

Louisa told the officer that she felt a sense of duty because she had been a secretary in a Jewish firm for eleven years, but she was not generally friendly to Jews. This Byzantine distinction apparently satisfied the German. Louisa was given permission to go to Westerbork.

"I didn't feel safe," she recalls. With two suitcases packed, she went to her minister to ask him to accompany her.

"If I go alone, I may never come back," she told him. "I think it's better if you go with me, because you are a known personality."

The minister, who was in the underground, agreed to the journey.

It was a two-hour bus ride to Westerbork, which was in a flat, wide-open farming province north of Groningen. The camp was simply a fenced-in area about two kilometers square on the edge of town, right across the street from some lovely old houses.

Louisa and her minister alighted from the bus and started walking toward the guards in front of the barbed-wire fence. An elderly woman sitting in her breakfast nook noticed them heading toward the camp. She began knocking furiously on the window, beckoning them in.

"Are you going into that place?" she asked, astonished.

Louisa and the minister nodded silently.

The woman glanced quickly up and down the street. "Are you crazy?" she whispered. "You'll never come out."

"Maybe we will," Louisa replied. "We're Christians."

The woman gazed at them a long moment. Then she said, "Well, at least come in for a cup of tea before you try."

Over tea she urged them to turn back, but Louisa refused. As they left the kind woman's house and approached the camp a second time, Louisa was shocked to recognize one of the guards posted at the fence. It was the bookkeeper from the sleepwear factory where she had once worked. He was clearly uncomfortable. Louisa stared him down.

"So you've gone over to the Nazis?" she asked.

His face turned red and he protested weakly, "Don't look at me like that just because you picked the wrong side."

After a moment's silence, Louisa told him why they had come and asked him to take her into the camp. Looking over to his superior officer, who nodded, he shrugged and opened the gate.

From the outside, the camp was quiet. A dozen or so barnlike buildings lined the grounds, each one surrounded by black-uniformed soldiers with fixed bayonets. Louisa heard nothing but birdsong and a faint sound as if people were shouting from inside the barracks.

But once the group approached one of the buildings and the door was opened, the screaming became overwhelming. Inside were at least two hundred people with nothing to sit or lie down upon except a few benches. It was total chaos. Mothers frantically shoved through the crowd in search of their children, babies in corners cried, and toddlers stood frightened in the center of the room, looking for a familiar face.

"What are you doing here?" one woman shrieked at Louisa. "Don't you know you'll never get out alive?"

"We'll see," Louisa said coolly. "We're Christians, not Jews. I'm looking for Anna Marie Marcus of Groningen."

The woman pointed out a dark corner of the barracks where several people from Groningen were congregated. Mrs. Marcus wept openly when she saw them and the suitcases full of clothing. She thanked them profusely. After twenty minutes inside the barracks, Louisa and her minister left without incident.

Louisa's courage in this episode borders on—if not crosses over into—a form of temporary insanity. She risked her life to bring a pair of suitcases full of children's clothing into a transit camp. The recipients of the gift were soon on their way to Auschwitz. It would not have been an unlikely event for Louisa to have been tossed on the train along with them.

All of Louisa's rescuing activity, from helping Mrs. Marcus to the way she treated fugitives in her home, reveals an affirmation of normalcy and a high regard for maintaining decent living conditions no matter what the circumstances. But it also shows her flamboyant, dramatic defiance. Risky though the trip to Westerbork was, it probably served to strengthen her ability to withstand stress. Had this foray been less successful, she might not have had the inner stamina and confidence to take on the much greater danger of harboring Jews.

Louisa's child-naming incident, her performance under interrogation, and her trip to Westerbork, taken together, manifest an upward curve of risk similar to Stefania Podgórska's. With each successful challenge, her sense of her ability as a resister to authority was enhanced—enabling her to transcend the inherent terrors of a situation and take action when others who may have shared her humanistic values were paralyzed with fear.

The Steenstras' rescuing activity started as a continuation of their normal routine, in that they had rented the upstairs portion of their house to Jewish lodgers and continued to allow them to live there after it was forbidden.

Their first lodger was Emmanuel Marcus, Anna Marie Marcus's brother-in-law. He had come to the Steenstras' home just after the German occupation.

The Steenstras could see firsthand the effect that the Nazi decrees had on their boarder. First he had to sew a Star onto his coat; then he could no longer leave the house at all except at certain times during the day; and finally the order was posted that all Jewish males should report to a work camp on the outskirts of town.

"If you want to, you can stay here with us," Louisa told Emmanuel. "We probably will have people in hiding here."

"No, thanks." He smiled. "I'll give the work camp a try."

The Steenstras tried to talk him out of it. They argued that even if the work camp wasn't so bad, once he registered the Germans would never let him get away.

"We saw it coming—that they would kill all the Jews," she remembers. "But he didn't believe it."

The Steenstras saw Emmanuel a few times after he was sent into the work camp; it was slave labor, building a road for no money, but it was not a prison. He was given occasional days off. Louisa figured that the strategy was to seduce the Jews into one place, in order to make them easier to transport. The underground was informing everyone about the rumors coming out of Poland, that the Nazis had extermination camps where thousands of corpses were burned each day. She told Emmanuel of these reports, but he always gently refused to listen.

At last the road was finished, and Emmanuel was transferred to Westerbork. Louisa was certain she would never see him again. Exhausted and depressed, she went to The Hague to visit a friend. While she was there she got a call from Albert, who told her to return home "because our little dog Manny came back."

Stunned, Louisa caught the next train to Groningen. "I went home and came upstairs," she recalls. "There he was sitting." Albert said that when he had knocked on the door, he was nothing but "mud and mud and mud."

Emmanuel had at last heeded the words of his Dutch friends, and escaped from Westerbork in an empty German food truck on a stormy night. About thirty kilometers outside the camp he jumped the truck, and had walked the rest of the way back to Groningen. He had planned the escape for two weeks before attempting it.

Soon after Emmanuel's return, another Marcus brother, Carl, came to live with the Steenstras. He had been married to a Gentile girl in Amsterdam, and she stayed in the house as well for a few days before moving back. Carl lived with the Steenstras for more than a year, then was passed on by the underground.

Meanwhile, the economic effects of the war were beginning to take their toll. Albert had four adult mouths as well as a baby to feed.

It got so bad with food and everything. My husband . . . was manager in a winery. He was given bottles of wine at the end of every week. He went to the farmers and exchanged the wine for some food—meal, flour, whatever he could get. He worked for the company until the end . . . but by that time we were eating tulip bulbs to stay alive.

With two Jews living upstairs and Albert's connections with the underground, it became necessary to create a secret hideout in the house. Louisa asked a friend of hers, a building contractor, to fix up the walk-in closet in the bedroom so she could keep her husband safe in case of a raid. She could tell her friend that Albert was in the underground, but not that they were hiding Jews.

"The hiding place was so safe." Louisa chuckles. Albert came home from work that day and Louisa surprised him by telling him there was a hiding place upstairs. He went into the spare bedroom and looked around.

"Where is it?" he asked, puzzled.

"Guess." She smiled.

After half an hour, he still could not find it. It was an inner wall in the closet, painted over so cleverly it could only be opened with a knife and was literally invisible from the outside. The hiding place, in a pinch, could fit five people.

It was not a live-in hideout, however. As a rule, Emmanuel and Carl were able to wander freely throughout the house and sleep in the spare bedroom. They only went into hiding when guests came to the house.

Albert's underground connections began supplying the Steenstras with a steady stream of fugitives, Jewish and Gentile alike. One of their charges was a young man who had lived in a town where a German officer had been shot and wounded by the resistance. The Nazis rounded up all the men in the town and shot them—about 400 —in the main square. Louisa's resident had been riding his bike in the countryside when he heard the shooting; she didn't know exactly how he had come to her house, but she took him in.

Louisa believed that *she* was carrying on a revolution. Her motivations of nationalism and anti-Nazi feeling were subtle, but strong. Louisa clearly considers herself a member of an active resistance and not simply a helping hand for victims. The network supported her even as it called on her to make greater and greater sacrifices.

They always had at least two illegal occupants. When one left, the underground would soon bring another. Some got out of the country, others were passed on temporarily. But as the war progressed, Louisa became a professional rescuer—providing for fugitives from the Nazis as a full-time occupation.

Every day, for three years, Louisa lived at home with her death sentence. She drank coffee with it in the morning, discussed the weather with it in the afternoon, and prepared a fleshless dinner for it when her husband returned in the evening. No matter that it came in human form, as Jews and members of the Dutch resistance; no matter that she thought her hiding place completely safe. Louisa Steenstra spent three long years drinking with, talking to, and cooking for—for all she knew—her own and her family's doom. The images of death which permeated her consciousness during those three years will never leave her.

> I am still nervous from that time. It is always on your mind—every day. It is on your mind. . . . The little things—the human things—people don't know. . . . I had a friend and her husband who had a daughter who was sixteen years old. She was walking on the street and she saw two German soldiers bringing a guy in. She said hello to him. So the Germans thought the girl was in the resistance too. They arrested her. She just said hello. They arrested her and she was sent to a concentration camp. She wasn't an hour there and she was dead. She talked back to one of the women guards. She was shot. Sixteen years old. I don't know.

As she shared this story, I could not help but think of Louisa herself, naming her baby girl Beatrice Irene in the bed next to the newborn of a Nazi. Had it been Louisa who had, in all innocence, greeted a member of the resistance on the street, she would surely have died as well—for the crime of having a prideful sense of flair.

Throughout the war, Louisa's anger and her success at rescuing sustained her. But overall, the situation was not as risky as that of some. Although her neighbors probably suspected she was sheltering Jews, they kept quiet. The house was comfortable, the hideout secure. Of course, the risk was always there, but after two and a half years it did not seem as real as it had at the beginning.

Then the Nazis occupied the Dutch coast and took over all the houses along the shore of the North Sea. Rather than murder all the occupants, which might have been the solution of choice had the neighborhood been Jewish, they decided to forcibly relocate them. Suddenly Louisa's home was inspected by Germans, and then an elderly Dutch couple arrived at her doorstep.

They were a fussy pair, Louisa remembers, who kept to themselves. Emmanuel and Carl were put out of their bedroom and had to sleep on the floor. The Dutch couple was surprised to find Jews in their new home, but did not want to rock the boat at first.

Because they were fellow Netherlanders who had been deprived of their home by the Nazis, Louisa thought that they were fairly safe. But still it was nerve-racking to have total strangers living in a house where criminal activity was taking place. For a few months the situation seemed well in hand,

But then one day Emmanuel had a bit of trouble with the couple. He said stupid things, I think. I don't know. We had soup on the stove in the kitchen. The older lady came downstairs and she lifted up the lid to see what it was. Mortie—the Jewish guy —saw that. He said, "It's not ladylike to lift the lid from the pot in the kitchen." I said to him, "Be careful what you say! Here life is at stake! Don't make any trouble here!"

I had the feeling fourteen days before it happened. I said to my husband that we had to go away. He said I was crazy.

Louisa insisted that Carl and Emmanuel leave; her brother took Carl in. Carl was cooperative because he was aware of how chancy even a small tiff could be. But Emmanuel, true to form, refused to believe that such a nice old couple would turn them in just because of a minor comment like the one he had made. He would not go.

He did not realize that Mrs. Tarkes, the elderly woman, was on the verge of reporting them anyway. She had refrained only out of politeness to Louisa and Albert, whom she considered her hosts—but she was no rescuer herself.

Emmanuel Marcus's actions, in hindsight, may seem incredibly reckless. Had he simply kept quiet, or left the house with his brother, the Steenstras' tragedy would never have occurred. But he had been a member of this family for years—even before the war. He considered himself an old friend. The Tarkeses were the intruders, not he. Additionally, as he demonstrated by his willingness to go to the Nazi work camp earlier, his status as a hunted minority was not entirely clear to him.

Mrs. Tarkes went to the police and told them the Steensras had a Jew in hiding. She went to great pains to ensure that no ill fortune should come to the Dutch couple, but she said she wanted the police to take the Jew away.

She did not know that the officer to whom she complained was one of the 3 percent of Netherlanders who had joined the Nazi Party. Years later, when Mrs. Tarkes was brought up on charges by Louisa and the Dutch government, she was found innocent because she could not have assumed that the Germans would learn of the Steenstras' Jew.

Two weeks later, the Gestapo raided the house. They came with a German shepherd, who quickly discovered the Steenstras' wonderful hiding place.

It began at four o'clock on a clear Sunday afternoon. Albert had just returned from taking Beatrice on a sled ride in the park. There was no coal in the house, and the Steenstras had already burned almost all their furniture for heat, so Louisa busied herself gathering blankets for her chilled husband and daughter. The Tarkeses were out; Emmanuel was upstairs.

They heard a bang and a crash, and raced down to the front door as Emmanuel slipped into the hideout. There were three SS officers, one of whom was Farber—an agent famous throughout Europe for his cruelty. The officer behind Farber held the big, snarling German shepherd on a leash.

Terror-stricken, Albert stood his ground. Farber told him they knew he had a Jew in hiding, and he would go easy if Albert confessed.

Albert shook his head. Farber made a quick movement, and the officer behind him released the dog. The dog leaped over to Albert and bit deeply into his hand. Louisa began screaming as her husband's blood spurted on the floor.

"Confess!" Farber ordered, and Albert, writhing in pain, shook his head again. This time the dog bit his ear off. Louisa covered Beatrice's face with her hand, begging them to stop.

The junior officers dragged Albert, screaming incoherently, with them as the dog bounded up the stairs. Farber stayed with Louisa and Beatrice, who were wild with terror. Louisa heard the dog barking and one of the officers shouting in German. Farber took off up the stairs. Albert shrieked Beatrice's name, and then two gunshots rang out.

Trying not to think about what was happening upstairs, Louisa picked her daughter up and peeked out the door. There was no guard. Without a moment's hesitation she ran across the street to her mother-in-law's house.

When Louisa got across the street, her mother-in-law was hysterical. The whole neighborhood had heard the shots and the screams. "Take Beatrice, I have to go," said Louisa hurriedly. "Keep her safe."

Her mother-in-law seemed not to hear, and called out her son's name. "I must go to him," she insisted, pushing Louisa out of her way and making for the door.

Louisa grabbed her. "No! If you go they'll shoot you! Take care of my baby girl—I'll be back!"

She ran to the home of another neighbor, whom she knew was a member of the underground. The neighbors hid her in their basement.

During our interview, Louisa was visibly upset by reliving her memories of the past. At different moments in her narrative she told three different versions of the events of that Sunday—all agreeing, but increasing in detail and emotion with each retelling.

"The dog—he bit off my husband's ear," was an oft-repeated phrase, even when it was somewhat out of context. That moment was the most dreadful of Louisa's life. At the sight of her husband's blood and his agony, she knew they were as good as dead—but could hardly imagine how horrible their manner of dying would be.

And yet she retained the presence of mind to escape with her little girl in the few seconds that were open to her—leaving her husband screaming, the dog barking, and the sound of gunfire upstairs. In the end, her inner resources saved her and her daughter. Pride made her thirst for survival, rage gave her strength, and her innate sense of the dramatic—as well as her previous experiences deceiving the Nazis—allowed her to distance herself sufficiently from what was happening to continue to act.

For a contrast we can examine Louisa's mother-in-law's reaction as implied in Louisa's narrative. When the elder Mrs. Steenstra heard her son screaming from across the street, she took leave of her senses with grief and helplessness. Had she run to the house as she wanted to, alerting the guards to Louisa's escape, they would all have been killed.

The underground was concerned not only with Louisa's safety but also that she not fall into the hands of the Nazis. She knew too much. Once the situation had cooled, Louisa made a rendezvous with a man from the underground who said he could get her out of the city.

"I had slippers on and an old coat from my mother-in-law," Louisa remembers. "Nothing. Nothing. Nothing. But I knew my girl was safe with my mother-in-law. . . . I knew my girl was okay."

That night a man from the underground in another district brought Louisa to the outskirts of a park. An empty milk truck was waiting for them. She had to climb to the top of the tank and open the lid. A sour stench overpowered her for a moment, and she drew back; the man from the underground pushed her in.

At the bottom there were a few other people; Louisa will never know who they were, because they were all told to keep quiet. "I am a nervous person," says Louisa now, "but not because of nothing."

On the border of Friesland province, the truck was stopped by a Nazi guard. Louisa's heart was pounding so hard she could almost hear it reverberating in the resonant milk tank. She felt an urge to cough, but held it back in desperation.

"Go ahead," said the German guard. It had been the second time in as many days that Louisa had felt close to death.

In Leeuwarden, Louisa found herself sheltered. For the final months of the war, she lived in an attic with five others. She does not say whether any of them were Jews, but she does mention the extreme religiosity of her rescuers. "We didn't have much to eat," she says. She weighed ninety pounds by the end of the war.

After only three days in Leeuwarden, however, she began feeling desperately anxious about Beatrice. "I said, 'I need my little girl. I have to have my girl with me. I need my girl—I don't know where she is and what's happening to her.' . . . I was crying day and night."

The man who had brought Louisa to Leeuwarden in the milk truck volunteered to cycle the sixty kilometers to Louisa's mother-in-law's and pick up the child. When he arrived, the elder Mrs. Steenstra refused to surrender the girl to a stranger but would tell him where the child was if he came back with a note from Louisa. Beatrice had been hidden with still another neighbor just hours before the Gestapo learned that Albert's mother lived right across the road and came back to tear her house apart.

Louisa's underground contact, whose real name she never knew, cycled back to Leeuwarden for the note and then returned on his bicycle to Groningen. Bicycling was the safest form of transportation; cars were inspected and pedestrians occasionally rounded up, but for the most part bikes were left alone.

The man picked up Beatrice on a dark, gray afternoon, and rode with her in a terrible storm. He stopped off in the house of a fellow resistance member at the border, but refused shelter for the night. He knew Louisa was terribly anxious.

At three o'clock in the morning he arrived in Leeuwarden and, according to a prearranged signal, tossed a few pebbles against the attic window where Louisa was waiting. Louisa raced downstairs. Her daughter was sitting, streaming wet, behind the man on his bicycle. When she saw her mother she screamed and ran to her. Louisa was torn between gratitude, fury, and overwhelming grief. "She was such a little thing," she says now. "So many things happen in this world."

Louisa was nurtured and supported by the network until the war's end. But her urge to defy the Nazis outlasted the war. The day after Canadian tanks entered Leeuwarden, Louisa marched right up to the commander of their unit and told him her story. He authorized a jeep and an accompanying soldier to help her find her husband and reclaim her property.

The house was empty. Only the piano was left, eerily, in the living room. The Germans had taken everything in her house, because she was a criminal and had no rights. All that remained of Louisa's past was a huge puddle of dried blood on the floor upstairs.

A neighbor had gone to the coroner's office to identify the bodies. Albert had been shot in the neck, he told her, beneath the ear that the dog had torn off. Emmanuel had been shot in the back of the head, and his eye had been hanging out of its socket.

After the war Louisa immigrated to Canada, where she had cousins. She could not bear to be in her home country anymore. Today she lives on a monthly allowance from the Dutch government, which she receives in recognition of her trauma for the sake of the Dutch people, and a small stipend from the Jewish Foundation for Christian Rescuers, which she reluctantly accepted.

But the most vulnerable and helpless victim of the experience was Beatrice.

She has managed to repress her memory of the events of that day, but when she was three and a half years old she had recurring nightmares that a dog was trying to kill her. She did not eat for six months after their arrival in Leeuwarden. Even today, she refuses to speak about the past. Her children do not know how their grandmother helped the Jews.

"She would never do what I did," says Louisa. "She says, 'I will never do what you did, Mom. I never had a father. Is it worth it?' I say, 'Trix, you think about it. Every life is worth something.' But she says, 'Did it help?'

"What do you think?" Louisa asks me, sounding helpless and depressed. "Did it help?"

· 7 ·

RELATIONSHIPS

ACTS OF RESCUE created relationships. They had beginnings, middles, and ends; they had purposes and sets of roles and responsibilities which sustained them. Rescuing relationships were subject to internal and external forces which could nurture or challenge them, make them seem worthwhile or unreasonably burdensome.

The theme of the rescuing relationship was altruism; its product, the creation of a safe harbor in a hostile world. Its basic "contract" was this: the rescuer committed to harboring a Jew—to take care of his daily needs, to warn him of danger, to maintain a façade of "normal life" behind which the Jew would be safe. The Jew was dependent, but was expected to cooperate—making as little trouble as possible, using personal resources to help out in daily life, and staying relatively invisible.

As in any relationship, things happened which strained the original terms. Few, if any, could have known in the beginning how long these relationships would go on, or what new demands would be made as others needed help, or food ran out, or fear created family tension and strange behavior. As each set of expectations was replaced with new ones, each individual's roles and responsibilities had to be redefined, new problems had to be overcome, and new strategies developed.

Rescuers lived with the knowledge that they had put themselves and their loved ones in jeopardy. At the same time, they knew that at any moment they could reverse their decision. Each day as they struggled to feed their two households—their immediate family and their hidden family—they also contended with the dreadful awareness that it was possible, just possible, to change their minds.

The story of shy and unprepossessing seamstress Jean Kowalyk illustrates how complex the rescue relationship could become. This young woman agreed to hide Dr. Solomon Berger and ended up caring for seven people. Each day she fed them, washed their clothes, and discarded their waste. One of her charges, a married woman whose husband was in hiding with her, openly carried on an affair with another man, also in hiding. From time to time, they left the attic and slipped behind the emergency double wall to have sex. The husband and his wife's lover fought constantly. On one occasion the shouting match turned into a noisy brawl with blood spilling on the floor. Kowalyk was furious. She was petrified that the loud voices of two men would arouse the suspicions of her neighbors, and they all would be shot. Kowalyk had enough. She was ready to throw them out. They pleaded with her, promised to reform, and begged her to reconsider. In the end, she relented.

What compensated Jean Kowalyk and others like her for these great efforts? Many rescuers, I discovered, had suffered a recent loss of someone close to them or an incapacitating childhood illness which caused them to identify with the Jewish victims. In the humiliation of her charges, Jean Kowalyk saw her six-year-old self lying helpless from a fall that broke her spine and stunted her growth.

In World War II Europe, the motivations that lay behind rescuing relationships were rarely straightforward. Most people had both stated and hidden agendas. A rescuer who agreed to harbor a child, for example, might have done so to save a child's life but also because the family wanted to adopt a child. Or a rescuer who initially agreed to hide Jews for money may have continued to do so for reasons that had nothing to do with economics. In some situations a rescuer at first simply wished to save a Jewish child, agreeing to raise that child as a Jew, but later began to try to convert the child to Christianity.

Situations were fluid in this regard. As circumstances fluctuated and time passed, the relationship between those in hiding and those who hid them changed.

Israel and Frania Rubinek's rescue story is an example of how muddied rescuer motivations could be and how complicated the relationships could become.[1] In 1941 with a little money Frania Rubinek scraped up, she and Israel opened a general store in Pinczow, Poland. At first they could not afford much merchandise. When their farm customers came in, Frania kept them entertained with stories, while Israel took what cash was available and went out to buy what his customer wanted at a wholesale place down the street. After a few months, business was booming. Farmers liked to come in to buy things and to visit with the entertaining couple. One day Zofia Banya, a farmer's wife from Wlochy, a village three kilometers from town, came into their store. She needed several items, but was short fifty groszy (less than a quarter). Israel Rubinek told her never mind, she could pay him back next week. She could not get over the fact that he had trusted her. This happened week in and week out. She never forgot it.

By hiding in a bunker constructed by Israel, the Rubineks escaped the roundup and slaughter of the Pinczow Jews. They were on the run when they heard from another escapee that Zofia Banya was searching the woods for them. Zofia was determined to save the lives of the couple from the general store who had trusted her.

The Rubineks made their way to Zofia Banya's farm. There the good woman welcomed them, but asked almost immediately if they had any money. She and her husband, Ludwig, were impoverished. They did not have enough for themselves and their seven-year-old boy, Maniek. Without extra money, Zofia certainly could not feed extra mouths. The Rubineks told her they had money, with an easy assurance they did not feel, and told her they could get more. Thus began the stay in a one-room farmhouse that would last twenty-eight months. Frania Rubinek slept on a ledge above the oven where, if she stretched out her legs, they dangled in the faces of the Banyas sleeping below. Israel Rubinek, when not keeping watch by the door, slept on the floor beside Maniek. Beneath the stove and covered by a small door was a potato cellar just big enough for the Rubineks to cram into in an emergency. Actually the Banyas' cramped quarters worked in the Rubineks' favor. Although neighbors began to suspect Ludwig's new prosperity, they assumed he could not possibly be hiding Jews because he had no place to put them.

While Ludwig welcomed the Rubineks' money to buy their basic necessities, he was scared that the Germans would discover that he was harboring Jews and would kill them all. He was a crude, illiterate man who bragged to Rubinek that he had once killed a man he did not like by throwing him into a burning oven. The more frightened he became, the more often he beat his wife and demanded that the Jews leave. Zofia Banya pleaded with Ludwig to let the Rubineks stay. Neither gave up. Zofia Banya was determined to live up to the trust the Rubineks had placed in her. She would not abandon them. So the beatings and pleading over the presence of the Rubineks continued. Once when the Rubineks were hiding in the potato cellar, they overheard Ludwig tell his wife that he was sick of keeping the Jews and that he was going to get his ax and cut off their heads for the reward of two kilograms of sugar that the Nazis offered.

To protect himself, Israel Rubinek slept with a knife and became determined to make Ludwig his friend. He began to read the newspaper to Ludwig and explain political events to him. On Sunday when farmers came to visit, Ludwig repeated what Israel had told him. In no time at all, Ludwig became known as the most politically savvy man in the village.

Finally, toward the end of the war, the Rubineks' money ran out. Instead of promptly throwing them out, Ludwig treated them more nicely than ever and shared with them what little food he had. He wanted to show them that he was not as crude a man as they thought. Moreover, just as the Rubineks came to love the Banyas' son Maniek and taught him to read and write, so too Ludwig had grown fond of his charges. Ironically enough, the warm, emotional attachment felt by Zofia Banya toward the Rubineks spread to include in its glow the man who never wanted to save them in the first place.

I have listened to and read hundreds of stories, and I am continually astounded by the strength of rescuers' commitment to individuals that almost everyone else considered inconsequential. To most people, the Jews were getting what they deserved; they merited no special help or consideration.

All of the postwar social-psychological studies which were designed to pinpoint the kind of behavior and circumstances that elicit helping behavior illustrate how unlikely rescuing was. Some studies prove that when people perceive that the need for help is legitimate (and not the result of the victim's own actions such as a drug overdose), they are more likely to help. Other studies show that people are most likely to help those who dress or look similar to them or who share their political ideology or ethnic background. Other research demonstrates that before helpers volunteer aid, they weigh the costs of helping and back away if it seems too high.[2] In Nazi-occupied territories, where the cost was enormous, and the differences between Jews and others accentuated, few helped.

The bonds that developed between rescuers and their charges were built on the knowledge that a careless misstep by either party meant death for both. With this in mind, there was a hierarchy of desirability. At the top—that is, most preferred—were Jewish women who could pass for Aryans and who, in addition, had false identification papers. The most difficult to place were males who "looked Jewish": dark eyes, long, curly hair and a beard, a large nose, big ears, and accented speech. The old and the sick had hardly any chance at all. They required medical care that was impossible to get without the rescuers endangering their lives.

Girls were more desirable than boys, whose circumcised penises gave them away as Jewish. Preverbal youngsters were easier to hide than four- to ten-year-old children, whose unpredictability gave rescuers pause. Such children could all too easily blurt out unintentional information that would bring in the Gestapo.

Rescuers and their charges were like comrades in the same foxhole, pinned down by the same hostile fire. Many, such as the Banyas and the Rubineks, lived together in close quarters. They shared food, beds, anxieties and dangers. The relationship called for mutual forbearance and trust. They relied on one another to avoid detection. For victims such as the Vreedenburgs and Rubineks whose Jewish looks gave them away at once, this meant darting into cramped hide-outs at a moment's notice. For others who could pass for Christians, it meant hiding true feelings and fears. Survivor Elizabeth Grayson remembered how difficult this was. In 1942, Grayson, fleeing deportation, ran to the Berlin apartment of a woman she knew only slightly, Liselotte Muhe, and asked if she could spend three nights with her. That short visit stretched into a three-year stay. During that whole time Muhe and Grayson played their parts of normalcy. Grayson held up her end:

> I gave up being myself and played a role. We had to make it seem perfectly natural for me to be living there in that apartment house. I had to look happy and prosperous and couldn't show how afraid I was that at any minute I might be discovered. We had to lie all the time, and had to be careful to let nothing slip out that would give us away.[3]

Because rescuers' illegal acts of mercy put them on the same footing as their charges, their empathy for their plight changed into an identification with them. Rescuers grew to feel psychically at one with the Jews, even feeling victimized. Polish rescuer Alex Roslan can remember the exact moment when his feelings changed:

> After the Polish Uprising, when my son was killed, and I had to flee with my wife, my daughter, and two Jewish children . . . I felt that people were looking at me. I felt like I myself was a Jew. I was a Jew, I could be killed for no reason. Whatever happened to Jacob would happen to me. I was frightened all the time.

Stefania Podgórska's identification with her charges and her feelings of victimization were so great that she ignored her own power to rescue herself. When the Gestapo ordered her out of her home, she refused to save herself and her sister Helena and to abandon the thirteen Jews she harbored. Instead she prayed.

The possibility of discovery and death lent the rescuer-rescued relationship a feverish intensity. This intensity, combined with the wartime atmosphere of Nazi occupation, air raids, bombings, and daily exposure to death, made actions seem surreal. In such an environment, nothing was inconceivable. Improbable relationships became possible. Rescuers fell in love with their charges. Nannies became mothers to the children they rescued. Childless couples became parents. Servants became masters. Patients listened to analysts' problems.[4]

During this time, the rescue of children had a special fairy-tale quality. Polish dressmaker Maria Niemiec had always wanted a girl. But she had boys one after another. Now she was too poor and too old to bear another child. In 1941, however, it seemed to her that her dream for a daughter might come true. Dr. Samuel Licht, an old, dear family friend, wrote from the Lvov ghetto to ask her if she would take in his daughter Teresa, six years old, and a four-year-old cousin to live with her. Niemiec agreed.

Niemiec's boys all liked Teresa, or Terry as they called her, and they were instructed by their mother to treat her like a sister. The little cousin, however, cried all the time, and Niemiec was forced to find him a place with another family in town. A year later, Terry's little cousin was playing outside with other children in the street when he accidentally let slip what his real name was. The children told their parents, who in turn reported the incident to the Polish police. The whole family was arrested and killed.

When Maria Niemiec heard the story, she panicked. She feared that neighbors were also talking about her. Without telling her own children where she was going, Niemiec grabbed Teresa and fled with her to Warsaw, where Teresa's parents were hiding in the apartment of a Russian noble lady.

Maria's attachment to Terry was extraordinary. Terry was the daughter she had longed for but never had. To save her and her family too, Niemiec had to abandon her own children. Was that the case? Or did attachment to this little girl alter her thinking?

The large majority of rescuing families were warm and loving; they sought to re-create the same loving family environments in which they were raised. Their spouses came most often from the same socioeconomic background, and, like them, were raised in caring homes where at least one parent or caretaker served as an altruistic role model. Most rescuers married for love. If they had children, they repeated the examples of their own parents and involved their children in their altruistic activities.

These rescuing families viewed marriage as an equal partnership and were able to share their fears and responsibilities. Some couples divided the tasks of caring for their charges. Aart and Johtje Vos split the responsibilities for running their safe house. Aart Vos took care of providing the food, obtaining the necessary provisions for their extended family that amounted to thirty or more extra bodies, and maintained network communications. Johtje Vos oversaw household matters and was responsible for the emotional care and feeding of their charges. As Aart Vos explained to me, it was rugged work:

> My wife kept [people's spirits] up. She tried to keep the people laughing. She tried to give them hope. She would say, "I hear the Germans are losing." She said that to keep the boat floating. You cannot just let fifteen or twenty people sit there with nothing to do but think about death. You cannot just sit. I let them go into the woods to cut wood for the stove. I let them work in the garden. I let them do something in order not to sit in a chair all day long. I kept them moving.

The emotional support that these couples provided for each other was critical in sustaining their commitment to their charges. They helped each other through frightening times and drew courage from one another.

However, those family members who might not approve of rescuers' actions were either ignored or kept in the dark. Elena Ivamauskiere, for instance, did not bother to consult her husband when a twenty-year-old woman—Ninute—confided to her that she had escaped the ghetto with a young man who also needed shelter. Ivamauskiere's husband readily agreed to hide Ninute. But she knew that he would be too afraid to shelter a Jew who did not look Christian. So without his knowledge, but with the help of her two daughters, Ivamauskiere secreted Ninute's friend in the barn.

It was similar for the children in rescuing relationships. In my conversations with rescuers and those they saved, the themes of sisterly love and empathic identification with their adopted Jewish "siblings" came up again and again. The certitude that they were valued and loved members of the family allowed the children of rescuers to love rather than to resent the new members of their family. Cornelia Knottnerus was one of many such examples. When her family took a teenage boy and girl into their home, Cornelia welcomed them. She felt very protective of them and grew to love them both. In fact, she adored the fourteen-year-old Sarah. For the two and one-half years they lived together, Cornelia and the Jewish girl were "extremely close, like sisters." The feeling was reinforced one day when Cornelia borrowed Sarah's coat:

> We didn't have many clothes during the war and I [needed to go out] into the cold. Sarah said, "Please, take my coat," because she could not go out of hiding. Though we had removed the Jewish Star, a yellow stain remained, and I remember how frightened I was. Boarding the train I finally realized as I had never before what it meant to be marked as a Jew, and I was very sad and terribly afraid.

The experience deepened Cornelia's empathic engagement. She remembered trying to comfort Sarah, who would often cry when she thought about her mother and father. In these moments of anguish, these two girls transformed the pain into anger against the Nazis.

Early on, Cornelia and her own younger sister "learned to keep secrets. Under no circumstances were we to reveal anything to the Germans." During a neighborhood raid, German soldiers burst into the house with guns and conducted a violent search which destroyed the house. Sarah and the Jewish boy were hidden in a secret closet, and though held at gunpoint, Cornelia did not give them away:

After the war a friend of my mother said, "You were a very brave child." I didn't understand what she meant and then she said, "You were afraid, and yet you never said to the Germans, 'The Jews are in the closet.' " The thought would never have occurred to me.

In retrospect Cornelia explained:

When you are young, you love a challenge. I thought of myself as a little hero against the big Nazis. The best antidote to fear is action, and we did not become brave all at once. Little things added up. We brought this paper there for the underground . . . we took in these children . . . we made out false passports . . . our involvement got deeper and deeper . . . but we were not brave all at once. The times forced us to give in and be a quisling [collaborator] or to fight back, and we would rather have died than cooperate with the Nazis.

After the war, Cornelia kept in contact with Sarah, her Jewish "sister." To this day she retains a strong feeling for the Jewish people and often speaks in synagogues about her wartime experience as part of a rescuing family. The themes of "sisterly" love and empathic identification with the "adopted" Jewish children came up again and again in these interviews. These close sibling bonds generally lasted into adulthood. In Cornelia's case, her "sister" Sarah even looked like her ("We were both dark and had curvaceous figures") and this feeling of likeness, combined with Cornelia's capacity for empathy, may have strengthened their sibling bond or may have facilitated her initial warm acceptance of Sarah.

What Schlomo and Eva Geritsen remember is the closeness. In 1942, when Schlomo and Eva's father was incarcerated in Westerbork their socialist and religious Jewish mother went underground and crossed the border into Belgium, and stayed hidden there until the underground advised her to hide the children.[5] Eva and Schlomo were smuggled back across the border, separated, and four-and-a-half-year-old Schlomo waited, terrified, until Johannes DeVries came along. Frightened Schlomo immediately felt the love and warmth of Johannes, but when Schlomo arrived safely at the DeVries home, he "cried and cried and then they put me to bed." Night after night, Schlomo cried until finally he was able to communicate his sadness to Johannes and his wife, Janke. "I told them that I wanted Eva, who they finally understood was my sister." Johannes DeVries immediately said, "If I can take in one child, I can take in two. Don't worry." Johannes alerted the network and asked that little Eva, only three years old, be put in his charge. Not long after, Eva arrived. She recalls, "I was only three but I remember seeing their big, nice dog." Their daughter, Greta, recalls, "I was twelve at the time they reunited. They were so happy to be together again that it really broke your heart." Greta was very fond of the children:

> They were like a brother and sister. The little boy had asthma, and when he cried, it made me so sad that I cried too. I didn't know if they would like me at first; they were so small. But I felt sorry for them, and helped my mother tend to them and I read them lots of stories. The children in the neighborhood asked questions but we knew enough to keep quiet. We trained Eva and Schlomo to say they were orphans who were bombed out of Rotterdam and they played their roles well.

Schlomo and Eva were told by their mother not to reveal their Jewish names to anyone. They took it literally and did not even mention their names to the DeVrieses. Even though they trusted them "completely," and felt Janke DeVries was "very warm . . . a true mother," they waited till liberation to share their secret!

Eva felt *she* was "babied and spoiled. I was loved and cared for . . . I played happily on the street with the big dog. In fact, when the war was over, I didn't want to leave the DeVries family." Neither did Schlomo. But the children were returned to their mother, who in 1948 became very ill with cancer. Hearing the news, Greta, then seventeen, moved to Amsterdam so that her "brother and sister" would not be put into a foster home. When the children's mother died in 1948, Johannes attempted to legally adopt them, but their mother had left notarized instructions that the children were to be sent to Palestine. Johannes was furious, and could not understand how he'd been considered "a good enough parent in wartime, but not good enough now." Despite the DeVrieses' protests, Eva and Schlomo were sent on a children's transport to Palestine, where they lived on a kibbutz. They eventually reestablished contact with the DeVrieses. When he visited Israel to plant a tree on the Avenue of the Righteous, Johannes DeVries saw how fulfilled the children were in their surroundings and he finally understood why the children's mother had wanted them to grow up in Israel. They are both happily married. The DeVries family, with the exception of their son, is still in very close contact with both Schlomo and Eva, whom they call, with pride, "our Jewish children."

At times children in rescuing families were envious of their new siblings because their own parents seemed to give preferential treatment or more admiration to total strangers. The fourteen-year-old Rex DeVries was very jealous of his foster siblings, Schlomo and Eva. According to Rex's father, Rex was very spoiled by his mother. Johannes warned Rex, "If you say one bad thing to these children I will kill you." When I interviewed Schlomo and Eva they were not aware of Rex's resentments, and Eva even recalled Rex as "a big brother, very protective." Rex has not kept in touch with Eva and Schlomo or with his own family for more than twelve years. Johannes did not even know Rex's address when I was interviewing the family.

Maintaining secrecy was particularly burdensome for children and created problems with relationships outside the close-knit family. The fact that they could not bring other children home rankled. While I did not hear a murmur of complaint from most rescuers' children about sharing beds, food, and clothes with their adopted siblings, this constraint was often mentioned. It was arduous enough growing up in wartime, but carrying around a secret they could not even share with their best friends made it yet more difficult. It isolated them from their schoolmates and made them avoid friendships.

Late in the spring of 1944, a Hillegom, Holland, schoolchild tried to befriend eleven-year-old Esther Warmerdam. Esther's silence and distance from others had aroused the schoolchild's curiosity. She wanted to see Esther's house and tried to wangle an invitation, but Esther steadfastly ignored her hints. Her home housed her father's hardware store in the front and living space for Esther and her eleven siblings in the back. It also at any given time sheltered one or more of a total of 200 fugitives.

"Show me the inside of your house," Esther's schoolmate demanded.

"I can't."

"Why not?"

Esther gave the family's standard pretext. "We have a big family, and my mother doesn't want any more around the yard."

But that did not stop the girl. Day after day she followed Esther home, hinting to be invited in, but Esther would put her off, using one pretext or another. Finally, in late autumn, the situation came to a head. "There's something mysterious going on in your house," the girl told Esther. Esther stood immobilized. Her lack of a reply enraged the girl. She grabbed Esther's hair and pushed her down and held her head in snow. Esther managed to fight back and run away. For days she waited in terror for her family to be reported, but nothing happened. The girl never spoke to Esther again.[6]

With no one else to play with, their adopted siblings became, by default, their playmates of choice. Close personal ties were formed that would last a lifetime. Nelly Trocmé, daughter of Le Chambon's pastor André Trocmé and his wife, Magda, who was thirteen years old at the time of the German invasion, grew very close to the two girls sheltered at her house:

> When you are thrown together the bonds are very strong. Remember, we shared the same room, went to school together, were part of the same Scout group. Because I did not have a sister, these girls became my sisters. We shared the trauma of adolescence and became extremely close.

The sibling bonds that developed between rescuer children and the Jewish children who were hidden within their families were marked and have endured in the period since liberation. The loving family atmosphere created by the rescuer parents fostered normal relations between the children. The rescuer children were made to feel part of the meaningful and humane act of rescue. Their active participation in protecting their "Jewish siblings" was an experience which "shaped [their] lives" and enhanced their self-esteem. Because rescuer children had been taught tolerance long before the Holocaust and were not deprived of love once the family expanded, they could love and accept their "Jewish siblings." When the rescuers' children played active roles in the rescue, they did not develop a high degree of jealousy or envy. Some identified with their new siblings; others developed maternal or paternal feeling toward them. Again and again, the Jewish children—no matter how different in age and background —were described by rescuer children as being similar to them, so similar that it was easy for them to form a brotherly or sisterly bond with them. When they seemed different, the relationship took the character of nurturance or protection.

The closeness between rescuers and their charges was reinforced by their isolation. Liselotte Muhe even sent her own mother to live in a small town outside the city rather than risk the possibility that her mother might accidentally let slip some piece of information disclosing Elizabeth Grayson's true identity. Similarly, Franciczka Subkowa, a Polish nanny who hid her two adored Jewish charges and their mother, engineered a fight between her sister and herself. She did not trust her sister not to turn her charges in for a reward.

Individuals and families were not the only ones to care for and form strong attachments to Jewish refugees. In such places as Assisi and Secchiano, Italy; Nieuwlande, Holland; and Le Chambon and the region of the Cévennes, France, whole towns conspired to hide Jews. They formed what French survivor and filmmaker Pierre Sauvage has called a "conspiracy of goodness." The conspiracy involved the entire population of a town. In the case of the Fullenbaum family, 600 citizens of the central Italian town of Secchiano banded together to help. Led by two families, villagers harbored Wolf and Esther Fullenbaum and their four-year-old daughter, Carlotta, for more than a year. Their presence was a matter of public knowledge and private pride. Villagers housed the German Jewish refugees on the second floor of the village schoolhouse. The townspeople saw to it that the Fullenbaums had food even when they had no money left. When Nazi soldiers invaded the village—as they did from time to time—villagers took them out into the fields to blend in with the other workers. To hide their thick German accents, villagers told authorities the Fullenbaums were local deaf-mutes. Despite the arrest and deportation of their village priest for harboring fugitives, no one ever cracked and disclosed the Fullenbaums' presence. The family was helped to British territory and survived the war.

The village of Le Chambon in south-central France, made famous by Pierre Sauvage's television documentary *Weapons of the Spirit* and Philip Hallie's book *Lest Innocent Blood Be Shed,* was but one of several villages that took part in a communal effort to save Jews. Less well known was neighboring Cévennes, a rural community that also conspired to hide Jews and others fleeing the Third Reich. French pastor Marc Donadille pointed out that even those villagers who backed the Vichy government kept their mouths shut about the refugees. It was part of a country habit and frame of mind that accorded neighbors a wide berth.

Dutch rescuer Wilto Schortinghuis, who with his wife operated a safe house for the underground, made the same point. He remembered the fall of 1944, when the Germans attempted to evacuate the entire city of Arnhem. Schortinghuis was forced to take in a Dutch family of four. Schortinghuis already had five Jewish people in hiding. Fortunately, the relocated family did not inform on them. According to Schortinghuis, such passive support was central to the success of any rescue operation:

> The whole environment of the country helped us to rescue. This is not something you do alone. The underground provided false identity papers and food coupons. For three years our neighbors put up a protective shield around us by acting as if they did not notice anything. We were only the tip of the iceberg.

For their part, Jews were aware that they lived only through the good graces of their rescuers, and most did everything possible to hold up their end. For David Frital, currying favor became a survival plan. Frital was a bank clerk in Lotczk in the western Ukraine. When the Germans took over his town, Frital was moved into the ghetto. From time to time, he would slip out to look for a hiding place. Returning from one of his outside forays, Frital saw the German killing squads at work in the ghetto. Desperate and in a panic, he ran to the home of a fellow employee, Irena Bron, and asked for shelter for one night. Despite the fact that Frital was by no means an intimate friend of theirs, the father, Zigmund Bron, agreed.

In the morning Frital realized he had nowhere to go. Hoping to prove himself a useful addition to the household, he went into the kitchen and started a fire and peeled potatoes for breakfast. Pleased and surprised, Zigmund Bron went off to work while Frital stayed at the house caring for Bron's sickly wife and doing assorted house chores. With nothing said, Frital stayed another night and then another.

Through instinct and shrewd assessment, David Frital was employing a gambit that social psychologists have dubbed "the foot-in-the-door effect." Studies show that when people are asked for a small favor and comply, they are more likely to agree later to a larger favor than they would be if they had been asked first for the larger favor.[7] In Frital's case, he asked for shelter for one night and then finally asked Bron if he could stay the winter with him. He promised he would leave in the spring to join Ukrainian partisans in the forests. Bron agreed. He hadn't the heart to send him out to face the harsh winter weather. Still, the tension in the house caused by Frital's presence was almost palpable.

Frital was determined to do everything he could to alleviate the tension. He realized that to keep the Brons' fears at bay he could not act like a victim. On the contrary, he needed to appear strong, competent, and resourceful. So from time to time he slipped into the city and visited with people he knew. He came back from these visits with information, gossip, and stories of other Christian families who were also sheltering Jews. This gave the Brons enjoyment and the temporary courage to continue. But their sleepless nights did not end until they confided their secret to their priest, who gave the Brons his blessing. On May 12, 1942, Frital left of his own accord. The open windows and pulled-up shades required by the warmer weather made hiding more difficult. Germans were capturing more and more Jews. Frital decided the time was ripe to move on.

Even under the most extreme conditions, Jews tried to make themselves as useful as possible to their rescuers. On a farm outside of Radin, Lithuania, four refugees from the massacre of the nearby ghetto sat in a shallow ditch. The four, Fegel Yurkansky, a woman in her early twenties, and a rabbi's wife, Esther Fischer, and her son and daughter, were peeling potatoes. They were determined somehow to repay the risks Jan Adamowicz was running by hiding them on his farm.

Adamowicz was the town drunk. Partisans steered clear of him because they were afraid that in a drunken stupor he would give away vital information. Yet when a villager stumbled on the four refugees in the forest he brought them right away to Adamowicz. The villager knew that beneath Adamowicz's grizzled and often inebriated exterior was a caring man with a sense of integrity. The villager was confident that Adamowicz would take care of them.

And he did. Although he was too frightened to bring them into his home, Adamowicz dug a ditch in the forest where the Jews could hide, and each night sent one of his five children out with food. To repay Adamowicz for his kindnesses, Fegel Yurkansky and Esther Fischer peeled potatoes. Fegel had already sewed a dress for one of Adamowicz's little girls, which resulted in a temporary scare when people did not believe her mother had sewn the dress. Fegel then sewed another dress and had the mother do the final alterations in order to convince the town skeptics. Afterward she confined herself to kitchen chores.

But this too proved dangerous. A policeman dropped in on a routine check on the Adamowiczes one day and saw the extra peelings. Immediately he accused the Adamowiczes of hiding Jews. Apparently Poles peel potatoes in little pieces, but these peels were done in the Jewish fashion, one long swirl. The Adamowiczes made up a convincing lie, but that small favor nearly cost them all their lives.

Not all Jewish refugees were aware of the seriousness or precariousness of their position and some were not particularly grateful. Esther Warmerdam recalled coming home one day when she was eleven years old and meeting a little girl named Suzy, who, her father said, would be visiting because "her parents can't look after her right now." Two weeks after Suzy's arrival, a woman came to the house. "I'm Suzy's mother," she announced. She was a dark, well-dressed, patrician-looking woman with a manner that suggested she was accustomed to giving orders. She proceeded uninvited to inspect the Warmerdams' house from bedrooms to root cellar. She opened the food cupboards, inspected Suzy's clothes, and looked for dirt on the laundry drying in the yard. She then launched into a list of complaints. The clothes were threadbare, the toys scarce, the food improperly prepared.

The Warmerdams tried to calm her.

"Your Suzy's doing fine," Mr. Warmerdam said with a smile.

"We're doing our best," Mrs. Warmerdam said stiffly.

For four weeks the mother kept up her visits. Every few days, she would arrive like a cloud, issue instructions, and leave. Her visits upset the family equilibrium. Esther's mother resented the slurs about her and how she ran her household. Finally Mrs. Warmerdam had enough. "If our care isn't good enough, take her somewhere else," she told Suzy's mother.

"I will," the mother shouted.

By the end of March, Suzy was gone. The Warmerdams never saw Suzy or her mother again.

Rescuing relationships could end in different ways, the most complete being at the time of liberation when the charge had been protected until the danger was past. In other cases, circumstances or personal choice made it impossible to continue. Someone could have been hiding Jews for several years when denunciations in the community became too threatening; a new child could be born; a rescuer's spouse or child became uncooperative and therefore dangerous; food could become scarce, neighbors suspicious, authorities inquisitive. The charges might be asked to leave, either by the rescuer or by a network; the decision could be mutual or one-sided. In all cases, the impact of the relationship lasted for a lifetime.

PART II

MOTIVATION

"We must have a language that allows us to
explain to ourselves and others why we are
doing what we do. And in an individualistic
society, where caring is sometimes seen as an
abnormality, it becomes all the more
important to be able to give an account of
ourselves. An adequate language of
motivation is thus one of the critical
junctures at which the individual and the
society intersect: being able to explain why
is as important to our identity as a culture
as it is to our sense of selfhood as individuals."

—Robert Wuthnow, Sociologist

IN MY TRAVELS in the United States and abroad, speaking to various groups about rescuers, one fundamental question comes up time and again: Why did they do it? Why did they risk their lives and the lives of their loved ones? I give a complex answer to the question, which listeners resist. People want a simple explanation. General audiences, people who feel that they are good-hearted, find it impossible to imagine themselves doing what these rescuers did. As I talk, they begin to appreciate the array of circumstances, people, and solutions. Still there are always some who feel that at bottom there is no accounting for why this handful of people did what they did.

I sympathize with and am irritated by the romantic idea of an unfathomable mystery. Clearly, human behavior is complex, inconsistent, and changeable. Reason does not always prevail. So much of how rescuers reacted depended on singular combinations of circumstances, personalities, feelings, and personal history, crystallized into a single moment.

Rescuers are unable to articulate all the reasons why they participated in altruistic acts. When I asked them, "Why did you do it?" I often evoked feelings of discomfort and even annoyance. Aside from their irrational guilt, feeling that they should have done more, many were embarrassed because their honest explanations ("It was the right thing to do," or "I couldn't live with myself if I let these people die") were, from an interviewer's point of view, so unrevealing. Even so, researchers took rescuers at their word and lumped Holocaust rescuers into a single category of people who believed in and acted on the idea that all people were part of a fellowship of mankind. Political scientists began referring to them as John Donne's people.*

> No man is an island, Intire of itself;
> every man is a piece of the Continent, A part of the Maine; . . .
> Any man's death diminishes me, Because I am involved in
>   Mankinde;
> and therefore never send to know for whom the bell tolls;
> it tolls for thee.
>
> —John Donne, *Devotions,* XVII

Psychoanalysts believe that rescuers' acts derive from self-centered unconscious motivations. For example, for certain civilians, the act of rescue enabled them to express their rage against the Third Reich. Saving the lives of Jews provided them with the narcissistic gratification of outwitting their oppressors and the pleasure of having a person or persons totally dependent on them. Most analysts would argue that self-gratification rather than altruism underlay rescuers' deeds. Anna Freud, for one, felt that there was no such thing as altruistic motivation. To her, people who help others receive the benefit of a personal gratification from their helping behavior.

Unconscious motivations certainly played a role in turning a bystander into a rescuer. Yet intangibles such as personal gratification and enhanced self-image were small rewards indeed for the vast risks these people undertook.

Empirical research and analysis has begun to yield clear social and psychological patterns beyond the unconscious. In tracking what

---

* The term "John Donne's people" was coined by Kristen Monroe, a political scientist at the University of California at Irvine. It is an imaginative way of expressing the rescuers' vision of common humanity among all peoples.

prompted an individual's initial rescue effort, five distinct categories become clear: *moral*—people who were prompted to rescue Jews by thoughts or feelings of conscience; *Judeophilic*—people who felt a special relationship to individual Jews or who felt a closeness to the Jewish people as a whole; *network*—people fueled by anti-Nazi ideology, joining others who were politically opposed to the Third Reich; *concerned professionalism*—people such as doctors or social workers who held jobs in which helping was a natural and logical extension; and *children* who helped rescue Jews at the behest of their families.

Of course, not everyone with whom I spoke fit precisely into one of these categories. Motivations were complex and sometimes straddled more than one category. Should a nanny who rescued a beloved charge be considered a "Judeophile" or a "concerned professional"? Should someone, such as Friesland rescuer Theresa Weerstra, who initially took in a little girl and ended up as an integral part of an underground network, be considered a "moral" or a "network" rescuer? Should a man who rescued his Jewish wife and then went on to rescue more Jews be considered at all?† If so, how should he be categorized? "Moral"? "Judeophile"?

Real situations, which ranged from rescues lasting hours to rescues lasting years and included the changeability of rescuing relationships, interfered with my neat categories. Nonetheless, despite all the exceptions, fine lines, and tangled reasons surrounding initial rescue efforts, these motivational categories provided me with valuable insights into the nature of altruistic behavior. They pierced the veil of mystery that surrounds rescuers' deeds. Viewed from the perspective of these five motivational groupings, rescue activity appeared more intelligible, but no less amazing.

These categories define not only the initial motivations of the rescuers but in large measure the essence of who they were as people. Rescuers saw themselves as helpful, competent people who took responsibility to save Jews. But they also had their own particular set of reasons. They were moral, ideological, or professional people who saved lives. They were admirers of the Jewish people, or they were

† Yes, according to Yad Vashem, if that rescuer also saved non-family members.

children who helped their families' rescue. The rescuer self took a quiet pride in its ability to maintain moral integrity, ideological beliefs, professional standards, or humane relationships.

From this discovery, other insights followed. I found that the motivational category to which a rescuer belonged influenced not only how the rescue was carried out but also the way in which the rescuer self was integrated into postwar daily life. Moral people continued to live out their lives with a strong commitment to religion or another moral code. Professionals continued helping people through their work; some ideological rescuers went on to another morally committed ideology; Judeophiles continued their relationships with those they rescued or with the Jewish community; and child rescuers resumed helping in their adult professional lives. Whatever rescuers did afterward, their lives expressed their motivational core.

Assigning rescuers to one of the five categories according to their initial motivation was therefore more than an intellectual reshuffling of the deck. On the contrary, an examination of the circumstances and motives that led rescuers to their initial rescuing acts pinpointed the salient aspect of the rescuer. It was this aspect—moral, Judeophile, ideological, professional, or duty-bound child—that continued after the war as a central part of the inner lives of these individuals. It is this part of a rescuer's self that gave many rescuers tremendous satisfaction and direction.

· 8 ·

MORALITY AS
MOTIVATION

MORAL RESCUERS were people who, when asked why they
risked their lives to save Jews, often answered, "How else should one
react when a human life is endangered?"[1] Their concept of right and
wrong was so much a part of who they were and are, that it was as if I
had asked them why they breathed.

This clear sense of right and wrong was called "autonomous"
morality by child-development expert Jean Piaget. As Piaget saw it,
morality has an intellectual as well as an emotional dimension. Young
children from ages four to eight have a "heteronomous" morality—
that is, their behavior is subject to another person's law. For children,
their law is the law of adult authority. The child's respect for authority guides his concept of what is right and wrong. Acts that are wrong
are those punished by adults. Duty is understood as obedience to
authority.

For the rescuer, morality was relative rather than absolute. Justice
was a matter of reciprocal rights and obligations within a social
group.[2] This is the "autonomous" morality Piaget describes as devel-
oping after age eight. It derives from the mutual respect that peers feel
for one another.[3]

Eli Sagan of the New School for Social Research takes Piaget's concept of autonomous morality a step further, arguing that morality, or conscience, is an independent psychic function. Sigmund Freud had contended that guilt, shame, and fear of punishment regulate a person's superego, the part of the psyche that enforces moral standards and blocks unacceptable impulses. In Freud's view, the superego is a repository for parental values, good and bad. The same internalized voice that commands the self to tell the truth, respect others, and be honorable can also permit the self to hate blacks, despise women, or repress sexual pleasure.

Sagan feels that Freud's superego does not sufficiently explain moral behavior. What happens when values come into conflict: "All men are created equal," yet some men own slaves. What happens when the impulses of the superego are pulled in opposite directions? How does the superego sort it out? Sagan contends that conscience operates as a powerful, autonomous entity within the psyche. Separate from the psychic drives, conscience develops in infancy through the nurturing of a caretaker, and is thereafter regnant. In Sagan's view, conscience reigns not through fear of punishment or castration, as Freud believed, but through love. A child who receives love wants to give it back. In Sagan's terms, a moral rescuer was simply a person trying to return the love he received as a child.[4]

Moral rescuers, however, were doing more than just reciprocating affection. Moral rescuers had a strong sense of who they were and what they were about. Their values were self-sustaining, not dependent on the approval of others. To them, what mattered most was behaving in a way that maintained their integrity. The bystanders who ultimately became rescuers knew that unless they took action, people would die.

Moral rescuers did not leap at *any* opportunity to right wrongs. On the contrary, this category of rescuers rarely initiated action. Unlike rescuers with other types of motivation (such as network people who were propelled by hatred of the Third Reich), moral rescuers typically launched their rescuing activity only after being asked to help or after an encounter with suffering and death that awakened their consciences. Scenes of Nazi brutality touched their inner core and activated their moral values, which had been developed early in life and may have remained dormant. For the most part, when asked to help, moral rescuers could not say no. Magda Trocmé's "Naturally, come in, come in" comes to mind. Magda Trocmé did not know these people; it was simply the right thing to do. In rural Holland, Poland, and France inhabitants may have never seen a Jew before the Nazi occupation.

Rescuers' morality was of three types: ideological, religious, and emotional. *Ideological* morality was based on rescuers' ethical beliefs and notions of justice. A congruence between moral beliefs and actions had always been a part of their lives. They stood up for their beliefs; and so, when they were asked to help, they did. They were also more likely than other moral types to be politically involved. Some belonged to socialist or Communist parties or in a few cases to nationalist parties.

Religious-moral rescuers described their sense of right and wrong in religious rather than ethical terms. Their morality was based on religious tenets such as "Do unto others as you would have them do unto you" and precepts about how to treat others and how to live their lives. Religious values, including a tolerance for people who were different, were unshakable and permanent in these rescuers. During the war and after, when faced with dire circumstances or morally complex questions, these rescuers relied on their faith to see them through crises.

The war placed religious-moral rescuers in a double bind. Their act of rescue pitted them against their government and often against their church leadership. Of the two relationships, their ruptured connection to government was of much less concern than was their break with the church. After all, the government was a legal, amorphous tie. A break with their church, however, was a different matter entirely. Their rescue activities left them feeling alienated from their religious community, which for many amounted to their extended family. Often religious-moral rescuers had to break a bond with a beloved priest or pastor who was a Nazi collaborator. Because of their rescue activities, these rescuers could no longer comfortably engage in normal religious dialogue, such as in Bible study groups or in confession, lest they reveal their true thoughts and actions. As was the case with the Jews they harbored, religious-moral rescuers felt cut off from the most meaningful part of their lives.

Some fundamentalist Protestant sects and Calvinist Protestants taught that Jews were God's "chosen people." This teaching should not be confused with the teaching of religious values of tolerance. Nonetheless, it is of interest that many Dutch rescuers were members of the Anti-Revolutionary Church Party, a group whose members were taught about Jews in positive terms. Members of this party felt a spiritual connection with Jews through stories from the Hebrew Bible and through stories about Jesus. Jews were brothers and sisters to them, not alien beings.

Spiritual religious feelings were not limited to those affiliated with traditional religions. A deep spiritual conviction and dedication to the principles and practices of nonviolent action motivated pacifists. Dutch rescuer Wilto Schortinghuis was such an individual. A registered conscientious objector well before the German invasion, Schortinghuis and his wife looked to Mahatma Gandhi and Albert Schweitzer for their inspiration and their own consciences for motivation. When I asked Schortinghuis why he and his wife hid twenty Jews on his farm, his answer was simple: "We feel life is sacred."

Emotional-moral rescuers felt a compassion for victims of Nazi persecution that compelled them to help. Emotional-moral rescuers were the rarest type of moral rescuers. They responded to the helping situation out of compassion and pity, not just from an ideological sense of right and wrong. Theirs was a morality based on caring and responsibility, the same morality that Harvard University psychologist Carol Gilligan celebrated in her groundbreaking book *In a Different Voice*. Gilligan proposed that a morality based on compassion and concern for others was more prevalent among women than among men.[5]

A majority of these emotional-moral rescuers carried out more than five separate incidents of rescue each. More than any other category, emotional-moral rescuers were engaged in rescuing children. Alexander Roslan, who sneaked into the Warsaw ghetto to take a peek and could not forget what he saw, was but one example of this type of rescuer. Roslan's care and love for Jacob, and later Sholom and David, extended far beyond a desire to do the right thing. As was the case with other emotional-moral rescuers, Roslan's activity stemmed from a sensitivity to the needs of others. In time, his caring grew into an emotional attachment that brooked no obstacles or objections.

Nowhere is the example of a moral rescuer better illustrated than in the story of Irene Gut Opdyke, who, once she became aware of the plight of Jews, was determined to save them no matter what the costs. For years, Gut's rescuing relationships were central to her life and to her being.

Irene Gut, as a nineteen-year-old nursing student, had become aware of the plight of the Jews from the moment she pushed back the curtains from the window of the hotel in Radom where she worked as a waitress for the Nazi Major Ruegemer. She had seen the misery of the Jews in the ghetto outside and could not forget that misery. Irene and her sister left food for the Jews, but when the Nazis closed down the ghetto behind her hotel, they could only watch in helpless horror from across the street.

One day she and her sister heard shooting. Major Ruegemer, seeing how upset Irene and her sister were at what they had just witnessed, excused them from the day's work. As the two headed home, they heard still more shooting. They followed a group of Gestapo to the edge of town. There Gut and her sister saw a mass of shallow graves. The gestapo stood people in front of the graves and opened fire with machine guns. "The earth was shaking with the breath of those who had been buried alive," Gut recalled. That day, that moment, Gut made a covenant with God. She asked Him for the opportunity to do something. "I asked God to give me responsibility, to bring me the opportunity to help, even if my own life should be taken," she said.

Gut's first rescue activity, that of leaving food at the ghetto fence, was motivated by an empathy and a conviction that these were human beings like her, not something "other." She saw that these people were suffering, and her sense of humanity compelled her to act. Gut's case shows just how complex the classifications can be. I placed her among the ideological moral rescuers because, although she was a deeply religious person, her initial act stemmed from an ideological rather than a religious belief. Although the Gestapo killings compelled Gut to pray to God for the opportunity to help, her impetus was an ideological one.

When the major was assigned to head an ammunition factory near the Russian border at Tarnopol, Gut got her chance to do more. She and her sister went along with the major on his new assignment. Gut discovered almost immediately that there were 300 Jews working at the factory in Tarnopol. Eavesdropping on the major's conversations at dinner with the local Gestapo, Irene learned that young, healthy Jews were being picked up in the ghetto to work in a labor camp. When Gut was given the responsibility of supervising the laundry, she was thrown into close contact with a dozen Jews who had come there from the ghetto.

At first the Jews did not trust Gut. She set out to earn their trust. On one occasion, a Jewish woman wanted to visit her parents in the ghetto. Gut managed to obtain a pass from the major by telling him that the woman was sewing dresses for two German secretaries and needed to bring the dresses to the ghetto to get buttonholes made. When, on the following day, the woman had not returned from her visit, Gut asked the major for permission to go look for her:

> It was the day after a raid on the ghetto, and what I saw was unbelievable. . . . It was an unbelievable feeling, first of all to see blood everywhere. Then you feel that people are looking at you, but you cannot look at them. I went to the house of her parents . . . nobody was there. And when I started calling her name I found she was hiding under the stairs. Having heard my voice, she came out of her hiding place. I told her the raid was over, and that she should come with me. But she didn't want to come. Her parents had been taken away and she didn't care anymore. I put all kinds of things in her basket and with the pass we got out. I played a German *Fräulein* at the gate and [told the German guard] she had to carry my things.

From that time on, Gut listened carefully to Gestapo mealtime conversation so that she could warn the Jews in the laundry room of impending raids. Those Jews would then pass on the news to Jews behind the ghetto walls.

One day the head of the Gestapo informed the major that the entire ghetto would be liquidated in June. Gut was helpless; she knew no one with enough room to hide her dozen friends from the laundry. But a few days before the final liquidation of the ghetto, the major was assigned new living quarters. When Gut saw the villa into which he was to move, she felt that God had sent her deliverance. That night, when the Germans were fast asleep after a drinking bout, Gut stole the keys to the villa from the major and locked his door behind her. One by one she moved each of her laundry friends down the coal chute to the villa's cellar.

The next morning the major asked her if she would mind supervising some painters who were coming to spruce up the villa, and she jumped at the opportunity. But when she got to the cellar her friends looked "like desperate little children." Without wasting a second, Gut moved everyone from the cellar to the attic because the cellar was scheduled to be painted first.

It was the end of June, and the windowless attic was unbearably hot. Gut locked the Jews in, promising to return with food and a chamber pot. She remembered this day as the most frightening day of her life. "I remember trying to serve lunch while simultaneously manipulating the workers away from where the people were hiding," she told me. "Then we discovered that the architect, who was Jewish, had known what was coming and had built in a hiding place." The hiding place was under the garden and was reached by slipping through a crawl space underneath the coal chute. Gut packed food, water, and a pot and escorted the group to their new hideout.

One night, one of the Gestapo took his *Fräulein* for a romantic rendezvous in the gazebo. Gut was afraid that the people below would be caught, especially since one of them had a cold and was using a pillow to muffle the sound of her coughing. It was impossible to warn them directly, so Gut decided to divert the couple with a light snack and drinks. The officer was furious and yelled at her for interrupting them, but his shouts served as a warning to those beneath the gazebo that someone was there. Fortunately, he took his lady to a more secluded area, and the people in hiding were safe.

Aside from providing for the twelve Jews under the gazebo, Gut regularly brought food to the forest, where more than 200 Jews who escaped from the ghetto were hiding. Gut had always known there was danger in helping Jews, but one day in September the penalties were made graphically clear. Gut was shopping in the town when she saw a Polish family, children and all, hanged with a Jewish couple and their young child in the center of the marketplace. The public hanging was the Nazis' way of letting the people know what would happen to those who befriended Jews.

After witnessing the fate of those the Nazis branded "Jew-lovers," Gut was more careful about taking precautions. She began locking the kitchen doors from the inside so that visitors would have to ring a bell before entering. But one day someone failed to lock the door and the major opened the door to find four Jews and his loyal Polish servant preparing food for the others.

Gut had no choice but to throw herself at the elderly major's feet and beg for mercy. "They are my friends," she pleaded with him. "I had to help them. I couldn't let them die. Nobody has a right to kill. If you cannot forgive me I will have to give my life. There is nothing else I can do."

The major dismissed Gut, saying they would discuss everything later. When Gut went back to her friends, she found them ready to commit suicide. She begged them to wait. Later that evening, the physically repulsive major summoned Gut to his room. He pulled her onto his lap and then took her to his bed. He insisted that she have sex with him; had she resisted, she would have placed the Jews in mortal danger. Eventually, the major promised to let the Jews stay. Gut never told the people whose lives she had saved what she had done to make their safety possible.[6]

The major became accustomed to the Jews. He grew to enjoy their cooking and baking and called them by their first names. They, in turn, called him "Grandpa." They all lived together in this manner until February 1944, when the Russians marched into Poland. Orders came from Berlin to evacuate the villa.

Though the major was quite nervous, Gut refused to abandon the Jews in the villa. "In a war you never know how long it will be before rescue comes," she explained. Gut was even protective of the life of an unborn baby in her band of refugees. One of the women had gotten pregnant and wanted to abort. Gut would not hear of it. "I saw so many babies killed," she told the mother-to-be. "Please don't do it. You'll see—you'll be free by the time you have to give birth. You will be liberated." Events proved her right. The Russians liberated the city, and all the Jews, including the newborn, were saved.

As was true for all rescuers, Irene Gut Opdyke's altruistic behavior during the Nazi era was not an aberration. On the contrary, rescuers' acts grew out of their basic character, their core values and self-images. As a student nurse, Gut thought of herself as a caring, empathic, and helpful individual. During the war, this image was transformed into that of an ideological-moral rescuer. This was because Irene Gut witnessed Nazi atrocities not as a detached spectator but rather in an all-encompassing, transforming manner which summoned up a deep sense of responsibility. All previous goals took on a new meaning in light of this new identity. This changed self, which was an evolution of her previous self, was expressed by her own strong sense of humanity and justice. She felt responsible for others and that became the central reason for her being. It was, in the end, what led Irene Gut Opdyke to risk her life for twelve strangers in a laundry room and 200 Jews hiding in the nearby forest.

Coupled with a sense of morality that sprang from an ideological commitment was Irene Gut's belief in a common, caring kinship of humankind under God. The combination of these factors culminated in a daring repudiation of Nazi authority and an intense dedication to save Jews.

CHRISTIANITY TEACHES the values of respect for life and disobedience to immoral earthly authorities. Magda Trocmé's daughter Nelly remembered that she and the other children of Le Chambon were taught "the importance of doing what was right, and learned to listen to our own conscience. We saw our parents disobey the law and were taught that a system that persecutes *must* be disobeyed."

There was, to be sure, ancient precedent for such a position. Religious rescuers took their cue from stories from Christian Scripture. Some identified with the Good Samaritan. Others saw themselves as biblical protectors, such as those who shielded the infant Jesus from Herod's soldiers, or Jesus himself, who ventured into the leper colony. Identifying with such images helped Christians cope with the stress of rescue and overcome their fear. It also led many of them to renew or deepen their religious group connections. In turn, many of these religious groups became rescue networks.

Religious-moral rescuers can best be understood in the context of their church affiliation, their country of residence, and the period of their rescue behavior.

At first, church officials welcomed the rigid morality of the Third Reich. The new government was viewed as a refreshing change from the decadence of the Weimar Republic. Even maverick church leaders such as Martin Niemöller and Dietrich Bonhöffer, who were later deported to concentration camps for their anti-Nazi sermons, did not initially take issue with Nazi racial laws. The 1933 Vatican Concordat, in which the Roman Catholic Church agreed not to interfere in state matters in exchange for Hitler's promise to leave the Church alone, smoothed the way for early cooperation between the Holy See and the Third Reich.

As a result of the Concordat, Catholic religious leaders were very slow to denounce Nazi racism and later to marshal their forces to help Jews. St. Raphael Verein, a Catholic organization presided over by Bishop Wilhelm Berning of Osnabrück, Germany, that protected German émigrés, announced in November 1933 that for the time being non-Aryan Catholics would be considered *Gastvölker* ("guests"). Assistance from the Catholics came in 1935, when the Nuremberg Laws, which defined a Jew as anyone who had one Jewish grandparent, were passed. But this assistance was directed at aiding these 140,000 non-Aryan congregants—Christians of Jewish descent —not at Jews. (In 1938 alone, the organization helped 1,850 non-Aryan Catholics emigrate.) Three years later, when the Nazis passed a law requiring Jews to wear a Star in public, German bishops tried to intervene again on behalf of non-Aryan Catholics. These Catholics faced the humiliating prospect of wearing the Jewish emblem to mass. In Berlin, Bishops Heinrich Wienken and Wilhelm Berning personally asked the Gestapo to exempt their congregants from this directive, but the request was denied.[7]

As would be the case throughout the war, the efforts of less lofty church officials—individual parish priests and nuns—proved to be the most effective in saving Nazi victims. On August 3, 1941, the Catholic bishop Clemens Count von Galen of Münster vehemently denounced the Nazi euthanasia program. As a result of his outspokenness, Nazi leaders halted the program but apparently allowed for a possibility of its resumption.[8]

Protestant groups were likewise slow to denounce Nazi racism. In 1936, Protestants who protested the Nazi decree that forbade non-Aryans to be members of the clergy or to hold church office set up an Office for Christians of Jewish Descent in Berlin. The main task of this office was to assist non-Aryan Christians and Jews to emigrate from Germany. It also provided jobs, material and legal aid, and—for converts—religious support. After August 1939, when children of converts and mixed marriages were not permitted to attend secular public schools, the Office for Christians of Jewish Descent founded Christian schools for these children in Berlin.

In the early years of the Third Reich, to be a rescuer was to defy one's religious leaders. The Society of Friends—the pacifist Quakers —was a notable exception. The Quakers were distinguished for their willingness to help Jews and anyone else who required refuge in Nazi Germany. Early on, they funded Jewish emigration from Germany; and later, when emigration was no longer possible, they provided hideouts, food, clothing, and escorts to aid in escape. In 1949, the American Friends Service Committee and the British Friends Service Committee won a Nobel Prize for their efforts during World War II.

Despite the fact that Jehovah's Witnesses were rounded up along with the Jews, they too came to the aid of the Jews.[9]

The passivity of most of the German Catholic bishops in the face of mass extermination of the Jews stands in sharp contrast to the conduct of the French, Belgian, Dutch, and Italian Catholic bishops. In Holland, the Church, as early as 1934, denounced the participation of Catholics in the Dutch Nazi movement. Later Catholic leaders forbade Catholic policemen to hunt down Jews even if it meant losing their jobs. In Belgium, members of the Catholic episcopate actively supported the rescue efforts of their clergy. In France, the highest dignitaries of the Church repeatedly used their pulpits to denounce the deportations and to condemn the barbarous treatment of the Jews. The Protestant leader Marc Boegner was the first to publicly protest the anti-Jewish laws promulgated by Vichy. Priests and other members of the clergy used their monasteries, parish houses, and private homes to hide Jews. In the hallowed tradition of sanctuary, which held that fugitives from justice were immune from arrest in churches or other sacred places, clergy sheltered those fleeing the Third Reich.

Nowhere was this tradition of sanctuary more remarkably demonstrated than in Assisi, Italy. There, in the home of the Franciscan order of Catholic monks, the bishop of Assisi, Giuseppe Placido Nicolini, found refuge for hundreds of Jews. He and Don Aldo Brunacci, a professor canon at the San Rufino Cathedral, procured false identification for Jews and even arranged kosher meals for some. Don Brunacci hid Jews in cloisters such as the Convent of the Stigmata, and also set up a school for Jewish children to study their own religious and cultural heritage. They never attempted to convert them to Catholicism. Father Brunacci was arrested in 1944, but was spared through the intervention of the Vatican, upon his agreement to leave Assisi. All in all, some 200 Jews sought sanctuary in Assisi. All were saved.[10]

The Catholic international religious orders for women did not have a set policy or program on racial persecution. Harboring Jews and other fugitives therefore became a personal choice, at times guided by a mother superior. In Poland, at least 189 convents hid more than 1,500 Jewish children, mainly in Warsaw and the surrounding area. This was a small effort compared with the rescue of children in Belgium and France, because in Poland nuns themselves were persecuted and incarcerated, and went into hiding in areas occupied by the Reich after October 1939. Those nuns who lived in areas occupied by the Soviet Union until June 1941 were forced to work as far away as Siberia and were forbidden to wear religious garb.[11]

Ultimately it was each individual who made a moral choice. For religious-moral rescuers the sense of responsibility was rooted in religion. Theresa Weerstra was confronted with a friend's plea to shelter a four-year-old Jewish girl. According to the friend, the girl's father had been shot and her desperate mother had hidden the girl in a closet. "Don't cry, and wait," the mother told her before fleeing with her other child. "Some Christians will come and help you." Now this little girl stood before Theresa.

Weerstra had learned what happened to Jews from a friend who had escaped from a concentration camp. Without consulting her husband, who was off at work, and without much deliberation, she took responsibility for the child.

When I interviewed Weerstra, she referred to her first rescue act as an "impulsive" one. But in the course of our conversation, I found that her decision to help was not as capricious as it might appear. Her humanitarian response was derived from an inner core of religious values. These were values cultivated in childhood by parents who were deeply religious and who served as altruistic role models. Religious values led Weerstra to look at this little Jewish girl and to see no difference between her and any of her own three children: What if this was my child, my mother, or me needing shelter? What would Christ have done?[12]

Weerstra empathized with the child and her mother. She assessed her own ability to care for the child, to protect her from harm, and to keep her own family safe. She remembered the teachings of her church. This thought process was very quick. So quick, in fact, that she does not remember making a deliberate choice, but thinks she acted on impulse. She placed the Jewish child in bed with three of her own children.

When Weerstra's husband came home that evening, he had a different reaction. He was frightened. "What are you doing?" he demanded. Weerstra told him that if they turned the little girl out she would be gassed. "What about the safety of our own children?" he asked. Later, when the children were asleep, Weerstra and her husband talked it over. "Remember the story of the Good Samaritan?" Weerstra asked him. "Martin, do you want to be like the first two travelers who looked away and turned their backs?" That night they agreed to shelter the little Jewish girl. The little girl was the first of 450 Jews, Allied pilots, and Dutch boys escaping German labor roundups that this courageous couple sheltered during the war.

As was true of other religious rescuers, Theresa Weerstra and her husband felt that rescue work was in accordance with Christ's teachings. Many felt that God had chosen them for the special task of saving lives. The feeling that they were doing God's work tipped the balance toward action. Fear fought with compassion. Self-interest battled with decency and human kindness. It was an emotionally charged inner debate, and some rescuers made mistakes.

For religious-moral rescuers, communal support, as in Assisi, was the exception rather than the norm. For the most part, personal faith sustained such people. Near the end of the war, twenty Germans surrounded the Weerstras' house, where ten fugitives were hiding. Although threatened with death, Theresa Weerstra was defiant. "You may shoot me, but I am not afraid," she told the soldiers. "You will shoot only the body, while my spirit goes straight to heaven." As the Nazis continued to search her house and turned to cross-examine her husband, Weerstra managed to burn a stash of false identification cards that would betray their network activity.

Clinical psychologist Nancy McWilliams of Rutgers University, in her studies of people who have dedicated their lives to helping others for moral reasons, found that altruistic individuals who were religious tended to sound the same themes. McWilliams, who studied people who represent an extreme of altruism such as a woman who cares for children of lepers in the Far East, found that even people from very different religious backgrounds described their feelings in surprisingly similar terms:

> I was fascinated to find, in talking to these subjects, how central to their humanitarian work their belief systems were . . . considering that there were four different denominational affiliations represented, it was striking to me that they all described their religious orientation in virtually identical terms. All [were] strongly religious, and all [were] observant of religious practices, but not in an empty or rigid ritualized way. All described the feeling of awareness of the presence of God in the world, and in their own good works. All [felt] that their humanitarian efforts somehow [helped] to strengthen their faith. All tended to make certain distinctions between truly holy and superficially observant worshippers.[13]

The distinction between "truly holy" and "superficially observant worshippers" is an important one. It is similar to that made in an earlier study conducted by the renowned personality theorist Gordon Allport in his exploration of how religion enhances or hinders the development of a tolerance for difference. Allport differentiated between two types of religious motivation: intrinsic and extrinsic. Extrinsically motivated persons value religion as a social institution. They enjoy the community feeling and social aspects of church attendance. Intrinsically motivated religious people, on the other hand, derive satisfaction from internalizing the precepts of the religion. They connect emotionally to what is said and taught each Sunday. Allport pointed out that the two types of religious people are not necessarily separate, but in those cases where they are, Allport found that intrinsically oriented religious people are less prejudiced than the extrinsically motivated.

Gordon Allport's distinction explains how it was that Stanislaw Falkowski, a twenty-four-year-old assistant parish priest—and resolute antisemite—ended up saving the life of a Jew.[14]

The son of a poor farm family in Piekuty Nowe, Poland, Father Falkowski was a devout Catholic and a passionate believer in the

Church's teachings. Those teachings included the traditional belief that the Jews killed Christ. His father died when Father Falkowski was a youngster and he and his mother scrimped to save enough money so that he could become a priest.

One day in November 1942, in answer to a knock at the window, Father Falkowski looked out and saw a boy of fifteen shivering in the cold. Although the boy looked like any other poor Polish villager, Father Falkowski knew immediately he was a Jew. He was filthy, covered with lice and scabs, and bone-thin. Despite Father Falkowski's belief that the Jews were being rightly punished for their sins, he could not turn the boy away. He invited the boy inside and, with little prompting, the boy's story poured out.

His name was Joseph Kutrzeba. He had been living in the Warsaw ghetto with his family, but they had all been deported to the Treblinka death camp. He too was bound for Treblinka, but during the night he had managed to open an air vent and jump from the train. He had been wandering from town to town ever since. Another priest had directed him to Father Falkowski.

The priest looked at the boy. Like other antisemites, Father Falkowski thought Hitler was God's way of punishing the Jews for killing Christ. But unlike those who hunted down Jews like rabbits, Father Falkowski also believed that it was his Christian duty to "love his neighbor." For him, the two concepts were not incompatible. God worked in mysterious ways. The priest would leave God to do what He would do. Meanwhile, Father Falkowski needed to help the boy.

The priest took Joseph in, cleaned him up, and nursed him back to physical and spiritual health. He taught Joseph Catholic rituals and prayers in order for him to pass as a Christian. The two became like father and son.

Despite this relationship, Father Falkowski never changed his mind about Jews. But, as with other religious rescuers, he believed that it was his obligation to conduct his life according to the Christian principles of compassion and charity. Indeed, this conviction among religious rescuers—that they were accountable to a higher and more fearsome authority—was the most salient aspect of their rescuer self.

It overcame antisemitism, transcended fear, and impelled them to action. This was what defined religious-moral rescuers before, during, and after the war.

It was also this aspect of the rescuer self that allowed them to maintain secrets, role-play, lie, steal, cheat, and do whatever was necessary to save lives. Theresa Weerstra explained what happened to her and her husband after her decision to take in the little Jewish girl brought to her doorstep:

> From then on, the door was open. Many entered, many went, many came in the night, fleeing. Many were so disturbed they almost lost their minds. I could lie at that time very well. I did not lie to sin, but I did lie to protect. When you are a Christian you see the world differently. You see the need. They were His people.

The Weerstras and other religious believers were acutely aware of the slippery ethical slope they descended when they lied, stole, and deceived others in order to save lives. Each day brought a reexamination of their beliefs and the correctness of their course. They never doubted that their course was true, but each step demanded careful consideration lest they wind up in the morally bankrupt position of the ends justifying the means. Alert to this danger, they relied on Christian Scripture to guide them. Theresa Weerstra solved potential conflicts or moral dilemmas that she encountered by asking herself, "What would Jesus do?" Similarly, network rescuer John Weidner, son of a minister and a devoted Seventh-Day Adventist, constantly looked inward. Every time he negotiated the safe passage of refugees across the border, he dug a little deeper into his conscience. His internal conversation went something like this:

> Am I doing what is right in this work? We are saving people from certain death, but we are using illegal means to gain their freedom. We forge identification and travel papers; we ask guards to renounce their appointed job when they help us. We falsify, evade, outwit. As a Christian, am I doing right in this?

Weidner found resolution to his questions through prayer and through probing his own motivations to make sure that hatred or personal gain did not prompt his rescue work. Such self-examination eased the guilt he felt in committing illegal acts and led to his growing conviction that he was doing God's work. He came to feel that his rescue work demonstrated God's love of and compassion for those persecuted by the Nazis.[15]

Hitler's military and racial war created moral dilemmas for everyone, not only for religious rescuers. The Nazi doctrine of collective responsibility ensured that an individual's act of humanity toward a Jew placed the rescuer's family in danger. Was not a rescuer's first duty toward his family? What kind of love and compassion required putting the lives of loved ones at risk? Within the rescuer self, an internal debate raged from moment to moment. Who had the greater claim? The needs of family or the lives of total strangers? Which need must be met first? The answers varied from person to person and within the family itself. Johtje Vos clearly remembered the conversation she had with her mother in which she was forced to articulate how she had resolved the issue in her own mind. Not long after the Voses began their rescue activities as part of the Dutch resistance effort, Johtje Vos's mother came for a visit. The true nature of what went on in the house was apparent, and it dismayed and frightened Johtje's mother. She reproached her daughter, arguing that Johtje had no right as a mother to jeopardize her life, much less put her children's lives in danger by her actions. But Johtje Vos saw the situation quite differently:

My husband and I talked to her and said, "We find it more important for our children to have parents who have done what they felt they had to do—even if it costs their lives. It will be better for them—even if we don't make it. They will know we did what we felt we had to do. This is better than if we first think of our safety." My mother fully understood this and agreed.

The Voses began their rescue activity, as Johtje Vos said, with "a suitcase, a child, and a piano." Their initial motivations, however, were quite different. Johtje Vos was motivated by her friendship with Jews. I therefore placed her in the Judeophile category. Aart Vos, however, came to his rescue activities through his strong feeling of compassion and pity for any suffering person. Similarly, Alexander Roslan's pity and sympathy for the dead and dying children of the Warsaw ghetto spurred him to offer help. Aart Vos and Alex Roslan were emotional-moral rescuers. They felt; therefore they acted. Vos said:

> It is like a tidal wave. When it comes over a village you are lucky you are alive and can save people. You do it. You do not sit and ask yourself, "Will I do it?" It is part of your body; the will is part of your body. You do it. You feel and you do it.

Many of the emotional-moral rescuers harbored children. Polish rescuer Maria Byrczek, for example, looked at a five-month-old baby girl brought to her by a neighbor and realized that she was this mother's last desperate hope for the survival of her child. The Alex Roslans and Maria Byrczeks of the world, however, were relatively rare.[16]

Oddly enough, those few rescuers motivated to rescue children out of compassion were subject to various suspicious conjectures. They were suspected of hiding children for money, free labor, permanent adoption, or the chance to convert a young soul to Christianity. Of course, not all of those who rescued children were emotional-moral rescuers, just as not everyone who rescued was motivated by moral considerations. John Donne's people were far too complex to fit into so neat a package.

In fact, there were people who risked their lives to help victims who looked upon their charges not with compassion, but with opportunism uppermost in their thoughts. They would shelter a child for as long as the money held out, or the labor was needed, or to fill a family void. With their attention focused elsewhere, historians and researchers at first tended to lump altruistic rescuers of children with opportunistic ones. It was, and is, a thoughtless characterization of individuals who, at the very least, merit a true account of their actions.

The actions of emotional-moral rescuers are no different from the actions of those moral rescuers who were motivated by an ideology of social justice or religious duty. The essential characteristic of moral individuals is that they do not remain passive when faced with conflicting choices. Their conscience can transcend an evil society because that conscience is independent and has its origins in early childhood.

· 9 ·

JUDEOPHILES

LIKE MANY OTHER budding German entrepreneurs, Oskar Schindler followed the Third Reich and opportunity into Poland. Schindler's aim was to buy a business, at a bargain, in the newly conquered territory. At a textile plant in Cracow, where he stopped to get advice from its German-appointed head, the young industrialist met Itzhak Stern, the plant's Polish-Jewish accountant. It was a fateful meeting for both men. Stern was a thin, erudite man with the manners and philosophical mind of a Talmudic scholar. Even during their first meeting (about a local enamelware factory Schindler was thinking of buying), the two engaged in a philosophical discussion about Christianity's Jewish roots. Schindler, who fancied himself a deep thinker, enjoyed talking with and learning from Stern. For his part, Stern, a member of the Zionist underground, judged Schindler to be that rare breed, a "good" German. A friendship was formed. It was a relationship that in time evolved into the love and respect of a father and son.[1] The fatherly Stern became chief accountant at Schindler's Cracow enamelware factory and his chief moral stimulus. Stern urged Schindler to protect Jews by hiring them for his factory. To please this man, whose mind and business acumen he so admired, Schindler did so. In the first year of his factory's operation, the number of Jewish workers employed at his factory increased from 7 to 150. Later, at

Stern's request, Schindler sheltered Jews who were too old and debilitated to work.

His relationship with this Jewish accountant initially placed Schindler in the motivation group that academics label "philosemites," and which I call "Judeophiles."[2] Judeophiles were those people whose rescue activity arose out of a special feeling or love for individual Jews or the Jewish people as a group. In Schindler's case, his initial impetus to rescue Jews stemmed from his desire to please his scholarly accountant. The transforming encounter that Schindler experienced watching a little girl dressed in a scarlet coat and cap as she witnessed the German soldiers murdering ghetto residents transmuted that desire into something more.[3] That episode fired Schindler's resolve and hardened his determination to help. But it was his relationship with Itzhak Stern that first led Schindler in a "rescue" direction.

As a group, Judeophiles represented the second-largest motivational category among rescuers I interviewed.[4] This love for individual Jews or of the Jewish people was the most prominent aspect of this group's rescuer self and became a central part of their essence. How such relationships resolved themselves differed from person to person and from situation to situation. For many, this relationship brought happiness and meaning to their lives. After the war, some married those whom they had saved; some converted to Judaism; and some moved to Israel. Some did all three. For others, the relationship dissolved after the war into a muddle of guilt, rage, isolation, and grief. Relationships were cut off abruptly. Some were severed deliberately; others were torn apart inadvertently by the chaotic conditions of war.

The sisterly attachment between Elizabeth Bornstein and Ilse Lowenberg survived the war and their resettlement in the United States. The Christian Elizabeth Bornstein lived in an apartment in Berlin with her Jewish husband and their five-year-old daughter. The apartment amounted to little more than a large living room, divided by a curtain to create a bedroom and a kitchen. From there, Bornstein ran a blouse-making business that employed three or four Jewish workers. One of her private clients was Ilse Lowenberg, an Orthodox Jewish woman who would drop by from time to time with material for blouses for herself, her sisters, or her mother. Between the Christian seamstress and the Orthodox Jewess, there seemed to be an instantaneous rapport. Lowenberg often stayed to chat or play with Bornstein's daughter. It seemed to both women that they had known each other all their lives and they felt a sisterly love for each other.

The fact that Elizabeth Bornstein's husband was Jewish (he had converted to Christianity when they married) prompted the couple to an early and vehement opposition to the Nazis. Her love for her husband extended to other Jews as well. When the restrictions against the Jews tightened so that it was illegal to employ them, Bornstein risked arrest by ignoring the Nazi prohibitions. She not only continued to employ her Jewish workers, but provided them with extra milk and food ration cards for their families. When the deportations began, Elizabeth Bornstein did still more. She offered to hide her friends, Ilse Lowenberg and her husband, in her own apartment. The Lowenbergs gratefully accepted her offer. Armed with false Aryan papers, the Lowenbergs wandered around Berlin during the day so that no one would suspect that they did not hold regular daytime jobs. At night they slept in the Bornsteins' kitchen.

For months the two families, five people in all, lived in conditions of cramped terror. One day the Nazis discovered the Lowenbergs' true identity, arrested them, and deported them. Ilse Lowenberg, however, jumped from the deportation train and made her way back to Berlin. She telephoned Bornstein, who managed to tell her that her apartment was no longer safe and mentioned another friend with whom she could stay. Lowenberg survived the remainder of the war in this hideout. Lowenberg's husband was not so fortunate. He died in the concentration camp to which the deportation train was headed.

After the war, the Bornsteins and Ilse Lowenberg (who had remarried) emigrated to the United States. Bornstein settled in New Jersey and Lowenberg in Queens. Throughout the passing years, their friendship and love for each other never abated. Although Lowenberg is an Orthodox Jew, she now joins the Bornsteins for their Christmas celebration. Ilse Lowenberg was the Bornsteins' only family.

Workplaces afforded many non-Jews opportunities to know and

establish special rapport with Jews. Certainly Miep Gies came to know Otto Frank and his family through her work as a bookkeeper and administrator at his food and spice export firm. Farmers traded with or were customers of Jewish-owned businesses. They shared a camaraderie of the marketplace that in more than one case became a lifeline for a Jew. Zofia Banya, for one, never forgot general store owner Israel Rubinek's trust in her to repay the money she owed him. But it was not all bonhomie and selflessness. Some non-Jews tolerated and protected Jews because they felt it might be economically beneficial. Part of Zofia Banya's determination to save the Rubineks stemmed from her knowledge that they had money that would help her and her family survive. This economically based Judeophilism was a factor in many rescues. If money were the only consideration, then these rescuers would be considered opportunists and exploiters, not "Righteous Among the Nations." But the hope of gaining a share of their charges' resources was sometimes mixed with a genuine desire to save people for whom they felt a special bond. The notion that they might also get some money out of the act of rescue may not have been a particularly noble thought, but it was a very human one.

An affinity toward Jews could come from many sources. Some Christians had childhood friends who were Jewish. Others remembered being *shabbos goyim,* or non-Jews whose job it was to turn on lights, light fires, and perform other minor household tasks for Jews who strictly followed the Jewish injunction not to do any work on the Sabbath. Non-Jewish children often received candy and other treats for their help, and they carried fond childhood memories of Jews.

A surprising number of Judeophiles had or suspected they had Jewish blood.[5] Swedish envoy Raoul Wallenberg had a great-great-grandfather and another relative, both on his mother's side, who were Jews.[6] (Of course, some Nazis suspected that they had Jewish blood in their background. These individuals, in order to appear above suspicion, became virulent antisemites.) Others had been in love with Jews and been forbidden by their families to continue their relationships. In these cases, the love not only remained for the lost sweetheart but was extended in general to the Jewish people. Still others thought that they themselves might be the illegitimate offspring of a secret Jewish liaison.

Walentyna Zak was such a case. This young girl from a small Polish town, who helped the Morgenstern family and their friends escape from the Warsaw ghetto and sheltered them, always suspected that she was the illegitimate result of her mother's first love, a Jewish man whom her grandmother prevented her mother from marrying. Walentyna's mother instead married a Polish construction supervisor, a widower with three children of his own. Eventually Walentyna and three other children followed. Walentyna was the oldest of the new brood, and while her father was not particularly loving toward any of them, she felt he disliked her especially. He forbade her to associate with Jews or to patronize Jewish stores. When she was seventeen years old, she fought with him, disobeyed him, and finally fled to the Polish city of Lvov, where she worked as a hospital nurse for a group of Jewish doctors.

For the same reason—that of probable paternity—Walentyna felt herself the adored, special child of her mother's. She recalled that once, during a visit home, her mother came into her room and, thinking her asleep, straightened her blanket and kissed her foot. Such loving devotion made up for the cruelty of her punitive father. Walentyna kept her suspicions to herself about who her real father might be. Finally one day, she mustered enough nerve and confronted her mother. Her mother scolded her for entertaining such a notion, but she did not deny it directly. That was confirmation enough for Walentyna. She did not push the issue further. It was enough to make Walentyna believe that she had a special Jewish connection, a connection that gave her a heartfelt desire to rescue. Her help and feeling for the Jewish family she saved from the ghetto was such that when capture by the Nazis seemed imminent, she refused to save herself by running away. "If they kill you and let me live, I'll have nothing to live for," she remembered telling them. "I will not run away. We will all go together."

Most Judeophiles began their rescuing activities by sheltering Jews they knew. The Bloms, for example, hid Janny Blom's ex-boss and friend Samuel Vreedenburg and his wife. Stefania Podgórska began by feeling compassion for one of the sons of the owner of the grocery where she worked. During two of the numerous episodes of terror in her war experiences, Stefania had an overwhelming spiritual revelation that allowed her to continue functioning. She committed her soul to God's care, and, to her way of thinking, God responded with miracles. But her original motivation to rescue was not religious, but Judeophilic, based on her emotional attachment to the family, and to one son in particular. As was the case with two-thirds of the other Judeophiles I talked to, Stefania's rescue activity did not stop with saving the life of just one Jew. The rescuer self that emerged with the initial rescue longed to do more, and most Judeophiles in the end saved a number of other Jews as well; Stefania saved thirteen.[7]

In small villages such as the one in which Jean Kowalyk grew up, Jews (if there were any) were known to everyone. They were not mysterious or alien beings. The Kowalyks knew the two Jewish families who lived in their village as neighbors and friends. Kowalyk's father was mayor of the village and was friendly with everyone, including the two Jewish families. Kowalyk recalled that one Jewish family in town owned the general store, and at Christmas or some other Christian holiday, the owner brought Kowalyk's father a bottle of whiskey or some fish. At school, Jean Kowalyk's best friend was Blumka Friedman, a Jewish girl who was a member of the town's other large and poor Jewish family. "We were very close," Kowalyk recalled. "When the Jewish Easter came, she brought me matzo. I loved it." As Jean Kowalyk described her childhood and her friendship with Blumka, who was murdered along with most of her family, Kowalyk's grief was still apparent. Her love of the Passover matzo was, and is, connected in her mind with her love of her Jewish friend.

Given the prevailing antisemitic attitudes of her village and country, Kowalyk's and her family's ability to overcome the prevalent negative myths about the Jews as "Christ killers" was remarkable. Today, of course, researchers have identified a number of factors that make this acceptance more understandable. Social psychologist Stuart W. Cook, for instance, has pinpointed five conditions that lead to favorable attitudes toward people who are different. First, a person's contact with the "other" cannot be superficial. A person must get to know the other as an individual. Second, both people must be in the same economic and social status for authentic interaction to transpire. Third, a more favorable impression is gained when the atmosphere is informal or friendly rather than businesslike. Fourth, the interaction between the two should be cooperative rather than competitive in nature. Finally, it is generally helpful if the "other's" personality, interests, and background are somewhat similar to those of the majority person.[8]

Thus, despite centuries-old antisemitic attitudes, particularly in Eastern Europe, it was possible under the right conditions for some to overcome bigotry. For example, the Zahajkewyczes, a Ukrainian family, had a tradition of Judeophilism that was passed from one generation to the next. Victor Zahajkewycz, the family's grandfather and patriarch, had been a theologian and teacher who had consoled his Jewish students when they were roughed up and befriended them whenever he could. He was a Greek Orthodox Ukrainian who had married a Roman Catholic Pole. Perhaps his own mixed marriage gave him more tolerance for people from other religions. In any case, he loved his Jewish students. When he died, the Jewish newspapers referred to him as a "Jewish father."

His son, Bohdan Zahajkewycz, inherited both his father's educational talent and his Judeophilism. In September 1939 when the war broke out, Zahajkewycz, his wife, and their four children were living in Peremyshl, a western Ukrainian city of 50,000. At first they lived in an apartment on the outskirts of the city. Among their neighbors were the Shefler family, an Orthodox Jewish couple with four boys. Unlike most Ukrainians, the Zahajkewyczes knew many Jews and had many Jewish friends. The Sheflers soon became their closest friends. Mr. Shefler, a former grocery store owner, was a skillful storyteller who amused the Zahajkewyczes' children with his tales and surprised them with treats. Three of the sons worked, but the youngest, Edzo Shefler, was still in high school. He, along with the other Zahajkewyczes, celebrated all the festive Jewish holidays with the Sheflers.

When the Sheflers moved into the city, the two families continued to see one another. The two wives visited, gossiped, confided in one another, and gave each other advice. It was an uncommon friendship in any case and certainly uncommon for a Jew and an Ukrainian.

Toward the end of the 1930s, events rocked the lives of these two families. In 1936, Mr. Shefler died. The two older brothers married and moved to other cities. During the Soviet occupation of Peremyshl, the Zahajkewyczes' seventeen-year-old son disappeared and was never seen again. In 1941, the Germans bombed the city and then invaded Peremyshl. The thirty or so Jews who lived in the Zahajkewyczes' apartment building looked to the schoolteacher for advice. He calmed their fears and told them to stay. Like most Ukrainians, Zahajkewycz felt that the Germans would be better than the Russians. They hoped the independence of the Ukraine might be restored and that food supplies might be more plentiful. Zahajkewycz was quickly proved wrong. Conditions under the Germans were worse than under the Russians. Food supplies were as scarce as ever. Eventually, Jews were forced to wear armbands emblazoned with the Star of David, and they were moved into a barbed-wire ghetto area. The Sheflers were forced to move into the ghetto.

The Zahajkewycz family remained together, but in 1942 the mother died and Helena, twenty-one years old and the eldest child, assumed responsibility for the household. Her father was no longer teaching, but was working full-time for the Ukrainian Relief Committee. Her brother Orest, who was sixteen years old, was recruited to work for the Construction Division of the German City Government. Helena was left to care for her six-year-old sister. One night Helena Zahajkewycz woke up to the sound of hushed voices. To her surprise, she saw her father talking with a former student and his wife who had managed to obtain two false identification cards. As if it were yesterday, she remembered what the Jewish student told her father:

> Professor, yours is the last door we knocked on. We knocked on the doors of many of our friends' homes and no one would let us in. We know you have children, and don't want to cause you trouble. We won't hold it against you if you refuse to help. But if you're willing, we'd like to stay a day or two. In that time maybe

your son or daughter could buy us tickets to Warsaw. Then we'll leave.

Despite the fact that the Zahajkewyczes lived across the street from a Ukrainian police station, Zahajkewycz told the couple that they were welcome to stay. The next day Helena and her brother bought them train tickets to Warsaw and then escorted the Jewish couple safely to the station.

The couple was just one among a number of Jews and other Nazi fugitives the Zahajkewyczes helped. One evening, later in the war, the Zahajkewyczes' doorbell rang, and outside their apartment stood Edzo Shefler with his new wife. In broken sentences, the pale and emaciated fugitive told them of ghetto conditions. His brother, Samyk, was still alive in the ghetto, but their mother had been deported and his two other brothers had disappeared. Shefler and his wife had escaped by pretending to be shot. Their bodies were thrown on a truck with Jewish corpses and dumped into a mass grave outside the ghetto. In the darkness, they managed to crawl out of the grave undetected and to flee.

The Zahajkewyczes held a family conference. Together they decided that they would shelter the Sheflers as long as necessary. Helena's father warned everyone of the danger and took particular care to impress on Helena's seven-year-old sister the importance of secrecy. The Sheflers stayed with the Zahajkewyczes for ten months, until the Russians liberated the city. Over the years, the Zahajkewyczes have kept in close contact with their extended family. Samyk survived the war only to die several months afterward in a car accident. Edzo Shefler and his wife, along with a baby born in a displaced persons camp, emigrated to Israel. In 1985, they were all reunited when the Zahajkewyczes flew to Israel to receive their Yad Vashem honors.

I discovered this story in the files of Yad Vashem. There I also found Helena Zahajkewycz Melnyczuk's name and New Jersey address. Her telephone number was unlisted, but once back in New York I decided to take a chance and drove out to see if she still lived at the same address. A small, intelligent-looking suburban matron came to the door. When she said, "How can I help you?" I knew I had the right address and had found the right person.

JUDEOPHILE RESCUERS who were married to Jews did not just worry about their own loved ones; their emotional affinity to Jews extended beyond the immediate family. Hungarian Helena Alias saw and got to know Jews at a very impressionable time of her life. Alias, who was born out of wedlock to a beautiful but simple peasant woman and an aristocratic father, lived with her father. Her mother married a Romanian Jewish artist and successfully fought for and gained custody of her daughter. At age ten, Alias moved to Romania and lived very happily with her mother and stepfather, a loving and kind man whom she adored. As an adolescent, she saw Jewish children beaten in her Romanian neighborhood as they walked to school and local shops vandalized and burned simply because their owners were Jews. It was something she was never to forget.

Alias married a Jewish factory owner, and for a while they lived happily in a big house in Yugoslavia. But the war soon caught up with them. Alias's husband was denounced by collaborators and imprisoned. A local priest, who was also a dear friend, arranged for a certificate of conversion to Christianity for Alias's husband, and after six grueling days he was freed. Alias began to rescue others, and eventually, with the "conversion" certificates, freed 180 other imprisoned Jews. Soon afterward, Alias's husband was arrested again, this time for distributing flour to starving Jews. Alias did not know that her husband had been arrested, but she saw Jews being herded to the train station for deportation. Terrified for the fate of these Jews, Alias followed the crowd to the station and gave water to people stuffed into stifling cattle cars. A German officer caught her distributing water and beat her, crushing her back, leaving her bleeding, and inflicting her with injuries that would be with her for life.

Still crippled by her beating, Alias went to Hungary to search for her husband. Eventually she located him, smuggled black-market goods into the concentration camp where he was imprisoned, and effected his escape and that of seven others. Alias and her husband fled to Yugoslavia, where he remained hidden in the basement of his factory for six months until liberation. During that time, she continued her rescue activities. She distributed clothes, food, and false identification papers to Nazi fugitives and helped a group of Serbo-Croatian resisters to escape from Yugoslavia by boat down the Danube.

Like Jean Kowalyk, whose love of a Jewish girlfriend predisposed her to find hiding places for Dr. Berger and the other Jews who came to her home, Helena Alias's rescue effort grew to include total strangers. Alias's deep awareness of the persecution of Jews was etched in her mind. This awareness prevented her from thinking only of her husband's and her own safety and comfort. That awareness, combined with her love of Jews that began with a stepfather and a husband, set her rescuer self in an outward, helping direction.

Still others felt a closeness to the Jewish people that came from their reading and understanding of the Hebrew Bible. Fundamentalist Christians, who grew up with biblical stories, felt a love for this ancient people. Some of these Judeophiles had never met a Jew, but when given an opportunity to rescue one, they were more than willing. They felt a religious connection to Jesus, a single Jew, or to those people the Hebrew Bible said were chosen by God. Amfian Gerasimov, a Latvian rescuer, was one. Gerasimov was the only surviving child of a Latvian couple who had divorced. After an unhappy period living with his newly remarried father, fourteen-year-old Gerasimov wound up living with his mother in Moscow. His parents' divorce and the shock of the Russian revolution sent Gerasimov on a quest for stability and meaning. In time he became convinced that the Jewish people were the anchor and foundation for all religions. He joined the sect of Sabbath Observers, but still longed to feel more a part of Jewish history and continuity. He wanted to move to Palestine. Instead, war interrupted his plans, and he and his family, which now included a Sabbath Observer wife, six children, and his mother, moved to Riga. There Gerasimov worked as a postman, and was soon involved in delivering messages and goods to Jews in the ghetto. Gerasimov did not know the people he was helping very well. They asked Gerasimov to keep their belongings safe, and he did. They were rich and he was but a civil service worker. But persecution was a great leveler. Rich or poor, stranger or acquaintance, Gerasimov identified with their suffering. He wanted to help.

Here again, a rescuer's motives are not unmixed or entirely self-less. Just as Gerasimov felt a special attachment to the Jewish people, he also undeniably felt an elevated sense of importance and prestige. He was a simple, poor man who was suddenly crucially important to people who were his social and economic betters. It was a heady experience that compensated in some small measure for the frightful risks he took by secretly delivering their possessions to them. The Jews then bartered for food and favors. In this way, Gerasimov indirectly saved a number of lives. His feelings of increased social importance in no way lessen this accomplishment. The most salient aspect of his rescuer self was broad-based identification with all Jewish people, not only wealthy or socially prominent ones. After the war, he and his son were circumcised, and his family moved to Israel.

· 10 ·

CONCERNED
PROFESSIONALS

NOT ALL RESCUERS felt an emotional bond with the Jews. In fact, members of one group—a group that sociologists label "concerned-detached professionals" and that I call "concerned professionals"—were drawn into rescue by virtue of their occupations. Although they made up only 5 percent of those I interviewed for the Rescuer Project, they were a varied and fascinating group. These diplomats, doctors, nurses, social workers, and psychologists did not necessarily love Jews—or even much like them. They were, however, ideologically opposed to the Nazi regime. When some social workers saw that, without help, Jewish families would be split apart and members of these families would have to face a deadly destiny alone, they felt obliged to help. When doctors saw men hunted by Third Reich butchers, they made an effort to intervene. And when certain diplomats saw people of different nationalities stripped of their basic citizenship rights—indeed of their dignity—they felt compelled to act. Unlike moral rescuers, who saw human beings who, with a little empathic imagination, could be just like them, these professionals saw what they were accustomed to seeing day in and day out: clients in trouble, patients in need, strangers in distress in a foreign land.

194 ~~~ CONSCIENCE & COURAGE

To concerned professionals, Jews were similar to those who customarily crowded into their offices, jammed their waiting rooms, or milled about their anterooms. To be sure, Nazi persecution made their cases more urgent. But these professionals were supremely confident in their ability to help. It was what they were trained to do. Thus, the rescuer selves that emerged from this group's helping activities were little different from their usual professional demeanors. They were competent, independent, and dedicated to doing their jobs well. They were also a bit aloof, keeping an emotional distance between themselves and their charges. They did not maintain relationships with those they rescued, and the people they helped most often did not provide testimony for recognition at Yad Vashem.

Dutch psychologist Jopie D., who had studied with Jung and Adler, was a divorced mother with two teenage daughters. By insisting on a professional distance from her charges, she was able to hire and keep a Jewish girl as a maid even though her home was right across the street from Gestapo headquarters and an SS officer lived next door. This same professional distance permitted her, when she was frightened and hungry at the war's end, to give her charge a bicycle and another address for shelter.

Jopie D. told me her detached attitude was purposeful and clear from the start. The rescue began when Jopie D. was called on the phone and asked if she could adopt a dog. Jopie D. thought this message sounded strange and it must be something that had another meaning. Jopie D. answered, "Yes, what kind of dog? A male or female?" It was a female. Jopie D. agreed; she understood that she was being called upon to adopt a human being. Jopie D. never knew who the caller was. Jopie D. must have been known by anti-Nazis because she had refused to take a pledge of allegiance to Hitler and so was denied her doctorate until after the war.

Jopie D. created a scenario that would protect her in case she was caught. She immediately advertised for a live-in maid in a local paper, and when an eighteen-year-old Jewish girl named Hannie arrived, Jopie showed her the ad and started rehearsing a script with her. Hannie, on the other hand, wanted to tell Jopie D. her story, but

Jopie D. said, "No. I don't want my fingernails pulled off." This was what the Germans did in order to force confessions.

While Jopie D.'s insistence on a professional distance may seem heartless, it was the way her rescuer self could operate best. With her emotions in control, fear did not paralyze her.

Jopie D. and Hannie rehearsed an imagined story based on false identification papers Hannie carried. And Jopie D. prepared for the worst. "If ever the house is searched, be sure that you don't turn your face. You don't have to be polite to the Germans. They don't expect it. You stay where you are and busy yourself in the kitchen cleaning something."

Indeed, one time the house was searched by a group of German soldiers from Leiden who every morning had to walk to Haarlem—a tremendous distance—and search houses for men, because they were needed for labor in German factories. Next door, three men were hidden, and so Jopie D. tried to keep the soldiers as long as possible so they would have to return home and not search any more houses for the day. Her scheme worked and so did the role-playing with Hannie.

Another close call with Hannie took place when they went on vacation. Jopie D. warned Hannie that if she saw anyone she knew, she must tell Jopie D. right away. Hannie did recognize someone and Jopie D. immediately told her to return to the address from where she originally came. The suspects questioned Jopie D. and she informed them, "A Jewish girl? What do you mean? The girl you saw is my maid. She just got a message that her mother is very ill and I sent her back to take care of her mother."

In her private psychology practice, Jopie D. played it very safe. She avoided patients' political conflicts. In one of her sessions with a client, Jopie D. was told by the patient that he belonged to the Nazi Party. Her instinctual response: "Like a flash I thought about what we discussed in previous sessions." Then he said, "After talking with you I want to get out of the party." Jopie D. immediately thought this was a trap. She responded, "That's one thing I cannot help you with. You have to find out for yourself." The client came back the following week and said he left the party. Jopie D. jotted it down and asked him, "How did you do it?" The client went to a party meeting, sat in full view of everybody, and then exposed himself. Party members thought that was terrible and kicked him out. Again, Jopie D. noted it down. When the war ended, the list of people who were members of the party was found and an official came to Jopie D. and asked about this man. She replied, "I can tell you the date because I have my notes." He was not imprisoned.

As with rescuers in other motivational categories, concerned professionals had a sense of obeying a higher law than that dictated by political considerations. Whatever their particular job—social worker, nurse, teacher—these rescuing professionals adhered to the highest ideals of their profession and applied them to the situation at hand.[1] So it was, for example, that Adelaide Hautval, a thirty-six-year-old French psychiatrist, refused to anesthetize prisoners for Nazi sterilization experiments. Hautval, who was deported to Auschwitz for protesting the ill-treatment of Jews by the Germans, told authorities that such experiments were against her principles as a doctor. "You cannot see that these people are different from you?" a Nazi doctor told her. "There are lots of other people different from me," she told him, "starting with you."

Other doctors felt the same way. Almost routinely, doctors hid Jews in rooms marked with quarantine signs during German round-ups. Still other doctors used their medical expertise to devise ways to hide a male's circumcised penis. Josef Jaksy, a Czechoslovakian urologist and surgeon, made a small incision on patients and then gave out a medical certificate that stated that they had just recently been circumcised for purely medical reasons.

Other doctors attached skin from another part of the body to the penis as the foreskin in order to hide circumcision. Polish surgeon Feliks Kanabus started performing these operations on his own. He felt "totally dependent on his own skill and imagination, especially since these operations had to be performed secretly." His assistants during the operations were his wife, Irene, and his brother-in-law, both doctors, but not surgeons.

After a few months of performing this surgery, Dr. Kanabus

found two other doctors who were doing a similar procedure. They pooled their knowledge and among them performed about 140 anti-circumcision operations. Half of the medical procedures were successful.[2]

Professionals in other fields also held fast to their humanitarian ideals. Despite the danger, social workers Irena Sendlerowa and Gertrud Luckner dedicated themselves to helping those most in need. Sendlerowa, who worked in the Social Welfare Department of the Municipal Administration of Warsaw when the Germans invaded Poland, set up a secret welfare network that forged documents to get Jews desperately needed food, medicine, and clothing. Part of the success of her efforts stemmed from the fact that a welfare network formed by Christians and Jews was already in place when the Warsaw ghetto was formed. That network, which was established to assist families broken apart by the war, had a youth branch that helped children and teens deal with the war and provided them with normal activities.[3] Sendlerowa transformed this structure into an underground operation that smuggled 2,500 children out of the Warsaw ghetto and hid them with families in the non-Jewish part of the city.

Gertrud Luckner, a social worker with the German Catholic Caritas Association, did not stay within her job description either. She acted as a secret courier, ferrying emigration money and information to Berlin Jews and checking on their welfare. It was a mission fraught with danger. With each visit to a Jewish family in hiding or in transit, she risked arrest. Eventually she was caught by the Gestapo, who demanded to know who was behind her operation. "My Christian conscience," she told them. It was not an answer designed to please Nazi officialdom, and the Gestapo grilled her for nine weeks. Finally, Luckner was sent to the Ravensbrück concentration camp, where she survived a two-year imprisonment. After the war, she continued her social work, devoting her life to improving relations between Christians and Jews.

Nowhere was the determination to uphold the highest ideal of their profession more apparent than in the cases of those rare diplomats who disobeyed their countries' foreign service directives in order to save Jews. Japanese consul Sempo Sugihara, based in Kovno, Lithuania; International Committee of the Red Cross (ICRC) representative Friedrich Born, based in Budapest; and Portuguese consul Aristides de Sousa Mendes, stationed in Bordeaux, all acted against the official policies and directives of their governments, following their consciences instead. In May 1944, Born was sent by the Red Cross to be the chief Red Cross delegate in Budapest. His initial instructions were not to interfere with the internal affairs of Hungary. Those instructions were modified somewhat when the news leaked out that Hungarian Jews were being deported not to labor camps but to the gas chambers of Auschwitz. Born was told to help the Jews the best he could, but it was clear that his efforts were to be confined to traditional diplomatic channels. Born did not hesitate to go far beyond his headquarters' directive. Following the examples of Swedish envoy Raoul Wallenberg and Angel Sanz-Briz of the Spanish legation, Born proclaimed innumerable hospitals and buildings to be the sovereign territory of the International Committee of the Red Cross and issued passports and forged identification papers to those who lived in those facilities. In addition, Born established a "Jewish affairs" department within his office and hired 3,000 Jews, thereby saving them from deportation. Despite complaints about his conduct from a fellow ICRC delegate, Born continued to act on behalf of the Jews.[4] His reports of Nazi atrocities were in part responsible for the international pressure that caused Adolf Eichmann to temporarily suspend the Hungarian deportations. Later, when Eichmann resumed his activities, Born courageously visited the deportation camps to deliver his outraged protest in person.

Giorgio Perlasca, an Italian, undertook the same sort of work in Budapest as did Born. Perlasca's transforming encounter, witnessing the murder of a Jewish boy by a Nazi mob, turned him from an Italian meat salesman to a volunteer member of the diplomatic corps of Angel Sanz-Briz's Spanish legation. One of Perlasca's tasks was to scout places to house the holders of the Spanish letters of protection that Sanz-Briz was handing out. In three months, Perlasca filled eleven apartment houses with 5,200 Jews. From each building hung the flag of Spain, serving notice to the Germans that the occupants were protected by Madrid. It did not matter that the occupants slept on stairs, used melted snow for drinking water, or went without plumbing. It did not matter that sometimes they ate food purchased with Perlasca's meager savings. For a while, at least, they were safe.

In late November 1944, disaster struck. Angel Sanz-Briz, the last legal representative of Spain remaining in Budapest, was forced to leave the country. At a loss over what to do next, Perlasca decided to check on the welfare of the Jews in the houses he had. When he arrived at one, the police were there rounding up people for deportation. The officer in charge told Perlasca that since Sanz-Briz had left the country, diplomatic relations with Spain were ended and the residents of Spanish houses were no longer protected. Without thinking twice, Perlasca improvised a dangerous, magnificent lie: "The legation is still in business," he told them. "Sanz-Briz has gone to Switzerland for a diplomatic conference. The flag is still flying. I am in charge. I am the legal representative of Spain."

The Hungarians, confused, agreed to allow the Jews to remain in Perlasca's houses. Suddenly, Perlasca was Spain's new chargé d'affaires in Budapest, nominated and confirmed by himself and recognized by the Hungarian government. It was his most magnificent moment. Nothing he did afterward ever measured up to the importance and success of his Budapest ventures.

In Kovno, Lithuania, Japanese consul Sempo Sugihara followed a similar scheme, with one important distinction. Whereas Born and Sanz-Briz took some liberties with their instructions from the home office, Sugihara ignored his instructions completely. Responding to an initial request from a Dutch yeshiva student who had managed to obtain from the local Dutch consul an entry permit for the South American colony of Curaçao, Sugihara issued him a transit visa through Japan. The Curaçao entry permit together with Sugihara's transit visa was a passport out of German-occupied Europe, and Sugihara knew it. He wrote the transit visa and then cabled the home office for permission to issue it. Permission was denied. In the meantime, the Dutch yeshiva student shared his plans with others and they lined up to receive a similar transit visa. Undaunted, Sugihara issued visas at a furious pace, writing nearly nonstop. At the end of the day, his hands would be so stiff that his wife would have to massage them back to life. Three times the government ordered him to stop issuing transit visas, and three times he defied instructions. When the Russians closed the Japanese consulate, Sugihara, with the aid of his wife, continued his rescue operation from a hotel room. He was still writing transit visas as his train pulled out of the Kovno station. By his own estimate, he saved 4,500 Jews. Others put the number as high as 10,000.[5] Although he paid a high personal price after the war for his insubordination, he never regretted his actions.

Diplomats' rescuer selves were different from those of ordinary citizens. As diplomats, disobeying home-office directives took on greater significance, since their actions were seen as representing the official stance of their countries. What Wallenberg, Born, Perlasca, and Sugihara did or failed to do was interpreted as a deliberate political message by the Third Reich and the host country. Diplomats were well aware of this. It made their dilemma all the more intricate. A personal, private decision to defy authority immediately became a public and highly charged political decision. Their rescuer self had no secret self. It was not possible. Moreover, there was no need for one. The decision to use diplomatic tools to rescue those persecuted by the Nazis was public by its very nature—issuing visas and filing official protests. Fortunately, diplomatic status also shielded them from the immediate consequences of their acts.

For diplomats, the reckoning came later, when their governments punished them for disobeying orders. Government policy, even one that is morally wrong, must be heeded. As the rescue was public, so often was the punishment. For his defiance, Sugihara was drummed out of the diplomatic corps and ostracized by other Japanese. He was denied an official recommendation for work in the private sector, a courtesy ordinarily granted to ex-diplomats. His whole family suffered isolation and shame. Eventually Sugihara found a job as Moscow representative of a Japanese trading company.

Perhaps nowhere was the dilemma diplomats faced more clear and the punishment so harsh as in the case of Aristides de Sousa Mendes, the wealthy, Catholic Portuguese consul general stationed in Bordeaux, France. Over a three-day period in the early summer of 1940, the fifty-five-year-old Mendes, helped by his wife and two oldest sons, signed entry visas for 30,000 refugees. He did so against the direct orders of his government that under no circumstances were Jews to be issued visas. But Mendes chanced to meet Chaim Kruger, the Orthodox chief rabbi of Brussels, who was fleeing across France with his wife and five children. Kruger told Mendes of the persecution awaiting Jews if the Germans took control. Mendes, without waiting for permission from the home office, not only issued visas for Kruger and his family but thereafter dedicated himself to saving as many Jews as he could. As he explained to his family: "I have to save these people, as many as I can. If I am disobeying orders, I'd rather be with God against men than with men against God."[6]

Mendes and his sons wrote and stamped visas daily from eight in the morning until two or three o'clock the next morning. When the official forms ran out, they used writing paper. When writing paper ran out, they used scraps of paper that bore the consular seal. Applicants walked for days to see the consul. They slept on chairs, stairs, and the floor and skipped meals rather than risk losing their place in line. One French political refugee arrived with four potato sacks filled with gold. He promised half to Mendes if he would give him a visa. Mendes refused his offer, but issued him a visa nonetheless.

With the fall of France, Lisbon recalled Mendes. Two officials were sent to escort him and his family back to Portugal. On their way out of France, in the city of Bayonne, Mendes saw a crowd of refugees outside the Portuguese consulate. Mendes stopped the car and demanded to know why the vice-consul was not issuing visas to those outside. The vice-consul replied that he was simply carrying out Lisbon's orders. "I have not been removed," Mendes shot back angrily. "I am still your superior." Countermanding the vice-consul's decision, Mendes wrote visas for the scores of Jews standing outside. Further on, at the French border town of Hendaye, Mendes issued still more visas to another group of refugees and then escorted them across the border to Spain.

Back in Lisbon, the Foreign Ministry punished Mendes for his insubordination. After thirty years of service, he was dismissed from the diplomatic corps and his pension rights were canceled. His colleagues shunned him and his friends avoided him. He retired to his château in Cabanas de Virato, a small mountain town 350 kilometers north of Lisbon. Those he saved would seek him out there and would applaud him when he emerged from his home. Nonetheless, his general public disgrace shamed him so much that he no longer could practice law. Cut off from a livelihood and friends, his energies became focused on seeing his reputation restored. He wrote every member of Portugal's parliament, arguing that what he had done was in keeping with the Portuguese constitution, and was a reflection of the benevolence of the Portuguese people. He received no reply. No one would cross Portugal's dictator, Antonio de Oliveira Salazar, whose political stance during the war was that of neutrality and appeasement. To support his family, Mendes sold one possession after another, and finally the château itself. In 1954, he died penniless, but entreated his children to clear his name.

Eventually Mendes's name was cleared. The first formal acknowledgment of his valor came in 1966 when Yad Vashem issued a commemorative medal in his name. After years of petitioning Portuguese ministers, Mendes's family succeeded in carrying out his last wish. In May 1987, President Mario Soares bestowed Portugal's Order of Freedom posthumously on Aristides de Sousa Mendes. In March 1988, Portugal's national assembly voted to restore Mendes's position in the Foreign Ministry and to distribute his back pay among his family.* As the vote was taken, all the deputies rose to their feet in Mendes's honor. His rescuer self had been validated at last.

---

*As of July 1994, Portugal's Prime Minister Cavaco Silva had still not given the Mendes family any financial remuneration, and furthermore has refused to give up the idea that Aristides de Sousa Mendes disobeyed orders.

· 11 ·

NETWORK
RESCUERS

IT IS GENERALLY ACKNOWLEDGED among sociologists that an ideology can only be defeated by a group effort. Individual attempts to counteract prevailing beliefs are futile. People for whom Nazism was anathema instinctively knew this. They sought out other people who saw the world the way they did, felt the way they did about Nazism, and wanted to do something about it. They gathered in political halls, university fraternity and sorority houses, church basements, and public school classrooms. They met in social welfare offices and in hospital staff rooms. They rallied in churches that had reputations for humanitarian endeavors such as Holland's Anti-Revolutionary Church and Germany's Confessional Church. And in towns like France's Le Mazet, Fay, Tence, La Suchère, Montbuzat, and Le Chambon and Italy's Assisi—towns with a tradition of harboring the religiously persecuted—they worked together to shelter strangers. They joined in what sociologist Georg Simmel has called "secret societies."[1]

Secret society members were both Jews and non-Jews. Unlike moral rescuers or Judeophiles who acted because they were aware that unless they did so a person would die, network rescuers were initially motivated by a fear and abhorrence of Third Reich policies. Non-Jews were enraged by Hitler's racist and dictatorial tactics. Nazism was the antithesis of their deeply held beliefs and humanitarian values. They felt personally violated. Even today, network rescuer Hetty Dutihl Voûte can barely contain her anger as she recalls her feelings about the German takeover of Holland:

> Right from the first day, I [was bursting with] rage toward the Nazis. They lied to us about not invading our country, they occupied our land, shot our soldiers, humiliated us, stole our provisions, arrested those who were our best men. Even now when I am writing this to you, I can feel my rage rise again![2]

Anti-Nazi rage was the tie that bound network rescuers together. Freud noted that a psychological group is formed when individuals have a common interest or a similar emotional bias in a particular situation. The higher "this mental homogeneity," the more readily people form a group, and the more striking are the manifestations of a group mind.[3]

I found network (underground) members to be remarkably homogeneous. Most came from business or professional families. Many were young adults who began anti-Nazi activities as university students. More than half had attended college or graduate school. All had at least some high school education. Although they were only the third-largest motivational category (ranking behind moral rescuers and Judeophiles), they were by far the most cohesive.[4]

These young people were early opponents of Hitler. They passed out anti-Nazi literature, organized protest strikes, and eventually undertook acts of sabotage. They were more likely than others to have shown their defiance of Hitler early on by ignoring the racial laws that prohibited non-Jews from having any sexual, social, or business contacts with Jews. Disobeying those laws was their first act of resistance. Even so, their focus was on opposing Hitler, not on saving Jews. Later, at the urging of Jewish network friends and as the plight of the Jews became more desperate, rescue became part of their general resistance efforts.

Such was the case in the most famous network operation of the war, the Danish underground's boat rescue. A tip from a courageous, high-ranking German official that the Germans were planning to transport all Danish Jews to concentration camps galvanized the network into action. In a matter of two months, the Danish citizenry spontaneously formed networks and whisked almost the entire Jewish population of Denmark to safety. It was the crowning achievement of an underground network comprised of students, doctors, taxi drivers, clergy, and others.

In the early days of German occupation, however, the Danish people were lukewarm in their support for the resistance. Initially the German occupation of Denmark was relatively benign. The Germans admired the Aryan-looking Danes and therefore curbed their bullying. Since Danish production, especially food, was needed for the German war effort, German occupiers did not interfere much with Danish government affairs.

For two and a half years, between 1940 and August 29, 1943, the Danish underground organized only small acts of sabotage. The approximately 20,000 members of the Danish underground were equally divided between Communists and other political groups, which in turn were divided into half a dozen major, independent operating networks. Each had a slightly different aim, philosophy, and political objective. Some were pacifists with a primary interest in gathering intelligence and publishing illegal papers. Others focused on attacking German military supplies and railroads. The Danish Student Organization had a "flying squad" that could be mobilized by a series of telephone calls. Whenever the Danish police suspected that the Germans were about to stir up trouble, a sympathetic policeman would alert the flying squad, who would then warn the concerned parties. The police had a tacit agreement with the underground that they would not interfere as long as the underground did not disrupt Danish factories and production.

The agreement broke down, however, when the Germans began to demand that Danes shift their production from food, clothes, and other peacetime goods to the manufacture of war materials. This shift raised moral questions among the Danes, questions that until then they had been able to ignore. As Harry LaFontaine remembered it, the question became:

> "How far could you go without becoming a partner in the war?" In the underground we said, "If you do anything that can help Germany win the war, you were a partner with the Germans." And indeed everybody was aware that if the Jewish question was ever raised in Denmark, that would be the [breaking point]. The government would refuse to carry out orders.

Should the Germans move against Danish Jews, the Danes, particularly in networks, were ready. When the Danish government and king resigned on August 29, 1943, the half dozen or so resistance networks were coordinated into one overall structure: the Freedom Council.

On September 28, 1943, Georg Duckwitz, the German shipping attaché stationed in Copenhagen, at great danger to himself leaked the Germans' plans to begin deportation of the Danish Jews starting the night of October 1. Duckwitz alerted Danish officials, and ordinary citizens dropped everything to help family members, neighbors, or friends. A taxi driver was reported to have telephoned every person with a Jewish name he could find in the telephone directory.[5]

Over a two-month period, they organized an informal "fishing armada" that transported Jews across the sea to safety in Sweden. More loosely structured networks joined efforts with the more organized resistance network.

All this took place under the constant surveillance of German authorities and patrol boats. Jews, dressed as warmly as possible, were stashed aboard boats. Some huddled in the bottom of the hull and were hidden under a tarpaulin. The boats were often stopped by German patrols. The boats had to seem to be simple fishing boats, and the fishermen's cover stories had to be solid. The hour-and-a-half-to-three-hour boat trip to Sweden was cold and nerve-racking.

The coordination and the level of participation in this remarkable rescue effort are indicative of the powerful influence of group norms on individual actions. Taxi drivers, fishermen, and students alike were caught up in the spirit of the enterprise. The English psychologist William McDougall suggested that men's emotions are stirred in a group to a pitch that they seldom or never attain under other conditions. In a group, individuals lose themselves in the group's emotions and are carried away by a common impulse.[6] In the case of the Danes, the impulse was a humanitarian one. The power of a group to influence uniform beliefs among its members is described by Alvin Zander, an expert on group dynamics at the University of Michigan.[7] It should be noted that this same dynamic, a group effort that allowed people to express their feelings and disobey authority, was what first catapulted Hitler and his National Socialist German Workers' Party to power.

Anti-Nazi networks followed Hitler's conquests across Western Europe. In Holland, networks were organized to resist the German occupation and also to protect endangered resisters and Dutch men and boys in their efforts to escape being drafted into the German work force. These fugitives needed hideouts and false identification and food ration cards; money was raised to support underground activities. Thus, when Jews began to be deported, the systems were in place to help hide them or to arrange for their escape. These loosely joined networks did not form in a vacuum. As sociologist Charles Kadushin, an expert on networks at the Graduate Center of the City University of New York, explains, social circles such as these grow out of existing formal structures.[8] In Holland these were individual Protestant or Catholic church groups, political groups, liberal or anarchistic intellectual circles in universities, all of which served as a core for anti-Nazi reserve activities.

But not all resistance groups expanded their activities to aid Jews. Some religious groups narrowly focused on helping only members of their own sect. Some armed resistance movements (such as the one my father joined in Byelorussia) believed that the main business was to defeat the German usurpers and the Jews could look out for themselves.

Eventually most Western European networks expanded to include rescue operations. Some moral rescuers (religious or otherwise), as well as Judeophiles and concerned professionals who started their rescuing in isolation, began to join networks. Working with a group gave solo rescuers the necessary resources they needed to continue. Networks provided extra ration cards, money, counterintelligence, and safe hideouts. The knowledge that they belonged to a group strengthened individual rescuers' resolve and gave their rescuer selves immeasurable psychological support. Backed by a group, network rescuers felt what Freud described as "an unlimited power." Such psychological support gave some rescuers permission to step outside their normal selves and lie, steal, and do whatever had to be done to save lives.[9]

Among religious rescuers in networks, this feeling of power was augmented by the conviction that they were doing God's work. Members of religious networks like France's CIMADE (Comité d'Inter-Mouvements auprès des Evacués) felt this. This group, along with other Christian groups, and the French Catholic Church, in courageous and notable contrast with the Vatican, banded together to save Jews.[10] In particular, they dedicated themselves to rescuing children from deportation to death camps.

A noted leader in organizing a religious network was Seventh-Day Adventist John Weidner. He was a devout businessman and son of a minister whose "Dutch-Paris" network was funded by the World Council of Churches.

In 1940, southern France had not yet been occupied by German troops. The region became a magnet for Jews and others fleeing the Nazis. But once the refugees reached the South, the pro-Nazi Vichy government put Jews into detention camps located in places like Vernet-les-Bains, Gurs, Venissieux, and Rivesaltes. From there, the government cooperated with the Germans by regularly handing over detained Jews to German authorities for deportation to concentration camps.

Weidner's group engineered the escape of Jews from these camps and guided them across the border to Switzerland; simultaneously, a coalition of French religious networks worked to save Jewish children. Pastors of the villages in the Haute-Loire, which included Le Chambon and the neighboring southwestern region of the Cévennes, also formed a spontaneous and informal network. Marc Donadille, pastor in the village of St.-Privat-de-Vallongue in the Cévennes, picked up Jewish children from Aix and Marseilles and hid them in villages and farms throughout the region. His brother, who was director of the railroad, helped by scheduling trains to Le Chambon to suit the convenience of network operatives.

Shelters for Jewish children were also found in various abbeys and churches. In Nice, Monsignor René Remond opened his bishopric to underground activities and allowed rescuers to canvass families to find ones who would take in Jewish children. In August 1942, French religious networks kidnapped 108 children from the detention camp at Venissieux near Lyons.[11] The children were sheltered in religious institutions under the protection of Cardinal Pierre Gerlier, assisted by Father Pierre Chaillet. For his efforts, Father Chaillet was arrested and confined to a mental hospital for three months. When Vichy officials pressured him to give up the children, he replied:

> The children are entrusted to us; they will remain in our care and you will only know their place of residence if we have a formal promise from the government that they will not be handed over to Germany.[12]

Working with Jewish groups, these networks of French Christian organizations saved an astounding 7,000 Jewish children living in France.[13]

The central fact of networks—that the rescuer self did not operate alone—was both its greatest benefit and its greatest peril. John Weidner's "Dutch-Paris" escape network, for example, included 300 people who forged papers, found temporary shelters for fugitives, obtained money, and escorted people across borders. Yet one weak link—Suzy Kraay—endangered all. She was caught in Paris carrying an address book with names of network contacts. As she was being taken to police headquarters, she surreptitiously dropped the address book on the sidewalk. An elderly Frenchman saw her and, not understanding the situation, returned it to her. "Mademoiselle has dropped this," he told her gallantly. The results of Kraay's slip were devastating. Half the members of the network, some 150 people, were traced and arrested, among them Weidner's sister, Gabrielle. (Gabrielle died in a concentration camp ten days before it was liberated by the Russians.)[14]

The danger, the intensity, and the urgency of rescue work drew members together. Network rescuers grew to feel they were part of a large, enveloping family. They felt they could rely on and trust only these "family" members. University of Toronto sociologist Bonnie Erickson observed:

> Participation in a secret society tends to be absorbing: the excitement and comradeship of shared risk can lead to stronger and stronger affiliation with the secret society and with other members. Participants may gradually restructure their networks, interacting more and more with other participants and less and less with outsiders.[15]

Saving Jews became an all-important, all-consuming task. Network rescuers' activities infused their lives with meaning and purpose. Rather than just talking about their values and beliefs, network members had an opportunity to act on them. For many, the experience was so deeply gratifying they would spend the rest of their lives trying to recapture it.

No two networks were the same and no two network experiences were exactly alike, but they have some common characteristics.[16] Kadushin defines a network as "a set of social objects onto which is mapped a set of relationships or 'flows' not necessarily in a 1:1 fashion," and explains that a circular relationship exists between individual members with no clear boundaries. Members do not all have direct interaction with everyone else. In fact, often the flow of interaction occurs via one or two other people, particularly if there is no set formal structure or leadership. However, some members play a more central role than others.[17]

Networks organized around a leader whose charismatic personality and forceful presence attracted those seeking ways to express their anti-Nazi rage are extremely vulnerable. If a network has a known leader, such a person is more susceptible to being denounced and killed. Furthermore, such a role is idiosyncratic and difficult to replace. Leaders such as John Weidner and Joop Westerweel were men of strong beliefs and unswerving principles, men who inspired others, attracting them to the enterprise. They were people with a knack for obtaining the resources necessary to carry out their plans successfully.

John Weidner ran a prosperous textile business in Paris, which he closed when the Germans took over Paris. He moved to Lyons and, despite stringent wartime restrictions, started another textile business from scratch. Joop Westerweel was a Dutch school principal whose innovative educational ideas and strong humanitarian ideals attracted a large following of teachers and students.

Joop Westerweel and his wife, Will, were Montessori teachers in Rotterdam whose passionate belief in individual freedom drew an informal group around them, known as the Westerweel Group. This group consisted of current and former students, other teachers and colleagues, Jews and non-Jews.

When the Germans took over Holland, Dutch resisters handed out leaflets and put up posters urging resistance to Nazi directives. As the Jews' situation worsened, the network's activities expanded. At its peak of activity, the Westerweel Group was involved in arranging escapes from the internment camps; finding safe hideouts; operating forgery and printing operations to churn out identification papers and ration cards; and, their most spectacular accomplishment, leading 300 to 400 children from Holland across Nazi-occupied Europe to Spain, Switzerland, and finally to Palestine.

At the center of this activity was Joop Westerweel, a teacher, an idealist, and a quick-tempered man who acted on his beliefs. In 1941, when he and his family returned from a summer vacation and found a Jewish family staying in their apartment, they insisted the Jews stay. (A friend of the Westerweels only meant to use their apartment temporarily until she could help the family escape. But her plans went awry, and the Jews were still there when the Westerweels returned.) Joop, Will, and their three children moved to nearby furnished rooms. Later they would move again to make room for Jewish children who needed to be hidden.

The Westerweel Group's intense activities, however, did not start until a year later. Until that time, the Nazis had pursued the Jews in their usual methodical way. Anti-Jewish ordinances were issued, goods confiscated, and all Dutch Jews were pushed into the Jewish quarter of Amsterdam. But on July 14, 1942, the first *razzia,* or roundup of Jews for deportation, began and networks were shocked into immediate action, much the way individual rescuers were stimulated by a transforming encounter. Saving Jews from the concentration camps became a top network priority.

In August 1942, a former student of Joop's, Miriam Finkhauf, asked him and his group to help her hide a Jewish youth group, Palestine Pioneers (in Hebrew: Hachshara). The 400 members of the group were in Loosdrecht in the province of Utrecht learning agriculture in preparation for their eventual emigration to Palestine. They had run out of time, and without help from non-Jews they would be rounded up and deported.

Joop Westerweel and his wife immediately agreed to help. They sent their children to stay with friends so they could focus their full attention on rescue work. Jews and Gentiles worked together to find hiding places for the children of Loosdrecht. The Westerweels recruited friends, family, and colleagues to help. They, in turn, recruited other trusted family members and friends. Networks and families became intertwined.

Westerweel's recruitment efforts were unending. He continually had to convince and reassure people that the cause was just and worth the risk. New members were always needed to replace those who were arrested or to staff new projects.

Hideouts were found for Jews, as well as for leaders of Jewish rescue efforts (also subject to deportation if caught). But hideouts were just a temporary solution. A more permanent one had to be found. In October, a group of thirteen youngsters attempted a border escape, but they never made it. No one knew precisely what happened, but it was clear that no other attempt could be made until a safer route was found. Joop Westerweel and Shushu Simon, a Palestine Pioneer leader with whom Joop had developed a close relationship, went to scout escape routes through the Swiss and Spanish borders.

Meanwhile the Jews of Palestine Pioneers waited. Will Westerweel and other members printed false identification papers and ration cards. Others visited the hidden children to calm them and see to their needs. Still others engineered the escape of friends from the internment camps of Westerbork and Vught.

Finally a border-crossing route was planned, and was ready for trial. Joop Westerweel led the children across Nazi-occupied Europe to Spain. From there they made their way to Palestine. In December 1943, however, Will Westerweel was arrested. She had offered a bribe to the wrong internment guard. Three months later, her husband was captured. As it happened, Joop was carrying a false identity card with the name of a man who was wanted by the Nazis for killing a German. Joop Westerweel was imprisoned and tortured by the Nazis for five months. He died without revealing a single name or activity of his group. Will Westerweel survived imprisonment and the war, and in 1964 was honored at Yad Vashem.

Leaders such as Joop Westerweel were the exception rather than the rule. The central focus of a network could not be static, it had to change with changing situational demands. Arrests occurred with great regularity; leaders were denounced, incarcerated, and killed. This meant that networks often could not depend on any one person to be the leader. When network members who were pivotal to the operation were caught the center of the operation and the leadership shifted.

Most networks, like the ones in the South of France, were informal and loosely organized. They grew from the spontaneous actions of friends, co-workers, and neighbors. These were democratic organizations that operated without formal rules.

Some networks did not even have a name. The Utrecht Children's Rescue Operation was the name given to a group after the war when historians and others needed a reference. But to those university students in the group such as Hetty Dutihl Voûte, it was just "friends together."

In 1940, Hetty was in Amsterdam studying at the university to be a biologist. She belonged to a sorority that included Jews, and she was close to many of them. But when Hetty realized war with Germany was inevitable, she was not thinking about her Jewish friends; she just wanted to do something to stop the Nazis. She volunteered for the Red Cross Auxiliary, at first cleaning the rooms and then helping with the wounded.

When Holland was defeated, Hetty returned to her studies. Her oldest and youngest brothers began an underground newspaper, and Hetty, the youngest of seven children, soon was recruited to distribute it. The first newspaper was called *Bulite #3*. The idea was that if the Germans should find the newspaper and confiscate it, they would drive themselves crazy searching for the nonexistent first and second issues. After a few issues, however, the newspaper ceased publication when Hetty's oldest brother was caught trying to escape to England with intelligence material. He was imprisoned in Holland and later sent to a camp in Germany.

When I asked Hetty what her family's reaction was to her brother's imprisonment, I was surprised to hear that her parents said, "Go on, go on with everything!" (As it turned out, five of the Dutihls' seven children were imprisoned during the war. The two others were less active in anti-Nazi activities because they had young children. All the Dutihls survived the war.)

Hetty, who was staying at her parents' home in Utrecht for the summer, heard about the deportations when a woman came to Utrecht with ten Jewish children in tow. The children, who had been abandoned when their parents had been deported, needed to be hidden before the Germans found them and deported them too. The woman had hoped that her Utrecht friend, whose son was a friend of Hetty's, would help. The son, desperate for help, called Hetty and all his other student friends. The students worked feverishly to place the children, who now were pouring into Utrecht, as Jewish parents began to fear what resettlement in the East really meant. Like Joop Westerweel and other network rescuers, Hetty dropped everything and gave herself the full-time "job" of saving lives. Nearly every day, Hetty, her sorority friend Gisela Wieberdink (who was the group's Amsterdam liaison), and a core of ten or twelve other student friends met to sort through what needed to be done and discuss who would do it. Foster homes for the children

needed to be found, false identification papers and ration cards secured, and follow-up visits to those already in hiding had to be
assigned. It was a tremendously complex and dangerous operation. Hetty and Gisela had no background or qualifications, just a
youthful eagerness to help the hunted Jewish children. Indeed,
Hetty Dutihl Voûte's recollection of events of that hectic time is
honest:

> We didn't know anything. We had to [find] foster parents, give
> them money, [food] distribution cards, everything. July and Au-
> gust were holidays, so there were lots of students who helped,
> and transported, and got distribution cards. Then in September
> they went to study again. [Of those] who were left, we knew who
> we could trust and rely on. That same core group stayed together
> until the end.

Just obtaining a ration card for a child was a complicated and
slow process. Distribution centers issued ration cards that were good
for buying products listed on the card. The cards were issued
monthly. Initially, the Utrecht students looked for trustworthy people
who worked in the distribution centers to issue cards to them. (Later
they would steal and forge them.) Hetty discovered some reliable
sources in southern Holland. So every month she traveled south to
pick up the cards, and then, stuffing them into her clothes, she smuggled them back to Utrecht.

To raise money for their operation, the students printed 10,000
copies of one of their poems and sold it for five guilders a copy.
People bought the poem knowing that the proceeds were going to
feed the hidden children. In addition, the archbishop of Utrecht contributed money and asked all his bishops to support the Utrecht
rescue operation as well.

In September 1942, the network had placed so many children
that they had to start an administrative card system. Hetty kept track
of it all. Her administrative record, which looked like an ordinary
book on her bookshelf, contained the names of all the children, their
aliases, their identity card numbers, and where they were located. By

the end of the war, there would be more than 300 names in the book.[18]

In the first month, the Utrecht group busied itself placing children who came to town. Later, as networks in other countries did, they went to Jewish parents and tried to convince them of the urgency and necessity of giving up their children. It was not an easy job. Parents were reluctant to trust the word of a stranger that their children would be safer with her. In Belgium, network members overcame the problem by working closely with Jews who would help convince parents of the necessity of entrusting their children to strangers.[19] In Poland, Irena Sendlerowa's circle in the Żegota, which rescued children from the Warsaw ghetto, was successful because Jews and Christians had known each other and worked with each other before the ghetto and the deportations.[20]

But Sendlerowa's people and the Żegota, the section of the Polish Home Army that was devoted to helping Jews, had little success convincing Jews to give up their children if the destination was a convent or some other Christian refuge.[21] Jews feared that rescuers would try to convert their children. In fact, sometimes that did happen. Polish historian Ewa Kurek-Matiunin, who interviewed Polish nuns who hid Jewish children in their convents, noted that while religious network rescuers were united in their goals to save lives, their motivations for doing so often differed. Some believed that their duty required saving not only Jewish lives but their souls too. This put them in a spiritual and moral conflict with others in their religious network who felt the children's religious background should be respected. Yet even the nuns who respected the children's religion realized that the failure to observe such Christian practices as communion or confession could lead to discovery. Kurek-Matiunin found that each nun handled these dilemmas her own way. Those more ecumenical in spirit compromised by tolerating more proselytizing of the children than they thought seemly, but made sure that after the war their charges were returned to their parents or the Jewish community.[22]

In Utrecht, Hetty and the other students pleaded with parents to give up their children. When the parents consented, the child was brought to a train station where two network members were waiting. They removed the Jewish star from the child's clothes and then the three of them would travel to the child's new home. The foster homes were all over Holland.

Like other network rescuers, the students of the Utrecht operation often could not remember their first rescue experience. (Both Hetty and Gisela were vague on this point, although Gisela thinks her first rescue was a Down's syndrome toddler who stayed at the sorority house for one or two nights.) People passed in and out. Unlike Judeophiles and moral rescuers whose rescuing had a definite beginning, middle, and end, most network rescuers did not have any relationship at all with those they saved. It was too dangerous to exchange names. Code names were routinely used in networks to guard against exposure and arrest. They also served a notable, if unintentional, psychological purpose. Being called by a code name made the rescuer self seem more real and more important. It was part of one's identity.

In June 1943, Hetty and Gisela's rescue activities came to an end. As they were returning from a visit to a couple they suspected might be Nazi sympathizers, the Gestapo arrested them. It was Hetty's twenty-fifth birthday.

She and Gisela were sent to a concentration camp at Vught and then sent on to the Ravensbrück camp in Germany. But the Utrecht Children's Rescue Operation continued. Other students took up the slack. Hetty's administration book was found and taken over by the archbishop of Utrecht and another network member. When the network ran out of children to place, they shifted their efforts to helping downed British pilots escape.

Informal social networks like the Utrecht Children's Rescue Operation were fluid entities that had no clear center of leadership, no single focus, and only a hazy idea of who was part of the group and who was not. Hetty Dutihl Voûte knew the dozen or so students in her group, but after the war she was surprised to find a number of other people who were also connected to the Utrecht rescues. I discovered that among the children she hid were members of the Palestine Pioneers, the same group the Westerweel Group rescued.[23]

The rescuer self in a network had the solace of being part of a group and an added burden and responsibility. The advantage was that more resources were available. If food, clothing, ration cards, or false identification papers were required, other network members helped procure these basic necessities. If a charge became ill, the network found a reliable doctor. If any problems arose with a charge, the rescuers could get help. For example, if a rescuer's home became an unsafe hideout, the charge was not just thrown out into the street to fend for himself. The rescuer was able to inform his or her contact in the network that a new hiding place was needed.

The disadvantage was responsibility for the welfare of many others: if they got caught, would they be able to maintain the secrets? Fear of jeopardizing the safety of others kept many network rescuers from reaping the full benefit of group support. Most network rescuers wanted to know as little as possible so that if they were caught, they would not have much information to divulge.

While all rescuers faced difficult moral decisions, network rescuers were enmeshed in a tangle of operations and sometimes conflicting obligations. The incident that led Johtje Vos to stuff incriminating papers into her son's sweater was a case in point. It was the day Jon, their friend and fellow underground member, had been caught by the Germans. The Voses assumed the Gestapo would torture Jon into revealing other network names. That was a given. It was as much part of the dangerous game they played as was the geranium they put in front of a certain window of their home to signal that all was safe. "We agreed among ourselves that we would never judge each other's thresholds for pain," Johtje Vos said by way of explaining her expectations.

But as Johtje was to discover, the game's rules were not always so clear-cut. What might best benefit the group might not be best for an individual, or vice versa. The Voses knew Jon had the names of all network members and the real names of those they were hiding. The Voses' first concern was to get those lists before the Nazis did. Aart Vos raced to retrieve them, together with the stamps they used to forge identification papers. He buried the whole lot in his garden.

A few hours later the Voses were sitting at the kitchen table, sorting through real and false identification papers in preparation for moving their charges to a safer house, when a black Gestapo car pulled up to the house. Aart Vos and the fugitives ran for the tunnel under the coal bin, while Johtje Vos gathered up the papers and stuffed them into her son's sweater and told him to disappear. Alone, she stayed to face the Gestapo.

Standing at the door with a Dutch collaborator and a Gestapo officer was Johtje's network friend Jan. He begged her to save his life and hand over the forgery stamp she had. If the Gestapo got them, they would not kill him, he told her. Johtje Vos was faced with an impossible decision. She could save her family, their charges, and herself or save her network friend. There did not seem to be a way to do both. It was a terrifying and morally excruciating situation. (To this day, Johtje Vos cannot retell this incident without shaking all over.) She did the only thing she felt she could: she denied knowing what Jan was talking about.

Just then Aart Vos, worried about Johtje, telephoned the house. Before he could say anything that might incriminate them, Johtje described what was happening at the house and with feigned puzzlement asked him if he knew anything about a stamp. Thinking quickly and stalling for time, Aart suggested that a man named Dick, whom he knew the Nazis would not be able to apprehend, had the stamp.

By this time, Jan's wife, Mieke, came running into the house. She had heard that her husband and the Gestapo were at the Voses' home. Suddenly Johtje got an idea how she might be able to save Jan's life. She turned to Mieke and asked her if she knew where Dick was. Mieke said she did, and Johtje told her to go find him and bring back the stamp. At the door, she whispered to Mieke to meet her in two minutes at the corner of the woods.

When Jan's wife left, Johtje went back into the room and sat down again. Then she turned to the German and told him she thought she knew where her husband was and that perhaps he could help them in their search for the stamp. Her children were upstairs sleeping, she told him, so he need not be afraid that she would not return. The German gave her ten minutes.

Johtje ran out of the house. She found Mieke and told her, "I have those things but we have to risk our lives to get them out. Are you willing?" Mieke said that she was, so together they sneaked back to Johtje's house. Lying flat on their stomachs so as not to be seen, they crawled underneath a window to the garden and dug with their hands to retrieve the package Aart had buried earlier. If they had been seen, they would have been shot on the spot.

Luckily, nobody saw them. They retrieved the package and agreed that Mieke would take the stamps and return to the house in twenty minutes, pretending she had just bicycled back from Dick's house and had gotten the stamp from him. Meanwhile Johtje ate the dirt off her hands and wiped her hands on her underpants so that she could return to the house without arousing any suspicions.

She reentered the house and, breathing as if she had been running, told the waiting officials that she had looked everywhere, but she could not find her husband. In twenty minutes, Mieke returned with a stamp she claimed she got from Dick and threw it on the table. It was not, however, the right stamp. After a tense moment, Mieke volunteered to see Dick again and get the right stamp. She left, retrieved another stamp from the unearthed package, and returned. The officials were satisfied. Oddly enough, the Germans never bothered to go after Dick. Johtje was not arrested, and Jan's life was saved. For the moment, the secret society was safe.

· 12 ·

CHILD
RESCUERS

ESTHER WARMERDAM clearly remembers the exact moment she became aware of her parents' rescue activities. Until that moment, the German occupation of Holland had not really changed her life in Hillegom. The eleven-year-old Dutch girl still went to school, played water polo, and helped take care of her eleven brothers and sisters. Sometimes strangers would come and stay with them in their big house outside of Amsterdam. Esther's father had explained that the strangers were hungry people from the city who wanted to stay for a while in a place where food was more plentiful. In fact, some weeks earlier, her father had introduced her to Paul, a boy about her own age. Esther knew that this hungry stranger from the city must be staying for some time, or else her father would not have bothered to introduce him to her. But she did not pay much attention to the newcomer because she disliked him. With his wavy black hair and aloof airs, Paul looked like a foreign prince. The Warmerdam children nicknamed him Zandhaas, after a sand rabbit that prefers to stay in the dunes and not mix with other animals. Paul hated the name and withdrew even more.

Then one day as Esther and her siblings were playing in the

street near the front of their home, Paul burst out the front door. "I'm not a rabbit!" he screamed. "I'm a Jew! I'm a Jew, a Jew!"

Esther and her brothers looked at each other in fright. They did not understand what Paul's screaming was all about, but sensed it meant trouble. Quickly they grabbed him and dragged him, still screaming, back into the house. After Esther's mother had hurried Paul into another room, the children asked their father to explain the boy's rantings. Reluctantly, Esther's father abandoned his efforts to shield them and told them that Hitler was murdering the Jews. As he talked, Esther began to comprehend the terror of the adult world around her and knew that her days of childhood play were over. Her father asked them all for their help. He trusted them to be quiet about Paul and the others who stayed with them. They were never to tell anyone what went on at home.[1]

From that day on, Esther became a full-fledged rescuer. She kept friends and classmates away from the house (even to the point of fighting one who was determined to come in) and accompanied her father on his missions to pick up food and escort home "divers," a term the Dutch used for those who needed a place to hide. During 1942–45, the Warmerdams helped more than 200 children escape deportation. Some children stayed for a day, some for a week, a few for the entire war. Esther helped take care of them.

Like adults, child rescuers developed a rescuer self that shut out all else and focused on protecting and caring for their charges. But there were important differences. A child's rescuer self was launched as a result of his or her parents' actions. Like Esther, they were enlisted in a cause; they did not volunteer. Their initial motivation was a wish to please their parents. Children who took the initiative were rare. Most children began rescuing activities because their parents asked them to help.

The nature of that help varied. The vast majority of children's involvement in rescue activities was passive. They were rescuers by virtue of living in the same house as the Jews their parents hid or were helping elsewhere. All the same, child rescuers were subject to the same risks. If a raid found Jews hiding in their home, children were as likely as adults to be hanged, shot, or shipped to a concentration camp. Some children were too young to understand the gravity of the situation and so they were not told the truth. Instead, young ones were told that the newcomers were distant relations whose houses had been bombed or whose family had been killed in the war.

In other cases, parents recruited their children and employed them as trusted lieutenants in their rescuing operations. They were the expedient choice, and the adult rescuer self used whatever was needed for the job at hand. At their parents' command, children became couriers, espionage agents, and guides. They learned to lie convincingly to authorities or feign innocence if caught. Their presence lent even the most dangerous activities an air of guilelessness and harmlessness. Often it was Christian children who were sent into the ghettos to escort Jews past the Nazi guards, through the gates, and to safety. On more than a few occasions, a child's presence on the scene saved people's lives. Johtje Vos stuffed incriminating evidence into her son's sweater and sent him outside to play. Jean Kowalyk's nephew saved the lives of the Jews in hiding as well as the extended Kowalyk family with his impromptu lie about smoking and playing cards in the attic with his friends.

Twelve percent of those rescuers I talked with were child rescuers. They ranged in age from five to twenty-one. Many of them attributed their ability to withstand fear to the naïveté of youth. Young people ignore danger either through a deliberate if unconscious misjudgment of the seriousness of the situation or by making light of danger altogether. This youthful sense of immortality led child rescuers to see their activities as a lark or an adventure. Dutch rescuer Cornelia Knottnerus, who was ten years old when her family took in Sarah, thought of herself as "the little hero against the big Nazis." Many children, particularly adolescents, found it hard to believe that their lives were really in danger. The Zahajkewycz family lived across the street from a Ukrainian police station, yet Helena said that she and her younger brother were not afraid. Naturally, they were cautious about keeping their Jewish charges concealed, but they did not live in constant fear of discovery:

Mostly the months passed for us—no matter how paradoxical this sounds—without worries. It may be that we who were young did not have many anxieties, and were naïvely fond of risks. And it may be that, under Father's strong influence, we were all unconsciously certain that we were protected by God and that He would keep us from harm.

The danger was real enough. Esther Warmerdam's home was raided a number of times. At those times, Esther would help the Jewish children dash to their hiding places. Everyone knew where to go (out the girls' bedroom window, along the eaves trough, past the chimney, and onward to the flat sunroom roof at the back), since Esther's father was continually running races and games with the children as a way of rehearsing them for such an emergency.[2] On one raid, a German soldier searched the house while another took her father outside and put a gun to his head. Esther's mother ran outside and told the soldier to leave her husband alone because he was a deaf-mute. Esther described what happened next:

> Suddenly we heard a shot and we thought it was over. A few moments later, he came into the house smiling. He told us how proud he was that we kept our mouths shut. . . . If only he knew how I had felt inside. I was ready to run outside and tell them. . . . Enough was enough. Tears were not there anymore, only anger. Anger at my parents and the whole stinking world. We had not asked for this.

Like Esther, many child rescuers had ambivalent feelings about their family's involvement in saving Jews. On the one hand, children felt proud that their efforts caused lives to be saved. Their work enhanced their self-esteem and gave them a feeling of competency and importance. In many families, children were included in family councils and given a voice in rescuing decisions. Parents listened to their concerns and children felt that their contributions were valued. All this was a mighty counterbalance to the powerlessness they felt because of their age and circumstances.

On the other hand, rescue took over every aspect of family life. All other concerns were pushed aside. (Joop and Will Westerweel gave up family life altogether by sending their children away.) No matter what troubles or problems a child might have, they appeared insignificant compared with those that faced Jews. Guilt, shame, and anger vied with the child's feelings of love and pride. They empathized with the plight of the Jews while at the same time they resented them. They were angry at their parents for undertaking a humanitarian role in which they were forced to take part, while admiring them for their altruism. Above all, they could not help asking the question that haunted Esther Warmerdam decades later: "Why were my parents doing this to me?" They chose to put their children's lives in danger. Why? Just posing the question brought back Warmerdam's old feelings: "It hurt so much inside to be so scared and lonely."

A startling one-quarter of all those rescuers I interviewed said they risked the lives of their children to save others. Parents, who sometimes used children as young as five years old as couriers or decoys, felt guilty that they risked their children's lives to save the lives of comparative strangers. Such guilt often prevented parents from praising their children's efforts at the time or discussing their rescue activity after the war.

Moreover, parents did not fully grasp the enormity of what it meant to ask a child to keep his or her activities secret. By making such requests, they were burdening their child with the staggering responsibility for the well-being of the family as well as those they harbored. Young children felt the weight most keenly. They were at the mercy of two authorities: the Nazis and adults at home. They did not want to displease either one. Six-year-old child rescuer Annie P. was as much afraid of letting down her stepfather as she was of the Nazis. She suffered a vicious booting to her spine rather than tell Nazi officials where the Jews were hidden and have to face her stepfather afterward. After all these years, she still has nightmares in German in which she hears over and over again her Nazi interrogators.

Like adults, children developed a rescuing self that took over their beings. They were Davids against Goliaths. They were on their guard at all times to remember a cover story or to avoid letting a

telling detail slip. Such guardedness deprived many of their childhoods.

Teenagers were particularly affected. Adolescents depend on peer
support and yearn for peer approval. By identifying with peers, adolescents ultimately develop their own identity. But once the rescuer
self took over, a teenager could no longer truly belong to a peer
group. A wall went up between them and their friends. They did not
partake in any antisemitic slurs, rarely invited friends home, and, in
Germany, avoided the Nazi youth movement.

In his work on child development, psychoanalyst Erik Erikson
has emphasized that each developmental stage builds on and requires
the previous one. In Erikson's model, after adolescence comes intimacy, "the capacity to commit oneself to concrete affiliations and
partnerships and to develop the ethical strength to abide by such
commitments."[3]

The adolescent child rescuer's situation interfered with the natural unfolding of intimacy. With the end of the war, the necessity for
the rescuer self disappeared, but secrets continued for many child
rescuers. They still feared that revealing too much would be dangerous. They felt isolated from their peers, and many had trouble culti-
vating intimate relationships.

Yet despite such problems, few of the rescuers I interviewed—
parents or children—wished that they had done things differently.
Reluctantly and with the same feelings of inner conflict they underwent at the time, parents said they would make the same decisions;
proud of what they did, most child rescuers would have had it no
other way. The rescuer self that emerged, at first motivated by a desire
to please a parent, took on a life of its own, as a child's action began
to reflect personal awareness and conscience. So it was that Orest
Zahajkewycz began bringing home friends who were evading the Germans' forced-labor roundups. They stayed in the Zahajkewyczes'
apartment until their escape plans were set. Still later, through Orest's
initial contact, the family harbored a Jewish doctor who had escaped
the Nazi liquidation of the ghetto.

In the same vein, Wendelgard von Neurath and her mother
befriended the Jews from the local prison camp who came each day to

help on the farm. But Wendelgard soon took actions on her own. One day after Christmas, she came across a prisoner sitting slumped over in the greenhouse. His face was covered with red spots and his lips were raw and cracked. He had scarlet fever, a highly dangerous and contagious disease. The other prisoners warned her that if the SS found out the man was diseased, they would kill them all. Ignoring the danger to herself, she asked two other prisoners to help her take the sick man to a small house next to the greenhouse. For the next two days, she nursed him. During the day, he was her patient. At night he reported back to the camp. Then one day the other prisoners did not bring him to the farm. Wendelgard speculated that they killed him so the guards would not find out about the scarlet fever.[4]

Sometimes children's sensitivity and conscience compelled them to go beyond their parents' efforts. Antosia Adamowicz was ordinarily a dutiful daughter, but she could not sleep in her warm bed knowing that the four Jews huddled in the ditch on her father's Lithuanian farm were freezing. Her parents had forbidden her to go outside in the snowstorm, but the Jews, who had sat in that ditch and made dresses and peeled potatoes for them, had not had anything to eat or drink in two days. Unless someone went out with food, she knew they would die. Disobeying her parents' orders, the sixteen-year-old took a kettle of water and a loaf of bread and went to find them. The storm had died down and so to cover her tracks in the snow, she took off her heavy boots and went barefoot, brushing her footprints clean with a branch as she went. The Jews heard someone approaching and, assuming the Germans had discovered their hideout, began reciting the Sh'ma, the holiest Hebrew prayer and the last one they thought they would live to say. Instead they heard Antosia's voice calling, and the food she brought saved their lives.

Like adults, children grew to an awareness of the conditions around them. But a child's understanding of that world was vastly different from an adult's, and seen through their eyes, wartime activities often took on a different color and shading. Polish rescuer Pania Wywiad was nine years old when she heard the grown-ups in her family talking about the possibility of war with Germany. Soon recruitment posters were all over Warsaw urging young people to register for antiaircraft and anti-gas defense duty. Young men went off to register and returned dressed in dashing military uniforms. The city was bustling with activity and anxiety. Pania felt the city's vibrations and the grown-ups' fear. "We knew something terrible was coming," she recalled. Pania, her older brother and younger sister, were worried that their father, a baker, would be called for military service. When he was summoned for duty, the family was desolate. He went off to defend Warsaw, and his family was left to cope as best as they could.

When the Germans bombed Warsaw, Pania's family scrambled down to the basement of their apartment house. Their apartment was near the railway station, so they spent a lot of time in the basement. Pania remembered feeling more angry at the destruction and terror the Germans had unleashed than frightened of the bombs. Her sister and older brother, however, were terrified. Her sister became hysterical at the sound of every siren, so Pania held her hand tightly so she wouldn't cry. Her brother said nothing, but as the bombing went on day after day, he began to develop a stutter. (He still stutters today.) As best she could, Pania comforted them both, and provided for the family by running through fires and gunfire to get water. On one such trip, she saw dead Polish soldiers. It was a sight that shocked her into early adulthood and readied her for action:

> I saw their glassy eyes and I was speechless . . . and ran home
> to tell my mother. This terrible sight worked a revolt within me.
> I began to hate . . . I too would be rebellious and strong.

Pania's initial experiences in her apartment basement were the beginnings of her rescuer self. She discovered she could overcome fear, take action, and be helpful. (Dutch child rescuer Cornelia Knottnerus later would make that same discovery. "The best antidote to fear is action," she observed.) Seeing the soldiers was a transforming moment that even at such a young age fixed Pania's resolve.

Pania's father returned unharmed. The Polish defeat had been quick and the German occupation was swift. Within two days of Pania's father's return, they were watching Nazi soldiers force their Jewish neighbors to clean the streets and dig ditches. Pania saw it all and listened to the grown-ups as they speculated on Hitler's plans and discussed their own. Pania's father had already made up his mind. He joined the Polish opposition movement, the Home Army. Her sister was sent to a nearby village for safety.

While Pania's father worked in the underground, her mother took in Jews and other fugitives from the Nazis. Their apartment became a home to an odd assortment of characters. But Pania, listening and watching, appreciated it all:

> In our house were women with children, women without husbands, workers, children, the unemployed as well as the intelligentsia. Everybody in this house was *equal*.

This message of democratic acceptance of others was reinforced by an antifascist woman teacher whom Pania deeply admired. The teacher, whose husband had been taken prisoner, ran an underground classroom of general studies, which Pania attended.

With three models of moral courage before her and the confidence to know that she could overcome fear and act, Pania's rescuer self was ready to surface. Soon Pania's father was using her as a courier for the resistance. She began to deliver letters, food, and medicine to rebels via the underground canal system in Warsaw. "My mother and father made it clear that we—every one of us—had certain functions to fulfill," she related. Among her functions was counterintelligence. She watched the movements of German soldiers and listened to their raid plans. For a spy, she cut a very unprepossessing figure. She was a small girl with a head and eyes inclined to one side, a result of her constantly looking about for German soldiers. Her main job, however, was escorting Jews, contacts of her father, out of the Warsaw ghetto and finding hiding places for them. To overcome her fear, Pania playacted. She pretended she lived near the spot where she had to bring the Jews. This allowed her to go confidently on her way, stopping every now and then in front of a windowpane to check in the reflection if she was being followed. Once she transferred an entire Jewish family from the ghetto to a hiding place in the Aryan part of the city. The mother had to bleach her hair blond, but she and the two girls were easy for Pania to escort. The father was more difficult. He looked Jewish, and Pania was afraid. It took her two weeks to do it, but she managed to transport them all out safely.

In August 1944, Jews and the Polish resistance fought back in what was known as the Polish Uprising. The streets became a battleground, and Pania's father and brothers joined the fight. The battle lasted for two months. During that time, Pania and her mother scrounged for food as best they could. Gas, electricity, and water were all cut off. The Germans marshaled their forces to crush the Uprising. Pointing rifles at Pania and her mother, the Germans commandeered their apartment and pushed them out into the street. The streets were littered with corpses, among them Pania's father and brother. The scene was mayhem. Germans were shooting anyone who might be a member of the resistance. The resistance sporadically returned fire. Ukrainians roamed the streets raping any women they saw. At any moment Pania and her mother expected to be shot. Instead, soldiers drove them away, and the next morning packed them into a cattle car of a train bound for Auschwitz.

They arrived at the Auschwitz station at noon, but stayed there until evening guarded by soldiers with dogs. Everywhere Pania looked she saw wired gates and naked men who looked like walking skeletons. Pania was now fourteen years old. As she stood there, she felt this was the end for her. She couldn't imagine anyone coming out of this place alive.

Pania was assigned to cellblock #16 and her mother to cellblock #17. In her block there were 600 girls of all ages. Eight children slept on a wooden shelf, three girls to one cot. To survive, they banded together. Those who slept together were united. Children from the same room were close to each other. They nursed each other when they were sick, held each other up through roll calls, and looked out for one another.

> I found myself sleeping with two girlfriends on one cot, with girls from my house, and we really felt like members of one family. We helped one another. When in sleep we pulled the blanket away we felt the other was cold. When one was sick and

still had to present oneself in the roll call we gave her our own robe so she should be warm. Getting sick was equal to death.

By now, Pania was an experienced hand. She was a four-year veteran of surviving and helping others. But never had her rescuer self been so tested as it was in the inhuman conditions of Auschwitz. She was separated from the three adults she loved and admired most: her teacher, her mother, and her father, who was dead. Pania looked for other adult role models to pattern herself after. She found one.

It was at a time when Pania had been moved to another camp and placed in a cellblock for the sick. She was ill and despairing and all around her she saw more black depression and death. But one day a Russian mother came into the cellblock. The woman, who like all the prisoners was starved, went over to her child and, after carefully looking about, unwrapped a precious piece of bread she had hidden in her clothes and handed it to her. It was a moving moment and a lesson in charity that gave Pania hope.

The Russian woman had reaffirmed her values and revived her faith in humankind. Pania's rescuer self—that part of her that coped with fear, overcame obstacles, and helped others—was validated. On January 12, 1945, Pania and her mother were freed by the Russians and made their way back to Warsaw. Despite the lost years, she finished her schooling and went on to be a special education teacher. She has worked for the past thirty years at the Institute of Pediatrics at the Academy of Medicine in Poland with sick and chronically ill children.[5]

Child rescuers such as Pania Wywiad were a vital part of rescue operations, yet their role has been almost entirely ignored. In Yad Vashem testimony, survivors rarely mention children's participation in their rescues despite the fact that in many cases children risked their lives to save others. Children were considered too young to fully appreciate, or sometimes even remember, the situation. Most researchers do not distinguish children's rescue efforts from those of their parents. They were seen as part of a family endeavor. The children lived at home and were subject to their parents' authority. As such, they were merely the dutiful agents of their parents' will to rescue, or so the thinking goes. Whatever they experienced was not materially different from what their parents underwent.

Of course, nothing could be further from the truth. A child's perspective and interests were quite separate from his or her parents'. On occasion, they even conflicted. Danuta Bronska, the ten-year-old daughter of a Polish air force captain, lived in Warsaw with her mother. Her father spent most of the war flying out of England with the rest of the Polish air force. From the early moments of the war, her family was part of the underground resistance movement. In fact, she used to deliver notices about underground meetings to trusted people about town. When the Nazis began to herd the Jews into the Warsaw ghetto, her mother took in a Jewish boarder, Nathan Hart. Danuta did not like Hart. She sensed an emotional attachment between her mother and this refugee from the ghetto and she was jealous.

Nathan Hart was soon joined in hiding by four other Jews whose expenses were covered by the Polish underground. Danuta helped her mother by running errands, and, when necessary, accompanying Jews around the city. Her blond hair deflected any suspicion that the adult with her was Jewish. In August 1944, the Warsaw Uprising started. While the others ran off to join the resistance, Hart stayed behind with Danuta and her mother. One day a series of bombs hit Danuta's building. Panic ensued. People were buried under the rubble, and Danuta was separated from her mother. Amid the screams, Danuta finally heard her mother's voice. But the voice was not calling for her, but for Hart. "Nathan! Nathan!" her mother screamed frantically. It was a moment that the young girl would never forget or forgive. Years later, after her mother divorced her father and married Nathan Hart, the hurt in Danuta's voice was still apparent. She felt her mother's love extended only as far as her usefulness to Nathan and her other charges. Her mother's cries of "Nathan! Nathan!" still rang in her ears.

The unpredictability of war thrust some children into a rescuer role never intended or foreseen by their parents. In 1941, Polish underground activist Stanislaw Wlodek agreed to hide a Jewish acquaintance's two-year-old son. Wlodek figured he and his wife could handle the responsibility of another child. Besides, the Weglaszyn school principal felt that his nine-year-old and seven-year-old sons were at an age when they could help out too. The Germans, however, interfered with his calculations. A year later on a routine search, the Germans found a shortwave receiver in Wlodek's house. Wlodek managed to escape to nearby woods, but his wife was arrested. (She died in Auschwitz in 1943.) At ages ten and eight, barely more than babies themselves, Janusz Wlodek and his brother Krystn became de facto parents.

For a time, the family survived on the food stored in the house. When that was gone, Janusz and Krystn worked for neighboring farmers in return for food. Sometimes they took their "nephew" Jurek with them to work. At other times, one went to work while the other looked after the child. On occasion, they had to leave Jurek alone for hours at a time. At those times, they could only hope that if the Nazis raided their house, as they did from time to time looking for their fugitive father, Jurek wouldn't give them all away.

The boys survived in this ad hoc, day-to-day way for several months. Each day brought the hope, shared with them by their neighbors too, that their mother would return. Each day also brought the icy fear that Jurek in his innocence would give himself away by blurting out his true identity or by urinating in the open where anyone might observe his circumcised penis and thus know he was a Jew. Finally, a village woman who knew the Wlodek family saw Jurek and began spreading the word around town that he was a Jew. In the woods where Wlodek was keeping a distant watch over his family, Stanislaw Wlodek heard the village gossip. Quickly, he arranged for his sister, who lived in a nearby village with her shoemaker husband and two children, to take in Jurek, who survived to be reunited with his mother after liberation. Wlodek's sons survived on their own.

A child who witnessed a botched rescue or a failed escape attempt was often shaken to the core. The sense of helplessness, already so intense in a child trying to operate in a world of older, bigger, and more knowledgeable adults, was overwhelming. In the case of Bronislaw Jachym, the intervening decades have not quite subdued his initial feelings or blurred his memory of events.

Bronislaw Jachym wrote to me in response to a brief article

about my work that appeared in the *Gazetta,* the Solidarity newspaper in Poland, which requested information about the experiences of children. In the summer of 1941, he wrote, he lived in Smegorow, a small Polish village near Tarnow. His farm was near a forest where Jews who had escaped from the ghettos in neighboring cities had taken refuge. The Nazis regularly patrolled the area, using German shepherds to hunt fugitives. The dogs were efficient and the soldiers ruthless. Most locals stayed away from the Jews, and the Jews, knowing of the soldiers and their dogs, stayed clear of farmyards.

The few farmers who wanted to help found that the safest way for all concerned was to throw bread over the farmyard fence when Jews were seen coming across a field. (Nazi fugitives never walked on the roads or used paths lest the German patrol dogs sniff them out.) Bronislaw wrote that his mother often gave him a piece of bread with the order to "give it to the children" and not eat it himself. Bronislaw was impressed by his mother's generosity, as they were poor themselves. He would do as she instructed, while she observed him secretly from the house.

Occasionally the Jewish wanderers were mothers with little children. They needed milk as well as bread. When Bronislaw and his mother saw a group like that coming, Bronislaw would run to the farmyard gate, unlatch it, carefully place a cup of milk and bread on the path outside, shut the gate, and run out of sight. It had to be a quick and careful operation. Any spilled milk or human smells on the cup would lead the dogs to the farmyard and to the Jews. As soon as the mother and child had finished feeding and passed on, Bronislaw would jump out, retrieve the cup with an especially long stick, and immediately dunk it in a kettle of boiling water.

One day around noon, a Jewish woman with two children roamed along the back paths toward the village. The woman, whom Bronislaw remembers as being "round and beautiful," walked as if in a trance. She carried a two-year-old in her arms, while another child walked beside her and held on to her dress. Bronislaw recalled thinking that all three, with their thick, dark curly hair framing their faces, looked like biblical cherubs. With his own blond, straight wirelike hair, he was jealous of these strangers.

When Bronislaw's mother saw the three Jews through her window, she stood up and without a word poured a double portion of milk and cut off a double portion of bread. Bronislaw ran to put the food on the road and then scurried back to a shed to watch secretly as the mother and her children rushed for the food. They ate and then walked off, heading in the direction of the Bren River.

A half hour later, two Germans and a barking German shepherd straining at its leash appeared. To young Bronislaw, the dog looked huge and the two Germans seemed gigantic. Like hunters tracking a fox, the trio halted at the spot where the Jews had eaten their meager meal. They took off again at a trot, following the same trail the fugitives had taken. Bronislaw watched them in helpless horror. He knew that the Jewish woman and her two children couldn't be very far ahead. Later he learned that the Germans had caught up with them near the village of Stanki and killed them immediately. After the Germans left, a villager buried them at the edge of the forest.

Bronislaw Jachym wrote that these reminiscences of childhood never left him. The experience transformed him and hardened his resolve to save lives. He became a doctor. But he wrote that with the passing of time, his thoughts become more obsessive and more intense. The slightest stimulus triggers the past. The child he was still mourns these people he never knew.

In the same way their parents' experience marked them, child rescuers' experiences made an indelible impression on them. They changed them and in many cases altered the course of their lives. After the war, many child rescuers pursued health care or other helping careers. Stefania Podgórska's sister, Helena, who helped care for thirteen Jews, remained in Poland and became a doctor. Like many other young child rescuers, she suffered from speech problems and years later was still awakened by nightmares. Yet because of those same experiences, she chose a career dedicated to saving lives. Clearly the rescuer selves that emerged during the war powerfully shaped the lives of child rescuers, just as they did their parents'.

· 13 ·

MEN AND WOMEN RESCUERS

IN 1986, Alice Eagly and Maureen Crowley published a review article on helping behavior which concluded that women and men helped differently. Running throughout the various literature they described was the assumption that women were more likely to help than men unless the situation was dangerous. In those cases, the presumption was that men were more likely to have the skills necessary to undertake risky rescues. It was also thought that masculinity and accompanying notions of chivalry led them to offer help more readily to strangers. The female gender role, on the other hand, led women to acts of caring for others.[1]

I have found rescuing behavior to be infinitely more complex and varied than these stereotypical, gender-based assumptions with men as risk takers and women as nurturing and caring helpers. A number of factors increased the likelihood that an individual—male or female—would help: having a personality inclined toward risk taking, emotional involvement with Jews, special abilities, available resources, various situational elements, ability to confront complex moral questions, and, ultimately, trust in one's competency. In fact, my research leads away from the traditional thinking. As social psy-

238 CONSCIENCE & COURAGE

chologist Carol Tavris has said: "We can think about the influence of gender without resorting to false polarities."[2]

Freud recognized that "character-traits which critics of every epoch have brought up against women—that they show less sense of justice than men, . . . that they are more often influenced in their judgments by feelings of affection or hostility—all these would be amply accounted for by the modification in the formation of their super-ego." But "as a result of their bisexual disposition and of cross-inheritance, they combine in themselves both masculine and feminine characteristics so that pure masculinity and femininity remain theoretical constructions of uncertain content."[3] Nevertheless, distinctions have been made.

Piaget, using hypothetical dilemmas to measure moral judgment in children, found that boys, unlike girls, tended toward organized games with elaborate rules. Therefore he concluded that boys were more concerned with justice than girls. It was the fairness and impartial, abstract justice of rules that Freud, Piaget, and others believed was the essence of an individual's morality.

In the 1960s, Harvard University psychologist Lawrence Kohlberg refined Piaget's early work by charting moral development through six distinct stages, each one more advanced and mature than the one before. Kohlberg created hypothetical moral judgment stories. (For example, your wife is very sick and will die unless she gets a very expensive medicine that you cannot afford. Should you rob the drugstore?) From the answers, Kohlberg concluded that individuals at stage six, the highest level of moral reasoning, were those who had the ability to consult their consciences and act on universal ethical principles. At that level, an individual was motivated by abstract, ideological beliefs of justice. He asks himself, "What would I consider fair if I was in the other person's place?" and proceeds from there. (Later Kohlberg backed away from this strict hierarchy, acknowledging that stages four, five, and six are also "alternative types of mature responses.")[4]

In the 1970s, psychologist Carol Gilligan challenged the prevailing views of psychological development, which up to that time had been based almost entirely on research with men. Gilligan agreed with

Freud that women and men differ in what they regard as "ethically normal," but she maintained that women's moral reasoning was not faulty; it was simply different.

Gilligan argued that there are two kinds of morality which stem from two different kinds of motivation. One is a morality based on an impartial idea of justice, and the other is a morality based on compassion and care. Gilligan believed that the value of caring in human relationships, which coincides with Kohlberg's stage three, is as important as justice (stage six). What matters ultimately to women, Gilligan found, is being responsive to human feelings—that is, judging by "hearing a human voice." A woman's need to make and maintain interpersonal connections plays as important a role in moral decision making as fairness does in the understanding of rights and rules. When facing a moral decision, women do not think about what is fair so much as "who will be hurt the least."[5] According to Gilligan, compassion for others is not a sign of weakness or a symptom of neurotic dependency but another dimension of moral development.

Gilligan was the first theorist to place caring and justice on an equal footing. To her, morality was not an abstract concept of right and wrong to be charted in a classroom setting. Justice and mercy, responsibility and care were learned through human interaction. This morality of care implied empathizing with another's distress and actively offering support and aid.

Gilligan's notions of "female" morality as contrasted with "male" morality would lead one to expect that emotional-moral rescuers (morality based on compassion for Jews) and Judeophiles (morality based on emotional attachment to Jews) would be mostly women and network rescuers (motivated by anti-Nazi ideology) would be male. This is not what I found. In all groups, men and women were nearly equally represented.

Women undertook dangerous missions. Women were involved in high-risk activities like slipping Jews past German patrols and guiding them safely across the border. On the other hand, men were motivated by feelings of compassion and pity, with some still emotionally shaken by their experiences, weeping unashamedly as they relived that time.

I saw, in my research, the two kinds of moral reasoning Gilligan describes. But the link between gender and reasoning style was not as strong as Gilligan's analysis suggested it would be. Both men and women showed morality based on caring and attachment. Both men and women had emotional responses to the plight of the Jews. Both men and women came to the aid of victims through an outraged sense of justice.

In the course of my research and work at ADL's Jewish Foundation for Christian Rescuers, I talked with men who were so emotionally affected by what they saw that they turned their lives upside down, jeopardizing everything in order to save Jews. The story of Alexander Roslan was certainly the most dramatic example of this. The sight of the bodies of children in the Warsaw ghetto so affected Roslan that he risked his life, fortune, and emotional stability to save Jacob, Sholom, and David. Roslan characterized those scenes he witnessed in the ghetto as the most difficult moments for him during the war. "You can't eat," he remembered. "You can't sleep. If you see things like that, you can get sick." It was this emotional reaction that transformed Roslan into a rescuer.

Roslan's love for Jacob, Sholom, and David transcended any cognitive moral imperatives of fairness or justice. He nurtured three youngsters even more than his wife did, who could never completely overcome her fears of discovery and death. Similarly, the responsibility for the emotional care and welfare of the two Jewish children sheltered with the Stenekeses fell to John Stenekes rather than his wife, Berta. Even at the start, when the children were staying with Stenekes's sister, John kept a paternal eye on Jacques and Anna and gave them bakery treats when they came around. It was he who offered to hide the children when his sister lost her nerve and planned to put them into a hotel. John Stenekes empathized with their situation, took to heart their need, and felt compelled to act. He was the one who broke the news to his wife that the two children who played with their baby were Jewish and that unless they took them in, the children would be killed. Berta Stenekes agreed to shelter them, but John shouldered the responsibility for looking after them.[6]

The work of University of Massachusetts social psychologist Ervin Staub shows similar findings. Staub found that gender did not necessarily predispose a person to be caring. Staub, who as a six-year-old child was rescued in Budapest by Raoul Wallenberg, developed a scale to identify people with altruistic natures. Those who scored high on his scale were more concerned with the welfare of others. Staub found both men and women who scored high. Staub concluded that while there may be a tendency for women to be compassionate and caring, this was largely due to early socialization, and men were just as capable of having such feelings and acting on them. It is the development of caring and responsibility in boys that enables them to be just as kind as women.[7]

While male rescuers sometimes used Gilligan's "female voice," women frequently displayed temperaments and attitudes that Freud attributed to his model of "moral man." In women such as Marion van Binsbergen Pritchard and Louisa Steenstra, Hitler's philosophy and Nazi policies triggered deep-seated revulsion. They were outraged by seeing justice so perverted. Witnessing German soldiers carelessly tossing Jewish children into trucks and watching as two passersby tried to stop them left Dutch rescuer Marion van Binsbergen Pritchard shaking with anger. Louisa Steenstra's anger at the German bombing of Rotterdam and the unjust killing of 30,000 people in one day shocked her into action. "When you hear that, how can you not act?" she said. "I couldn't stand it. I hated the Germans." This anger consumed her and consumes her still. Anti-Nazi anger and rage at the human race for its proclivity for cruelty were themes to which she returned time and again in her conversation with me.

Recent research has further undermined the notion that men and women differ appreciably in their moral reasoning, or that women have a permanently different voice because of their early closeness to their mothers. Anne Colby and William Damon found little scientific support for Gilligan's claims for general gender-based distinctions. They concluded that "to the extent that differences of this sort do exist, there is no evidence whatsoever that they are due to early and irreversible emotional experiences between mother and child."[8]

But Gilligan's research was not the only body of work which led me to believe that there might be differences in the way men and women reacted to Hitler's war against the Jews. Philip Friedman, one of the first historians to write about Holocaust rescuers, suggested that women may have been more sensitive than men to the plight of the Jews. Friedman hypothesized that women's nurturing and caring natures might have made them a soft touch, especially when those in danger were children. Women might have been "more easily moved by their emotions and thought less of the consequences."[9]

Frances Henry, a Canadian anthropologist who studied a Bavarian community whose pseudonym is Sonderburg, reported that in her study more women than men helped. Henry, whose grandparents and ten other Jews lived in Sonderburg and were helped by locals for three years until their eventual discovery and deportation, felt that this was because most of the help involved giving the fugitives housing and food. Unlike the administrative tasks of obtaining forged documents or lining up escape routes, food and domestic arrangements were the traditional province of women. This same point was made by Pierre Sauvage, the filmmaker who as a boy was saved by rescuers in Le Chambon. Sauvage noted that most often it was the women, who were home most of the day and in charge of the domestic arrangements, who were the first ones approached to take a stranger into their homes. That first important and critical decision, to help or not, was theirs to make. In Sauvage's mind, the women of Le Chambon were the "backbone" of that community's rescue effort.[10]

Yet an early study by German political scientist Manfred Wolfson contradicts Henry's findings and Sauvage's observations. In 1966, Wolfson, who was working in the United States, solicited letters and other documents from seventy Germans who helped Jews between 1938 and 1945. He concluded that more men than women helped.[11]

Running through all these various inquiries was the assumption, sometimes implicit, sometimes overt, that in dangerous situations men would be more likely to help. I too assumed that women would undertake less physically taxing or hazardous tasks and leave the heroics to men.

Time and again I was proven wrong. Women told of how they had acted as decoys, couriers, double agents, and border runners.

Women such as Czechoslovakian historian Vera Laska were an integral part of both resistance and rescue work. Laska was a Czech resistance fighter who also led Jews and other fugitives to safety in Yugoslavia. German patrols made these border crossings extremely dangerous. Nonetheless, men and women such as Laska and John Weidner gambled that their wits and luck would see them through.

Polish resister and rescuer Jan Karski felt that women were better suited for undercover or conspiratorial work because they were quicker to perceive danger, less inclined to risky bluffing, and more optimistic of the outcome. In particular, he praised the role of the network liaison woman or courier, whose job it was to warn of impending raids, move the hunted from house to house, and carry information from one network member to another. Marc Donadille, the French Protestant minister who led the Cévennes escape network, years later paid public tribute to such women:

> I want to praise the operator in the post office in St.-Privat, whose name I don't remember. She was Catholic, but shared our feelings and our concerns. One day she said, "The phone calls between the police at Florac and the brigade at St.-Germain come through to me. I can pass that information on to you."
>
> Then, rather than relay information, she simply hooked my line into these conversations so I could listen directly. . . . Then she told me that she had orders to intercept my mail. "I'll put your mail aside and you can get it at night from my house. Then you can remove the compromising letters and I will send [the rest] on. This we did regularly.[12]

The telephone operator was playing a very risky and dangerous game. Had the Nazis caught her, she would have faced the same possibility of imprisonment, torture, or execution as Donadille or any other male resistance worker. She did have, however, one advantage: officials in some countries, particularly the Netherlands, were sometimes loath to pronounce a death sentence on a woman. A woman who was caught often stood a better chance of being sent to a concentration camp than being summarily executed. Hetty Dutihl Voûte, who was caught for her illegal Utrecht children's rescue work and sent to Ravensbrück, thought that had she been a man, the Nazis would have shot her.

Given the opportunity, women proved to be good spies, smugglers, and saboteurs. Yet their deeds were largely overlooked. In the postwar celebration of men's daring deeds, the quiet bravery of women was ignored. The traditional hero was a swashbuckling male, and heroes who did not fit that model were ignored. Movies and made-for-television features portrayed male heroes. Women, if they had any rescue or military role at all, were cast in minor roles.

World War II represented an opportunity for women to escape their normal domestic concerns and express their anti-Nazi outrage by taking action in behalf of a just cause. "We think of war as a male activity and value," social psychologist Carol Tavris noted, "but war has always given even noncombatant women an escape from domestic confinement—the exhilaration of a public identity—and a chance to play a heroic role usually denied them in their private lives."[13]

The chance to escape normal boundaries and become an important part of a larger cause sometimes gave women the courage they needed to undertake risky ventures. Certainly this was the case with Anje Roos, a woman whose implacable opposition to Nazism grew from small acts of kindness.

In 1940, when the Germans took over Holland, Anje Roos had nearly completed her training as a psychiatric nurse. Roos had no illusions about Hitler's intentions. Her parents, who lived in Alkmaar, a town twenty miles north of Amsterdam, had told her and her seven brothers and sisters often enough that the Führer meant what he said. He aimed to rid the world of the infirm and the racially impure and rule the world. With the Germans now in charge, Roos knew psychiatric nursing did not have much of a future. She changed direction and began to study to be a midwife.

Soon after the Germans took over, they banned Jews from professional employment. Jewish doctors and nurses were no longer permitted to work at the hospital. Roos, who in addition to taking courses at the hospital worked in the tuberculosis ward, was outraged.

The patients were too. Together with the head nurse, Roos wrote a petition asking that the order be withdrawn. All the patients signed it, and it was sent off to the Austrian governor in charge of the occupation. It proved to be a futile effort, but for Roos and the patients it was, nonetheless, a healthy tonic. "It didn't help; no reply ever came. But there was a kind of elevation around the ward that they did something," Roos explained. "It was important for them as well as for us to do something—to demonstrate—to tell them we didn't like it and we were angry."

In the spring of 1941, Roos completed her training and rented a house in Amsterdam with three other nurses. Her roommates had many Jewish friends, and on Fridays it became the custom for Roos and her roommates to buy goods for them that they were not permitted to purchase. Through these new friends and through the Jewish family she worked for as a baby nurse, Roos's awareness of the plight of the Jews increased. She felt close to her employers and knew the dangerousness of their situation. The precariousness of their position became evident one day when she answered a knock at their door. It was the Gestapo hunting for Jews to deport. With the family safely out of sight, she faced the Gestapo and told them no Jews were there. They had already been arrested. "You do *such wonderful* work," she told them sarcastically.

With little time to lose, Roos arranged for the family to travel to Utrecht and be hidden in a home there. (Later she learned the family was captured by the Germans when they naïvely went for a walk in town.) Roos returned to work at the hospital, but it was clear to her and her friends that the Jewish situation in Amsterdam was rapidly deteriorating. When Jewish friends who belonged to the Palestine Pioneer movement asked her for help she was ready, even eager. Her anti-Nazi rage needed an outlet.

By day, Roos bicycled around town hiding Jewish children and delivering documents, food, and money to those in hiding. By night, she worked at the hospital, where, along with her nurse friends, she stole as many drugs and hospital supplies for the underground as she could. Her day duties for the Palestine Pioneers, a network affiliated with the Westerweel Group, were arduous and not always predictable. She was frequently late for work or absent altogether. Her nursing supervisor told her to shape up or she would be fired. Roos did not know what to do. Both jobs were important to her, but she did not know how she could manage both. So she turned to her parents for advice. As she recalled, her parents told her, "If you want to help the Jews—and you should—then do that and don't work with the nurses anymore. They don't need you there. They need you at the Pioneers."

Her parents' blessing broke Roos's last restraints. A new persona, free of the ordinary expectations of female behavior, was born. She immersed herself in rescue work. She involved her whole family. Roos picked up Jews and transported them to her parents' house. From there she would find safe houses for them in other parts of northern Holland. Through friends and Christian religious circles, she found safe places for all her charges.

The Palestine Pioneers was only one of several networks for whom Roos worked. Along with one of her brothers, who was a police officer, Roos joined the Arondius Group, an underground sabotage organization. Members of the group, Jews and non-Jews, were on the Germans' most-wanted list. In March 1943, the Arondius Group decided to raid the Nazi registration office to burn the files that held the names and addresses of all the Jews in Amsterdam. They thought that without such information the Nazis would find it more difficult to round up and deport the Jews.

Dressed like police officers, the saboteurs overpowered the night watchman and set the place on fire. The mission was a success, but their victory was short-lived. Careless talk among network members gave them away and a month later Roos, her brother, and the others involved in the raid were arrested. Roos's brother and twelve other Arondius members were tried and shot. Roos was sentenced to serve one year of hard labor in Ravensbrück.[14]

A year and a month later, Roos came home. She was weak, painfully thin, and ill with tuberculosis. That slowed but did not stop her. As soon as she was physically able, she rejoined her friends and the Amsterdam resistance. She worked as a courier for an underground newspaper, distributing news and false identification papers as needed.

Roos does not fit the customary image of a female rescuer. Her rescuer self was not that of a resourceful, home-based caretaker. While she and her roommates hid fugitives in their house, most of her rescue activities took place outside the home. Her rescuer self was adventurous, daring, and bold. It was a persona that many women, particularly those in networks, chose to adopt.

The existence of heroic women seemingly contradicts other social-psychological research which suggests that daredevil women would be rare. In experimental situations requiring one-time heroic actions (such as jumping into a river to save a drowning person), researchers have found that men tend to be more responsive. Women are more apt to size up the situation as too dangerous to attempt to do anything.[15]

During the Holocaust, women confronted a myriad of situations —not a one-time experience—that required heroic intervention. By "heroic" I mean deliberate actions which place the person in sharp danger. Without question, rescuers who hid Jews in their homes were heroic people; their actions, however, were not. They had all the comforts and familiarity of home and neighborhood. They did not repeatedly seek dangerous missions. Heroic rescuers did. From one night to the next night Roos never knew where she would sleep. Laska did not even know what country she would be in the following day.

The work of Kay Deaux, social psychologist at the Graduate Center of the City University of New York, helps explain the apparent gap between my findings and the work of others. Deaux found that skill level matters in moral acts as well as in more commonplace ones. For instance, a woman who was a good swimmer would be just as likely to jump into a river to save a drowning person as a man who was a good swimmer. The key variable is swimming ability, not gender or morality. Women did not avoid danger or hang back from risk per se. If women felt they had the skills useful in a particular situation, they helped.[16]

Much of the time skills are divided along stereotypical gender lines. Fifty years ago, most women were full-time housewives and mothers. If they worked outside the home, they were most likely to be factory workers and farmers or to hold jobs in traditional women's fields of teaching, nursing, or social work. Very few women were printers, mechanics, or captains of industry. In wartime resistance activities these distinctions between men and women were not absolute. There were women forgers, saboteurs, and money launderers. But for the most part, women undertook or were assigned rescue tasks that centered on their household and child-rearing skills.

At home, women took responsibility for the people they were hiding. It was difficult work. Quarters were often cramped, nerves frayed, and hunger constant. Each simple task, from hanging out laundry to emptying chamber pots, contained the possibility that someone would spot something suspicious and report it to the authorities. It was left to one member of the household to keep things running and to keep people's spirits up in the process. That job usually fell to the woman of the house.

The Voses, for example, divided up the chores. Aart Vos was responsible for the house's outside liaisons with the underground and obtaining food while Johtje was in charge of the household. Each of them had a dangerous task. Aart traveled all over the countryside on his motorbike, calling on his dairy-farm contacts to scrape up supplies to feed his burgeoning household. He knew that anyone caught transporting food over a road was subject to arrest.

Johtje Vos oversaw the domestic arrangements of the household. She acted as a combination traffic controller, cook, arbitrator, psychoanalyst, and entertainer. She hosted candlelit parties for which the fugitives dressed up in clothes borrowed from one another. She led the children in games, like "Who remembers what a banana looks like?" Johtje did anything she could think of to distract them from dwelling on their discomfort and fears. Aart Vos realized how demanding a job his wife had:

We had thirty-six people hiding in our house at one time. When you have a home, not a big one, and you have it filled up with Jewish people coming in and out the whole day, every day, not for a week but for four or five years, you can't understand what that takes out of a woman. I was out on my bicycle, but she had to keep everyone together.[17]

When the Nazis suspected the Voses of possessing the stamps to forge illegal documents, it was Johtje who was left to deal with the Gestapo and connive a way out of a lethal situation. Her ability to act took charge, bluffing, stalling, and finally strategizing their charges' way to safety. Johtje Vos's bravery underscores recent studies, which, according to sociologist Cynthia Fuchs Epstein, show that "behavior that we link to gender depends more on what an individual is doing and needs to do than on his or her biological sex."[18]

At times, however, the roles of men and women in rescue activity were determined by gender stereotypes. For example, when children needed to be transported, hidden, and cared for, women usually saw to it. Many of the networks that were engaged primarily in the rescue of children were headed by women. Irena Sendlerowa in Poland, Anje Roos Geerling and Hetty Dutihl Voûte in Holland, and Andrée Guelen Herscovici in Belgium led their countries' efforts to save children. Those children rescue networks not headed by women, like NV (short for Naamloze Venootschap, the Dutch equivalent of "limited company," or "Ltd.") and the Piet Meerburg, boasted of an overwhelmingly female membership.

Of course, there were exceptions. In Belgium, Abbé Joseph André was very much involved in the rescue of children, and in the South of France, churchmen played a critical and active role in rescuing children.

But for the most part, it was women who led or rallied behind efforts to save children. There were a number of reasons for this. To some extent, women were more actively called upon than men to rescue children because women's efforts were perceived as having a greater probability of a safe outcome. Networks assigned tasks according to skills, and most male network leaders assumed women were better suited to care for children. Jewish parents made the same association. They were more likely to trust the safekeeping of their children to a Christian woman than to a Christian man. Among Jewish parents, nannies were the rescuers of choice. When that was not an option, parents looked for the next-best thing, a single young woman. A couple was not as desirable. Jewish parents feared a couple would try to convert their children and that a couple, who represented a ready-made family, would be more reluctant to return their children to them after the war.

Network leaders knew that and assigned the job of prying Jewish children from their parents to women. Belgium schoolteacher Andrée Guelen Herscovici, for example, was recruited by the Comité de Défense des Juifs (CDJ) to call on Jewish parents and lead their children to safe houses. The Gestapo had a list of all the Jews who still lived at their official addresses, and the CDJ had the same list. It became a race between Herscovici and the Gestapo over who would get there first.

Yale historian Deborah Dwork, who interviewed rescuers of children in the NV and Piet Meerburg networks, found that women couriers were the mainstays of both operations. The groups, most of whose members were university students, specialized in saving children because they felt their age would undermine their authority and effectiveness with older victims. Piet Meerburg, the student who formed the network, told Dwork why 90 percent of his members were women: "It was much more suspicious for a boy of twenty to travel with a child than a girl. It was absolutely a big difference. We went to fetch the children from the crèche [nursery] together, but then the woman student accompanied them on the train to Friesland and Limburg."[19]

There was still one other role that women, and only women, played in the rescue efforts, and that was the role of "single mother." Nannies, friends of the family, and even strangers—often found through network contacts—were asked by Jewish parents or by intermediaries to shelter a child. Those who agreed needed to make up a story to cover the sudden arrival of a baby or a child. Exactly what the cover story was and how believable it was depended on the individual and the circumstances. Many young women moved to other villages and posed as married women whose husbands were at the front. Still others claimed the child was a relative whose parents had been killed in a bombing raid. Whatever cover the rescuer self scripted, the person had to act it convincingly. Husbands, wedding days, tragic war events—a whole family album of lies—had to be fabricated to lend an air of authenticity. No man could ever get too close. Secrets kept them on their guard at all times. These "mothers" did not want to place their own family and friends in danger. The others, they dared not trust.

Single mothers created stories that were inventive, daring, and frequently unbelievable. Relatives and old friends doubted the existence of a husband they had never heard of or seen. The suspicion among neighbors, the gossip around town, labeled them unwed mothers. All of a sudden, they were young women of uncertain reputations who were no longer desirable as potential wives. In a Catholic country like Poland, such whisperings were devastating. These women were considered social outcasts. To escape the gossip and any suspicion of the truth, they moved to other villages. When the whisperings and suspicions started up again, they moved on.

These women willingly paid a huge personal price. Their reasons were no different from anyone else's. Like men and other women rescuers, they faced danger and gambled their lives to alleviate suffering and satisfy their sense of justice. What they did and how they did it reflected their individual personalities, talents, and societal roles. In the end, Carol Gilligan's different voice was not so different after all. It was a shared voice of common decency and humanity.

· 14 ·

EARLY
CHILDHOOD

"Example is not the main thing
in influencing others.
It is the only thing."

—Albert Schweitzer

IN THE COURSE OF MY WORK with Holocaust rescuers and those they saved, I have attended ceremonies which have honored them. On those occasions, I am struck with what a varied assortment of individuals they are. They look nothing alike. Their economic and social circumstances are quite different. They speak different languages. Some are barely articulate, pleased but nervous at all the attention. Others are fluent in eight languages and do not seem at all intimidated by the honors. When one looks at them from the audience, the group seated on the podium always seems to be as random a gathering of people as a group of subway riders who are seated in the same car.

Yet they were not just a haphazard collection of individuals who chanced to rescue Jews, but people who have surprisingly similar humanistic values. It was not a whim that led these people to risk their lives and those of their families, but a response, almost a reflexive reaction in some cases, that came from core values developed and instilled in them in childhood. These childhood experiences and influences formed a leitmotif that played through the histories of most rescuers. I began after a while to wait for the recital of one or more of those well-known passages: a nurturing, loving home; an altruistic parent or beloved caretaker who served as a role model for altruistic behavior; a tolerance for people who were different; a childhood illness or personal loss that tested their resilience and exposed them to special care; and an upbringing that emphasized independence, competence, discipline with explanations (rather than physical punishment or withdrawal of love), and caring.

Of course, not all rescuers experienced one or more of these factors, but a majority did. Nor were these childhood influences by themselves enough to transform bystanders into rescuers. The circumstances, timing, and opportunity for rescue had to be just right.

Yet interviews with rescuers left me with no doubt that the experiences and values inculcated in them at an early age had an impact on their ability to stand up to racism and empathize with those persecuted. Frieda Suss, whose family helped the Kissingers escape from Bavaria, recounted an incident from her youth, recalling it as vividly as if it had happened yesterday. Frieda Suss was with her mother one day when they heard screams in the village. Suddenly they saw hundreds of Orthodox Jews being chased by a mob. The local merchants incited the crowd, shouting, "Dirty Jews, go back where you came from!" Suss recalled how in the face of the angry mob, her mother, a simple peasant woman, stood her ground: "Listen, you idiots," Suss remembered her mother scolding the crowd. "That is not nice what you are doing. And especially all you children. Never, ever judge anybody according to his race or his dress. Only judge people according to the way in which they behave toward you."

It took a certain kind of environment, however, for such lessons to take hold. Most Holocaust rescuers came from loving families that instilled in them a sense of self-worth and love. When they were children, their interests were encouraged and their talents praised. Irene Gut Opdyke grew up with such tender memories of her close, well-to-do Catholic family (who championed her dreams of becoming a nurse) that she began her first interview with me by eulogizing her parents.

In fact, many rescuers attributed their strength to their parents' love. Many felt themselves to be the adored favorite of one parent. As a child, Latvian rescuer and Judeophile Amfian Gerasimov, who as a mailman served as a go-between to Jews in the Riga ghetto, was an adored child. Seven siblings who were born before him died in childhood, so Gerasimov was understandably his mother's cherished son. Once when his mother tried to discipline him for some misbehavior, Gerasimov told her in all seriousness, "I am Jesus." His mother calmly corrected his mistake ("No, you are my son"), but, most significantly, she never contradicted the feelings of self-esteem and importance behind that pronouncement.

Sociologist Eli Sagan argues that conscience (or morality) has its genesis in the original nurturing situation between children and their primary caretakers. He contends that "love is not the result, but the foundation of conscience."[1]

According to Sagan, the development of conscience falls into three distinct stages. The first stage, and one of the most important factors in the development of moral capacity, centers on the love and nurturing that caretakers give children. When the child-caretaker bond is strong, full of love and tenderness, children develop sound and robust consciences. In Sagan's second stage, children begin to identify with their immediate family. They want to give back both the affection and the comfort they have received. It is in this second stage that compassion and pity, Freud's basis for moral action, are developed.

In Sagan's last stage of moral development, children's consciences reach full maturity. They want to give love and comfort to those outside their immediate family. It is this capacity to act lovingly toward people whom one does not even know that is essential for the development of a social conscience.

While researchers in helping behavior may put it a different way, most of their studies do show a high correlation between parental nurturing and altruism. In 1948, in one of the earliest studies of anti-Nazi behavior, psychoanalyst David Levy found that when he compared twenty-one anti-Nazi German men (not necessarily involved in aiding Jews) with passive German bystanders, the resisters' childhood homes were more accepting and less rigid. Their parents were de-

scribed as comparatively more affectionate and less restrained, featuring a strong and affectionate maternal influence and no severity in
paternal discipline. New York psychologist Frances Grossman's 1984
analysis of nine rescuers uncovered the same general pattern. Grossman found that a warm, loving relationship with at least one caretaker
and a sense of independence and confidence were key elements that
separated rescuers from bystanders. She noted that in childhood rescuers experienced a loving and trusting relationship with an affectionate mother, had a communicative and nonauthoritarian father, and
were often an only or a favored child.[2]

My research and work with rescuers support and build on the
findings of Sagan, Grossman, and other researchers. Indeed, I found
that as children, many rescuers felt not only loved but protected. Gitta
Dubro Bauer recalled how her father became fierce if he felt any one
of his daughters was threatened. Bauer, who was the second oldest of
four daughters, remembered a time when she saw the ferocity behind
her father's ordinarily gentle demeanor. One Sunday morning a Nazi
cousin, who was considered decent enough but was the black sheep in
her own vehemently anti-Nazi family, was visiting. Bauer and he got
into a heated political discussion. In the excitement of the moment,
Bauer called SS chief Heinrich Himmler a pig. Bauer described what
happened next:

> My cousin flew into a rage and threw something at me. It was
> something soft—a piece of underwear or something. Something
> struck me—a button—and I cried out. My father had been in
> the bathroom shaving with a real shaving knife. He had heard
> the discussion and my [remark], and he came out of the bath-
> room with his knife in his hand. He told my cousin, "If you ever
> dare to put your hand on one of my daughters, I will use this
> knife on you!"

Developmental psychologist Carolyn Zahn-Waxler and her colleagues at the National Institute of Mental Health, on the other hand,
argue that "love is not enough" to foster altruism. Love has to be
combined with reason and firm guidance. Zahn-Waxler found that

altruism was best and most effectively communicated in homes where parents exerted a firm control over their children. Her studies showed that children who were altruistically inclined had parents who tended to explain to them the consequences of hurting other children and to do so with an admonition such as "I don't like to be with you when you act like that."[3] In Aart Vos's childhood home, his father, Floris Vos, told Aart and his seven brothers and sisters in no uncertain terms when their behavior crossed the line. Vos remembered that once at dinner he made derogatory remarks about some people. He could not recollect exactly what he said about whom, but he never forgot what happened next. After dinner his father called him into his study for a talk. The essence of the lecture was that all sorts of people inhabit this planet and that it was God's will that it was so. "If you talk against other people, you are going against God's will, and you are causing people pain," Vos remembered his father chiding him. "Do me a favor. Think it over and stop it."

Floris Vos's approach to disciplining his son was typical of the approach of most rescuers' parents. They reasoned rather than threatened. They eschewed what New York University social psychologist Martin Hoffman calls the "power-assertive" technique of discipline. Hoffman, who has studied parental techniques of discipline and its effects on altruism, found that parents who explained rules and used inductive reasoning instead of harsh punishment tend to have children who care for and about others. After all, parents who voluntarily relinquish the use of force in favor of reasoning send their children a message about how the powerful should treat the weak.

Rescuers' parents talked to their children about what was acceptable behavior and then clearly laid out rules. But rational conversation did not always carry the day. When Wendelgard von Neurath expressed trepidation about hiring a half-Jewish woman as a gardener, her mother refrained from talking her out of her prejudice. Perhaps von Neurath felt that arguing with a German teenager, especially one who knew that Jews were dangerous, was futile. Instead she sent Wendelgard down to the gardener's house to get to know Hanne, the new gardener. "I went under protest, but to my surprise Hanne was a very nice person," Wendelgard recalled. Hanne told her about her brother, who was in a labor camp, and how she was worried about her elderly parents, who lived in Berlin and did not have much money. "We sat together on her bed talking for a long time," Wendelgard recounted. From then on, as often as she could, Wendelgard would visit Hanne. The fact that she was half Jewish never bothered Wendelgard again.[4]

Such gentle but firm guidance is far different from an authoritarian parent's habitual, peremptory commands. Swiss author Alice Miller, who has studied authoritarian families in which rules are laid down for the child without discussion or justification, points out that children from these kinds of households have trouble making independent judgments. Given little or no explanation, all directives seem, from the child's perspective, arbitrary and irrational. So they give up and do what they are told.[5]

The ability to think and act independently was, of course, a key element in rescue activity. Coming to the aid of persecuted people required an independent mind. A person had to be accustomed to reasoning through a problem and coming to a conclusion not based on what others thought or what the laws mandated. Those raised in authoritarian families were not likely to resist the pressure to conform.

However, not all rescuers were raised in lenient, democratic homes. Some, particularly those who grew up in religious homes, had fathers who were stern patriarchs and strict disciplinarians. Johtje Vos's father, a career army officer who later became the town mayor, literally put the fear of God into her. He was the local chairman of the Anti-Revolutionary Party of the Christian Reformed Church. (The Christian Reformed Church, affiliated with the Dutch Reformed Church, was founded by Johtje's grandfather Dr. Abraham Kuyper, Prime Minister of the Netherlands.) "I was actually scared to death of God," Johtje recalled. Her father did not inspire that kind of fear, but in all domestic matters, his word was law. No explanations were offered; the children only knew that parents must be honored and obeyed. Johtje and her two sisters were not allowed to ice-skate on Sunday or do anything else that violated the injunction to rest on the Sabbath. No one dared challenge their father's authority. Johtje chafed under such restrictions and ran off to study journalism in Paris.

This kind of strict discipline, however, did not crush the self. On the contrary, rescuers' families nourished an independence of mind and spirit. They set direction, lent support, and then sent the children out on their own.[6] A year before her grandson's graduation from the gymnasium (the equivalent of high school), Jan Karski's grandmother gave him a bicycle and money and told the fifteen-year-old to get to know his country and "see how all people live." That trip was his first foray by himself into the world beyond Lodz. (This same boy would later become a Polish diplomat and risk his life escaping from Nazi-occupied Europe to bring word of Hitler's Final Solution to Western leaders.) He saw people in eastern Poland—Ukrainians and Byelorussians—living in poverty. Some had no windows in their houses. Others lived with animals. To see people living in such squalor was "one of the greatest shocks in all my life," Karski said.

In talking with rescuers from all kinds of different homes, I found that one quality above all others was emphasized time and again: a familial acceptance of people who were different. This value was the centerpiece of the childhood of rescuers and became the core from which their rescuer self evolved. From the earliest ages, rescuers were taught by their parents that people are inextricably linked to one another. No one person or group was better than any other. The conviction that all people, no matter how marginal, are of equal value was conveyed to children of both religious and nonreligious households.[7]

This acceptance and tolerance of differences was developed in various ways. Le Chambon villagers were descendants of the once-persecuted Huguenots, so that tolerance for other religions was a natural part of their culture. But in other regions and other towns, tolerance had to be learned in a more visceral way. In some cases, rescuers' families were the odd family in the community. Irene Gut Opdyke's father, who was an architect, and Jean Kowalyk's father, who was a train conductor, had jobs that initially required them to move their families around a great deal, often making them strangers in a close-knit community. (It was not until Jean was eight years old that her family settled in one place.) Others were local curiosities. The Roos family was the only Protestant house in an otherwise all Roman

Catholic block in a poor neighborhood in Alkmaar. Will Westerweel's Amsterdam house was the only non-Jewish home on their street. While most rescuers felt very much a part of their larger communities, their positions were sometimes just unusual enough to give them an appreciation for ideas and people out of the ordinary.

In many cases, an acceptance of various people of different beliefs was a legacy of a mixed marriage. This allowed many rescuers, particularly those in Poland and the Ukraine, to stand apart from the pervasive antisemitic Christian doctrines of the time. Ukrainian rescuers Jean Kowalyk and Helena and Orest Zahajkewycz came from families of different Christian beliefs. Jean Kowalyk's mother was Roman Catholic and her father Ukrainian Catholic. Helena and Orest Zahajkewycz's grandfather was Greek Orthodox and his wife a Polish Roman Catholic. In these families, children and grandchildren were taught to respect religious differences. This same religious tolerance was part of the Bauer household too. Gitta Bauer's father was Protestant and her mother was a devout Catholic. While Gitta and her three sisters followed in their mother's footsteps, the women in the family still saw to it that their father polished his top hat and went to his Protestant church on Good Friday and on Reformation Day. At formal mealtimes, Bauer's mother insisted on prayers and then crossed herself when they were over. Gitta's father said the prayers with them, but did not cross himself.

The ability to accept individuals who were different was so ingrained in those who ultimately became rescuers that the racist propaganda of the Third Reich had little effect. They were able to see Nazi claims of Jewish conspiracies as the grotesque lies that they were. A few rescuers such as Father Stanislaw Falkowski were antisemites, but they were rare. More often, those who grew up in homes in which parents displayed antisemitic attitudes went on to be involved in resistance groups or to oppose the Nazis through sabotage and disseminating anti-Nazi literature. Although this type of resistance is noteworthy, it was not these individuals who risked their lives to save Jews.

It was not just values of tolerance taught at home that made rescuers less likely to adopt antisemitic attitudes. In many cases, rescuers and their families had close ties to individual Jews. Their friends, neighbors, co-workers, and teachers were Jews. They were Judeophiles in temperament, if not in initial motivation. Irene Gut Opdyke, Stefania Podgórska Burzminska, and Will Westerweel grew up playing with Jewish children. Stefania Podgórska Burzminska can still hear the cries of the protective Jewish mothers in her Polish village shouting to their children to stay away from the Gentiles: "Don't play with the *shikse* [Gentile girl]." "Don't touch the *shaygetz* [Gentile boy]." Happily, no one paid any attention to them, and the children all played together. Polish dressmaker Maria Niemiec, who abandoned her four sons and husband to carry a little Jewish girl to a safer hideout, and Dutch pacifist Wilto Schortinghuis grew up in homes in which Judeo-Christian friendships spanned generations. Maria Niemiec's mother was the wet nurse to the Licht family, the same family whose little girl, Terry, Niemiec later rescued. Over the years and through at least two generations, the Lichts and the Niemiecs visited one another at Christmas and Hanukkah time. Similarly, Wilto Schortinghuis's grandfather shared a duplex with a Jewish family and as a boy Wilto would often visit them with his grandparents. "We did not know any fundamental differences, except that they ate dry matzos at Easter," Schortinghuis recalled. "We ate the matzo they gave us with butter and sugar and felt quite privileged."

Still other rescuers, whose families did not know any Jews, had to discover for themselves the proper moral stance. At age sixteen, Stefania Podgórska had not given Jews a thought. But when the Germans took over Peremyshl and began issuing anti-Jewish ordinances, she was forced to examine the matter. Notices began appearing in the streets: Jews had to wear a Star of David on their clothes; Jews could not own businesses. Native Poles avoided meeting the eyes of their Jewish neighbors. Young Stefania was perplexed. What was behind this? Her Jewish employers, the Diamants, seemed nice enough. Was there something wrong with the Jewish people that she, in her inexperience, had not known? Or were the Germans just being unfair?

It was the first moral debate she had ever had with herself, and it took her a while to decide what was right. She described the incident that crystallized her thinking:

A Jewish boy, maybe ten years of age, was walking down the street. Another boy, who was not Jewish, started to yell a little at this Jewish boy. And so an ordinary worker, maybe thirty, asked the non-Jewish boy, "Why do you yell at him?" And this boy said, "Well, because he is a Jew." And this man said, "So what he's a Jew? Look at him. He is the same as you. You see he is not different. Just the Germans make the difference. . . . Look at him. He is a Jew. Okay. . . . But look at him—the same skin as yours, as mine, like everyone. . . . You have to be friendly. There is a war now, and when the war finishes we will all again be friendly." And the man told the boys to shake hands and be friends.

For me, this was something new. And you'll laugh when I say this, but when I came home, I looked at my skin. You see I looked, and I said [to myself], "Of course we are the same!"

At sixteen Stefania was old enough to realize that she need not obey authority. But she was still young enough so that the notion that Jews were human beings like herself came as a shock. For other rescuers this idea was not a novel one. In Anje Roos Geerling's childhood home, the message that people were people was always clear and explicit. Her father forbade anyone in the house to make derogatory comments about Jews. In other homes, the message was tacitly understood. Irene Gut Opdyke's father, for instance, worked with people of many different nationalities, and according to his daughter, he never cared about the differences. "He never said, 'He is a Jew' or 'She is a Gypsy,' " she told me.

It seems logical that an individual who understands that everyone is part of a common humanity would also believe that all people should be treated equally. The Oliners, in their Altruistic Personality Study, called this democratic principle "inclusiveness," or "a predisposition to regard all people as equals and apply similar standards of right and wrong to them without regard to their social status or ethnicity."[8]

While most rescuers grew up in loving homes that nourished independence of mind and spirit, a few did not. Walentyna Zak's father was a hateful man whose imperious ways led the teenage

Walentyna to repeatedly defy him. Walentyna found his demand that she not associate with Jews or patronize their stores so nonsensical that it helped convince her that her real (and certainly more loving) father was Jewish.

But rescuers' parents did not simply let it go at that. They backed their words with actions. The overwhelming majority of rescuers I interviewed, 89 percent, had a parent or adult figure who acted as an altruistic role model. Many rescuers, such as Irene Gut Opdyke, Amfian Gerasimov, and Jan Karski, revered their mothers, who were devoutly religious and who regularly helped others in need. Gut Opdyke described her mother as "a wonderful woman who always had an open heart for anybody who needed help." Her daughter, who fits that same description, remembered that in the winter her mother welcomed Gypsies who came to their house needing warm shelter and nursing. (Alexander Roslan had similar memories of his mother feeding Gypsies who stopped by their farm.) "Her motto in life was to always be ready to be helpful," Irene Gut Opdyke recalled.

Rescuers' parents were altruistic exemplars who, each day by word and deed, instructed their children. Helena and Orest Zahajkewycz's father, who was a teacher, bought books in quantity so he could give them away to his poorer students. Jean Kowalyk's mother smuggled bread to the local labor camp workers. The Roos family took in a Czech girl who needed refuge. And long before the labor camp inmates came to the von Neuraths' farm, Wendelgard's mother sheltered and fed tramps who had wandered on their property.[9]

Yet laboratory studies that have tried to gauge the impact of imitating an altruistic role model are mixed. Marian Radke-Yarrow and Carolyn Zahn-Waxler conclude that when a child has been observing an adult model in an experimental setting, imitation of honesty, generosity, helping, or rescuing behaviors are apparent for a short time and even may be applied to other situations. However, imitation has not been found to be universal, automatic, or even very long-term.[10]

Even so, nearly everyone I talked to mentioned a person who influenced their helping behavior. Hiltgunt Zassenhaus, the German interpreter for Norwegian and Danish political prisoners, told me that as a child she learned altruistic behavior from the actions of both her mother and her father. Her father was a schoolteacher who was kicked out of his job for his liberal political beliefs. Her mother spent much of her time secretly helping Jews flee Germany. When Zassenhaus was assigned to translate for the Scandinavian political prisoners in their dealings with the German authorities, she and her mother began baking bread and scavenging for goods to smuggle to them.

As it happened, one of the residents of the apartment building where the Zassenhauses lived was a black marketeer. Before each prison visit, Zassenhaus and her mother would barter with him for the supplies their prisoners so desperately needed. Little by little, Zassenhaus's mother traded away most of what she owned.

No china of worth was left, and now she had come to the silverware which we used only on special occasions. It had been her wedding present and she had kept it in a special box in the cupboard of our dining room which previously held the china too.

I was with her when she opened the box. She had twelve place settings and each piece was carefully wrapped in tissue paper. She took out one of the spoons and I saw her hold and weigh it in her hand, apparently far away in thought.

"Wouldn't you rather keep it?" I asked, and anxiously waited for her reply.

"Keep it?" she repeated after a long silence.

The spoon was engraved with her initials. She looked at them and suddenly smiled as if something had occurred to her. Putting the spoon down, she turned to me and took my hand. . . .

"You must learn to understand that only what you give, you'll have."[11]

Other rescuers pointed to their father as the one who most influenced them. Irene Gut Opdyke, Helena and Orest Zahajkewycz, Jean Kowalyk, and Johtje Vos, among many others, noted that their father showed by example as well as by instruction how to treat others. While Johtje Vos rebelled against her father's strict religious upbringing, she greatly respected his humanity. After Johtje Vos's father's army career, he served as mayor of a village in the northern province of Groningen. Farmers trusted his judgment. When they had financial difficulties, he advised them and frequently lent them money. Johtje could not help admiring these small acts of thoughtfulness. Unlike other mayors who delegated civil marriage ceremonies to their secretaries, Johtje's father put on his jacket, hung the official mayoral chain around his neck, and insisted of performing the ceremony himself. First, he asked the couple if they also planned a church wedding, or what the Dutch call "a blessing." If none was in the offing, he made sure the civil ceremony was very elaborate and gave an appropriate lengthy and solemn speech. At these civil ceremonies, the brides were often noticeably pregnant. (Farmers wanted to marry with the assurance that their prospective wives were fertile and could deliver the needed farm help.) Although sex before marriage was against his own religious principles, Johtje's father cheerfully overlooked their lapse. "My father would not judge people who lived and felt differently than he did," his daughter remembered. "That was always a point made to us."

As children, many rescuers were not just encouraged but were expected to help others. When a neighbor was ill or a school friend was in trouble, rescuers reported that their parents took it as a matter of course that they would help. In many religious homes, children were part of the whole family's charity work. Cornelia Knottnerus, who was the ten-year-old loving companion to Sarah, the Jewish girl her family sheltered, went on "neighborhood duty" with her mother. On such duty, members of the Anti-Revolutionary Church Party visited new mothers, the sick, and the elderly and offered to do whatever was needed. In the same vein, Irene Gut Opdyke followed the example of her mother, who often cooked extra food for her poorer neighbors, and regularly visited a local Jewish family whose daughter was bedridden.

Social psychologist Ervin Staub and other researchers suggest that this habit of helping behavior was instrumental in turning bystanders into rescuers. In his studies Staub found that involving children in efforts to help other children increased later helping behavior.[12]

Researchers have noted that helping behavior is most pronounced in older siblings, many of whom are accustomed to caring for younger children. Psychologist Nancy McWilliams found that some of the extraordinarily altruistic people she studied (a man who runs an adoption agency for crippled children; a woman who cares for the children of lepers) took care of younger siblings. Willard Gaylin, who studied men who went to prison for protesting the Vietnam War, reported that nearly all of them were firstborn sons and thus used to taking on responsibility and authority.[13]

Holocaust rescuers were not necessarily the oldest, but like the people in McWilliams's sample they were accustomed to assuming responsibility for younger siblings. Half of those I interviewed were firstborn, and most of them had siblings two or three years younger. Irene Gut Opdyke, for instance, was the oldest of five children and her mother relied on her to take care of the others. Irene did not let her down. She practically raised her youngest sister herself. Irene enjoyed doing it so much that she decided on a nursing career and volunteered at the local hospital.

Other social scientists argue that the predisposition to help others centers on a finely developed sense of empathy rather than a habit of helping. Martin Hoffman hypothesizes that a person's ability to connect to the emotional plight of others is an innate response. According to Hoffman, infants in the first days of life can differentiate a real baby's cry from a computer-generated crying sound. Hoffman believes that the reflexive crying of an infant in response to the crying of another infant is a primitive precursor of empathic arousal. During the second year of life, children begin to differentiate self and other and their emotional involvement in another's distress begins to become transformed from personal self-distress to sympathetic concern for the victim.[14]

Empathy with the plight of the Jews was indeed a critical part of rescuing behavior. Nelly Trocmé recalled that there was a concerted communal effort on the part of Le Chambon villagers to make the refugees feel at home:

In school it was an unspoken assumption that one was not to ask where or how these [foreign] children came into our midst. Despite the language barrier, we understood that they had suffered and that we should not add to their suffering by asking what could be embarrassing questions. We tried to make them feel welcome.

I found that empathic responses were especially keen in those rescuers who had suffered a death or a significant personal loss of some sort in childhood. When pressed, a majority of rescuers I interviewed admitted to having undergone at least one such traumatic experience. Many of them were young during World War I. Some lost fathers in that war, while others were just separated from them for a time.

Moreover, because medical care was considerably cruder, many children lost siblings to illnesses. The personal loss combined with exposure to an altruistic caretaker encouraged identification with the caregiver. McWilliams found that all of her subjects had suffered a loss in early childhood of a warm and nurturing caretaker. The loss of a loved one who was also an altruistic role model was a profound trauma, albeit one that propelled them in a positive direction.[15]

Initially, I had not thought to ask rescuers about personal losses in childhood, and most did not bring the subject up. But as a result of reading McWilliams's work, I began to probe this area. With some prodding, I found that when rescuers told me their background, they were apt to omit childhood memories of a death or loss. In some cases, the death occurred at such a young age that they had only vague memories of it. But in other cases, their recollections were too painful to mention.

The significant losses experienced by rescuers, however, did not necessarily have to be a death of someone close to them. The loss could be a separation from a parent, the loss of a home, or the temporary loss of freedom. Whatever the particular loss, the result was an increased sensitivity to the suffering of others. Miep Gies, who helped the Frank family in hiding, grew up as a sickly and undernourished child in post-World War I Vienna. When she was eleven, her parents sent her to Amsterdam, as part of an international program to help hungry Austrian children. With that one well-meaning parental decision, the young girl had lost her home, her family, and everything that was dear and familiar. Gies never forgot the consideration shown to her by her adopted Dutch family of seven:

> Despite the language problem, all the children were kind to me. Kindness, in my depleted condition, was very important to me. It was medicine as much as the bread, the marmalade, the good Dutch milk and butter and cheese, the toasty temperature of the warm rooms.[16]

For a number of rescuers, a childhood loss came from a serious accident or illness that rendered them virtually helpless for a long period of time. Johtje Vos suffered from heart problems that left her listless for much of her girlhood. Irene Gut Opdyke contracted tuberculosis in her early teens and was bedridden and isolated in a tent for months on end.

When Jean Kowalyk was six, she fell and broke her spine. Her family was not even sure she would survive. Jean was unconscious for three days and her doctors did not know what to do. In desperation Jean's mother carried her to the local church and prayed. Miraculously, Jean recovered.

The doctors and the power of prayer had saved her life, but still Jean was confined to a body cast for six months. It was a tough time for both mother and daughter. Jean worried that she would be stunted for life, and as time dragged on, her mother took out her anxieties by impatiently scolding Jean. Kowalyk recalled that her father was the one who protected her from her mother's irritability. It was also her father who urged her not to let her physical condition stand in the way of being an independent woman. She had a wonderful talent for sewing, he told her. Why not learn to be a seamstress? With that for an occupation, she could always earn her own way. She took his advice.

Despite Jean's childhood hardship and her later trials, she was not a bitter person. In fact, generally speaking, the vast majority of rescuers I met were positive and resilient people. They did not brood on their early misfortunes. On the contrary, their early childhood loss or adversity served only to fortify their inner strength. They had been tested by misfortune, and they had overcome it, emerging as stronger and more confident people.

Of all the accounts I heard, the story of Bert Bochove best illustrates those childhood influences that shaped rescuers. Bochove was born in Woubrugge, Holland, in 1910 to Protestant parents, who taught him to respect all religions. The youngest of eight children, Bert contracted polio at age two. His whole family, including a devoted nanny, rallied around him and encouraged him to overcome his disability. They helped him exercise his legs and included him in all the family activities. Bert's father, a shopkeeper and Sunday painter, often recounted stories of his own father to Bert. As one family story had it, when Bert's grandfather heard about a local minister who had risked his life to aid plague victims, Bert's grandfather felt such goodness should not go unnoticed. So he wrote a series of articles praising the minister's altruistic deeds.

At eleven, Bert's father died of cancer, and for a time Bert was inconsolable. His eldest brother helped him overcome deep depression and the two developed a strong bond. Although one of Bert's legs was lame from polio, this brother encouraged him to play soccer with the other children and to swim.

One time when Bert was playing soccer with his family near his house, thirteen-year-old Bert saw a boy fall from a rowboat into the canal. The boy was drowning. Without a moment's hesitation, Bert jumped into the canal and rescued the boy.

That was Bochove's first rescue. His second came during the Nazi occupation when a Jewish friend of his wife's asked if they would hide her. Before long, the Bochoves were harboring thirty-seven Jews in their home. They managed to rescue all, but there were plenty of close calls along the way. The closest came when one of their pharmaceutical workers wrote her Nazi boyfriend that she suspected her boss was hiding Jews. Bochove discovered her suspicions when a letter from her boyfriend arrived when she was on vacation. Bochove opened it. Her boyfriend wrote her that she should not worry about the Jews. He would see to it that they were cleaned out immediately. Sure enough, a day later the Gestapo arrived to search the premises, but by that time the Bochoves had moved everyone to another hide-out.

Bert Bochove's story, of course, is an atypical one. It touches on not just one, but all the familiar themes that run through a number of rescuers' childhoods. But in tying up all these loose ends in one such story, an important thread may get lost: At critical times in their upbringing, rescuers were cared for and loved. Bert Bochove's brother helped him persevere in an arduous time in his life. Jean Kowalyk's father and Irene Gut Opdyke's father gave their daughters the reassurance and love they needed to recover. When Jan Karski's father died, his older brother saw to it that Jan received money and a proper education. And so it went. Rescuers were people who as children had a person—a parent, a grandparent, a nanny, a brother or sister—rescue them when events threatened to overwhelm them. They never forgot that experience. Hitler's persecution of the Jews gave them the opportunity to return the favor.

PART III
POSTWAR

"The evil that men do lives after them,
the good is oft interred with their bones."

—**William Shakespeare**, *Julius Caesar*

· 15 ·

POSTWAR

IN 1945, the Russian and Western armies advanced across
Nazi-occupied Europe, crushing the Germans. After years of waiting
for liberation, rescuers were released at last from Nazi subjugation.
The days and nights of muffled sounds, cramped spaces, and gut-
wrenching fear were suddenly over. The Vreedenburgs could put on
their shoes and leave the Bloms' second-story bedroom and walk
outside in the daylight. Israel Rubinek could throw open the crude
plank door of the Banyas' dirt-floor cottage and strut around the yard,
as did the chickens he had enviously watched. Fegel Yurkansky and
her little group, crouched in the ditch on the Adamowiczes' farm,
could stand up, pull themselves out, and walk away.

But as both survivors and rescuers were to discover, it was not so
easy to walk away from the past. For both groups the past would
continue to haunt them and shape their future. The war had changed
them. The people who undertook rescue, whether it was for a few
days or for years, were fundamentally changed by the experience.
Those who saved the lives of Jews were farmers, housewives, nurses,
business people, seamstresses, nannies, and teachers. They were diplomats, professors, doctors, and wealthy entrepreneurs, or they would
go on to become these. Still, no matter who they were or would
become, their rescuer selves remained a critical part of their identities.

Wendelgard von Staden said as much when she told an interviewer in 1981 that "the camp played a very big part in my inner life for decades. It worked in me for thirty years."[1] Similarly, Annie P., who at age six suffered crippling kicks to her spine rather than tell a Nazi where Jews were hidden, felt that her childhood experiences with her charges and other rescuers strengthened her belief in God. "The faith shown by the people I met during the war was astonishing to me," Annie P. told me. "It comforted me then and became a guiding light and an integral part of my life."

The rescuer self that had grown from each individual's core values and basic moral integrity remained after the war. For most, having saved lives was a source of quiet pride and inner satisfaction. Belgian rescuer Andrée Guelen Herscovici, who found safe hideouts for Jewish children, looks back on her rescue activity as the time in her life that stamped her character and gave her life direction. Similarly, Bert Bochove felt that rescue activities gave his life a personal fulfillment hard to duplicate: "Despite several betrayals by Dutch collaborators, in some ways the war was the best time of my life," Bochove told me. "There were always so many people around, and I got such satisfaction from helping out, from keeping the Nazis from finding the hiding place."

For many years, that quiet inner satisfaction was all the reward rescuers could expect or want. Rescuers in Eastern Europe, the Ukraine, Poland, and Russia, who lived among Jew-hating neighbors, extracted promises from their charges not to reveal their rescue role, and then, with the utmost caution, they helped their charges scurry away. In Zorotowyci, Poland, Jean Kowalyk helped the seven Jews hidden in her attic to make their furtive escape. However, one of them, Dr. Berger asked Jean to marry him. After the intense involvement they had had with one another over the past two years, Jean found it difficult to refuse him. Moreover, while Jean loved her fiancé, a tailor, she never trusted him enough to share her secret rescue life. Jean felt the tailor would reject her if he knew about her hiding Jews and she was convinced that no one except a Jew would want to marry her, so she accepted the doctor.

But before Jean and the doctor could be married, Jean received an anonymous letter warning her that unless she left the country she would share the same fate as that of the Jews she *did not* manage to save. The letter scared Jean. It could have come from a camp guard, or from any of her neighbors, for that matter. Anyone was capable of carrying out this deadly threat. So, leaving her mother, her family, and her home behind, Jean fled the village with Dr. Berger. The two married in Czechoslovakia, and eventually Jean made her way to Canada and the United States.

In other Polish towns, villagers greeted the survival of Jews and those who saved them with the same undisguised enmity contained in the anonymous letter sent to Jean Kowalyk Berger. The Rubineks waited on the Banyas' farm outside of Pinczow for days after Russian liberation just to make certain it was safe to venture out and into town. For nearly two and a half years they had been in hiding. When the Rubineks met Poles they knew from their days running the general store they were greeted with cold surprise. "Oh, you're still alive?" the Poles inquired. Shortly after the end of the war, Lvov sewer worker and rescuer Leopold Socha was run down by a truck in Gliwice, Poland. No one knew if it was an accident, but some townspeople said God had punished him for saving Jews.

For Jews and their rescuers, postwar Poland was a hostile environment. Most Jews, and some of their saviors, felt they had no choice but to emigrate. In fact, the great majority of rescuers who left Europe did so because they continued to feel that their lives were in danger because they had saved Jews. Those who stayed in their countries remained wary. The rescuer self—the self they were forced to adopt to cope with the everyday practicalities of saving lives—stayed alert. Vigilance, secrecy, cunning, and role-playing were still needed for self-protection. Polish partisans and bandits roamed the countryside looking for Jews and "Jew-lovers" to kill.

Survivors who emigrated were unaware of the continued persecution of their rescuers. This reality plagued and tortured Franczek Chrostek for decades. At a reunion thirty-seven years later with the family he rescued, the Rosensteins, Chrostek finally revealed the postwar ending to his rescue story. The Rosensteins were friends of my parents, and so I was present when Franczek Chrostek told the complete story of the Rosensteins' rescue and its aftermath.

For two years, Franczek Chrostek and his wife hid members of the Rosenstein family in two ditches on their farm near Bialystok, Poland. Hearing the news of liberation, the Rosensteins cautiously stole out of their ditches and moved to another town where they were not known. They managed to obtain a cow, and one of the brothers, Pesach, returned to the Chrosteks to celebrate their survival and give the Chrosteks the cow as a "thank you" gift. During Pesach's visit, outlaws stormed the Chrosteks' farm, put a gun to Franczek Chrostek's head, and demanded, "Give us the money the Jews gave you! Give us the gold that the Jews gave you!" They started beating him as they repeated their demands. Pesach Rosenstein, who was hiding behind the oven, ran out of the house. The bandits saw him, chased after him, and then shot him in the head.

The bandits warned Franczek Chrostek they would kill him if he told anyone what happened. Chrostek never did. He dragged the body into the woods, buried Pesach, and then lied when Pesach's brother Abraham came looking for him. Abraham figured that his brother must have somehow been killed, but did not press Chrostek. The bandits, however, never let Chrostek alone. Every night they harassed the farmer, asking, "Where are the Jews?" Chrostek finally fled to another village, where his family joined him. They lost all contact with the Rosensteins.

Chrostek never got over his fears from the killing and harassment or his guilt surrounding the murder of Pesach. For almost twenty years he and his family had no peace of mind. Fear of being caught for their rescue activity and denounced as "Jew-lovers" was a daily terror. Whereas other rescuers were able to go on with their lives, the postwar trauma the Chrosteks experienced did not allow them to put their rescuing relationships aside.

In 1964, the traumatized Chrosteks emigrated to the United States. Franczek Chrostek was determined to find the Rosensteins and unburden himself of his guilty secret. Finally, three and a half years after the first correspondence, the Chrosteks and the Rosensteins reestablished contact and were reunited in New York. They celebrated the Sabbath together and the festivities continued for a few days. During the reunion, Franczek Chrostek finally told Abraham the secret that he had held in all these years, the torment that woke him in the middle of the night and which he attempted to escape through alcohol. Chrostek spilled out the details of Pesach's death and sought forgiveness from Abraham for what was never Chrostek's fault. The misaddressed letters, the losing of telephone numbers and addresses were expressions on both sides of the unconscious fears and ambivalence surrounding the reunion and confrontation with the past. By the age of seventy-one, Franczek Chrostek had lived long enough with his secret and he was ready to part with it and move on. His confession restored his sense of honor. Sadly, it did not heal his years of living with fear and guilt. He continues to drink and feels at home nowhere.

Most rescuers are aware that antisemitism did not end with the defeat of Hitler. Agnieszka Budna-Widerschal, for example, discovered that the defeat of Nazism muffled but did not extinguish hatred of the Jews. Before the war, Budna-Widerschal, a young woman from a very religious Catholic family, worked in a factory in Peremyshl. There she met and fell in love with a Jewish factory mechanic. They married, and when the Germans took over, Budna-Widerschal secured a larger apartment so she could hide her husband, his three brothers, and two friends. They struggled and somehow all of them managed to survive the war. In September 1945, Agnieszka gave birth to a daughter, Bella. Four months later her husband died of diabetes and Agnieszka and her baby moved to another Polish village where some of her family still lived. She married another Jew, Shimon, and for a while all was well. In 1954 when Bella was nine years old, a group of older schoolmates stopped by after school and asked her to take a walk with them. Bella delightedly accepted. They walked along the railroad tracks, and just as a train was about to rumble by, the children pushed Bella into its path. She was killed instantly.

At the funeral, neither the children nor their families expressed any remorse about killing a half-Jewish girl. "Better your daughter than mine," one mother told Budna-Widerschal in what was the closest expression to sympathy Budna-Widerschal received. In 1958, Agnieszka Budna-Widerschal and her husband emigrated to Israel.

Coping with the fear of Jew-hating retaliation was not the only thing that forced rescuers to keep the secret and role-playing aspects of their rescuer selves alive. Some rescuers had kept their helping activities secret from their immediate families and dared not confess what they had done. Circumstances forced others to continue to live the roles that their rescuer selves had invented.

Nannies and single mothers who cared for Jewish children were desperate to maintain their cover stories. Having told neighbors, friends, and family about fictional marriages or invented distant relations, these rescuers lived in fear that their lies would be exposed. They were terrified that the child's parents or relatives would return and claim the child whom the whole town believed to be theirs. How could a rescuer explain such a scenario and cope with subsequent humiliation and degradation? More important, how could they endure the loss? They loved their Jewish charges as much as if they had been their own children. The difficulty of explaining the sudden disappearance of their "child" or "niece" was nothing compared to the emotional pain of losing that love. Some rescuers were determined not to part with the Jewish child they saved. To evade those Jewish survivors who might be looking for children or relatives, some rescuers moved to different towns or villages where no one would be able to find them. In some cases the truth came out years later in rescuers' deathbed confessions. In hundreds of other cases, the truth was never revealed.[2]

While the good intentions of rescuers never wavered, their motivations changed. For some, such as Polish rescuer Maria Byrczek, what began as a compassionate act—the taking in and caring for a baby—was transformed by love into an implacable resolve to keep a loved one. Marysia, her five-month-old "niece," had become as dear to her as her own four children.

As it happened, Marysia's real mother, Erna Korngut, had managed to elude imprisonment in a concentration camp by wandering the countryside. Erna did not look Jewish and could pass for a Polish peasant. Throughout the war, she came to visit Byrczek in order to see her daughter. Erna dared not tell Byrczek she was the baby's mother because she feared Byrczek might turn her and her baby out. Instead, Erna told Byrczek that she was the baby's aunt. Despite the increased danger of sheltering still another Jew, much to Erna's surprise, Byrczek invited her to stay with her whenever Erna wanted to see her niece.

After the war, Marysia's mother told Byrczek her true identity. Erna explained to Byrczek that her husband had survived imprisonment in a concentration camp and the newly reunited family wanted their baby back. Byrczek did not believe this woman was the child's real mother. Byrczek refused to give the child up, and the battle for custody of Marysia dragged through the courts. Finally, the courts ordered Byrczek to hand over the now six-year-old Marysia to someone who was almost a stranger to her—her mother.[3]

After years of caring for and loving their charges, rescuers had to face the emotional anguish of relinquishing them. The personal satisfaction of saving a life and performing a good deed for a fellow human being seemed insignificant compared with the deep emotional loss caused by parting with a loved one. Maria Niemiec, who had left her sons to rush Terry, the daughter she always wanted, to a safe apartment in Warsaw, returned her to the Lichts and rejoined her own family. For a while the Lichts tried to live in Poland. They changed their name to a less Jewish one in an attempt to hide their Jewish identity. But the strain was too great, and after a time they emigrated to the United States. They kept in touch with the Niemiecs and sent them packages and medicine, but they could never convince Maria to come to the United States.

Other Jewish children were claimed by Jewish organizations whose mission was to nurture Jewish continuity and preserve Jewish heritage. After the slaughter of six million Jews, Jewish organizations regarded Jewish children as precious and endangered. Jewish children were critical to the regeneration of the Jewish people and necessary for the rebuilding of the Jewish nation in Palestine. Representatives of organizations such as Aliyat Hanoar (Youth Aliyah) and Vaad Hatzala (Rescue Committee) combed countries that had been occupied by the Nazis searching for orphaned children to resettle in Palestine.[4]

It was hard enough for rescuers to surrender their beloved charges to Jewish relatives, but relinquishing them to an impersonal organization was especially difficult. After the war, Aart and Johtje Vos wanted to adopt a girl they had hidden and whose parents had been killed in the war. Despite their love for her, the Jewish community maintained their policy of retrieving Jewish children from their rescuers and placed her in a Jewish orphanage in Holland. Throughout the years, however, the Voses kept in close contact with the child they always considered their daughter and who remembers her wartime years with the Voses as the best of her life.

The adjustment to peacetime tranquillity after years of military occupation and fear was not always easy. War had disrupted daily patterns and habits for so long that the return to normalcy—the freedom from curfews, blackouts, bombs, and arrest—was a major adjustment. Many also needed time to recover physically, particularly those who had been in concentration camps. Network rescuer Anje Roos, who was sent to a concentration camp for her role in the Amsterdam raid in which Nazi files were burned, contracted tuberculosis while incarcerated and was confined to a sanatorium for two years following liberation. Although she got better, the tuberculosis weakened her and made it impossible for her to bear children. "Dutch-Paris" network leader John Weidner was left with a speech impediment, a permanent result of the torture he underwent when he was captured by the Nazis. Brutal treatment in concentration camps left others, such as Danish underground leader Svend Aage Holm-Sorensen, nervous and anxious. They were mere shells of their former selves.

To help overcome physical and psychic war wounds, rescuers such as Hermann Graebe, John Weidner, and Anje Roos Geerling continued their anti-Nazi activities. Weidner worked with the Dutch government to prosecute those guilty of war crimes, while Roos Geerling and Graebe helped Allied commanders identify Nazis and then testified at their war trials. Still other rescuers unhesitatingly pitched in where help was needed. Aart Vos and Marion van Binsbergen Pritchard worked with refugees in displaced-persons camps. Gitta Dubro Bauer, free at last from the double life she had led as a German bureaucrat and rescuer, became a journalist and covered the 1945–46 Nuremberg Trials for an East German news agency.

All the activity and refocused energy, however, did not prevent many rescuers from noticing that postwar life was not what they had envisioned. The defeat of the Third Reich did not bring the paradise of democracy and fellowship that Weidner and other rescuers had dreamed of. To his dismay and disgust, Weidner saw Nazis and Nazi sympathizers regain positions of power. In a matter of months, the new world order of peace he was determined to help bring about fell victim to nationalistic infighting and partisan squabbling.

The world had been blown apart, then stitched together; yet little seemed to have changed except the rescuers themselves. Will Westerweel and Louisa Steenstra were widows. Irmgard von Neurath's only son, who had fought in the battles of Leningrad and Narva, came home brain-damaged. Alexander and Mela Roslan's son was killed. Countless other rescuers lost family, friends, and loved ones.

Death and horrific wartime remembrances intruded into post-war life and hampered many rescuers' efforts to rebuild their lives. Weidner continued to be haunted by memories of his dead sister, Gabrielle, and many of his murdered colleagues. Although Weidner reestablished his textile business in Paris, living in the same city and sometimes passing the church where the Nazis arrested Gabrielle eventually became too distressing. In 1958, he emigrated to Pasadena, California, where he founded the highly successful American Dietary Laboratories.

Wartime memories plagued other rescuers and prompted them to speak up. Hermann Graebe's testimony at the Nuremberg trials put a psychological wall between him and his German neighbors and colleagues. It is possible that Graebe's colleagues felt his presence to be an implicit rebuke of their own actions during the war. The Graebes, like many other rescuers, felt alienated from their community. They, however, had the additional burden of being harassed and ostracized. Having lost many possibilities for employment and with his son being threatened by other children at school, Graebe was forced to seek protection for his family by immigrating to San Francisco.

Those rescuers who remained in their old homes were disoriented for a time and somewhat at a loss. War had given them a sense of purpose; their lives were dedicated to a larger goal. Hitler's defeat, while it justified their sacrifices, also robbed rescuers of what had become their central reason for being. Their moral selves were cut adrift with no one to rescue and no cause to support. Those whom they had hidden, cared for, and risked their lives to save had left. While some Jewish survivors kept in touch with their rescuers, many others, desperate to reestablish their own family bonds and forget the horror-filled past, did not maintain relations with their saviors. The abrupt rupture of what often had been intense and caring relationships left rescuers feeling bereft and lost.[5]

In many cases, financial losses added to the emotional ones. In Eastern Europe, most upper-class rescuers lost their wealth and social status. During the war, their wealth and property had been confiscated by the Nazis. After the war, the Communists expropriated what was left. Those in Western Europe also saw hard times. In Holland, John Stenekes's bakery was overrun and destroyed by retreating Germans. As was the case with many who had nothing left and nothing to lose, the Stenekes emigrated. The Stenekes resettled in Canada. Others moved to the United States and Israel.

Despite the multiple losses most rescuers suffered, few took time to mourn. Instead, they cauterized their emotional wounds and pushed painful memories from their consciousness. Those who did look back were urged by social workers and others not to dwell on the past and waste time grieving, but to focus instead on the needs of the present and the possibilities of the future. The vast majority of rescuers needed little urging. They were eager to leave death and destruction behind and get on with their lives. Most rescuers, therefore, sealed off their past, burying their rescuer selves and their wartime recollections as they once hid their charges.

But willful amnesia was not always successful. From time to time, the uncontrollable terror of that time returned in nightmares or in repetitive anxiety dreams. Past fears resurfaced in unexpected flashbacks. Some rescuers suffered from insomnia, were easily startled, or had intense reactions to stimuli associated with their rescuing time.

Medical professionals helping Vietnam veterans adjust to postwar life identified these reactions as symptomatic of post-traumatic stress disorder, a malady common among those who had undergone a traumatic event.

Post-traumatic stress disorder refers to a person's feelings of helpless terror in the aftermath of a traumatic event. Traumatized people relive the danger of the past as though it were recurring in the present. Aside from Vietnam veterans, common sufferers of post-traumatic stress disorder include victims of violent crime, Holocaust survivors, and others who experienced close personal encounters with violence and death.[6] Although it has long been known that a traumatic incident involving a threat to life will affect the brain chemistry of white mice for a considerable length of time after the event, only recently have studies unearthed evidence that a similar phenomenon may occur in humans.

According to researchers, the brain reacts to terror by going into a kind of chemical overdrive. The part of the brain regulating the "fight or flight" impulse secretes a great deal more chemicals than normal, preparing the body for an emergency, while another brain system, closely linked to the emotional center, releases a flood of neurochemicals that blunt the perception of pain. Researchers speculate that during an extremely traumatic event, the brain may habituate itself to the heightened neurochemical output, resulting in a brain chemistry that is reacting continually to the stress of a single episode.

In the case of many rescuers, their brains may have been generating these higher levels of stress-related neurochemicals for *years*. Some evidence suggests that this prolonged state of elevated chemical output increases the likelihood of suffering from post-traumatic stress disorder later.

My intention is not to reduce rescuers' pain to a clinical discussion or to write it off as a chemical imbalance. However, it is important to understand the full effect that the war had on rescuers. Whether or not they were threatened, raided, interrogated, beaten, or incarcerated for aiding victims of Nazi persecution, rescuers were nonetheless victims of Nazi terror. Stefania Podgórska Burzminska, who in her late teens in Poland hid and cared for thirteen Jews in an attic, Alexander Roslan, who risked everything he had, in Warsaw, for three Jewish boys, and Louisa Steenstra, who brought food and clothing to inmates in Westerbork and later sheltered them in her home, all suffered from different manifestations of post-traumatic stress disorder.[7] Stefania struggled with fear and anger for years, suffering from recurring nightmares and extreme nervousness. Roslan sealed off his emotions and memories and remains emotionally numb. Steenstra's memory of her husband's death and the circumstances surrounding it never leaves her. She suffers constantly from the intrusion of flashbacks, and any conversation about the past repeatedly results in the visualization of a dog biting her husband's ear. These rescuers are still paying the price, first exacted by the Nazis a half century ago, of maintaining integrity during the Holocaust.

For the most part, rescuers are not familiar with post-traumatic stress disorder. In all my interviews, few rescuers described themselves as being traumatized by the war. They often do not understand the connection between their emotional well-being today and something that happened fifty years ago. Furthermore, if they admitted their own suffering, it would affect their image of themselves as normal people who simply "did what was right." Claiming some sort of special treatment, whether as a reward for their goodness or out of concern for their supposed ailment, was, and is, dissonant with their characters.

Yet those same qualities of compassion and empathic imagination that led rescuers to help are the same ones that do not allow them to forget what they saw. In a Dutch rescuer's case, the reaction came after twenty years. At age sixty-nine he suddenly began to burst into tears when he read newspaper articles or saw television programs about starving or suffering children. In addition, he suffered from terrible seizures. The seizures and the hypersensitivity were his delayed reactions to the tension he had lived under for so long during the war. The Dutch declared him a war invalid due to post-traumatic stress, and he was given a pension.

But even those rescuers who seemed to be well adjusted paid a price for their purposeful forgetfulness. In denying the past, they buried a crucial part of themselves—their rescuer self. It was a self that expressed the best, most honorable part of their essence. It was this self that allowed Oskar Schindler to be a captain of industry and a wheeler-dealer par excellence with the Nazis in order to save lives. Despite other business ventures, he would never again achieve the success he had under the Nazis. It was this self that gave the Italian meat salesman Giorgio Perlasca the courage, inventiveness, and boldness to declare himself the legal representative of Spain and thus save hundreds of Hungarian Jews. With no one on hand to acknowledge that self, and no one to believe his improbable wartime stories—when he returned to Italy, his wife and sister did not believe his tales—and eager himself to disassociate himself from painful memories, Perlasca's soul shriveled. He doubted himself to such a degree that after the war he had difficulty holding on to even menial jobs.[8]

The loss of the rescuer self was yet another loss rescuers neglected to mourn. I use the word "mourn" intentionally. In counseling Holocaust families, I have found the mourning process to be necessary so they can integrate their past and present-day lives. Each loss needs to be internally acknowledged and grieved over before it is finally accepted and a personal meaning can be found. None of this is easy. Mourning can be a long, emotionally draining process. It forces people to abandon denial and confront their intense feelings about death and loss. Mourners experience a wealth of emotions—rage, helplessness, guilt, depression. They feel both guilty and grateful to be alive, upset that they did not do more and proud of what they did do. Grief surfaces as each loss is acknowledged and felt: the deaths of those loved; the sudden disappearance of others; the loss of ideals, fortunes, health; and the disappearance of the rescuer self.

The overwhelming number of rescuers I met in the course of my work had not yet directly acknowledged how terrified they were during the time they were rescuing Jews. In the terms of the mourning process, this is called "denial." Holocaust rescuers despaired of ever being able to convey the reality of their experiences and so rarely talked about the war to anyone, including their own children. "You want to forget and pretend it never happened," Esther Warmerdam, the child rescuer whose parents sheltered more than 200 Jewish children, told me. "You put it in the back of your mind."

My interviews frequently nudged rescuers from one stage of mourning to the next. My questions forced them to confront their intense emotions surrounding the war that first led many of them to repress their memories. Many were initially apprehensive about the interview. When talking with couples, I found that the emotionally less volatile spouse would intervene protectively and answer questions that might cause the other to break out in tears. Alex Roslan's wife, Mela, for example, hovered protectively at his side during our talk. While supportive and helpful, Mela does not like her husband to talk about the war; she says it upsets him and makes his blood pressure skyrocket.

But in most cases, rescuers found that talking to an interviewer about their wartime activities was therapeutic. Until the interview, they did not fully appreciate the various ways their war experiences had affected them emotionally. Talking led them to connect their feelings to events long suppressed but not forgotten. It gave them a new understanding and integration of themselves.

For many, this interview was the first time they had told their story. Certainly it was the first time anyone sought to trace their rescue activities back to prewar childhood influences. They began to see themselves in a different light. Hiltgunt Zassenhaus, the German interpreter who saved Norwegian and Danish political prisoners, told me that questions about her early childhood, parental values, and her current life gave her a heightened sense of her own complexity. As the author of a book about her war experiences, she had been the subject of a number of magazine articles. My questions, however, made her realize that her rescue activity was not a singular occurrence brought on only by the dire circumstances of war, but was an act consistent with who she was before the war and who she is now.

Time, and the encroachment of old age, has played still another role in breaking the silence surrounding rescuers' activities. The passing years have made it more difficult for the rescuers to avoid thinking about the war. As they grow older, they are forced to review and find meaning in the past rather than plan for and anticipate the future. In psychoanalyst Erik Erikson's terms, they are passing through the last two developmental stages of life: "generativity versus stagnation" and "ego integrity versus despair."

According to Erikson, men and women in the twilight of their lives have a natural desire to pass along the wisdom distilled from their experiences to others. They have lived a long time and have gathered much experience. They want their children and grandchildren to be guided by their failures and by their successes. The result is what Erikson called "generativity," a term that includes a late burst of productivity and creativity.

Erikson's developmental theory explains in great measure why rescuers are now talking about what happened and what they did. Time has eroded their tendency toward reticence, and age has spurred them to action. The energy they formerly used to repress their feelings is now being channeled in constructive directions. The generativity of rescuers includes writing their memoirs, speaking out publicly for the first time about their wartime roles, and accurately documenting the historical record. When I last heard from Utrecht children rescuer Hetty Dutihl Voûte, she was busy compiling a list of those who perished in the Vught concentration camp so their names could be inscribed on the wall of the crematorium there. (Vught's crematorium still stands as a Dutch monument and memorial to Holocaust victims.)

But there is more at work than the selfless wish to guide future generations. Erikson's final developmental stage was "ego integrity versus despair." In Erikson's development model, this last stage is a person's final coming to terms with who he or she is. There is a reaching for self-understanding and self-acceptance.[9] Many of the rescuers are in the final, healing phase of mourning. In this last phase, mourners seek ways to extract personal meaning from the past. They have overcome denial, confronted and absorbed their losses, and finally integrated the rescuer self into their being.

Precisely how rescuers accomplished this depended not only on their individual postwar circumstances but also on what motivational types they were. Adjusting and integrating the rescuer self into their postwar life was different for an emotional-moral rescuer than it was for a Judeophile or a network rescuer. Those who could talk about their experiences with others, such as network rescuers or moral-religious rescuers who were part of a rescuing church group, fared the best. Emotional-moral rescuers and child rescuers, on the other hand, were more likely than others to suffer from post-traumatic stress disorder. The intense feeling of vulnerability combined with a terror of divulging the family's secret condemned many child rescuers to an adulthood of suspicion and nightmares.

Each motivational category incorporated the rescuer self into postwar life in its own way. Moral rescuers such as Irene Gut Opdyke and Aart Vos continued to channel their altruistic efforts in a very direct and personal way. The Voses, after they had resettled in Woodstock, New York, adopted a child and founded a home for children. Later, they established an international children's camp where city children came to work and play on their farm. All this activity went a long way toward assuaging the pain they felt at their failure to adopt the little Jewish girl they loved so much. Although a heart attack forced Johtje to close the camp, she is still active in a number of other social causes.

Other moral rescuers needed considerable time to recover from the war. Some never healed. Wendelgard von Staden's mother, Irmgard von Neurath, was crushed by the horror of what the Nazis had done. She lost confidence in her countrymen and her country. In the early 1950s, the von Neuraths sold their farm. Her husband, the baron, died in 1960, and she died five years later.

Irene Gut Opdyke escaped such despair by running away from any reminders of the death and destruction she had witnessed. She emigrated to the United States, where she rebuilt her life. Irene married a U.S. army officer, whom she first glimpsed in a displaced-persons camp in Europe but did not meet until she moved to New York. They married and moved to California, where Irene became an interior decorator. "I put a 'Do Not Disturb' sign on my mind," she recalled. Still, her rescuer self could not be totally denied. A friendship struck up with a blind woman led Gut Opdyke to invite the woman into her home. Gut Opdyke cared for the woman until her death years later.

In 1975, Gut Opdyke's mind was roused from its self-induced wartime slumber when she received a letter from a "revisionist" neo-Nazi group, spreading the lie that the Holocaust never took place. The denial of all she had witnessed and endured infuriated Gut Opdyke and set her on what has become her life's work. She has become a full-time Holocaust lecturer; she is dedicated to encouraging love and understanding among all peoples. Gut Opdyke asserts, "It is my mission!" And she adds, "I particularly want to educate the young. [With] every child I reach and change I am helping to change all of humanity." Gut Opdyke shared with me the hundreds of letters she receives from schoolchildren who say they are amazed they could be touched by a seventy-year-old grandmother, and after hearing her they find the courage to cope with their own problems.[10]

Among the rescuers, religious-moral rescuers had little difficulty integrating their rescuer selves into postwar life. They continued to live out their days according to the same Christian principles of compassion and charity they had during the war. Despite the hostility of the new Communist regime, the good-hearted Polish priest Stanislaw Falkowski went on preaching his peculiar brand of Christianity filled with antisemitic overtones. (Thanks to Father Falkowski, Joseph Kutrzeba, the fifteen-year-old Jewish boy he cared for, escaped to Germany—where there were many Polish workers, and he therefore was able to lead a more anonymous life—and ultimately the United States, where he became a successful radio producer for the United Nations, in addition to producing and directing films, theater, and television programs.) In 1950, Father Falkowski's outspoken sermons brought him to the attention of Poland's secret police, and in 1950 he was arrested for spreading the rumor that the Church was being persecuted by the Communist regime. (In the language of the court, Father Falkowski was charged with throwing "logs under the feet of those marching toward progress and socialism.") Throughout the years, including the two and a half years of Father Falkowski's imprisonment, Joseph kept in touch with him and even sent letters of

290 CONSCIENCE & COURAGE

support and presents to Father Falkowski's mother. Still later Father Falkowski's outspokenness got him into trouble with his church superiors, but Joseph's letter to the Primate of Poland, Cardinal Stefan Wyszynski, on his rescuer's behalf helped straighten matters out. It was a rare instance in which someone who had been saved was able in some measure to return the favor. "I owe you my continued spiritual life," wrote a thankful Father Falkowski to Joseph.[11]

Although Father Falkowski's antisemitism was rare among religious rescuers, his devotion to Christian principles was not. Religious rescuers were steadfast in their dedication to Christian beliefs and continued to act on them. Le Chambon pastor André Trocmé and his wife, Magda, founded an international organization, the House of Reconciliation, an institution based in Versailles, France, that is dedicated to creating a new understanding among people with opposing ideas. When Magda Trocmé looks back on her wartime activities, she is inclined to think too much is made of her altruistic behavior. She feels that she has received too much attention.

For other rescuers, however, their rescues and relationships with Jews were of central importance. These Judeophiles continued to feel a special closeness to Jews. A central part of their identity was defined by the feeling of a special connection. Friendships formed before or during the war continued to play a big part in their lives. For the rest of their lives, Miep Gies and her husband would be known around the world as the would-be rescuers of Anne Frank and Oskar Schindler would find emotional and financial surety only among his former factory workers.

Schindler had stayed with his workers until the last SS man left. He then headed west and into dreary postwar life made bearable only by his friendships with his former charges. Stripped of their nobler purpose, Schindler's business ventures failed. The nutria ranch he began in Argentina with $15,000 awarded him by the Jewish Joint Distribution Committee went bankrupt. A cement venture folded almost before it had begun.

In 1961, at the behest of some of his former workers, Schindler visited Israel for the first time. Two hundred Jews—Schindler's Jewish workers and their children and grandchildren—greeted him as he stepped from the airplane and gave him a hero's welcome. Articles about Schindler's exploits appeared in Israel and at home in Frankfurt.[12] All this publicity gave Schindler's life a schizophrenic quality. In Tel Aviv, he was hailed on the streets as a hero. In Frankfurt, where he lived, he was jeered at and pelted with stones. In 1963, he punched a factory worker who called him a "Jew-kisser," and the man lodged a charge of assault. The local judge lectured Schindler and then ordered him to pay damages.[13]

Such humiliations increased Schindler's dependence on the survivors. For the rest of his life he would spend some months of each year with them. In October 1974, Schindler's years of hard drinking caught up with him, and he died of a liver disease. He was buried in the Catholic cemetery on Mount Zion in Jerusalem. More than 400 "Schindler Jews" and their families attended his funeral.

Like Schindler, other Judeophiles clung to those they saved. Some married their former charges. Others, such as Polish rescuer Walentyna Zak and Gitta Dubro Bauer of Berlin, felt such a rapport with Jews that they later married one.

Such marriages were not always successful. As Jean Kowalyk Berger discovered, gratitude and a habit of distrusting non-Jews were not in themselves a solid foundation for marriage. After she supported herself as a seamstress in Canada and smoothed the way for her husband to gain an entry permit there and later to the United States, Dr. Berger left her. It was a postwar nightmare: she was alone and penniless in New York City. Not knowing what to do, she sat down on a park bench. As it happened, she sat next to a woman from Poland, a Jewish survivor, who advised her to go to the Hebrew Immigrant Aid Society and tell them her story. The society, however, refused to help her. A worker explained to Kowalyk Berger that they had to limit their help to Jews. Still Kowalyk Berger persevered. She found a room to live in on 148th street and a job sewing on 72nd street. To save the nickel subway fare, she walked the seventy-six blocks to work and back. The money she saved she sent to her family back home in what became Russia.

Kowalyk Berger's husband's betrayal did not shatter her Judeophilism or her charitable heart. After years of effort, she finally reestablished contact with the other Jews she saved who were now living in Israel and in 1985 she flew to Israel to be honored at Yad Vashem. Although Kowalyk Berger has difficulty walking and standing for long periods of time, she talks to the young about her wartime experiences in the hope that they will learn that a single person standing for what he or she believes to be right can make a difference.

After the war, more than fifty rescuers emigrated to Israel with the children they rescued, lovers they married, or in general to be with the Jewish people. Unbeknownst to one another, they struggled in Israel as Christians or as converts. Because they were not born Jewish, they were denied full government benefits and pensions. Many lived in poverty. Some were persecuted. Amfian Gerasimov, the Latvian postman who helped Jews in the Riga ghetto, converted to Judaism although he still believed in Jesus Christ. In 1976 he and his son moved to Israel to be with the people to whom, even as a Sabbath Observer, he had felt a strong connection. Fellow congregants did not accept Gerasimov's combined Jewish and Christian faith. Neighbors ostracized him, and one day after Sabbath services a group of children threw stones at him. Eventually Gerasimov found a synagogue that shared his faith, and before he died he felt that he had at last come home.

In 1985, *Kolbotek,* an Israeli television program similar to *60 Minutes,* documented the plight of the rescuers living in Israel. The program shocked the country. The government hastily voted rescuers a special stipend. A social support network where rescuers could meet, tour the country, get recognition, give lectures, and talk with one another was developed. Forty years after the fact, rescuers are honored in their adopted land.

Among all the groups, concerned professionals had the most seamless transition from rescuer to civilian life. Diplomats were a special case. Those who were social workers, nurses, doctors, teachers, and psychologists during the war continued to be the same afterward. Their professional identities, of which their rescuer self was a part, remained intact. War had not altered their professional outlook. They continued to help people in their usual way. Jopie D., the Dutch psychoanalyst who hired a Jew as a maid and then turned her out at war's end, maintained her professional distance with her charge and with her patients. On one occasion after the war, circumstance threw them together, but the survivor did not feel or express any gratitude. There was no need, as Jopie D. never allowed a personal relationship to develop.

Diplomats were the tragic exceptions to concerned professionals' generally smooth entry into postwar life. Sempo Sugihara and Aristides de Sousa Mendes were drummed out of diplomatic service for disobeying orders and ostracized by their countrymen. Raoul Wallenberg was arrested by the Russian liberators as a spy and thrown into jail. He was never heard from again.

While the lack of a personal relationship with their charges generally did not affect concerned professionals, it did make it more difficult for a few network rescuers such as Danish rescuer Svend Aage Holm-Sorensen to integrate their rescuer self into their postwar lives. As a key organizer of the Danish resistance, Holm-Sorensen never knew the Jews he was instrumental in saving. During the war a one-on-one relationship was not necessary or even desirable. What was important and critical for Holm-Sorensen and most other network rescuers was knowing that they were not alone in what they believed in or what they felt. There were others like them who hated the Nazis as much as they did and were willing to risk their lives and the lives of their families to defeat the Nazis.

After the war, the fortunate members of networks who knew others in their group were able to help heal themselves by reminiscing and confronting the past with others. Sharing their past with those who had undergone similar experiences was significant for the process of healing painful memories and calming fears. They no longer felt so neurotic for feeling ashamed for what their country did, or guilty for not doing more themselves. By talking about what they had kept hidden, network rescuers strengthened their acceptance of all that had happened. Their rescuer selves were validated and, in such a setting, became part of a collective consciousness.

For others, no such postwar conversation was possible. They did not know the other network members well enough to know how to reach them. The camaraderie engendered by facing a common danger dissipated, and friends drifted away. Holm-Sorensen emerged from his imprisonment in several concentration camps a nervous wreck, a victim of post-traumatic stress disorder. Of course, this diagnosis of his condition was not made at the time; he had to recover on his own while living among the Danes who had denounced him to the Gestapo.

Most network rescuers continued to be politically active. The same political instincts that made them oppose Hitler compelled them to fight other politically oppressive parties. In Czechoslovakia and other Eastern European countries, underground networks formed around opposition to the new regimes. Network members in other countries found other causes such as nuclear disarmament and world hunger. Anje Roos Geerling demonstrated against the Vietnam War and protested nuclear armament. In addition, she carries on a correspondence with and sends money to a foster child in Kenya and another in Honduras.

Of all the rescuers with whom I spoke, child rescuers seemed to have the most difficulty integrating their rescuer selves and their war experiences into their current lives. Most were *not* too young to understand the risks they ran in harboring Jews and so were terrified of being caught. Yet their sacrifices for and contribution to the family's rescue effort were rarely mentioned. Some parents deliberately ignored their children's help because to acknowledge their role meant admitting a reckless disregard for the safety of their own children. Others felt guilty when their children awoke with nightmares.

The habit of secrecy they developed during the war continued, hindering them from engaging in intimate relationships in adolescence and preventing most children from bringing the subject up with their parents. For some children the whole subject was too emotionally charged to talk about directly. Like Esther Warmerdam, many child rescuers were proud of their parents' altruism and at the same time appalled at how cavalierly their parents risked their lives for people they did not even know.

Eventually most child rescuers come to accept what their parents did and why the parents felt that they had to sacrifice their own children's safety. It is easier to understand this behavior if the child's contribution is acknowledged in some way by a family member, a survivor, or an organization. When I interviewed Jerzy Niemiec, one of the sons whom Maria Niemiec abandoned in her dash to a safer city with Terry, I was astonished not to hear him express any jealousy or anger regarding his mother's behavior. Of course, when I interviewed him, the event had taken place more than forty years earlier, and the boy was now an English professor in Poland. Whatever terror that time held for Niemiec had long since been suppressed, and he delights in Terry's survival, in which he played a role. A year earlier, Terry had come with her child to Poland to visit the Niemiec family. When I spoke with Jerzy Niemiec he was returning the visit—his first to the United States.

A surprising number of child rescuers were able to successfully integrate their rescuing past into their present lives. Gratified by their experience of saving lives, many entered service professions. Nelly Trocmé became a teacher. Annie P. worked as a paramedic. Pania Wywiad became a special education teacher for the chronically ill and disabled, while Helena Podgórska and others became doctors. But other child rescuers needed help coming to terms with their past. As other rescuers discovered, talking about their experiences with people who underwent similar experiences—be it other child rescuers or family members—helped heal their emotional wounds. Many child rescuers were not aware that some of their current fears of intimacy, or their proclivity for secrecy, were a reaction to events during the war years.

Through the existence of the Jewish Foundation for Christian Rescuers and interviews that have been conducted with rescuers, these individuals have been able to confront their past and find new meaning in their present. They are writing, lecturing, and serving as much-needed moral role models for the younger generation. All of this has been enormously gratifying to see. But how do the rescuers themselves feel? After being put to the test, was the inner satisfaction of

preserving their personal integrity and opposing a malevolent authority worth the anguish? In short, was the effort worth it?

Among others, Danish rescuer Svend Aage Holm-Sorensen has
asked himself these same questions. This, he told me, is his answer:

A few years ago, I was on a train on the way to an old-boys golf
tournament in Denmark when the train stopped in the university town of Roskilde. Three girls, sixteen or seventeen years of
age, boarded and about five minutes later one of them asked me
whether my name was Holm-Sorensen! I was startled until I
realized she had seen my name tag on the golf bag. But then I
really got a shock.

"Are you the one who was in German prisons and KZ [con-
centration] camps?" she asked.

I began to shake and feel cold and hot at the same time.
"Yes," I said. "But what do you know about that? And from
where?"

Then all three girls began telling me things that they knew,
things that I have never been able to tell my family. They said
they had to write about me in school and would I please tell
them something about that time. Before we reached my destination, I did tell them a few things, but I was glad, very glad to get
off that train.

Afterward, when I could collect myself, I came to think that if
some young people today are *that* interested in what happened
from 1940 to 1945, then it was time for me to write my story.
Time, at last, to tell my sons how love, belief, and will can help a
human being get through pain and evil times, where each minute
is an hour, each day a month, each month a year. Where you're
lucky just to be able to tell yourself that you've made it through
another day.

Above all, I want my sons—and young people, like those girls
on the train—to know that despite everything that happened in
the KZs what I did during the German occupation of Denmark,
I would do it again.

I do not say this lightly. I've asked myself many times whether
my work in the resistance was worth losing my health, my marriage, and ten years of my life, which is what it took before I

could get hold of my nerves, get my energy back, and give myself completely to my work. Was it worth those endless nights for years after the war, waking up from terrible nightmares, fighting, screaming, and soaking wet? . . . Was everything I did in the resistance *really* worth everything I went through in the KZs, and would I do it again?

My answer is still the same: Yes. Because without freedom, life is *nothing*. *Never, never,* do I want to live—or have those I love live—in hate, fear, and suppression. And *yes, yes,* I would do it again. And again and again.

· 16 ·

MYTH, REALITY,
AND MEMORY

"The memory of the righteous
is a blessing."

—Proverbs 10:7

THE FRENCH WRITER and philosopher Voltaire said, "History is mythology re-created by each generation." In the belated move to honor rescuers and acknowledge their moral courage through public memorials, myth and reality collide. This collision is important, for it is through public memorials that a nation conveys to its citizens the character and values it most cherishes. Until very recently, most World War II memorials, statues, gardens, and plaques honored those people whose deeds cast the national character in a patriotic and heroic light. The medals and ceremonies recognized military war heroes, not the milkman who left extra bottles of milk for a family sheltering Jews. In building a new, postwar national identity, heroes needed to be larger than life and so military leaders such as Charles de Gaulle and those active in armed resistance were glorified. In France, everyone eagerly claimed to belong to the *maquis,* or resistance. No one owned up to supporting the collaborationist Vichy government. In Denmark, every citizen claimed to have taken part in the remarkable boat rescue that saved the lives of 7,500 Danish Jews. No one admitted to having been one of the thousands of Nazi sympathizers.

In Holland, myth has it that the valiant Dutch hid Jews, formed underground networks, and successfully resisted Nazi occupation. In fact, denunciations were rampant and in the end the vast majority of Dutch Jews perished.[1]

However, saving the lives of Jews or rescuing Jewish children from deportation and certain death was not considered material for glory. This suited most rescuers, who felt that what they had done was a private matter. The very idea of anyone paying tribute to them for an action that they considered a natural response made them uncomfortable. As time went on, they shared their experiences with researchers because they knew they were part of a large behavioral study on altruism and they wanted to help. The spotlight was not solely on them. Danish rescuer Harry LaFontaine, who was a member of the Danish resistance and did take part in the boat rescue, took pains to remind me of the network's standard policy:

> Immediately after the war in 1945, all the commanders agreed that all the blame and all the credit would be accepted as a group. We wouldn't single out any specific person. We had, of course, some people that started writing some books after. But anytime anyone needed to verify something, he would meet the solid Danish front of the Freedom Council that would say, "Yes, we did the sabotage, but who specifically did it, we're not going to release."

To keep the historical record as accurate as they could, Danish resistance workers in 1948 established a museum in Copenhagen— the first one of its kind—and filled it with wartime exhibits such as illegal printing presses, homemade weapons, forged documents—even two cells ripped from the Danish prison. Resistance workers figured that if people saw it, the actual stones and bars as well as the writing and other artifacts, no one could deny the reality of what happened.

But the dispute over whether the Holocaust really happened was yet in the future. The more immediate event was the 1961 trial of Adolf Eichmann in Jerusalem. The Eichmann trial was a watershed moment in history. The chillingly dispassionate eyewitness accounts of Nazi inhumanity and sadism were broadcast worldwide. (Eich-mann himself described an inspection visit he paid near Minsk to *Einsatzgruppen* soldiers, who were busily at work shooting Jews. "I can still see a woman with a child," Eichmann told the court. "She was shot and then the baby in her arms. His brains splattered all around, also over my leather coat."[2]) As the prosecutors methodically presented evidence and painstakingly built their case, it was no longer possible to deny the past. Attention was riveted on the victims of these atrocities and the architects of it. At last, survivors could tell their story and people listened.

The brutal testimony of the Eichmann trial set off an urgent quest for evidence of human kindness during the war. People around the world needed to feel that the heart of man was not unrelievedly black. Rescuers were discovered. Oskar Schindler, who was visiting Israel at the time of the trial, was greeted at the airport by hundreds of his survivors and their families, and the written testimony of German rescuer Hermann Graebe was read at the trial.[3] With the Eichmann trial, the facts of history emerged. By facing past evil, the world was finally in a position also to acknowledge the heretofore invisible hero-ism and decency of rescuers. At the Eichmann trial, Gideon Hausner, Israel's Supreme Court Justice, paid this tribute to those citizens who risked their lives to save Jews:

> In the darkness that engulfed Europe there were some shining lights. The Jewish people have a long memory; it will never forget its benefactors as it will not forget its foes. Their names [will] be engraved in our memory forever, as we still [bear] in thankful memory the name of Cyrus of Persia, who enabled the exiles to return to the promised land.[4]

Hausner's tribute was not the first to rescuers or even the first Israeli acknowledgment of the tremendous debt of gratitude owed. In 1953, survivors had planted a forest in northern Israel to honor Dutch school principal Joop Westerweel. In 1957, the United States first publicly honored a rescuer. The Anti-Defamation League of B'nai B'rith dedicated a bronze plaque in New York City to commemorate the "Christian heroes who helped their Jewish brethren escape Nazi terror." The plaque was unveiled by Marie Hélène Lefaucheux, a French delegate to the United Nations and member of the French resistance who had helped Jesuit Father Pierre Chaillet save hundreds of Jewish children.[5]

Still, rescuers were reluctant heroes. They were not accustomed to speaking from a pedestal. While they realized that some consider what they did during the war notable, even noble, they were leery of those who would hold them up as moral exemplars. They were, after all, just human beings. Many rescuers lost their temper, acted petty, and sometimes said a thoughtless or unkind thing or two. During the war, they did only what needed to be done.

In the late 1970s, neo-Nazi extremists began asserting that the Holocaust was a Zionist hoax. Radical fringe groups claimed that the Holocaust was a figment of a fevered Jewish imagination. The gas ovens, the murders, the mass executions did not really happen. It was all a Zionist plot to garner world sympathy and smooth the way for the Israeli state. These allegations, preposterous as they were, were given more credence than anyone thought possible. Clearly, for some people it was easier to believe in a hoax than to come to terms with evidence of such evil. This movement propelled rescuers to come forward. They began to appreciate that unless they spoke out and told their stories, the reality of what happened would get lost and history would be misrepresented, in the guise of "revisionism" by antisemites. In the United States, Irene Gut Opdyke, after years of silence, felt a moral responsibility to speak up and educate young people, in part as a response to receiving revisionist mail at her home in California. In Canada in 1985, the trial of publisher Ernst Zundel galvanized Esther Warmerdam into action. Zundel was charged with causing racial hatred by knowingly passing out false information by distributing a pamphlet entitled *Did Six Million Really Die?* Warmerdam, the Dutch child rescuer who helped her parents shelter more than 200 Jewish children, had lived in silence about her activities. She had kept her war experiences a secret from her children, determined to leave all that behind her when she left Holland for marriage and a new life in Woodstock, Ontario. ("You put something like that in the back of

your mind, and you want to forget and pretend it never happened,"
she said.) But the trial and publicity surrounding Zundel's pamphlet
changed all that. Warmerdam was enraged by the very idea that the
Holocaust itself was on trial. That this terrifying historical reality was
in question at all was beyond belief to her. If the Holocaust never
took place, she angrily told a reporter for the Toronto *Star*, then she
for one would like to know the whereabouts of the parents of the
children she and her family hid during the war. "Why didn't Max's
parents come back? Elly's family? Yetty's parents? They must have all
gone somewhere. Let Zundel look Max, Elly, and Yetty in their eyes.
Let him see those who lost everything."[6]

Warmerdam's anger was tempered by her ingrained sense of
caution, a residue from the rescuer self of her war days. She allowed
herself to be quoted in the newspaper, but, fearing neo-Nazi reprisals,
used her maiden name. I found her when a friend sent me the Toronto *Star* article. I telephoned the reporter of the piece, who in turn
called her for permission to pass along her real name to me. Like Irene
Gut Opdyke, Warmerdam has rededicated her life to ensuring that
her Holocaust story becomes part of the historical mixture of myth
and reality. As is true of other rescuers, Gut Opdyke and Warmerdam
are powerful teachers and inspirational examples. By simply recount-
ing their experiences, they shake audiences out of their indifference to
evil and motivate them to take action.

California rabbi Harold Schulweis has spent his life seeing to it
that the public remembers the acts of the rescuers. He was the prime
mover behind the movement to find rescuers, support them, and
recognize them publicly. In this latter effort, he and the organization
he envisioned, the Jewish Foundation for Christian Rescuers, have
prompted others to memorialize the rescuers in books, films, photography exhibits, cantatas, children's stories, and ceremonies.[7] Although
the foundation's primary goal is to financially assist the rescuers in
their waning years, a corollary of its work is the education of future
generations.[8] The deeds of rescuers stand as much-needed models of
moral behavior. Every child knows the name of Hitler, but how many
know the name of Raoul Wallenberg? As recently as 1991, when
Mishi Harman, an eight-year-old Israeli boy, wanted to research the

life of Wallenberg for a school project, he found there was not one book in Hebrew on Wallenberg. If stories of larger-than-life figures such as Wallenberg are not translated into other languages, what chance do the stories of commonplace goodness have of being passed down from one generation to another? These will be lost in time, and will not be part of history.[9]

With this question in mind, Israeli Prime Minister Ben-Gurion proposed the establishment of Yad Vashem. The purpose was to make visible the anonymous and the hidden and to fulfill the biblical injunction "to vindicate the righteous by rewarding them for their righteousness" (Kings 8:32). The Commission of Righteous Among the Nations of the World at Yad Vashem has been tireless in its efforts to find these non-Jewish saviors. They have gathered documents, sifted through reams of testimony, and tracked down the rescuers so that they might be honored and their stories included as a vital part of Jewish history. And so they are. In January 1987, Israel's parliament, the Knesset, invited the rescuers who live in Israel to be honored guests at a regular session. In a gesture unprecedented in Israeli parliamentary history, the members of the Knesset stood in honor of these invited guests who had risked their lives to save Jews during the Holocaust.

Public recognition of rescuers' deeds, recalling as it does painful memories of those not saved and the shameful behavior of others, inevitably turns into emotionally charged events that lack the cool historical perspective found in other ceremonies. In 1990, Ely Ben-Gal, a historian at the Diaspora Museum in Tel Aviv who himself was rescued in Le Chambon, spoke to a historians' conference there and acknowledged that survivors' wounds may be too raw for them to achieve the historical objectivity necessary to please everyone:

> Some of you have the feeling that we either do too much or too little. A little while ago, a local merchant told my father he had sheltered a young Jewish girl, and he added, "She was like my daughter . . . but I never had any news of her." On the other hand, the Council of Reform Churches wrote to Yad Vashem that its medal risks "calling into question the profound sense of

spontaneous action, as if good was the exception and villainy the norm."

We ask you to understand that if we sometimes do too much and at other times not enough, it is because we experienced an internal wound which for this generation, at least, will not heal easily. . . . Perhaps now we can accept in a certain way that we were chosen: not God's chosen people, but the exact opposite, the people selected to be backed against the wall. So perhaps it is because of that we need—for ourselves, and using you as inter-mediary—to have a ceremony and a medal. We need it to be able to say to our children that they must not lose faith in humanity, that in our worst moments of abjection, we were not alone.[10]

Formal recognition of rescuers' deeds serves other purposes and constituencies as well. Children of rescuers understood the urgency and the need to do this, but it is one thing to understand, on an intellectual level, the importance of saving lives, and another to come to terms with the emotional price that rescue exacted. Many children of rescuers felt abandoned. The lives of rescuers and of their families were in disarray; rescuers were put in jeopardy in order to help people who were not related to them in any way. Public honors and recognition of their parents as moral exemplars have helped soothe the anger and hurt. Such recognition has given the children of rescuers the comfort of knowing that their parents' sacrifice and their own suffering made a difference.

The tales of rescuers saving Jews are not only about evil against good; they illustrate the complexities inherent in making moral decisions. These stories involve real concerns: dealing with conflicting responsibilities, coping with peer pressures, handling social ostracism, and making choices and living with the consequences of them.

Memorials ensure that the stories of rescuers will be told from one generation to the next. Without a concerted effort, the stories of these Righteous Among the Nations of the World will be lost. In the countries of the former Soviet Union, for example, students learn about World War II—"the Great Patriotic War"—in some detail. But these former Soviet citizens neglect to mention the two million Polish Jews who were killed in Russian territories. Needless to say, the exploits of people who saved some of these nonexistent beings are also ignored.[11]

Other countries are reluctant to acknowledge the contributions of rescuers. Honoring the exceptional few throws an unwelcome spotlight on the majority who did nothing or who collaborated with the Nazis. No one wants to dig up the shame and guilt of the past.

In Germany and Austria, even those who fought against the Nazis, and who saved approximately 7,000 Jews from among the 240,000 slated for extermination, feel that nothing can expiate the enormity of the crime. A memorial to those few who swam against the nationalistic tide would only serve as a shameful reminder that 90 percent of the Jewish population in those countries was in fact annihilated.[12] Austria has solved this problem of collective guilt by avoiding the subject altogether. No memorial of any kind acknowledges the persecution of the Jews, much less the few who risked their lives to save them.

In those countries, such as Belgium and Italy, where the rescues were carried out in large measure anonymously, these deeds remain unheralded. In Italy, an astounding 80 percent of the Jewish population was saved, but mostly by anonymous soldiers or nameless network workers. There is no one person to thank. In Belgium, many of the rescues were carried out by networks of Jews working with non-Jews. (It is not Yad Vashem's mandate to acknowledge the rescue of Jews by other Jews or to honor groups.) Moreover, Belgium is not a country that boasts a lot of national memorials, as it has never forged a uniform national character. It is a nation that is an amalgam of three cultures, Flemish, German, and French. The occasional friction that results from this ethnic diversity prevents the emergence of a single ethnic national character, and thus a lack of national Holocaust memorials. (However, in southern Belgium on the wall of the Reine Elizabeth Castle in Jamoigne, a plaque was recently installed to commemorate the rescue of eighty-three Jewish children.)

There are other reasons why nations are not eager to celebrate rescuers. In many cases, rescuers were in defiance of government regulations or direct orders. In any other circumstances they would be considered traitors. In Nazi Germany the deeds of such citizens as Oskar Schindler or Gitta Dubro Bauer were in fact treasonous. The most amazing instance of government defiance did not happen in Germany, but in Japan. Consul Sempo Sugihara saved thousands of lives by ignoring his government's instructions. Sugihara came from a culture that prized conformity and consensus. He was trained in a profession that valued following orders precisely and executing them intelligently and efficiently. Yet this man broke free of these restraints in order to follow his conscience. In 1992 in his hometown of Yaotsu, Japan, on a tranquil plateau along a mountain ridge, the "Hill of Humanity" was dedicated to Sempo Sugihara. This monument to a disobedient hometown son is extraordinary in its beauty and in its celebration of stubborn independence. Sugihara's memorial is a semi-circle of 160 different-size ceramic pipes. Surrounded by flowers, shrubs, and small trees, the pipes represent individual countries of the world. By computer command, the pipes can produce water, lights, and music. Rabbi Zerah Warhaftig, former Israeli Religious Affairs Minister, who received one of the first transit visas issued by Sugihara, planted one of the trees that encircle this exquisite monument.[13]

Despite national objections and obstacles, a number of memorials of one sort or another have been erected to honor rescuers. While they stand as examples of moral courage, they are also a testimony to Jews and Gentiles alike who were determined that rescuers' deeds be valued and honored. The rescue of the Jews of Denmark has been commemorated in several public spaces, including a neighborhood in Jerusalem named Denmark Square, where a skeletal boat sculpture rests. The actual hull of one of the rescue boats was transported to the port city of Haifa near the gate of Ha'aliyah, the reception camp for new immigrants in 1948. Another Danish rescue boat is displayed in the United States Holocaust Memorial Museum in Washington, D.C.

The April 1993 opening of the United States Holocaust Memorial Museum allowed government officials and American citizens to pay a long-overdue tribute to rescuers. Stefania Podgórska Burzminska sat with President and Mrs. Clinton and told an audience of thousands about her rescue of Joseph Diamant Burzminski and twelve other Jews. Later, in a touching moment in front of that same audience, Joseph himself thanked her for saving his life and that of his brother and friends.

When I spoke with Stefania several weeks later, she was looking at the photographs that President Clinton had sent her and was recalling the warm reception she received. Perhaps these photographs will help ease the darker memories of the terror of that time that she says yet haunt her. Perhaps, too, the inclusion of her name along with those of other rescuers, their photographs, and brief descriptions of their exploits that occupy a portion of this new museum will allow her to integrate her past with pride in herself. The exhibit, entitled "Courage to Rescue," highlights rescuers by country, featuring countries such as Denmark, Italy, and Bulgaria which saved Jews in large numbers. Memorabilia and photographs of Wallenberg's operation in Hungary and of the villagers of Le Chambon-sur-Lignon tell the stories of these heroic efforts.

In large measure, the United States Holocaust Memorial Museum owes its existence to the determination of Holocaust survivors and the postwar generation they have inspired. Unlike the early decades after liberation when survivors busied themselves with attempts to return to normal life, today they, and people of the next generation, feel it is their mission to make sure rescuers' stories do not die with them.[14] Documentary filmmakers Pierre Sauvage (*Weapons of the Spirit*, his story of being hidden as a child by the townsfolk of Le Chambon-sur-Lignon in the context of France under the Nazi occupation), Myriam Abramowicz and Esther Hoffenberg (*As If It Were Yesterday* [*Comme Si C'Etait Hier*], the story of the rescue of the Jews in Belgium), Sam Elfert and Arnold Foster (*Avenue of the Just*, interviews with rescuers and the Jews they saved, including Mela and Alex Roslan), Katherine Smalley (*So Many Miracles*, Zofia Banya's rescue of the Rubineks), Sy Rotter (*The Other Side of Faith*, the story of Stefania Podgórska Burzminska, and *Żegota: A Time to Remember*, a story about the rescuing efforts of a section of the Polish Home Army), and Robert Gardner (*The Courage to Care*, interviews with a number of rescuers) are just a few of those who have felt compelled to pay tribute and remember. The mission to tell the stories of rescuers extends to other art forms as well. Civic acknowledgments have come in the form of paintings, performance art, gardens, plaques, and statues. The James A. Michener Arts Center of Bucks County, Doylestown, Pennsylvania, boasts a George R. Anthonisen statue that depicts a rescuer's moment of choice. A mother and son are confronted with a refugee girl and her father, who look on beseechingly.

Jerusalem's Yad Vashem, where thousands of trees are planted in honor of an individual, family, or group who risked their lives to save Jews, has inspired other communities to grow gardens in their honor. Delaware, Chicago, and Warsaw all have their versions of Yad Vashem's tree-lined Avenue of the Righteous. In Delaware, the rescuers' garden was the inspiration of Halina Wind Preston, one of those who survived the war by hiding in the sewers of Lvov with the help of two sewer workers. Preston, who spent thirteen months of her life in dank darkness, spent the rest of her life as an educator shedding light on that period of history. In Warsaw, a tree of common memory bears the inscription: "To the common [*meshutaf*] memory of Polish Jews murdered at the hands of the Germans between the years 1939 and 1945 and to the Poles who died extending aid to the Jews."

This inscription is a rare example of an Eastern European country's acknowledgment of rescuers' deeds. (Another notable exception is the statue of Raoul Wallenberg that stands in a park on the outskirts of Budapest, Hungary.[15]) While most major Eastern European cities created memorials on the sites of their ghettos and concentration camps, the bravery of those who defied their regimes and saved Jews is not acknowledged in the same general and public way. As was the case with political leaders in Western countries, Communist government and party officials were not eager to honor people who defied authority. But there were other factors at work. In Poland, even the efforts of the Żegota, which among its other resistance activities rescued thousands of Jews, were purposefully overlooked. Many of those in the Żegota were Christians, and the postwar Communist government of Poland, along with many other Communist regimes, was interested in suppressing religion, not elevating it.

In some instances, individuals have made up for governmental indifference or oversight. In Kassel, Germany, a group of thirty-two high school students researched the life of Wilhelm Hamman, a schoolteacher imprisoned at the Buchenwald concentration camp by the Nazis for being a Communist. The German high school students, who were between fourteen and fifteen years of age when they undertook this research project, discovered that Hamman was responsible for saving the lives of 158 Jewish children and youths imprisoned in Buchenwald's cellblock #8. Amazed at their discovery, the students believed Hamman deserved Yad Vashem honors and went about finding those whom he had saved and urging them to write their testimony. In the early 1980s, due to these students' efforts and the book they published based on their research, Wilhelm Hamman received posthumous recognition by Yad Vashem.

In the United States, other individuals were determined not to forget the moral courage of rescuers. New Yorkers Frank and Maria Morgens, who passed themselves off as Polish Aryans during the war, vowed that if they should survive they would help the Poles who risked their lives to save them and others. They have made good on their promise. Throughout the years, the Morgens kept in contact with their rescuer, sending her letters, packages, money whenever they could, and bringing her to the United States several times, starting with their first reunion in June 1961.[16] In 1966, after the Morgens read a newspaper article that reported on a ceremony held at the Israeli Embassy in Warsaw that honored 12 Polish rescuers, they sent each rescuer a Christmas food package. Through thank-you letters, the Morgens got to know these rescuers, and in May of 1967 Frank Morgens traveled to Warsaw to meet them. He heard their stories, saw their needs, and began what would be a lifelong commitment to send eleven of them a small monthly stipend.[17]

Harvey Sarner, a retired Chicago attorney, is another remarkable individual who has devoted his time and his financial resources to ensuring that rescuers receive their proper place in history. In 1989, while researching a book, Sarner became aware of the fact that although the vast majority of rescuers recognized at Yad Vashem were from Eastern Europe, few trees had actually been planted in their honor. Since the Six-Day War in 1967, when Eastern European nations broke off diplomatic relations, Eastern European rescuers had not had the opportunity or the money to travel to Jerusalem for a tree-planting ceremony. Sarner set out to correct this. Using Yad Vashem's files, Sarner tracked down Eastern European rescuers and, at his own expense, escorted them to Israel for public recognition. On one occasion, he brought over a woman whose husband had left her because of her insistence that they save a Jewish baby. She went on to hide seven other Jews and their families. On her Sarner-sponsored trip to Israel, she complained bitterly that the Jews she saved had not bothered to come and see her, or even to write back, for that matter. As it turned out, her letter to them telling about her Israeli trip was the first time she had written to them in forty years. She wrote them at their old addresses, naïvely assuming that their names and places of residence had not changed in all that time.

Sarner's daughter had an idea as to how the survivors might be located on such short notice. She called Israel's two main radio stations and told them the story of this woman and those she rescued. The stations broadcast the rescue story and asked those having any information on the whereabouts of the survivors to call. In short order, the radio stations were swamped with callers. They did not have any information to give, but nevertheless wanted to show their gratitude by inviting the rescuer to stay with them for the remainder of her trip. Finally, the rescuer did hear from one of those whom she rescued. He had been in a grocery store when the grocer, who was listening to the radio, asked him if one of the survivors' names being broadcast was not his old name.

The reunion was but one among many that was arranged through Harvey Sarner's efforts. This extraordinary dedicated man, who is not himself a Holocaust survivor, has arranged for some 400 rescuers to be honored in Israel, reuniting many of them for the first time since the end of the war with those they rescued.

The tree plantings, sculptures, films, memoirs, and the gardens that honor rescuers' deeds serve as a reminder. But if they force an onlooker only to think of the valor of yesterday, these reminders have failed to get their message across. Contemplating the actions of rescuers should also compel every person to examine what he or she is doing in his or her own life to help those in need or to fight for tolerance among people. The price for such help is not death, as it was in wartime Europe, but the inconvenience of setting aside time in order to look out for someone else's interests.

Helping behavior is learned, and the gardens, statues, and films are ways to keep rescuers' stories vibrant and relevant for today. They are stories that show youngsters how, in the not so distant past, people came to other people's aid. These are lessons children appreciate. These are adults who did not lecture or talk about helping. They acted. They said yes and opened their hearts. Hannah Senesh, a Hungarian-born poet, emissary from Palestine who was tortured to death by the Nazis for attempting to free other Jews by parachuting behind enemy lines, described best the essential importance of rescuers. It is a fitting final memorial to them. While these words appear in Senesh's diary, they could have been written about the Righteous Among the Nations of the World:

There are stars whose radiance is visible on earth though they have long been extinct. There are people whose brilliance continues to light the world though they are no longer among the living. These lights are particularly bright when the night is dark. They light the way for Mankind.[18]

EPILOGUE

FIFTY YEARS AGO, the wholesale slaughter of millions of people was unthinkable. It took the brutal inventiveness of Nazi Germany with its gas chambers, crematoriums, and methodical killing squads to show the modern world that when it comes to racial hatred, no cruelty is beyond the realm of possibility. In the final analysis, this was Hitler's most enduring and terrible legacy: after the Holocaust, no inhumanity is beyond imagining, no barbarity is inconceivable.

In the recent past, the targets of hatred have been Jews, Gypsies, homosexuals, Jehovah's Witnesses, and Freemasons, among others. Today they are joined by Muslims, Croats, Turks, and Arabs. As I write, Serbs, playing out ancient hatreds, are slaughtering Bosnian Muslims and Croats. Following orders of their commanders, Serbian soldiers are committing mass murder, and are routinely raping Muslim women in their unapologetic pursuit of "ethnic cleansing." That military commanders consider such actions to be legitimate weapons of warfare is proof of social psychologist Stanley Milgram's observation that the conflict between conscience and authority exists in the very nature of society and "would be with us even if Nazi Germany had never existed. To deal with the problem only as if it were a matter of history is to give it an illusory distance."[1]

Yet Hitler's war against the Jews left the modern world with more than just hardened cynicism. There were some people who rose above their circumstances and acted bravely, compassionately, and, above all, humanely. They too have left a legacy; one that is being carried on today. Similar to their World War II predecessors, today's rescuers are not larger-than-life heroes, but ordinary people who see inhumanity and feel a personal responsibility to address it.

No matter when or where rescue takes place, the pattern of rescuing is the same. Awareness of dehumanization sets the process in motion when the condition is seen to warrant intervention. Personality and the situation converge, to act or not to act, in response to the need to save a life. Time is often of the essence in extreme situations. The decision to risk one's life happens quickly, coming from an inner core that automatically calculates the chances of success. Once rescue begins, a new "rescuer self" develops to take necessary actions and maintain secrets and a façade of normalcy. The stage, actors, and props may be different in each case, but the dynamics of the human response are always the same.

Who are today's rescuers? Many, such as the Kuwaitis who risked their lives to harbor Westerners right before the outbreak of the Gulf War in 1991, are anonymous. They helped Westerners by moving them from house to house in *galabiyas* (Arab garb). Those who eventually escaped never knew their benefactors' names and only revealed their lifesaving acts of courage at the war's end. In other cases, such as that of KGB Captain Viktor Orekhov, political shifts render continued anonymity unnecessary.

I learned about Captain Orekhov from Natan Sharansky, the writer whose efforts to emigrate to Israel brought worldwide attention to the plight of Refuseniks.[2] Refusenik was a pre-*glasnost* word that was applied to Jews living in the Soviet Union who had applied to Soviet authorities for permission to emigrate. The Soviets refused to issue Refuseniks exit visas. Refuseniks routinely lost their jobs, had their phones tapped, their mail opened, and were subjected to harsh interrogations and frequent searches by the Soviet secret police (KGB). Some, such as Sharansky, were imprisoned for their activities. Nonetheless, this harassment did not stop Jews from repeatedly requesting permission to emigrate.

In 1976, when a new wave of KGB oppression was targeted against the Refuseniks, Orekhov decided he could no longer tolerate the suffering he was inflicting on others. He began to inform dissidents of planned KGB actions against them. According to Sharansky, he and the others originally thought Orekhov's information was a KGB trap. But the intelligence he supplied of future arrests and searches proved to be absolutely accurate. The warnings saved hundreds of Jews from interrogations and arrests. In March 1977, Sharansky was tipped off that a Jewish activist close to him was in fact a KGB informer and that Sharansky's own arrest was imminent.

Years later, when Sharansky was in prison, he learned the identity of his anonymous benefactor. Unfortunately, so did others. Orekhov was sentenced to eight years in a special prison for former KGB and police officers. In 1991, when he was released from prison, Orekhov told reporters why he felt duty-bound to help the Refuseniks: "I was afraid [that unless I acted] my children would be ashamed of me."

Orekhov's words echo the sentiments of rescuers past and present. The motivational drive behind acts of conscience and courage are the same for today's heroes as they were for Holocaust rescuers. I have found that all altruistic individuals share the same reasons: morality, a special affinity with the victims, professional concern, a network or community with a shared anti-Nazi ideology, or children who help parents or other adults.

When I suggested these motivational types to Jennifer Davis, the executive director of the Africa Fund, a New York-based lobbying and grass-roots organization devoted to fighting apartheid in South Africa, she agreed wholeheartedly. Davis, whose life was threatened in South Africa for harboring black and Afrikaner activists, said my findings matched her experience and those of her colleagues who are fighting apartheid.

In pointing out that motivations for altruistic actions fall into five general areas, I do not mean to imply that all situations within those categories are the same. I am not comparing the government of South Africa with Nazi Germany, nor am I suggesting that the South African authorities are engaging in the systematic annihilation of a race. However, the unrelenting discrimination against South African blacks has become a moral dilemma for those who are the voice of conscience in that society. The disgraceful treatment of blacks has motivated a few white South Africans to risk their lives to see apartheid policies end. What motivated them? These social activists are influenced by the same factors as those who risked their lives decades earlier to save Jews. There are those like Jennifer Davis who are motivated for moral reasons. Someone asked her for help and, like other rescuers in a different time and place, she said, "Of course." She hid fugitives and sheltered activists until her activities became so notorious that she became a liability to the cause. Still, her rescuer self continues. Her life is devoted to fighting for justice and equality for black people.

Others joined the fight out of religious conviction. In the mid-1970s, Father Michael Lapsley was a student at the University of Natal in Durban. He was also a chaplain at two black universities and one white one. From all his various pulpits, he denounced the government's killing of black children in the streets. Someone took exception to his position and planted a bomb in a parcel of religious magazines. The resulting explosion blew away Lapsley's eye and both his hands and shattered his eardrums. The explosion crippled Lapsley but did not damage his beliefs and commitment. Today he is still speaking out against South African racist policies and lobbying for justice for all of South Africa's citizens.

Other equally committed South African activists are motivated for different reasons. Some are fueled by friendship and an empathy with the victims of oppression. Involvement for others, such as epidemiologists Zina Stein and Marvin Sasso or attorney Joel Carlson, was a natural outgrowth of their professions. Carlson, who is the author of *No Neutral Ground,* a book about his experiences fighting apartheid, marshaled the legal defense for black activists in the 1950s and 1960s. For his efforts, his life was threatened and his house was bombed. Still others are enraged at the injustice of the government's treatment of blacks and have formed a network with those of the same mind to fight racism. And last, throughout it all, there are children whose parents enlist their help on behalf of their moral and just cause.

But it is not just motivational forces that bind past and present moral heroes together. The process of transformation from bystander to participant is exactly the same as well. An awareness of a victim's plight, empathy, and an enabling situation together lead to action. As with Holocaust rescuers, modern-day models of moral courage display a willingness to see what others choose not to notice. There is a determination, some would say a stubbornness, to pursue the truth no matter where it leads.

Nowhere is this awareness and determined clarity more apparent than in the story of Anje Elizabeth Rosmus, the determined German woman depicted in Michael Verhoeven's film *Nasty Girl,* who single-handedly forced the citizens of the small Bavarian town of Passau to confront their past and themselves.[3] In 1980, at the age of twenty, Rosmus won the top German prize for an essay on privacy and public freedom in European politics and history. Delighted with the acclaim, Rosmus decided the next year to enter an essay contest sponsored by the President of West Germany. Her subject was "An Example of Resistance and Persecution—Passau, 1933–1939."

She approached her task with complete confidence in the official town version of antifascist heroics, which had been told to Passau's postwar generation in West Germany. "I was just an ambitious schoolgirl," she recalled in the television documentary *The Girl and the City, or What Really Happened?* "I wanted to win a prize, and I thought that the former resistance fighters and their relatives would have a lot to tell me."

Almost immediately, Rosmus's research hit a huge stumbling block. She could not find any documents or information about the Jews who lived in the Passau area. Were there any data? Did all the Jews leave before the war? Local newspapers from that time carried no mention of them, and townspeople's recollections were frustratingly vague. Desperate for information and unwilling to change her topic despite the unease it evoked, she wrote to the Jewish Community Center in Munich requesting any information they might have concerning the fate of Passau's Jews. The Center's director told her that he had no information but suggested she place an announcement in

Aufbau, a German-language Jewish paper that is published in New York and has a worldwide circulation.

Replies soon began coming in, and from these Rosmus started to piece together a history far different from what she had been told. Passau's current mayor was not the resistance hero he claimed to be but a member in good standing in the Nazi Party. The local priest, the same one who had married Rosmus, was a Nazi. Letters from survivors such as Robert Klein, who had owned a department store in Passau, described a town that was virulently antisemitic. Jewish businesses were confiscated and, with the full cooperation of the locals, soldiers rounded up Passau's Jews and deported them. The activities of Rosmus's own grandmother—activities that had been completely unknown to Anje—were in sharp distinction to those of the rest of the townspeople. These activities, written up in the Passau newspapers during the war, consisted of sheltering political resisters and sneaking food to labor camp inmates.

In the letters Rosmus received from Passau Jews, she felt the pain of their shattered lives. She vowed not only to uncover the truth but to find some way to make amends for the past. She became a woman with a mission. Justice demanded that the town acknowledge its true past and hold those responsible for the deportation of the Jews accountable for their criminal acts. Despite threats on her life, a firebombing of her home, and the increasing impatience of a husband who began to regard her interest in Passau's past as obsessional, she pursued her mission. But it cost her dearly. Her marriage ended in divorce and the local university ousted her when she insisted on turning her essay topic into a thesis. (However, after a five-year fight, Rosmus managed to get reinstated as a student and obtained an official apology from the German government.) She has not won many friends. When I asked Anje Rosmus if she had any supporters among the faculty for her Passau research, her answer was frank and direct: "No. But I have two people who are not against me."

In her attempt to make amends for the past, Rosmus established what has now become a town tradition. Each year Rosmus invites a Passau survivor to return home for a visit as a guest of the town. (Robert Klein, the town's former department store owner, was Rosmus's first honored guest.) The reunion serves as a way to inform the younger generation of Germans about the Jewish culture that was destroyed.[4] The visit also serves as a convenient news item prompting media discussion about the need to respect and tolerate different cultures and religions and to express moral outrage against the current racism toward foreigners, Turks, Gypsies, and others.

Tolerance—indeed, acceptance—of difference is a lesson that is particularly needed these days, not only in Germany but in other countries as well. In Israel for example, the Arab-Israeli conflict has led many Israelis to see Arabs as an implacable enemy. Their worldview is a simplistic one of "us" versus "them." As Bella Freund came to realize, anyone who sees things differently risks being judged an enemy too.

Freund, forty-year-old ultra-Orthodox Jew and mother of eight, was on her way to an appointment in a Jerusalem shopping center one day in June 1991 when she heard a great commotion. She heard shouts of "Terrorists!" and "Arab!" and through the crowd saw a man pinned to the ground by a guard. As it turned out, Adnan al-Afandi, a twenty-one-year-old Muslim extremist had just stabbed and slightly wounded a thirteen-year-old Jewish boy. Freund heard shots and felt that "something terrible was going to happen." Before she registered what she was doing, Freund threw herself on top of the Arab to protect him from harm. The mob reviled her, beat her, and called her "an Arab-lover" and a traitor. Still, she remained where she was until the police could escort the man to safety.

As a result of her action, Freund found herself the center of press attention and a fierce debate. Wives of the members of the *haredim,* a strict Jewish sect, were supposed to be submissive, bear lots of children, and keep out of the public eye. Freund had not only gone against these stereotypical notions but had saved the life of a man bent on the destruction of Israel. Added to this, the mother of the stabbed boy, Hanna Shahar, upbraided Freund for protecting a would-be murderer.

The Israeli press had a field day. Freund was interviewed almost nonstop for several days. She, Hanna Shahar, and her son appeared on the Israeli television program *Confrontation Line* and debated the incident. "I am very, very angry at this woman, more at her than at the terrorist," Shahar told viewers. "I would like to ask her: If they had stabbed her son, and I had protected the terrorist, how would she have felt?"

Moderator Dan Raviv asked Shahar whether she would have preferred the mob to kill al-Afandi. "Since we don't have [capital punishment], the people have decided that the time has come for us to take the law into our own hands and lynch these people because we can't go on like this," she replied.[5]

Freund was both incredulous and saddened by her experience. "I protected someone because he was a human being and found that I had to explain myself," said this modern-day heroine.[6] A child of Holocaust survivors, Freund was raised to believe human life is sacred. She never thought anyone would consider that idea a debatable point.

THESE DAYS nothing seems to be simple or straightforward. New situations raise old questions. What is the most effective way to stop the mass killing in Bosnia? What action will guarantee that the murders will not eventually resume?

Such moral quandaries are not limited to wartime situations. In the United States, the AIDS virus has pitted health professionals against one another. Some refuse to treat patients who carry the deadly disease for fear they will also contract it. Dentists have been known to stop in the middle of treatment, announcing that it is not their policy to treat AIDS patients. A Milwaukee heart surgeon was quoted as saying, "I've got to think about myself; I've got to think about my family. That responsibility is greater than to the patient."[7]

Yet other physicians feel a moral commitment to help persons with AIDS. Their Hippocratic Oath requires it; their consciences demand it. As is the case with Holocaust rescuers, these medical professionals do not focus on the question of how they can risk their lives for others. Rather, their question is: Can I live with myself if I say no?

This tendency to see things differently than most others is one of the distinguishing characteristics of the rescuers. It is a way of looking at the world that takes for granted the belief that an individual can make a difference. In Bella Freund's case, that difference amounted to saving a life. In Marshall Meyer's case, that difference has amounted to much more.

Rabbi Marshall Meyer was the leader of the Buenos Aires Jewish community and a leader and thinker known in international religious circles. In the 1970s, he and others witnessed what would become known as Argentina's infamous "Dirty War." Under the guise of squelching guerrilla activity, Argentina's military leadership went on a rampage of terror. The military purged Argentine society of anyone it deemed suspect. Thousands were victims of arbitrary arrest, detention, and torture. Some critical of the regime's policies were dropped from helicopters. Others were arrested and never heard from again. From 1975 to 1979, some 9,000 Argentinians disappeared.

Rabbi Meyer refused to be intimidated. He hid dissenters in his apartment and arranged for hiding places for others. He established an underground railroad that provided escape routes for enemies of the regime. But most important, he spoke up. He ignored repeated death threats and voiced his outrage. His prominence as a well-known religious leader protected him, and gave him an opportunity to call the attention of the world to the barbaric conduct of the military. He recalls those days as fearful times:

> Someone would call and say, "We know when your son gets out of school. He won't make it home." I lived with that reality for years. . . . A person is known by his enemies as well as his friends. I could not live with myself if I did not denounce the Nazi fascist dictatorship in Argentina. When things got really bad, we contemplated leaving, but didn't. I felt I had a commitment to the thousands of people who depended on me as a voice.

In 1985, two years after the election of President Raúl Alfonsín, who was committed to democracy, Rabbi Meyer and his family resettled in New York. As rabbi of New York City's conservative B'Nai Jeshurun synagogue, his commitment to social justice continues undiminished. He conducts special Passover seders for AIDS patients and oversees his synagogue's shelter program for the homeless, among other things. Reflecting the same sentiments as that of the Polish nuns who sheltered Jewish children, Rabbi Meyer feels involvement in social causes is an integral part of belief. "Ritual is not enough," he maintains. "Authentic religious practice needs to include programs that [help alleviate] human suffering."

I WOULD ARGUE that simply teaching tolerance and compassion is not enough.[8] Values cannot exist in a vacuum. Without ways to get people involved and put those values to practical use, altruistic impulses dissipate into good intentions. Government, religious and social institutions need to create programs in which people can channel their altruistic energies. For example, the U.S. Department of Education might insist that a certain number of community service hours be required before a student could receive a high school or college degree. The Treasury Department might stimulate more corporate pro bono work by offering firms large tax incentives. With more imaginative encouragement, people could become what Robert Lifton has called "species selves," people who can reach beyond their own nationality and race and embrace others.[9] This may well be a utopian fantasy, a Holocaust researcher's pipe dream. Even so, it is appealing to contemplate a day when those seeking moral heroes need only look as far as their mirror.

NOTES

Introduction

1. Ironically enough, the slaughter of Illyan Jews occurred during Purim. This Jewish holiday commemorates the Jews' narrow escape from the Persians' plot to kill them all.

2. One of the groups I later formed with Dr. Henry Grunebaum became the subject for an award-winning documentary, *Breaking the silence: The generation after the Holocaust.* The group members agreed to be filmed about very painful, personal struggles because they too felt a moral responsibility to share what they had learned. One of the members of the group, Moshe Waldoks, author and comedian, expressed the challenge of the Holocaust for our generation: "What do we tell our children, the third generation?"

3. In 1963 Rabbi Harold Schulweis started the Institute of Righteous Acts, at the Judah Magnus Museum, Berkeley, California, and urged Perry London, a psychologist in his congregation, to interview some of those who risked their lives to save Jews in order to study their motivation. The result was London's pioneering work on altruism (1970). The Rescuers: Motivational hypotheses about Christians who saved Jews from Nazis. In J. Macauley and L. Berkowitz (Eds.), *Altruism and helping behavior* (pp. 241–50). New York: Academic Press. Another psychologist, Stanley Coopersmith, also interviewed rescuers but his untimely death has only left us remnants of his

findings included in an article written by Oliner, S. (1982, June). The need to recognize the heroes of the Nazi era. *The Reconstructionist,* 7–14.

1 · A Still Small Voice

1. Hallie, P. (1979). *Lest innocent blood be shed: The story of the village of Le Chambon and how goodness happened there* (p. 120). New York: Harper & Row.

2. Rittner, C., & Myers, S. (1986). *The courage to care* (p. 30). New York: New York University Press.

3. Gies, M. (1987). *Anne Frank remembered* (p. 11). New York: Simon & Schuster.

4. The presence of God was revealed to the prophet Elijah through "a still small voice," which is similar to the voice of conscience to which the rescuers responded.

> . . . And behold, the Lord passed by. There was a great and mighty wind; but the Lord was not in the wind. After wind—an earthquake—fire; but the Lord was not in the fire. And after the fire—a still small voice. When Elijah heard it . . . a voice addressed him: "Why are you here, Elijah?" He answered, "I am moved by zeal for the Lord, the God of Hosts." [1 Kings 19:11–14]

5. Lanzmann, C. (1985). *Shoah: An oral history of the Holocaust* (p. 25). New York: Pantheon.

6. Bierman, J. (1981). *The Righteous Gentile: The story of Raoul Wallenberg, missing hero of the Holocaust* (pp. 96–97). New York: Viking.

7. Ibid., p. 92.

8. Schulweis, H. (1962). *The bias against man.* Paper presented at the Rabbinical Assembly, Kiamisha, NY.

9. Surprisingly, the recognition of "righteous Gentiles" is recorded as early as the rabbinic period. In Tosefta Sanhedrin 13:2, the teaching of Rabbi Joshua B. Hanania that "the righteous of all nations shall have a share in the world to come," became an accepted doctrine of traditional Judaism. Of

course, Jewish attitudes toward the Gentile world were largely conditioned by their political, economic, and social treatment. Repeated persecutions and expulsions of Jews from Christian lands explain the predominantly negative Jewish perception of Gentiles prior to the Enlightenment. Nonetheless, even during times of oppression, the rabbis never disavowed their belief in the potential worth of individual Gentiles.

10. I learned about the history of the development of the Yad Vashem's Commission on Righteous Among the Nations of the World from personal conversations with Judge Moshe Bejski, who chairs the commission. Judge Bejski also discussed this at a conference, "Rescue Attempts During the Holocaust," at Yad Vashem, Jerusalem, 1977. See proceedings of the Second Yad Vashem International Historical Conference, April 1974, pp. 627–47. Mordecai Paldiel, director of the Department of Righteous Among the Nations, has also been very helpful.

11. In 1963, Yad Vashem honored its first rescuer, Ludwig Woerl, a German political prisoner in Auschwitz who helped Jewish inmates.

12. Because of lack of archival or personal testimony, little is directly known about helpers who were motivated by a profit. Sociologist Nechama Tec discusses such a group of Poles from recollections of the survivors. She found that paid rescuers offered shelter to more than one person for extended periods of time, but only 11 percent offered food or money to their charges. Tec concludes that paid rescuers were more eager to discontinue sheltering Jews by throwing them out, killing them, or denouncing them to the Germans. Of course, there were isolated cases of a rescuing relationship intensifying, and, when the money ran out, paid rescuers becoming altruistically motivated. For detailed cases, see Tec, N. (1986). *When light pierced the darkness: Christian rescue of Jews in Nazi-occupied Poland* (pp. 87–98). Oxford: Oxford University Press.

Non-Jews who took money to guide Jews fleeing to neutral countries did not always bring them to their destination and sometimes escaped with the profits. Cases have also been reported of helpers who betrayed their Jewish charges.

13. There are several ways to spell "antisemite" and "antisemitism." I am using the academic acceptable spelling.

2 · The War Against the Jews

1. Bauer, Y. (1978). *The Holocaust in historical perspective.* Seattle: University of Washington Press.

2. Dawidowicz, L. (1986). *The war against the Jews 1933–1945.* New York: Holt, Rinehart and Winston. Dawidowicz's view that Hitler's hatred of the Jews was his central and most compelling belief—one that dominated his actions even to the detriment of the military war—is one that I share.

3. Ibid., p. 75.

4. Baker, L. (1978). *Days of sorrow and pain: Leo Baeck and the Berlin Jews.* New York: Macmillan.

5. Gordon, S. (1984). *Hitler, Germans and the Jewish question.* Princeton: Princeton University Press.

6. Dawidowicz, p. 49.

7. Gilbert, M. (1982). *Atlas of the Holocaust* (p. 39). London: Michael Joseph.

8. Ringelblum, E. (1958). *Notes from the Warsaw ghetto: The journal of Emmanuel Ringelblum* (pp. 86–89). New York: Schocken Books.

9. Gilbert, p. 39.

10. De Jong, L. (1990). *The Netherlands and Nazi Germany* (p. 6). Cambridge: Harvard University Press.

11. Ibid., p. 17. Dawidowicz notes that the resettlement lie did not need to be elaborate. In the ghettos of Poland, where hunger ravaged its inmates, offers of bread and marmalade were enough to induce thousands to turn up voluntarily for "resettlement" (p. 305).

12. At the time of the German takeover, 90 percent of Belgium's 90,000 Jews were not Belgian citizens. Most of them were foreigners, and many of them (15,000) were German Jews. This was the result of the Belgian government's earlier efforts. Working in cooperation with other groups, the government had set up a relief fund to help Jewish refugees. Thus when the Germans occupied their country, resistance workers had a relief structure already in place. Out of the total Jewish population of 90,000, 20,000 were

hidden and 25,000 escaped to neighboring France (unfortunately only to be deported from there). Grass-roots rescue efforts saved 8,000 Jewish children and 20,000 adults. Lucien Steinberg, L. (1974). *Not as a lamb* (pp. 131–55). Hants, Eng.: Saxon House, D. C. Heath.

3 · Awareness

1. Von Staden, W. (1981). *Darkness over the valley* (p. 29). New Haven and New York: Ticknor & Fields. I also interviewed von Staden and several of the Jews who were helped by her and her mother. Because her actions took place late in the war, some view them more as self-preserving rather than altruistic.

2. Ibid., p. 62.

3. Ibid., p. 70.

4. Ibid., pp. 70–71.

5. Wendelgard von Staden confessed to New York *Times* reporter Nan Robertson that the shuffling sound that the concentration camp prisoners made coming to and from her family's farm to work is a sound that still haunts her dreams. New York *Times,* August 10, 1981, p. B4.

6. Keneally, T. (1982). *Schindler's List* (p. 123). New York: Simon & Schuster. Keneally interviewed dozens of people Schindler saved. While his book is written in a novelistic fashion, the incidents and facts it covers are for the most part accurate. Schindler, however, died well before the book was written. I personally have interviewed survivors from Schindler's List, among them Judge Moshe Bejski, who worked closely with Schindler to forge documents and is the chairman of the Commission on Righteous Among the Nations of the World of Yad Vashem.

7. Ibid., p. 125.

8. De Jong, p. 16.

9. Gies, p. 119.

10. For text of the letter, see Hilberg, R. (1961). *The destruction of the European Jews* (p. 262). Chicago: Quadrangle.

11. Harvard University social psychologist Herbert Kelman broke down the process of dehumanization even further. According to Kelman, the process

of perceiving another person as subhuman involves stripping him or her of two essential life supports: identity and community. Identity means viewing another person as an individual entitled to live his or her own life according to personal goals and values. Community is the perception of self and others as part of a social network of individuals who "care for each other." Empathy and compassion can't exist without granting another person these two life-sustaining values.

12. I got this account from my interview with Jan Karski.

13. Lanzmann, p. 34.

14. De Jong, p. 41.

15. The whole town of Nieuwlande became involved in the rescue effort. Arnold Douwes funneled Jews from Amsterdam to the farm of Seine Otten. From there, Otten found Jews hiding places in the community. In 1943, Johannes Post, one of the Nieuwlande organizers, was caught and killed.

16. Von Staden, p. 81.

17. Keneally, p. 133.

18. The Catholic priest who was Gitta Bauer's father confessor was also an outspoken critic of the Nazi regime. He often prayed for "our brothers of Abraham's descent." According to Bauer, the Nazis arrested him for his outspoken opposition to their policies. He died in a cattle car on a train that was headed for Dachau.

4 · Action

1. Cialdini, R. B., Schaller, M., Houlihan, D., Arps, K., Fultz, J., & Beaman, A. L. (1987). Empathy-based helping: Is it selflessly or selfishly motivated? *Journal of Personality and Social Psychology, 52,* 749–58.

2. Experiments by Bib Latané and Judith Rodin found the diffusion-of-responsibility effect somewhat diminished if those witnessing an emergency situation were friends rather than strangers. Latané, B. & Rodin, J. (1969). A lady in distress: Inhibiting effects of friends and strangers on bystander intervention. *Journal of Experimental Social Psychology, 5,* 189–202.

3. Midlarsky, E. (1984). Competence and helping: Notes toward a model. In E. Staub, D. Bar-Tal, J. Karylowski, & J. Reykowski (Eds.), *Development*

and maintenance of prosocial behavior: International perspectives on positive morality (pp. 291–308). New York: Plenum.

4. Oliner, S., & Oliner, P. (1987). *The altruistic personality.* New York: Free Press.

5. Lynch, J. G., Jr., & Cohen, J. L. (1978). The use of subjective expected utility theory as an aid to understanding variables that influence helping behaviors. *Journal of Personality and Social Psychology, 36,* 1138–51.

6. Lewin, K. (1952). Group decision and social change. In G. E. Swanson, T. M. Newcomb, & E. L. Hartley (Eds.), *Readings in social psychology.* New York: Henry Holt.

Ross, L., & Nisbett, R. E. (1991). *The person and the situation: Perspectives of social psychology.* New York: McGraw-Hill.

7. Klingemann, U., & Falter, J. W. (1993). Hilfe für Juden während des Holocaust: Sozialpsychologische merkmale der nichtjüdischen helfer und charakteristika der situation (in press).

8. In the Rescuer Project, more than half the sample reported that they helped because they were asked as opposed to offering help on their own accord.

9. Lewin coined a new term, "psychological life space," to show "the totality of facts which determine the behavior of an individual at a certain moment." Lewin, p. 13.

5 · The Rescuer Self

1. Frank, A. (1952). *Diary of a young girl* (p. 131). New York: Pocket Books, Doubleday. Gies, p. 11.

2. In 1970, Perry London suggested that there was an element of "social marginality" among rescuers. This feeling of alienation made them more sympathetic to another outside group—namely, the Jews. He further suggested that this motivated them to help. London, P. (1970). The rescuers: Motivational hypotheses about Christians who saved Jews from the Nazis. In J. Macauley & L. Berkowitz (Eds.), *Altruism and helping behavior* (pp. 241–50). New York: Academic Press.

  Like London, Nechama Tec, in her study of Polish rescuers published in her 1986 book (*When light pierced the darkness: Christian rescue of Jews in*

Nazi-occupied Poland. Oxford: Oxford University Press), found that rescuers stood out within their environment—for example, an intellectual among peasants, a Communist among Catholics. However, Tec's explanation is different from that of London. She explains this characteristic of the rescuers as individuality or separateness which enabled them to stand up for their beliefs. These independent individualists had the capacity to stand up to a malevolent authority and not comply with the racist norms. Like Tec, I too found that the rescuers were rather independent people. However, in my study, as well as the Altruistic Personality Study, the vast majority of rescuers felt a sense of belonging to their community. In my initial interviews with a cross section of 100 rescuers, only 29 percent felt they were marginal figures or different from others. This difference may be attributed to the fact that my sample and the Altruistic Personality Study includes rescuers from different occupied countries. To have been a rescuer in a country long known for its antisemitic attitudes certainly took a rare individual.

3. Lifton. R. J. (1976). *The life of the self: Toward a new psychology.* New York: Touchstone Books.

4. Joutard, P., Poujol, J., & Cabanel, P. (Eds.) (1987). *Cévennes: Terre de refuge 1940–1944* (p. 242). Montpellier: Presses du Languedoc/Club Cevenol.

5. Gies, pp. 121, 150.

6. Bauer, Y. (1978). *The Holocaust in historical perspective.*

7. Gies, p. 161.

8. Keneally, p. 390. It also could be argued that Goeth's feeling that Schindler would be a good character witness attests to the paucity of candidates for this purpose rather than Schindler's acting ability.

9. Hiltgunt Zassenhaus also documented her rescue of Norwegian and Danish political prisoners. Zassenhaus, H. (1974). *Walls: Resisting the Third Reich—one woman's story.* Boston: Beacon.

10. Luitgard Wundheiler, whose family refused to submit to Nazi Party pressures, immigrated to the United States. She is a psychotherapist in private practice in Brooklyn. Wundheiler researched the activities of Oskar Schindler and has written on the subject of his moral development. I am indebted to her for the idea of Schindler's "developmental spiral." As she

sees it, Schindler's being defined by others as a compassionate and caring man made him see himself that way. As a result, he acted in line with that idea, which in turn reinforced others' view of him as a humanitarian, and so it spiraled. It is from Wundheiler that I learned of Schindler's request to the police to send Jewish escapees to him rather than turning them in to the Nazi authorities.

11. Lifton, R. J. (1986). *The Nazi doctors.* New York: Basic Books. Unlike the protean man Lifton wrote about in another book, *The life of the self,* who takes on and sheds values, rescuers were consistent in their values and views. They may appear protean-like because they risked their lives for others only during the Holocaust. But what disappeared was the immediate need for rescuing, not the rescuer's values. Asked if they would rescue again, most rescuers I interviewed said they "definitely" would. Not one told me, "Oh no, that was my rescuing phase."

12. Keniston, K. (1968). *Young radicals: Notes on committed youth.* New York: Harcourt, Brace & World. Rosenhan, D. (1970). The natural socialization of altruistic autonomy (pp. 251–68). In J. Macauley & L. Berkowitz (Eds.), *Altruism and helping behavior.* New York: Academic Press.

6 · Fear and Rescuing

1. Roundup of Jews for deportation.

7 · Relationships

1. Rubinek, S. (1988). *So many miracles,* Ontario: Viking. Filmmakers Katherine Smalley and Vic Sarin also documented the Rubineks' rescue story and filmed their reunion with their rescuer, Zofia Banya, in a 1986 documentary of the same name that aired on Canadian and American television. I have also interviewed the Rubineks and the filmmakers.

2. Much of this dependency research was done in field experiments. Potential helpers react to the source of dependency. For example, bystanders are slower to come to the aid of a drunk than to a sick man. This is illustrated in Piliavin, I. M., Rodin, J., & Piliavin, J. A. (1969). Good Samaritanism: An underground phenomenon? *Journal of Personality and Social Psychology, 13,* 289–99. When the cost is too great, the Piliavins found, bystanders think twice before acting, Piliavin, J. A., & Piliavin, I. M. (1972). Effect of blood on reactions to a victim. *Journal of Personality and Social Psychology, 23,*

353–61. The attractiveness of a recipient of help increases the rate of helping according to Daniels, L. R., & Berkowitz, L. (1963). Liking and response to dependency relationships. *Human Relations, 16,* 141–48.

3. Liselotte Muhe talked easily about her efforts to save Elizabeth Grayson. She, however, avoided discussing in any detail a Jewish man she fell in love with while hiding him. It was too painful a subject for her, as he killed himself before the war was over. On one occasion when Liselotte began to talk about him, she broke down sobbing and had to excuse herself to take medication. When she returned, she brought photocopies of newspaper articles about her rescue activities and her reunion in Connecticut with Elizabeth Grayson. Grayson's comments on role-playing are taken from an article Muhe shared with me in the October 6, 1946, edition of the Bridgeport *Sunday Post.*

4. The idea that analysts would confide their problems to their patients seems improbable enough, yet Jewish analysts had little choice. They needed their patients' help if they were to escape deportation. In Berlin, psychiatrist Herman Pineas accepted a patient's offer to hide him. After a few days holed up in her apartment in Vienna, it was clear to the doctor that she was acting out her fantasy that they would become lovers. As quickly as he could, the doctor arranged for another hiding place.

5. There were some attempts to smuggle Jews from Holland via Belgium to France, and from France to neutral Switzerland or Spain.

6. Esther Warmerdam with the assistance of William Butt has written her poignant memoir, *Behind the green doors* (1992), unpublished manuscript. I have also interviewed Esther over the phone and look forward to meeting her in person.

7. Among others, researchers W. de Jong and J. L. Freedman have documented this psychological phenomenon that is second nature to any encyclopedia salesman. De Jong, W. (1979). An examination of self-perception: Mediation of the foot-in-the-door effect. *Journal of Personality and Social Psychology, 34,* 578–82; Freedman, J. L., & Fraser, S. C. (1966). Compliance without pressure: The foot-in-the-door technique. *Journal of Personality and Social Psychology, 4,* 195–202.

8 · Morality as Motivation

1. Thirty-two percent of those interviewed for the Rescuer Project were coded as belonging to the moral rescuer category. Within that group, 14 percent were ideological-moral rescuers; 12 percent were religious, and 6 percent were emotional. In general, emotional-moral and religious-moral rescuers were more involved in saving children than ideological-moral rescuers.

2. Harvard psychologist Lawrence Kohlberg described the most advanced level of reasoning as reflecting an agreement with others to protect the rights of all individuals. Kohlberg, L. (1985). *The psychology of moral development.* New York: HarperCollins.

3. Piaget, J. (1965; originally 1932). *The moral judgement of the child.* New York: Free Press.

4. Sagan, E. (1988). *Freud, women, and morality: The psychology of good and evil.* New York: Basic Books. Sagan's contention of a separate conscience that limits the superego has informed and influenced my work. His notion of a conscience that passes judgment on the conflicting pulls in the superego is one that I share.

5. Gilligan, C. (1982). *In a different voice: Psychological theory and women's development.* Cambridge: Harvard University Press. Details of Gilligan's concept of moral development are elaborated below in a discussion about gender and rescue, in Chapter 13.

6. In 1981, Major Ruegemer was honored posthumously by Yad Vashem. It was very unusual for Nazi officers to be honored, but the Jews he saved wrote on his behalf. They never knew his cooperation was procured by Irene Gut Opdyke's agreement to sleep with him. The Jews knew him only as "Grandpa," a Nazi who did not turn them over to the Gestapo. In their testimony the survivors reported that because of Major Ruegemer's relationship with Irene he lost his post and was accused by a sergeant of having relations with Jews. In 1992, someone wrote Yad Vashem protesting the honor. The Commission on Righteous Among the Nations of the World at Yad Vashem is trying to verify the facts.

7. The role of the Catholic Church in Nazi Germany is thoroughly examined by Lewy, G. (1964). *The Catholic Church and Nazi Germany.* New York: McGraw-Hill.

8. Robert Jay Lifton elaborates on the complexity of the resistance to direct medical killing in his highly acclaimed (1986) *The Nazi doctors* (pp. 93–95).

9. Between 1933 and 1945, 5,911 of the 6,034 Jehovah's Witnesses living in Nazi Germany were rounded up and sent to concentration camps.

10. The usual source for the exploits of Assisi is a book by Ramati, A. (1978). *The Assisi underground: The priests who rescued Jews.* New York: Harcourt Brace Jovanovich. This account, however, has been challenged by a number of people, including Assisi rescuer Don Aldo Brunacci. According to Brunacci, Father Rufino Nicacci, portrayed as a key rescuer in Ramati's book, never had a principal role in saving the Jews. For the facts pertaining to Assisi, I have relied on my correspondence with Don Brunacci.

11. Ewa Kurek-Lesik, now known as Ewa Kurek-Matiunin, a Polish historian at the Catholic University of Lvov, has done extensive research on the role of the nuns in the rescue of Jewish children in Poland. Her findings are written up in (1992) *Gdy klasztor znaczyl zycie.* Cracow: Wydawnictwo Znak. The conditions of admittance and the social background of Jewish children saved by women's religious orders in Poland from 1939–1945. (1988) *POLIN: A Journal of Polish-Jewish Studies, 3,* 244–275.

12. In theories of moral development, empathy is viewed as a fundamental motivator in eliciting altruism and inhibiting aggression. Empathy refers to the experiencing of another's affective or psychological state. It has both affective and cognitive components. The cognitive component involves understanding the other person's experience and imagining oneself in his or her place. The affective component is the ability to match the other person's emotions (e.g., sadness in response to another's sorrow). C. Zahn-Waxler & M. Radke-Yarrow (1990). The origins of empathic concern. *Motivation and Emotion, 13* (2), 107–130.

13. McWilliams, N. (1976). *Helpers: A study in normal personality.* Unpublished doctoral dissertation, Rutgers University. McWilliams, N. (1984). The psychology of the altruist. *Psychoanalytic Psychology, 1* (3), 193–213. Quote is McWilliams, N. (1984), p. 207.

14. Allport, G. W., & Ross, J. M. (1967). Personal religious orientation and prejudice. *Journal of Personality and Social Psychology, 5,* 432–443.

15. Civil rights leader Martin Luther King, Jr., grappled with the same moral dilemma. His answer was explained in a letter he wrote from jail in Birmingham, Alabama. In that letter, King wrote that there are two types of laws: one just and one unjust: "One has not only a legal, but a moral responsibility to obey just laws. Conversely, one has a moral responsibility to disobey unjust laws. . . . an unjust law is a human law that is not rooted in eternal law and natural law. Any law that uplifts human personality is just. Any law that degrades human personality is unjust." Martin Luther King, Jr. (1963), "Letter from a Birmingham Jail," in *Why We Can't Wait* (pp. 81–86), New York: Harper & Row Publishers, Inc.

16. According to Dwork, D. (1991), *Children with a Star,* New Haven: Yale University Press, a mere 11 percent of European Jewish children alive in 1939 survived the war. One and a half million were killed (p. xi).

9 · Judeophiles

1. The father-son relationship between Itzhak Stern and Oskar Schindler has been commented on by a number of writers, notably Keneally (*Schindler's List*) and psychologist Luitgard Wundheiler. Wundheiler noted that when Stern died in 1969, Schindler was said to have cried inconsolably, as only a small child can cry at a parent's death. Wundheiler, L. (1986). Oskar Schindler's moral development during the Holocaust. *Humboldt Journal of Social Relations, 13* (1 & 2), 333–356.

2. Judeophiles could be found among the ancient Greeks and Romans. Aristotle mentioned that the Jews were a proponent of the "golden mean." He also found that they possessed all four cardinal virtues: temperance, courage, justice, and wisdom. Varro, a close friend and contemporary of the Cicero, was impressed by the purity of their monotheism. This positive feeling toward the Jews went against the grain of the populace, who denigrated the Jews for their rituals and beliefs. Feldman, L. H. (1958–1959). Philo-Semitism Among Ancient Intellectuals. *Tradition, 1,* 27–39.

Unlike antisemitism, Judeophilism is not a subject to which many scholars have given much thought or attention. Alan Edelstein, a sociologist at Towson State University, is a notable exception. Edelstein breaks philosemitism into six categories: religious, humanistic, social, intellectual, national, and economic. Through these categories, Edelstein lays out in precise detail the motivations behind Judeophilism. Edelstein, A. (1982). *An unacknowledged harmony.* Westport, CT: Greenwood Press.

Historian Celia Heller, who examined Polish philosemitism, has dispelled the myth that philosemitism was confined to the Polish left. She found philosemites among the conservatives, liberals, some without political affiliation, and leftists. Heller, C. (1992). The philosemites of Poland. *Midstream, 1,* 27–30.

3. This incident is described in more detail in Chapter 4.

4. The Rescuer Project found that Judeophiles comprised 28 percent of those who risked their lives to save Jews, ranking them just behind those in the moral rescuer category. Eighty-two percent of those classified as Judeophiles came from apolitical families and some 29 percent of them came from mixed marriages.

5. The fact that many of the rescuers suspected they had Jewish blood had escaped my attention until Harvey Sarner pointed it out to me. Sarner, a retired Chicago attorney, has dedicated his energies to finding Eastern European rescuers honored by Yad Vashem and flying them to Israel for the public recognition they deserve. Sarner observed that many of the rescuers he talked with told him they suspected that they had Jewish blood.

6. Wallenberg's great-great-grandfather came to Sweden in the late 1700s and converted to Lutheranism. According to his cousin Jacob Wallenberg, a businessman in New York, Raoul Wallenberg knew he had Jewish ancestry but was most influenced by being raised with love for humanity and compassion. In the late thirties, Wallenberg was in Palestine working as a banker in Haifa and met German Jewish refugees, from whom he learned firsthand the plight of the Jews. This awareness had tremendous impact on his willingness to help Hungarian Jewry.

7. Among the Judeophiles I interviewed for the Rescuer Project, 71 percent of them rescued more than one person. Most worked alone. Less than a third, 29 percent, were part of an underground network. For a more detailed narrative of Stefania's story, see Chapter 6.

8. S. W. Cook (1970). Motives in conceptual analysis of attitude-related behavior. In W. J. Arnold & D. Levine (Eds.), *Nebraska Symposium on Motivation* (pp. 179–231). Lincoln: University of Nebraska Press.

10 · Concerned Professionals

1. Professionals who obeyed a higher law, one that involved upholding an oath of office to serve mankind, did not necessarily have to take death-defying risks. In southern France, some gendarmes protected their citizenry and themselves by following their orders to the letter. Before carrying out an arrest, for instance, two gendarmes would go to a local bistro for lunch. In a loud voice, one might say to the other, "Look, Pierre, I see here that we have to pick up Max Cohen on 15, Rue Jacob." They would continue to enjoy their meal, hoping all the while that someone would pass the word on to Cohen. After lunch, they would go to arrest Cohen, only to be told he left the day before. They would then place an X next to the man's name. They had fulfilled their assignment. Alas, they had come a day too late to make the required arrest. This story was told to me by several French survivors.

Yad Vashem rarely recognizes policemen because while they may have saved Jews from deportations they concurrently were responsible for the incarceration of others.

2. Dr. Feliks Kanabus recounted his wartime exploits in a speech to the Jewish National Fund on September 20, 1965.

3. Irena Sendlerowa worked with five Jewish youth leaders who themselves did not want to escape. One of this group, known as Rachela, took children out of the ghetto when she went to work outside the ghetto. One day when she returned at the end of a workday, a Christian friend stopped her and told her that she would be killed if she returned without the children she left with that morning. She ignored the warning and was killed by the Nazis that evening.

4. Arieh Ben-Tov, an Israeli attorney, is to be credited for his significant research on the International Committee of the Red Cross and Born's exceptional role in this organization. Ben-Tov's report is published in (1988) *Facing the Holocaust in Budapest: The International Committee of the Red Cross and the Jews in Hungary, 1943–1945.* Geneva: Henry Dunant Institute, Martinus Nijhoff Publishers.

5. The wide range of estimates regarding how many Jews Sempo Sugihara saved is explained by the fact that a single transit visa might be photographed and used for any number of fugitives.

6. On many occasions I have had the pleasure of meeting and interviewing one of Aristides de Sousa Mendes's sons, John Paul Abranches, who serves as chairman of the International Committee for the Commemoration of Dr. Aristides de Sousa Mendes. Furthermore, the archives at Yad Vashem had testimonies as well as other publications. Among them: Clark, G. (1990, March). The priceless signature of Aristides de Sousa Mendes, *Reader's Digest,* pp. 137–42. Paldiel, M. (1986, December 5). The righteous diplomat who defied orders. *Jerusalem Post.*

11 · Network Rescuers

1. Simmel, G. (1950). The secret and the secret society. In K. H. Wolff (Ed.), *The sociology of Georg Simmel.* New York: Free Press.

2. From a December 12, 1992, letter to me from Hetty Dutihl Voûte.

3. Freud, S. (1960). *Group psychology and the analysis of the ego* (p. 21). New York: Bantam Books. Doug McAdam et al. also point out that the "greater the density of social organization, the more likely that social movement activity will develop." McAdam, D., Mccarthy, J. D., & Zald, M. N. (1988). Social movements. In N. J. Smelser (Ed.), *Handbook of sociology* (pp. 695–737, 703). Newbury Park, CA: Sage. The initial anti-Nazi activities among different social circles set into motion the mechanism for rescue of the endangered Jewish populations in many Nazi-occupied countries.

4. Network rescuers accounted for 22 percent of all those I interviewed. The majority had attended college (36 percent) or graduate school (27 percent).

Over 90 percent of rescuers in this group were involved in more than five incidents of rescue, which usually involved helping fifteen persons or more. Forty-one percent rescued 100–2,500 people, 23 percent rescued 15–50 people, and 18 percent helped 1–7 people. More than 90 percent were "professional rescuers," or people whose full-time occupation was rescuing.

It is interesting to note that "unusually high numbers of students and autonomous professionals are active in movements." Limited countervailing ties do not restrain members from the commitment that such activities require. McAdam, Mccarthy, & Zald, p. 709.

5. Silver, p. 47.

6. McDougall, W. (1920). *The Group Mind.* Cambridge, England: Cambridge, University Press.

7. Zander, A. (1979). The psychology of group processes. *Annual Review of Psychology, 30,* 417–451. The levels of collective relations in group growth is also described by Guy Swanson of the University of California, Berkeley: "People find that they need one another to do something but are unclear about what to do or how to do it. Through social interaction they arrive at a network of generalized interdependence based on their sense of needing one another and accepting one another as possible coparticipants in doing what may prove necessary" (pp. 97–98). Swanson, G. (1992). Doing things together: Some basic forms of agency and structure in collective action and some explanations. *Social Psychology Quarterly, 55* (2), 94–117.

8. Kadushin, C. (1976). Networks and circles in the production of culture. *American Behavioral Scientist, 19* (6), 769–784.

9. Ibid., p. 22.

10. The official body of the Catholic Church in France, the Assembly of Cardinals and Bishops, was silent from the beginning of the Vichy regime in June 1940 until the summer of 1942. Theologian Eva Fleischner, who interviewed French Catholics who saved Jews, theorized that the French Catholic Church backed the Vichy government because its Premier, Marshal Pétain, couched his political goals in religious terms. Although not a religious man, Pétain spoke in theological terms of repentance and expiation of sin. He called for France to return to traditional moral values. Fleischner, E. (1988). Can the few become the many? Some Catholics in France who saved Jews during the Holocaust. In *Remembering the future: Jews and Christians during and after the Holocaust* (pp. 233–247). Oxford: Pergamon Press.

Strictly speaking, the Catholic hierarchy in France supported Pétain because they hoped he would restore Catholic privileges that had been lost with the signing of the Concordat with Rome in 1901.

11. The coalition of French networks that worked to save Jewish children included: CIMADE (Comité d'Inter-Mouvements auprès des Evacués), Service Social des Etrangers, and Oeuvre de Secours aux Enfants (OSE). The OSE was a medically and socially oriented Jewish organization that was established in Russia before World War I and it slowly expanded in numerous European countries. After the Nazi occupation of France the OSE's Paris division moved to Montpellier. The organization received invaluable

help in finding shelter for children from the archbishop of Toulouse, Monsignor Jules-Gérard Saliège, and Monsignor Pierre-Marie Théas of nearby Montauban. Following their directives, the convents and other religious institutions in their dioceses were open to helping. Sabine Zeitoun elaborates on the rescue of children in France in (1988) Role of the Christian community in saving Jewish children in France during the Second World War, *Remembering for the future,* Supplementary Volume (pp. 505–25). Oxford: Pergamon Press. The activities of the Christian resistance in France is also documented in Henri de Lubac's (1990) *Christian resistance to Anti-Semitism: Memories from 1940–1944.* San Francisco: Ignatius Press.

12. Centre de Documentation Juive Contemporaine, CCXIV, 103.

13. Bauer, Y. (1978). *The Holocaust in historical perspective* (p. 73). Seattle: University of Washington Press.

14. I have interviewed John Weidner on several occasions. This particular incident, however, comes from his biography written by Ford, H. (1966). *Flee the captor* (pp. 245–64). Nashville: Southern Publishing Association.

15. Erickson, B. H. (1981). Secret societies and social structures. *Social Forces, 60,* 188–210, 201.

16. For details on the secret intelligence organization in Norway, which also rescued some Jews, see Aubert, V. (1965). *Hidden society.* New Brunswick, NJ: Transaction Books.

17. Kadushin, C. (1976). Networks and circles in the production of culture. *American Behavioral Scientist, 19* (6), 769–84.

18. I interviewed Hetty Dutilh Voûte, Gisela Wieberdink Sohnlein, and one of the children they rescued, Anita Meyers Budding, at a 1991 reunion. Budding, who now lives in New Mexico, had arranged for them to meet in New York at the First International Gathering of Hidden Children, sponsored by the Anti-Defamation League and Child Development Research. The conference, which I helped organize, brought together more than 1,600 Jews who as children were hidden during the Holocaust.

19. The Belgian resistance movement was successful because the files containing the names and whereabouts of Jews were burned. There were also fewer denunciations by neighbors. Belgians managed a collaborative effort between Jews and non-Jews to save children. Andrée Guelen Herscovici, a Belgian rescuer, held the notebooks that were used to record where each

child was hidden. Parents were not privy to such information lest they have an urge to say goodbye to a child before being deported.

20. For details on Jewish-Christian relations in Poland before and during World War II, see Bauer, pp. 50–62.

21. In Poland, some convents, monasteries, and orphanages (run by various Catholic religious orders) developed as rescue networks. But rescue networks did not develop among church members the way they did among members of the Confessional Church in Germany and Protestant and Catholic churches in Holland and France. The major group rescue effort in Poland was mounted by the Council for Aid to Jews through the Zegota, which was comprised of different political groups and social service experts who worked along with Jews.

22. Ewa Kurek-Lesik (1992). *Gdy klasztor znaczyl zycie*. Cracow: Wydawnictwo Znak.

23. Characteristics of these informal social networks were drawn from Kadushin's analysis of networks and circles, 1976.

12 · Child Rescuers

1. Warmerdam and Butt, pp. 38–46.

2. The Warmerdams played a number of games with their Jewish charges. Timed races through the house, dressing up, and tongue-twister games were all designed to evade the Gestapo's detection methods. After hearing that the Nazis had caught Jews disguised as women by throwing apples at them (the suspects had not caught the apples in their skirts as most women would have done, but in a masculine two-handed catch), Esther's father had everyone cross-dress and threw apples at them.

A few days later, he had everyone playing tongue-twister games. "*De kat die krabbelt de krullen van de trap*" ("The cat that scratched the wood shavings from the stairs"), he would mutter and then make all the children repeat the Dutch phrase after him as fast as they could. For weeks Esther's father had everyone in their house tripping over their own tongues on phrases only a native could pronounce. Later Esther learned the Nazis had captured downed British fliers with a tongue-twister test of Dutch pronunciation. Ibid., pp. 28–33.

3. Erikson, E. (1950). *Childhood and society.* New York: W. W. Norton, p. 263.

4. Von Staden, p. 100.

5. At Auschwitz, Pania Wywiad was the victim of the infamous Nazi doctor Josef Mengele. Mengele twice put dye in her eye, which changed its color and damaged a nerve ending. The Russians were nearing the camp, so Mengele did not get a chance to put dye in her eye a third time, which would have surely blinded or killed her.

13 · Men and Women Rescuers

1. Eagly, A. H., & Crowley, M. (1986). Gender and helping behavior: A meta-analytic review of the social psychological literature, *Psychological Bulletin, 100* (3), 283–308. The review article also mentioned that there was a slight tendency for women to help women more than men to help women.

2. Tavris, C. (1992). *The mismeasure of woman: Why women are not the better sex, the inferior sex or the opposite sex.* (p. 289). New York: Simon & Schuster.

3. Freud, S. (1925). Some psychical consequences of the anatomical distinction between the sexes. *Standard Edition,* 19:257.

4. Kohlberg, L. (1969). The cognitive-developmental approach to socialization. In D. A. Goslin (Ed.), *Handbook of socialization theory and research* (pp. 347–480). Chicago: Rand McNally.

5. Tavris, C. (1991). *The mismeasure of woman: Why women are not the better sex, the inferior sex or the opposite sex.* New York: Simon & Schuster. Tavris gives a clear and incisive analysis of Gilligan's place in psychological development.

Feminist psychoanalysts Nancy Chodorow and Jean Baker Miller attribute the origin of women's different voice to the psychodynamics of being raised primarily by mothers. Girls continue to stay attached to their mothers as they form their identities, whereas boys, in order to develop a male identity, separate themselves psychologically at an early age. According to Gilligan's view, the result is that adult women look for attachment and fear independence and men find security in independence and are threatened by separation.

6. My findings mirror those of sociologist Barbara Risman and Lenard Kaye and Jeffrey Applegate. Risman compared the personality traits of single fathers, single mothers, and married parents. She found that single men who had custody exhibited personality traits—specifically nurturing and caring —that were much more like mothers than married fathers. Similarly, in 1990 psychologists Lenard Kaye and Jeffrey Applegate, who studied 150 men who were spending sixty hours a week caring for their ailing parents or spouses, found that these men provided just as much emotional support as women traditionally do. The obligation of providing this care customarily falls to women, but when men do it, they do it just as well and lovingly. Risman, B. J. (1987). Intimate relationships from a microstructural perspective: Men who mother. *Gender and Society, 1*, 6–32. Kay, L. W., & Applegate, J. S. (1990). Men as elder caregivers: A response to changing families. *American Journal of Orthopsychiatry, 60*, 86–95.

7. Ervin Staub's extensive work on the tendency to help among men and women has been documented in various publications. Among them is a chapter published in 1974. Helping a distressed person: Social personality and stimulus determinants. In L. Berkowitz (Ed.), *Advances in experimental social psychology* (pp. 293–342). New York: Academic Press. Staub, E. (1978). *Positive social behavior and morality* (Vol. 1, pp. 39–73). New York: Academic Press.

8. Colby, A., & Damon, W. (1987). Listening in a different voice: A review of Gilligan's *In a different voice*. In M. R. Walsh (Ed.), *The psychology of women: Ongoing debates* (p. 327). New Haven: Yale University Press.

9. Friedman, P. (1955). Righteous Gentiles in the Nazi era. In A. J. Friedman (Ed.), *Roads to extinction: Essays on the Holocaust* (pp. 409–421). Philadelphia: Jewish Publication Society. Friedman's work, which preceded Gilligan's by some twenty years, suggested that women's morality was different from men's and was more emotional than intellectual.

10. Sauvage, P. (1986). Ten questions. In C. Rittner and S. Meyers (Eds.), *The courage to care* (p. 137). New York: New York University Press.
    Henry, F. (1984). *Victims and neighbors: A small town in Nazi Germany remembered*. South Hadley, MA: Bergin & Garvey.

11. Wolfson, M. (1970, April). *The subculture of freedom: Some people will not*. Paper presented to the regional meeting of the Western Political Science Association, Sacramento, CA.

12. Joutard, P., Poujol, J., & Cabanel, P. (Eds.) (1987). *Cévennes: Terre de refuge 1940–1944* (pp. 257–258). Montpellier: Presses du Languedoc/Club Cevenol.

13. Tavris, p. 68.

14. Anje Roos Geerling's brother Kais was a Dutch policeman whose beat was the Jewish quarter in Amsterdam. Like the rest of his family, he was an active rescuer. When the Germans raided the Jewish quarter, Kais Roos would round up as many Jews as he could and hide them. On occasion, he would arrest them and bring them into the Dutch police station for safe-keeping.

15. Statistics gathered from the Carnegie Hero Fund Commission appear to substantiate findings that show men to be more responsive to one-time heroic actions than women. The Carnegie Hero Fund recognizes individuals in the United States and Canada who saved or attempted to save another person's life. From its founding in 1904 through the end of October 1992, it had given out 7,673 awards. Only 761, or 10 percent of them, went to women.

Social psychologists Ted Huston, Gilbert Geis, and Richard Wright also found that individuals who acted as Good Samaritans in crime emergencies were males who saw themselves as "preeminently qualified to provide assistance." Huston, T. L., Geis, G., & Wright, R. (1976, June). The angry Samaritans. *Psychology Today,* p. 61.

16. Deaux, K. (1976). *The behavior of women and men.* Monterey: Brooks/Cole Publishing Company. Deaux did note a difference in the circumstances under which men and women offered help. Deaux observed that in situations that required an individual to take the *initiative,* men were more likely to offer their help. Deaux speculated that men's traditional roles may require them to be more aggressive in their everyday lives and so they had more of a tendency to intervene rather than react. But even this one distinction falls apart in modern times.

In 1990, Alfie Kohn, in *The brighter side of human nature: Altruism and empathy in everyday life* (New York: Basic Books), concluded that when it comes to real altruistic behavioral differences, "where gender differences do emerge, they are typically weak, partial, and buried in qualifications" (p. 82).

17. Block, G., & Drucker, M. (1992). *Rescuers: Portraits of moral courage in the Holocaust* (p. 82). New York: Holmes & Meier. Block's wonderfully expressive photographs of rescuers and Drucker's informed text and interviews powerfully demonstrate the incredible diversity of this group.

18. Fuchs Epstein, C. (1988). *Deceptive distinctions* (p. 99). New Haven, London, & New York: Yale University Press, Russell Sage Foundation.

19. Dwork, D. (1991). *Children with a star* (p. 53). New Haven: Yale University Press.

In a personal conversation with me, psychoanalyst Judith Kestenberg, who is an expert on the persecution of children under the Nazis, suggested another reason that Belgian women were so involved in the rescue of children. Kestenberg hypothesized that Queen Elizabeth of Belgium, who personally intervened with Nazi authorities at the Caserne Dossin deportation center in Malines to place children under six and adults over sixty-five years in orphanages and old-age homes, respectively, encouraged the rescue efforts of Jewish children. Her own efforts served as a role model for women who identified with the queen. In much the same manner, Danish men identified with the defiant attitude of King Christian X. Thus, the Danish resistance and rescue efforts were male-dominated.

14 · Early Childhood

1. Sagan, E. (1988). *Freud, women, and morality: The psychology of good and evil* (p. 164). New York: Basic Books. For Sagan's three-stage moral development process, see pp. 160–65.

2. Levy, D. M. (1948). Anti-Nazis' criteria of differentiation. *Psychiatry, 11,* 125–67. Grossman, F. (1984). Psychological study of Gentiles who saved Jews. In I. Charney (Ed.), *Toward the understanding of Holocaust and prevention of genocide* (pp. 202–16). Boulder, CO: Westview Press.

3. Radke-Yarrow, M., & Zahn-Waxler, C. (1986). The role of familial factors in the development of prosocial behavior: Research findings and questions. In D. Olweus, J. Block, & M. Radke-Yarrow (Eds.), *Development of antisocial and prosocial behavior: Research, theories and issues* (pp. 207–33). New York: Academic Press.

Zahn-Waxler notes that in the cases of children who had depressed parents, a role reversal took place. The children looked after the adults and were very sensitive to their emotional needs. Such awareness of the emotional distress of others frequently led these children to be altruistic adults.

4. Von Staden, *Darkness over the valley,* pp. 78–79.

5. Miller, A. (1983). *For your own good: Hidden cruelty in child-rearing and the roots of violence.* New York: Farrar, Straus, Giroux.
   Miller's findings confirm what had been reported earlier in the Authoritarian Personality Study. Researchers of that study saw clear differences in the households of highly prejudiced people and those who were not. Unprejudiced subjects attained considerable independence from their parents and made their own decisions. Less obedience was expected of them as children. Parents were more supportive, were unconditionally affectionate, displayed less conformity to conventional rules, and thus provided more freedom for individuality. Adorno, T., Frenkel-Brunswick, E., Levinson, D. J., & Sanford, R. N. (1950). *The authoritarian personality* (p. 385). New York: W. W. Norton.

6. While most of the rescuers considered themselves to be very much connected to their communities and families, there were some who considered themselves loners. This sense of themselves as separate from group influence helped them ignore group pressure.

7. Several studies of Holocaust rescuers have traced their motivation to the values ingrained in them as children. David Levy's study was but one (see note 2 above). Ute Klingemann, who studied German rescuers, also noted that role models even spoke specifically about Jews and stressed the fact that Jews were like all other people. U. Klingemann (1985, June). The study of rescuers of Jews in Berlin: A progress report. Paper presented to the Eighth Annual Scientific Meeting of the International Society of Political Psychology, Washington, D.C. Nechama Tec's analysis of Polish rescuers concluded that some Polish rescuers' motivation stems from "unique moral values of family life." Tec, N. (1986). *When light pierced the darkness* (p. 189). Oxford: Oxford University Press.

8. Oliner, S., & Oliner, P. (1988). *The altruistic personality,* p. 144. The Oliners found that 39 percent of rescuers' parents taught their children that moral values were to be applied universally, compared with only 13 percent of bystanders' parents.

9. A number of social-psychological studies of people who in other circumstances risked their lives for others show that a parental altruistic role model was a common childhood experience. David Rosenhan found that many of the civil rights workers who traveled South to participate in desegregation efforts described their parents as people who were actively committed to a moral or altruistic cause. One recalled his father carrying him on his shoulders to protest the Sacco and Vanzetti trial. A father of another civil rights worker fought on the Republican side in the Spanish Civil War. Rosenhan, D. (1970). The natural socialization of altruistic autonomy. In J. Macauley & L. Berkowitz (Eds.), *Altruism, sympathy and helping: Psychological and sociological principles* (pp. 101–13). New York: Academic Press.

10. Radke-Yarrow, M., & Zahn-Waxler, C. (1973). Learning concern for others. *Developmental Psychology, 8* (2), 240–60.

11. Zassenhaus, *Walls,* pp. 162–63.

12. Staub, E. The psychology of bystanders, perpetrators, and heroic helpers. *International Journal of Intercultural Relations,* in press.

In 1970, Staub conducted other studies that showed that children who were given responsibility for taking care of things in a teacher's absence showed a greater tendency to respond to cries of a child in an adjoining room than did children without such responsibility. Staub, E. (1970). A child in distress: The effects of focusing responsibility on children in their attempts to help. *Developmental Psychology, 2,* 162–64.

13. McWilliams, N. (1976). *Helpers: A study in normal personality.* Unpublished doctoral dissertation, Rutgers University. Gaylin, W. (1970). *In the service of the country: War resisters in prison.* New York: Viking.

14. Hoffman, M. (1982). Development of prosocial motivation: Empathy and guilt. In N. Eisenberg (Ed.), *The development of prosocial behavior* (pp. 281–313). New York: Academic Press.

15. McWilliams, *Helpers.* McWilliams, N. (1984). The psychology of the altruist. *Psychoanalytic Psychology, 1* (3), 193–213.

16. Gies, *Anne Frank remembered,* pp. 19–20.

15 · Postwar

1. Robertson, N. (1981, August 10). Growing up in Nazi Germany: A backward look. New York *Times*, p. B4.

2. In Poland, hundreds of Jewish children were hidden in convents separate from their families. Many of them were too young to remember their real parents and were never told they were Jewish. They grew up as Christian orphans, ignorant of their real ancestry and unaware that at least one of their parents had survived the war and was vainly searching for them.

When the Nuncio from the Vatican, wearing a big golden cross, came to meet with the Central Committee of Liberated Jews in the British Zone to offer them food and clothes, Dr. Hadassah Rosensaft (who could communicate with the Nuncio in French) replied, "We don't ask for food and not for clothes. I come from Poland, a Catholic country, and some of the inmates of Bergen Belsen who returned to Poland to retrieve their children who were hidden by Catholic families found that the families will not return the children to their parents. We are asking for a 'Call from the Vatican' to Catholics to give back Jewish children to their parents, relatives, or Jewish organization." Much to Dr. Rosensaft's dismay, the Vatican never issued a Call.

However, when Leokadia Jaromirska wrote Pius XII regarding a Jewish girl she rescued in Poland, Leokadia received a letter saying that she should give the child back to the father who survived. (For details see Hellman, P. (1980). *Avenue of the Righteous*, p. 237. New York: Atheneum.

3. There were incidents when Jewish parents, particularly in Poland and Holland, had to sue to get custody of their own children. Abraham H. Foxman, now national director of the Anti-Defamation League, was saved by his Polish nanny, who raised him disguised as a Catholic during the war but only relinquished her custody when forced by court order. These custody battles in Holland are depicted in a documentary and a book by the same author: Verhey, E. (1991). *About the Jewish child*. Amsterdam: Nyghvanditmar.

4. The governments of Belgium and France allowed Jewish organizations to determine the disposition of Jewish orphans. In Holland, however, the government wanted to avoid making a distinction between Jewish orphans and others and so established the Commission on War Foster Children (OPK) to

decide custody matters. The commission, which was Protestant-run, favored keeping the children with Dutch families. Opposing the government's commission was, among other Jewish organizations, Ezrat Hayeled, a private organization devoted to helping Jewish children remain Jewish and assisting them to emigrate to Palestine. The details of the struggles concerning guardianship of the war orphans in Holland was written up by Barsz, I. (1985, November 15). Strijd om Voogdij Oorlogspleegkiinderen. *NIW,* pp. 60–61.

Dr. Isaac Herzog, the chief rabbi of Palestine, supported by funds from the Joint Distribution Committee, set off on a journey to liberated Europe to seek out Jewish children, some of whom did not even know they were Jewish. Rabbi Herzog was a central figure and something of a one-man institution. He visited the Pope and received a promise that the Vatican would do everything it could to influence the church hierarchy in Poland to aid in uncovering and releasing Jewish children from monasteries and convents. Rescue Children, Inc., continued to assist children until they found a new home in Palestine with relatives or were adopted (see *An inventory to the Rescue Children, Inc., collection 1946–1985,* Yeshiva University archives, 1986).

5. One source of painful estrangement between rescuers and the Jews they saved was based on a bureaucratic requirement. In order for Jewish Holocaust survivors to receive postwar financial aid from their indigenous country, they had to ask their rescuers in Western European countries to certify that their charges "suffered from cold, hunger, and discomfort." Not understanding the administrative necessity of such documents, the simple people who had extended a helping hand were hurt by their charges' making such a claim.

6. Herman, J. L. (1992). *Trauma and recovery: The aftermath of violence—from domestic abuse to political terror.* New York: Basic Books.

7. These three rescue stories are discussed at length in Chapter 6.

8. When the Russians liberated Budapest, Perlasca was captured and put to work clearing streets of rubble and corpses and later deported in a cattle car to Istanbul. Ultimately he returned to Italy and an anonymous life of struggle. It was only in the late 1980s that Hungarian survivors remembered the man from the Spanish legation in Budapest who had protected them and saved their lives. Notices were placed in newspapers and efforts were made

to get testimonies from living survivors. In 1989 Perlasca was honored at Yad Vashem.

9. Erikson, E., *Childhood and society,* pp. 266–68.

10. Irene Gut Opdyke has written her own dramatic account of her wartime activities (1992). *Into the Flames.* San Bernardino, CA: The Borgo Press.

11. The story of Father Stanislaw Falkowski and Joseph Kutrzeba's fifty-year friendship is included in a documentary, *Messengers of hope: The hidden children of the Holocaust,* produced by Jeff Kamen, Jonathan L. Kessler, & Joseph S. Kutrzeba. For details write: 23 Fifth Street SE, Washington, DC 20003.

12. One article that appeared at the time contrasted the conduct of two Germans, Oskar Schindler and Adolf Eichmann, and quoted the preamble of a financial appeal Schindler's former workers wrote on behalf of their now impoverished boss: "We do not forget the sorrows of Egypt, we do not forget Haman, we do not forget Hitler. Thus, among the unjust, we do not forget the just. Remember Oskar Schindler." Keneally, p. 393.

13. Ibid., pp. 394–95.

16 · Myth, Reality, and Memory

1. In Amsterdam, the Franks' hiding place at 263 Prinsengracht has been preserved as a national memorial. The memorial exemplifies the discomfort of the Dutch on this issue. On the one hand, Holland has a tradition of Judeophilism that goes back to the period of the expulsion of the Jews from Spain. During World War II, as was the case with many other Dutch citizens, friends of the Franks helped the family hide. However, as was also common during that time, an unknown informant or informants betrayed the Franks' whereabouts to the Nazis.

Amsterdam boasts two other memorials to rescuers. One is a monument that commemorates the shipyard workers' strike on February 21, 1942, when the Nazis deported the first few hundred Jews. The other memorial is a war and resistance museum, which is housed inside the synagogue the Franks first attended when they arrived in the city from Germany.

More recently, the Dutch paid tribute to NV network leaders Jaap

Musch and Joop Woortman, who were killed by the Nazis for their efforts to save Jewish children, by naming a square in Amsterdam in their honor.

I am indebted to James Young for a few of the memorial sites for rescuers.

2. Adolf Eichmann made this comment during the interrogation at his trial, which is quoted in the chief prosecutor's book. Hausner, G. (1968). *Justice in Jerusalem* (p. 75). New York: Schocken Books.

3. Joop Westerweel's heroic deeds were also mentioned at the Eichmann trial by one of the witnesses.

4. Hausner, p. 397.

5. At the 1957 Anti-Defamation League ceremony honoring Christian heroes, guests were given a copy of Philip Friedman's *Their brothers' keepers*. This was the first English-language book on rescuers and had just been published.

6. Ernst Zundel was found guilty of knowingly spreading false information likely to cause racial hatred or religious intolerance. He was acquitted, however, on a second charge of the same nature. That charge involved another pamphlet, which argued that Zionists, Communists, Freemasons, and bankers were engaged in a conspiracy to rule the world.

7. The Jewish Foundation for Christian Rescuers, a project of the Anti-Defamation League, also sponsors an Honor-a-Rescuer program, which encourages synagogues, churches, schools, and organizations to adopt rescuers, assist them financially, and interact with them socially through letters and visits.

8. Rabbi Harold Schulweis's plea to support the rescuers via the Jewish Foundation for Christian Rescuers generated initial financial support by Mazon, Henry and Edith Everett, and Henry Ostberg. In addition to support from adults, youngsters donated a portion of their bar and bat mitzvah or birthday presents. Today the foundation provides monthly stipends to more than 1,200 rescuers in eighteen different countries and engages in a range of research and educational activities.

9. Sybil Milton, a historian and scholar-in-residence at the United States Holocaust Memorial Museum, has noted that establishing memorials was a three-stage process. The first stage was that of postwar adaptation, in which

survivors were concerned with starting a new life. The second phase began after the Eichmann trial and involved educating the new generation about the Holocaust. Finally, the third stage deals with ensuring that the education carries beyond one or two generations by erecting monuments and museums and organizing annual commemorations.

10. Ely Ben-Gal's remarks were part of a 1990 conference, "Le Plateau Vivarais-Lignon, Accueil et Résistance 1939–1944," held in Le Chambon. The proceedings were published in 1992. Le Chambon: Société d'Histoire de la Montagne, pp. 317–20.

11. Miller, J. (1990). *One, by one, by one* (pp. 158–219). New York: Simon & Schuster.

12. Dawidowicz, p. 403. Yad Vashem has honored fewer than 100 German rescuers. By far the vast majority of Yad Vashem-recognized rescuers are Polish and Dutch.

13. I am indebted to Esther Hautzig, author of *Remember who you are: Stories about being Jewish,* for this description of the Japanese memorial to Sempo Sugihara. Hautzig gave a speech at the opening ceremony of Hill of Humanity Park.

14. The making of many of these films became vehicles for reunions between survivors and rescuers. Pierre Sauvage also formed the Friends of Le Chambon to educate others about goodness, and Myriam Abramowicz was the moving spirit of the First International Gathering of Hidden Children, which paid tribute to the rescuers of children.

15. Among Holocaust rescuers, Raoul Wallenberg is the most widely honored individual. In addition to the statue in Budapest, there is also a Wallenberg Square located there. In the United States a Wallenberg organization keeps his memory alive through educational programs. A Wallenberg Square can be found in Los Angeles, and streets in New York City and Washington (the street that fronts the United States Holocaust Museum) are named for him. The town of Ramat Gan in Israel also boasts a Raoul Wallenberg Street.

16. The reunion was written up in a New York *Times* article by Ira Henry Freeman, "Reunion Here Recalls Rescues from Ghetto," June 3, 1961.

17. I first met Frank and Maria Morgens after delivering promised regards from their rescuer who converted to Judaism, married a Jew, and emigrated to Israel: Walentyna Zak, today Ala Sztajnert, whom I had just interviewed in Israel. I told the Morgens about my rescuer research, and immediately this energetic couple volunteered their assistance. Their help proved to be invaluable. Frank and Maria guided my work with Polish rescuers at the Jewish Foundation for Christian Rescuers. When an article about my research appeared in a Polish newspaper, hundreds of letters arrived. The Morgenses read them, translated them, and told me which ones needed immediate attention. Frank Morgens became the Jewish Foundation for Christian Rescuers' liaison with Poland. Through the Polish Society of Christian Rescuers, he set up an active search for more rescuers and a mechanism to follow up on rescuers who receive a monthly stipend.

18. Senesh, H. (1972). *Hannah Senesh: Her life and diary* (p. 13). New York: Schocken Books.

Epilogue

1. Milgram, *Obedience to authority,* p. 179.

2. Sharansky, N. (1991, April 25). A dissident in the KGB. Jerusalem *Report,* p. 41.

3. I first met Anje Elizabeth Rosmus on December 1, 1990, at the opening of the First Annual Jewish Film Festival in Washington, D.C. Wearing a sexy metallic gold jumpsuit that complemented her curly blond hair, Rosmus looked more like a movie star than a model of moral courage. Her speaking style, however, is direct and conveys her moral outrage at those Germans who are denying their Nazi past and those who are repeating racism in their actions today. As of the winter of 1993, 7,000 attacks have been reported of skinheads harassing foreigners and more than a handful of Turks have been killed.

4. One senses that Anje Elizabeth Rosmus is mourning along with the Jews. Her book *Exodus in the shadow of mercy: Jewish families in the region of Passau* traces the fate during the Third Reich of the thirty-two Jewish families who resided in Passau. Anje is completing her master's degree on Holocaust memorials in Germany.

5. Eliason, M. (1992, June 12–18). Woman who rescued Arab an unlikely heroine. *The Jewish Week, Inc.,* p. 22.

6. Haberman, C. (1992, June 8). New York *Times.*

7. Prager, K. M. (1987, October 23). What? Physicians won't treat AIDS? New York *Times,* p. A39.

8. People often ask me if children of Holocaust rescuers are more likely than most other people to become rescuers themselves. After all, they were raised in families who had risked their lives putting their ideals into practice. There are too many variables for a definitive answer. The opportunity to help may not arise or the situation itself might not lend itself to action. All that can be said is that children of past and present rescuers have a greater propensity to act in a morally courageous fashion.

9. Lifton, R. J. (1987). *The future of immortality and other essays for a nuclear age* (pp. 111–12, 133–35). New York: Basic Books; Lifton, R. J. (1993). *The Protean Self.* New York: Basic Books.

BIBLIOGRAPHY

Films*

Abramowicz, M., & Hoffenberg, E. (Directors) (1980). *As if it were yesterday* [documentary of Belgian rescuers]. New York: Films Now and Then, c/o Myriam Abramowicz.

Berri, C. (Director, Writer) (1966). *The two of us [Le vieil homme et l'enfant]* [feature film rescue in France]. New York: Corinth Films.

Blair, J. (Director) (1983). *Schindler* [film documentary]. London: Thames T.V.

Block, G. (Director, Producer, Writer) (1991). *They risked their lives: Rescuers of the Holocaust* [documentary]. Teaneck, NJ: Ergo Media & Santa Fe, NM: Gay Block.

Bundschuh, J. (Director) (1987). *Villa Air Bel: Varian Fry in Marseille.* Munich: Kick Films.

Chabrol, C. (Director) (1966). *Line of demarcation* [feature film on rescue in France]. Chicago, IL: Films, Inc.

*For details on many of these films, see Insdorf, A. (1989, 2nd ed.). *Indelible shadows: Film and the Holocaust.* Cambridge and New York: Cambridge University Press.

Christenfen, B. (Director), & Levinson, B. (Producer) (1967). *The only way* [feature on Danish rescuer]. Culver City, CA: Social Studies Service.

Collier, J. M. (Director) (1975). *The hiding place* [feature film on rescue in Holland]. Minneapolis, MN: World Wide Pictures.

Comforty, J. (Director, Writer, Producer), & Comforty, L. (Co-producer) (1994). *The optimists* [how the Bulgarian Jews were saved in the time of the Nazis]. Evansville, IL: Comforty Mediaconcepts Production.

Drach, M. (Director) (1973). *Les violons du bal.* Chicago: Films, Inc. & Los Angeles: Connoisseur Home Video.

Elfert, S. (Director), & Forster, A. (Writer) (1978). *Avenue of the just* [film documentary]. New York: Anti-Defamation League.

Erman, J. (1988). *The attic: The hiding of Anne Frank* [from Miep Gies's *Anne Frank remembered,* teleplay]. New York: CBS, Los Angeles: Telecom Entertainment, & London: Yorkshire T.V.

Feijoo, B. D., & Stagnaro, J. B. (Directors) (1988). *Under the world* [feature film on rescue in Poland]. Los Angeles: New World Pictures.

Flender, H. (Director, Producer, Writer) (1962). *Act of faith: Part II* [Danish rescue documentary]. New York: Anti-Defamation League & Clarksburg, NJ: Alden.

Gardner, R. (Director) (1985). *The courage to care* [film documentary]. New York: Anti-Defamation League.

Goodstein, D. (Director) (1988). *Voices from the attic* [rescue in Poland documentary]. Santa Monica, CA: Direct Cinema Limited.

Grede, K. (Director) (1990). *Good evening, Mr. Wallenberg.* New York: Swedish Film Institute.

Harel, D. (Director) (1983). *Raoul Wallenberg: Buried alive* [documentary film]. Los Angeles: Direct Cinema Ltd.

Holland, A. (Director) (1985). *Angry harvest* [feature film in Poland]. Washington, DC: European Classics.

Holland, J. (Director) (1993). *Rescue in October.* [Danish rescue documentary]. New York: Anti-Defamation League.

Imhoof, M. (Director) (1981). *The boat is full* [feature crossing border to Switzerland]. Chicago: Films, Inc.

Johnson, L. (1985). *Wallenberg: A hero's story* [teleplay by Gerald Green]. New York: NBC-TV.

Kaplan, R. (Director) (1989). *The exiles* [rescue of intellectuals to the U.S. by Varian Fry and others]. Los Angeles: Connoisseur Home Video and PBS.

Kijowski, J. (Director) (1992). *Warszawa—S703* [feature film on rescue in Warsaw]. Paris and Berlin: Molecule and Film Kunst.

Kjadegaard, A. (Producer, Director) (1993). *Exodus, or: a light in the dark* [documentary on Danish rescue]. Israeli Broadcasting Company & Danish Broadcasting Company. Washington, DC: National PBS.

Krents, M. (Director, Producer) (1957). *One man* [docudrama on Wallenberg]. Clarksburg, NJ: Alden.

Krents, M. (Director, Producer), & Flenders, H. (Writer) (1962). *Book seller* [docudrama on Danish rescue]. Clarksburg, NJ: Alden.

Lomnicki, J. (Director) (1991). *Still only this forest* [feature film rescue in Poland]. Washington, DC: Embassy of Poland.

Madsen, K. (Director) (1992). *A day in October* [feature film on Danish rescue]. New York: Castle Hills Productions & Academy Entertainment.

Malle, L. (Director) (1987). *Au revoir les enfants [Goodbye, children]* [feature film rescue in France]. New York: Orion Classics.

Marshall, R. (Producer) (1989). *Dark in the light* [documentary of rescue in sewers of Lvov]. London: B.B.C. & New York: Art Entertainment.

Mazer, V. (Producer, Writer) (1967). *Legacy of Anne Frank* [television documentary]. Clarksburg, NJ: Alden.

Mitrani, M. (Director, Producer) (1974). *Black Thursday [Les guichets du Louvre]* [feature film on rescue of children in France]. Chicago: Films, Inc.

Morley, P. (Director, Producer) and Sim, K. (Writer, Producer) (1980). *Women of courage* [documentary of German rescuer Hiltgunt Zassenhaus]. Yorkshire: Yorkshire Television.

Ornitz, A. (Director) (1972). *Denmark '43* [film documentary]. Waltham, MA: National Center for Jewish Films, Brandeis University.

Page, A. (Director) (1986). *Forbidden* [from teleplay, Leonard Gross's *Last Jews of Berlin*]. New York: Home Box Office.

Perlstein, D. (Director) (1990). *Escape to the rising sun* [documentary of Japanese rescue of Jews]. Waltham, MA: National Center for Jewish Films, Brandeis University.

Pounchev, B. (Director) (1988). *The transports of death* [feature film on rescue in Bulgaria]. Washington, DC: Bulgarian Embassy.

Ramati, A. (Writer, director) (1984). *Assisi underground* [feature film]. Los Angeles: Cannon Film and MGM/UA Home Video.

Randal, T. (Director, Producer) (1989). *To know where they are* [documentary film in Poland]. New York: Anti-Defamation League.

Rochlitz, J. (Director, Producer, Writer) (1987). *The righteous enemy* [documentary on rescue in Italy]. Waltham, MA: National Center for Jewish Films, Brandeis University.

Rosenberg, S. (1976). *Voyage of the damned* [feature film on the rescue efforts aboard the *St. Louis* ship].† Chicago: Films, Inc.

Rotter, S. (Director) (1991). *The other side of faith* [documentary of Stefania Podgórska Burzminska]. New York: Anti-Defamation League.

Rotter, S. (Director) (1992). *Żegota: A time to remember* [documentary on rescue in Poland]. Washington, DC: Documentaries International Ltd.

Sauvage, P. (Director) (1987). *Weapons of the spirit* [film documentary on rescue in Le Chambon-sur-Lignon, France]. Los Angeles: Friends of Le Chambon and Pierre Sauvage & New York: Anti-Defamation League.

† The German captain of the *St. Louis,* Gustav Schroeder, was recognized by Yad Vashem as a Righteous Among the Nations of the World.

Schneid, R. (Director) (1988). *Das letzte Visum* [*The last visa*] [documentary on the rescue work of Varian Fry]. Frankfurt: Hessen Television, Hessischer Rundfunk.

Segelman, G. (Director, Producer) (1991). *Choosing courage* [documentary, legacy of Lubberts, Dutch rescuer]. Rochester, NY: Bureau of Jewish Education.

Shapiro, P. (Director, Writer), & Cohen, J. (Writer) (1985). *Miracle at Moreaux* [telefilm adapted from *Ten and twenty*, about rescue of children in France]. Pittsburgh: WKED Atlantis Films.

Smalley, K., & Sarin, V. (Directors) (1987, 1993). *So many miracles* [documentary on Banyas rescue of Rubineks in Poland]. Waltham, MA: National Center for Jewish Films, Brandeis University.

Truffaut, F. (1980). *The last metro* [feature film on rescue in France]. New York: CBS–Fox Video.

Wajda, A. (Director) (1961). *Samson* [feature film on rescue in Poland]. Chicago: Films, Inc.

Wehan-Damisch, T. (Director) (1990). *Marseille–New York* [documentary on rescue efforts of Varian Fry]. Paris: French television.

Weiner, R. (Director) (1986). *The world of Anne Frank* [docudrama]. New York: Anti-Defamation League & Teaneck, NJ: Ergo Media.

Historical Background

Abrahamsen, S. (1991). *Norway's response to the Holocaust: A historical perspective.* New York: Holocaust Library.

Andreas-Friedrich, R. (1974). *Berlin underground.* New York: Henry Holt.

Arendt, H. (1973). *The origins of totalitarianism.* New York: Harcourt Brace Jovanovich.

Baker, L. (1978). *Days of sorrow and pain: Leo Baeck and the Berlin Jews.* New York: Macmillan.

Bartoszewski, W. (1987). *The Warsaw ghetto: A Christian's testimony.* Boston: Beacon.

Bauer, Y. (1977). Negotiations between Saly Mayer and the S.S. In Y. Gutman & E. Zuroff (Eds.), *Rescue attempts during the Holocaust: Proceedings of the Second Yad Vashem International Historical Conference, April 1974* (pp. 5–45). Jerusalem: Yad Vashem.

Bauer, Y. (1978). *The Holocaust in historical perspective.* Seattle: University of Washington Press.

Bauer, Y. (1982). *A history of the Holocaust.* New York: Franklin Watts.

Bejski, E. (1977). The Righteous Among the Nations and their part in the rescue of Jews. In Y. Gutman & E. Zuroff (Eds.), *Rescue attempts during the Holocaust: Proceedings of the Second Yad Vashem International Historical Conference, April 1974* (pp. 627–47). Jerusalem: Yad Vashem.

Ben-Tov, A. (1988). *Facing the Holocaust in Budapest: The International Committee of the Red Cross and the Jews in Hungary, 1943–1945.* Geneva: Henry Dunant Institute, Martinus Nijhoff Publishers.

Bethge, E. (1967). *Dietrich Bonhoeffer: Man of vision, man of courage.* New York: Harper & Row.

Braham, R. (1981). *The politics of genocide: The Holocaust in Hungary,* Vols. 1 & 2. New York: Columbia University Press.

Carpi, D. (1977). The rescue of Jews in the Italian zone of occupied Croatia. In Y. Gutman & E. Zuroff (Eds.), *Rescue attempts during the Holocaust: Proceedings of the Second Yad Vashem International Historical Conference, April 1974* (pp. 465–507). Jerusalem: Yad Vashem.

Chary, F. (1972). *The Bulgarian Jews and the final solution.* Pittsburgh: University of Pittsburgh Press.

Conway, J. (1968). *The Nazi persecution of the churches, 1933–1945.* New York: Basic Books.

De Jong, L. (1965, Spring). Help to people in hiding: A review of arts, life, and thought in the Netherlands 1940–1941. *Delta, 8* (19), 37–39.

De Lubac, H. (1990). *Christian resistance to Anti-Semitism: Memories from 1940–1944.* San Francisco: Ignatius Press.

Des Pres, T. (1979, May). Goodness incarnate: Sheltering Jews in Vichy France. *Harper's*, pp. 83–86.

Dietrich, D. (1988). *Catholic citizens in the Third Reich: Psychosocial principles and moral reasoning*. New Brunswick, NJ: Transaction Books.

Dwork, D. (1991). *Children with a star: Jewish youth in Nazi Europe*. New Haven & London: Yale University Press.

Fein, H. (1979). *Accounting for genocide: National responses and Jewish victimization during the Holocaust*. Chicago: University of Chicago Press.

Feingold, H. (1970). *The politics of rescue*. New York: Holocaust Library.

Flender, H. (1980). *Rescue in Denmark*. New York: Holocaust Library.

Frabre, E. (Ed.) (1970) *God's underground, CIMADE 1935–1945*. St. Louis: The Bethany Press.

Friedman, P. (1980). Righteous Gentiles in the Nazi era. In A. J. Friedman (Ed.), *Roads to extinction: Essays on the Holocaust* (pp. 409–21). Philadelphia: Jewish Publication Society of America.

Friedman, P. (1980). Was there an "other Germany" during the Nazi period? In A. J. Friedman (Ed.), *Roads to extinction: Essays on the Holocaust* (pp. 409–21). Philadelphia: Jewish Publication Society of America.

Fry, V. (1945). *Surrender on demand*. New York: Random House.

Fry, V. (1968). *Assignment rescue*. New York: Scholastic Books.

Gilbert, M. (1982). *Atlas of the Holocaust*. London: Michael Joseph.

Gilbert, M. (1985). *The Holocaust: A history of the Jews during the Second World War*. New York: Holt, Rinehart and Winston.

Goldberger, L. (1988). *Rescue of the Danish Jews*. New York: New York University Press.

Gordon, S. (1984). *Hitler, Germans and the Jewish question*. Princeton: Princeton University Press.

Hausner, G. (1966). *Justice in Jerusalem*. New York: Schocken Books.

Hilberg, R. (1961). *The destruction of the European Jews*. Chicago: Quadrangle.

Karski, J. (1944). *Story of a secret state.* Boston: Houghton Mifflin.

Kestenberg, M. (1985). Poland without Jews. *Newsletter of Jerome Riker International Study of Organized Persecution of Children, 1* (2), 1–2.

Kieval, H. J. (1980, October). Legality and assistance in Vichy France: The rescue of Jewish children. *Proceedings of the American Philosophical Society, 124,* 339–66.

Korbanski, S. (1968). *Fighting Warsaw.* New York: Funk & Wagnalls.

Laska, V. (Ed.) (1983). *Women in the resistance and in the Holocaust: The voices of eyewitnesses.* Westport, CT: Greenwood Press.

Lewy, G. (1964). *The Catholic Church and Nazi Germany.* New York: McGraw-Hill.

Marrus, M. R., & Paxton, R. O. (1983). *Vichy France and the Jews.* New York: Schocken Books.

Meed, V. (1973). *On both sides of the wall.* Beit Lohamei Hagettaot: Ghetto Fighters House Hakibbutz Hameuchad Publishing House.

Milton, S. (1983). The righteous who helped Jews. In A. Grobman & D. Landes (Eds.), *Genocide: Critical issues of the Holocaust.* Los Angeles: Simon Wiesenthal Publication.

Poliakov, L. (1950, August). Human morality and the Nazi terror. *Commentary,* pp. 111–16.

Poliakov, L., & Sabille, J. (1954). *Jews under the Italian occupation.* Paris: Centre de Documentation Juive Contemporaine.

Presser, J. (1969). *The destruction of the Dutch Jews.* New York: Dutton.

Ringelblum, E. (1975). *Notes from the Warsaw ghetto.* New York: Schocken Books.

Rossiter, M. (1986). *Women in the resistance.* New York: Praeger.

Rothfels, H. (1962). *The German opposition to Hitler.* Westport, CT: Greenwood Press.

Rothkirchen, L. (1982, June). The stand of the churches vis-à-vis the persecution of the Jews of Slovakia. In *Papers presented to the International Symposium on Judaism and Christianity under the Impact of National Socialism (1919–1945)* (pp. 273–86). Jerusalem: Historical Society of Israel.

Sloan, J. (Ed.). (1974). *Notes from the Warsaw ghetto: The Journal of Emmanuel Ringelblum.* New York: Schocken Books.

Steinberg, L. (1974). *Not as a lamb: The Jews against Hitler.* Glasgow: The University Press.

Steinberg, L. (1977). Jewish rescue activities in Belgium and France. In Y. Gutman & E. Zuroff (Eds.), *Rescue attempts during the Holocaust: Proceedings of the Second Yad Vashem International Historical Conference, April 1974* (pp. 603–15). Jerusalem: Yad Vashem.

Valentin, H. (1953). Rescue and relief activities in behalf of Jewish victims of Nazism in Scandinavia. *YIVO Annual of Social Sciences, 8,* 224–51.

Weigler, Z. (1957). Two villages razed for extending help to Jews. *Yad Vashem Bulletin, 1,* 18–20.

Zuccotti, S. (1987). *The Italians and the Holocaust: Persecution, rescue, survival.* New York: Basic Books.

Zuccotti, S. (1993). *The Holocaust, the French, and the Jews.* New York: Basic Books.

Holocaust Rescue Stories

Agar, H. (1961, May 7–11). Christians who dared death to save Jews. *Jewish Digest.*

Anger, P. (1981). *With Raoul Wallenberg in Budapest.* New York: Holocaust Library.

Arthur, B. (1976, February 2). Germans who saved Jews from Nazis. *Jerusalem Post.*

Bacque, J. (1992). *Just Raoul: The private war against the Nazis of Raoul Laporterie, who saved over 1,600 lives in France.* Rocklin, CA: Prima Publishing.

Bartoszewski, W., & Lewinowna, Z. (1970). *The Samaritans: Heroes of the Holocaust.* New York: Twayne Publishers.

Bauminger, A. L. (1969). *The righteous.* Jerusalem: Yad Vashem.

Bernstein, T., & Rutkoowski, A. (1963). *Assistance to the Jews in Poland.* Warsaw: Polonia Foreign Languages Publishing House.

Bierman, J. (1981). *Righteous Gentile: The story of Raoul Wallenberg.* New York: Viking.

Bishop, C. H. (1952) (illustrated by du Bois, W. P.). *Twenty and ten.* New York: Penguin.

Block, G., & Drucker, M. (1992). *Rescuers: Portraits of moral courage in the Holocaust.* New York: Holmes & Meier.

Boehm, E. H. (1985). *We survived: Fourteen histories of the hidden and hunted of Nazi Germany.* Santa Barbara, CA: ABC-Clio Information Services.

Breznitz, S. (1992). *Memory fields: The legacy of a wartime childhood in Czechoslovakia.* New York: Knopf.

Drucker, M., and Halpern, M. (1993). *Jacob's rescue: A Holocaust story.* New York: Bantam Books.

Ezratty, H. (1968, September). The consul who disobeyed: a Christian who sacrificed his career to save Jewish lives. *Jewish Digest, 8,* 54–56.

Fischman, W. I. (1964, December 1). The friar who saved 5,000 Jews. *Look,* pp. 66–71.

Flender, H. (1964). *Rescue in Denmark.* New York: Holocaust Library.

Ford, H. (1966). *Flee the captor.* Nashville, TN: Southern Publishing Association.

Friedländer, S. (1979). *When memory comes.* New York: Farrar, Straus, Giroux.

Friedman, P. (1957). *Their brothers' keepers.* New York: Crown.

Gies, M., with Gold, A. (1987). *Anne Frank remembered: The story of the woman who helped to hide the Frank family.* New York: Simon & Schuster.

Gross, L. (1982). *The last Jews of Berlin.* New York: Simon & Schuster.

Grossman, K. D. (1958). *Die unbesungenen Helden: Menschen in Deutschlands dunklen tagen.* Berlin: Arani Verlag.

Grossman, K. D. (1959, September). The humanitarian that cheated Hitler. *Coronet,* pp. 66–71.

Gruber, R. (1967, April 15). The heroism of Staszek Jackowski. *Saturday Review, 50,* 19–20.

Gruber, R. M. (1968, December). The Pole who saved 32 Jews. *Hadassah Magazine,* pp. 21, 36.

Gut Opdyke, I., with Elliot, J. M. (1992). *Into the flames: The life story of a Righteous Gentile.* San Bernardino, CA: The Borgo Press.

Hallie, P. (1979). *Lest innocent blood be shed: The story of the village of Le Chambon and how goodness happened there.* New York: Harper & Row.

Hellman, P. (1980). *Avenue of the Righteous: Portraits in uncommon courage of Christians and the Jews they saved from Hitler.* New York: Atheneum.

Herzer, I. (1983, June–July). How Italians rescued Jews. *Midstream,* pp. 36–38.

Hirt-Manheimer, A. (Ed.) (1978, October). The Christian conscience (Righteous Gentiles). *Keeping Posted, 24, #2.*

Horbach, M. (1967). *Out of the night.* New York: Frederick Fell.

Huneke, D. K. (1985). *The Moses of Rovno.* New York: Dodd, Mead.

Iranek-Osmecki, K. (1971). *He who saves one life.* New York: Crown.

Isaacman, C. (1984). *Clara's story.* Philadelphia: Jewish Publication Society.

Keneally, T. (1982). *Schindler's List.* New York: Simon & Schuster.

Kennedy, P. (1964, April). The Vatican pimpernal: Monsignor Hugh O'Flaherty. *Columbia, 44,* 26–27.

Leboucher, F. (1969). *Incredible mission.* New York: Doubleday.

Lester, E. (1984). *Wallenberg: The man in the iron web*. Englewood Cliffs, NJ: Prentice-Hall.

Leuner, H. D. (1966). *When compassion was a crime: Germany's silent heroes 1933–1945*. London: Wolf.

Lowrie, D. (1963). *The hunted children*. New York: W. W. Norton.

Lowry, L. (1989). *Number the stars*. Boston: Houghton Mifflin.

Mahler, E. (1962). How Granny saved Helenka from the Germans. In Y. Shilhav & S. Feinstein (Eds.), *Flame and fury*. New York: Jewish Education Committee Press.

Marshall, R. (1990). *In the sewers of Lvov*. New York: Charles Scribner's Sons.

Marton, K. (1982). *Wallenberg*. New York: Random House.

Meltzer, M. (1988). *Rescue: The story of how Gentiles saved Jews in the Holocaust*. New York: Harper & Row.

A *Moment* interview with Marion Pritchard (1983, December 1). *Moment*, pp. 26–33.

Neshamit, S. (1977). Rescue in Lithuania during the Nazi occupation. In Y. Gutman & E. Zuroff (Eds.), *Rescue attempts during the Holocaust: Proceedings of the Second Yad Vashem International Historical Conference, April 1974* (pp. 289–331). Jerusalem: Yad Vashem.

Oliner, S. (1979). *Restless memories*. Berkeley: Judah L. Magnes Museum.

Orenstein, H. (1987). *I shall live*. New York: Beaufort Books.

Orlev, V. (1991) (Translator Halkin, H.). *The man from the other side*. Boston: Houghton Mifflin.

Pritchard, M. (1984, April 27). It came to pass in those days. *Sh'ma*, pp. 97–102.

Ramati, A. (1978). *The Assisi underground: The priests who rescued Jews*. New York: Stein & Day.

Reiss, J. (1972). *The upstairs room*. New York: Bantam Books.

Rittner, C., & Myers, S. (Eds.) (1986). *The courage to care.* New York: New York University Press.

Rochman, L. (1983). *The pit and the trap: A chronicle of survival.* New York: Holocaust Library.

Rorty, J. (1946, December). Father Benoit: Ambassador of the Jews, an untold story of the underground. *Commentary, 2,* 507–13.

Rose, L. (1978). *The tulips are red.* New York: A. S. Barnes.

Rosenfeld, H. (1982). *The Swedish angel of rescue: The heroism and torment of Raoul Wallenberg.* Buffalo, NY: Prometheus Books.

Rotenberg, A. (1987). *Emissaries: A memoir of the Riviera, Haute-Savoie, Switzerland, and World War II.* Secaucus, NJ: Citadel Press.

Roth-Hano, R. (1988). *Touch wood: A girlhood in occupied France.* New York: Four Winds Press.

Rubinek, S. (1988). *So many miracles.* New York: Viking Penguin.

Sauvage, P. (1983, October). A most persistent haven: Le Chambon-sur-Lignon. *Moment, 8* (9), 30–35.

Silver, E. (1992). *The book of the just: The silent heroes who saved Jews from Hitler.* London: Weidenfeld and Nicolson.

Sobczak, S. (1983). How I hid twelve Jews. In J. Kugelmass & J. Boyorin (Eds.), *The memorial books of Polish Jewry* (pp. 175–76). New York: Schocken Books.

Stein, D. (1988). *Quiet heroes: True stories of the rescue of Jews by Christians in Nazi-occupied Holland.* Toronto: Lester & Orpen Dennys Limited.

Stix, H. (1978, June 23). A German who really cared. Los Angeles *Times,* part 4.

Tec, N. (1982). *Dry tears.* Westport, CT: Wildcat Publishing Company.

Ten Boom, C., with Sherrill, J., & Sherrill, E. (1971). *The hiding place.* Old Tappan, NJ: Fleming H. Revell.

Tokayu, M. & Swart, M. (1979). *The Fugu plan: The untold story of the Japanese and the Jews during WWII.* London/New York: Paddington Press, Ltd.

Vincent, S. (1970, June). Four Christians who were their brothers' keepers. *Jewish Digest, 15,* 78–80.

Vlcko, P. (1973). *In the shadow of tyranny: A history in novel form.* New York: Vantage Press.

Von Staden, W. (1981). *Darkness over the valley.* New Haven & New York: Ticknor & Fields.

Vos, J. (1952). *Like a cedar on the Lebanon.* Leiden: A. W. Sythoff Vitgeversmaatschabpy M.V.

Waagenaar, S. (1974, October 19). Unknown war hero: Rescue of the Jews by a Capuchin priest. *America, 131,* 210–12.

Weinberg, W. (1983, June 22–29). A Dutch couple. *The Christian Century, 20,* #20, 611–15.

Weinstein, F. S. (1985). *A hidden childhood: A Jewish girl's sanctuary in a French convent, 1942–1945.* New York: Farrar, Straus, Giroux.

Werbell, F. E., & Clarke, T. (1982). *Lost hero: The mystery of Raoul Wallenberg.* New York: McGraw-Hill.

Wolfe, J. (1981). *Take care of Josette: A memoir in defense of occupied France.* New York: Franklin Watts.

Yahil, L. (1969). *The rescue of Danish Jewry: Test of a democracy.* Philadelphia: Jewish Publication Society.

Zassenhaus, H. (1974). *Walls: Resisting the Third Reich—one woman's story.* Boston: Beacon.

Related Social Sciences
(Psychology, Sociology, Political Science)

Abraham, K. (1955). The rescue and murder of the father in neurotic fantasy formations. *Clinical papers and essays on psychoanalysis* (Vol. 2). New York: Basic Books. (Originally published 1922.)

Adorno, T. W., Frenkel-Brunswik, E., Levinson, D. J., & Sanford, R. N. (1950). *The authoritarian personality.* New York: W. W. Norton.

Asch, S. E. (1956). Studies of independence and conformity: A minority of one against a unanimous majority. *Psychological Monographs, 70* (9).

Atwood, G. (1974). The loss of a loved parent and the origin of salvation fantasies. *Psychotherapy: Theory, Research and Practice, 11* (3), 256–58.

Atwood, G. (1978). On the origins and dynamics of messianic salvation fantasies. *International Review of Psycho-Analysis, 5* (1), 85–96.

Bar-Tal, D. (1976). *Prosocial behavior: Theory and research.* Washington, DC: Hemisphere.

Bar-Tal, D. (1984). American study of helping behavior: What? why? and where? In E. Staub, D. Bar-Tal, J. Karylowski, & J. Reykowski (Eds.), *Development and maintenance of prosocial behavior* (pp. 5–21). New York: Plenum.

Beardslee, W. R. (1983). Commitment and endurance: Common themes in the life histories of civil rights workers who stayed. *American Journal of Orthopsychiatry, 53* (1), 34–42.

Berkowitz, L. (1972). Social norms, feelings, and other factors affecting helping and altruism. In L. Berkowitz (Ed.), *Advances in experimental social psychology* (Vol. 6). New York: Academic Press.

Blasi, A. (1980). Bridging moral cognition and moral action: A critical review of the literature. *Psychological Bulletin, 88* (1), 1–45.

Bryan, J. H. (1972). Why children help: A review. *Journal of Social Issues, 28* (3), 87–104.

Clary, E. G., & Miller, J. (1986). Socialization and situational influences on sustained altruism. *Child Development, 57* (6), 1358–69.

Colby, A., & Damon, W. (1992). *Some do care: Contemporary lives of moral commitment.* New York: Free Press.

Damico, A. J. (1982). The sociology of justice: Kohlberg and Milgram. *Political Theory, 10* (3), 409–34.

Damon, W. (1988). *The moral child: Nurturing children's natural moral growth.* New York: Free Press.

Darley, J. M., & Batson, C. (1973). From Jerusalem to Jericho: A study of situational and dispositional variables in helping behavior. *Journal of Personality and Social Psychology, 27* (1), 100–8.

Darley, J. M., & Latané, B. (1968). Bystander intervention in emergencies: Diffusion of responsibility. *Journal of Personality and Social Psychology, 8,* 377–83.

Ehlert, J., Ehlert, N., & Merrens, M. (1973). The influence of ideological affiliation on helping behavior. *Journal of Social Psychology, 89,* 315–16.

Erikson, E. H. (1968). *Identity: Youth and crisis.* New York: W. W. Norton.

Erikson, E. H. (1969). *Gandhi's truth.* New York: W. W. Norton.

Fogelman, E. (1987). The rescuers: A socio-psychological study of altruistic behavior during the Nazi era. Unpublished doctoral dissertation, Graduate Center of the City University of New York.

Fogelman, E. (1988). Psychological origins of rescue. *Dimensions: A Journal of Holocaust Studies, 3* (3), 9–12.

Fogelman, E. (1989, December 9). Forgotten heroes: Rescuers of Jews during the Nazi period. *America,* pp. 426–428, 434.

Fogelman, E. (1990). What motivated the rescuers? *Dimensions: A Journal of Holocaust Studies, 5* (3), 8–11.

Fogelman, E. (1990). In search of goodness: Finding and recognizing Righteous Gentiles. *Women's American ORT Reporter,* Spring.

Fogelman, E., & Wiener, V. L. (1985). The few, the brave, the noble. *Psychology Today, 19* (8), 60–65.

Freud, A. (1946). A form of altruism. *The ego and the mechanism of defense* (pp. 132–148). New York: International Universities Press.

Ganz, I. (1993). Personal and familial predictors of altruism under stress. Unpublished doctoral dissertation, Graduate School of Arts and Sciences, Columbia University.

Gilligan, C. (1981). *In a different voice: Psychological theory and women's development.* Cambridge, MA: Harvard University Press.

Goleman, D. (1985, March 5). Great altruists: Science ponders soul of goodness. New York *Times,* pp. C1–C2.

Grossman, F. (1982, July 22). Righteous Gentiles. *Scarsdale Enquirer.*

Grossman, F. (1984). Psychological study of Gentiles who saved Jews. In I. Charney (Ed.), *Toward the understanding of Holocaust and prevention of genocide* (pp. 202–16). Boulder, CO: Westview Press.

Haan, N. (1978). Two moralities in action contexts: Relationships to thought, ego regulation, and development. *Journal of Personality and Social Psychology, 36,* 286–305.

Harris, M. B. (1972). The effects of performing one altruistic act on the likelihood of performing another. *Journal of Social Psychology, 88* (1), 65–73.

Henry, F. (1984). *Victims and neighbors: A small town in Nazi Germany remembered.* South Hadley, MA: Bergin & Garvey.

Hoffman, M. L. (1963). Parent discipline and the child's consideration for others. *Child Development, 34,* 573–88.

Hoffman, M. L. (1975). Altruistic behavior and the parent-child relationship. *Journal of Personality and Social Psychology, 31,* 937–43.

Hoffman, M. L. (1976). Empathy, role taking, guilt, and development of altruistic motives. In T. Lickons (Ed.), *Moral development and behavior.* New York: Holt, Rinehart and Winston.

Hoffman, M. L. (1977). Empathy, its development and prosocial implications. In C. B. Keasey (Ed.) *Nebraska Symposium on Motivation* (Vol. 25). Lincoln: University of Nebraska Press.

Hoffman, M. (1982). Development of prosocial motivation: Empathy and guilt. In N. Eisenberg (Ed.), *Development of prosocial behavior.* New York: Academic Press.

Hoffman, M. (1984). Discipline, moral internalization, and prosocial motivation. In E. Staub, D. Bar-Tal, J. Karylowski, & J. Reykowski (Eds.), *Development and maintenance of prosocial behavior* (pp. 117–32). New York: Plenum.

Huneke, D. K. (1980). *In the darkness . . . glimpses of light: A study of Nazi era rescuers.* Report to the Oregon Committee for the Humanities.

Huneke, D. K. (1981–1982). A study of Christians who rescued Jews during the Nazi era. *Humboldt Journal of Social Relations, 9* (1), 144–49.

Huston, T. L., Geis, G., & Wright, W. (1976, June). The angry Samaritans. *Psychology Today,* pp. 61–85.

Huston, T. L., Ruggiero, M., Conner, R., & Geis, G. (1981). Bystander intervention into crime: A study based on naturally-occurring episodes. *Social Psychology Quarterly, 44* (1), 14–23.

Kelman, H. (1975). Violence without moral restraint: Reflections on the dehumanization of victims and victimizers. *Journal of Social Issues, 29* (4), 25–61.

Kelman, H. C., & Laurence, H. C. (1972). Assignment of responsibility in the case of Lieutenant Calley: Preliminary report on a national survey. *Journal of Social Issues, 28,* 177–212.

Kestenberg, J. (1984). *The response of the child to the rescuer.* Paper presented at the Acts of Humankind: Rescuers of Jews During the Holocaust Conference, Washington, DC.

Klein, D. (Ed.) (1993). A singular universe: Rescuers and hidden children, *Dimensions: A Journal of Holocaust Studies, 7* (1).

Kohlberg, L. (1981). *The philosophy of moral development.* San Francisco: Harper & Row.

Latané, B., & Darley, J. M. (1970). *The unresponsive bystander: Why doesn't he help?* New York: Appleton-Century-Crofts.

Lerner, M. J. (1980). *The belief in a just world: A fundamental delusion.* New York: Plenum.

Levy, D. M. (1946). The German anti-Nazi. *American Journal of Orthopsychiatry, 16,* 507–15.

Levy, D. M. (1948). Anti-Nazis' criteria of differentiation. *Psychiatry, 11,* 125–67.

Lief, L. H., & Fox, R. (1963). Training for detached concern in medical students. In *Psychological basis of medical practice* (pp. 12–35). New York: Harper & Row.

Lifton, R. J. (1961). *Thought reform and the psychology of totalism: A study of "brainwashing" in China.* New York: W. W. Norton.

Lifton, R. J. (1970). Protean man. In *History and human survival* (pp. 311–31). New York: Random House.

Lifton, R. J. (1976). *The life of the self: Toward a new psychology*. New York: Touchstone Books.

Lifton, R. J. (1982). Medicalized killing in Auschwitz. *Psychiatry, 45,* 283–97.

Lifton, R. J. (1986). *The Nazi doctors*. New York: Basic Books.

Lifton, R. J. (1987). *The future of immortality and other essays for a nuclear age*. New York: Basic Books.

Loevinger, J. (1970). *Measuring ego development*. San Francisco: Jossey-Bass.

London, P. (1970). The rescuers: Motivational hypotheses about Christians who saved Jews from the Nazis. In J. Macauley & L. Berkowitz (Eds.), *Altruism and helping behavior* (pp. 241–50). New York: Academic Press.

Lowe, R., & Richter, G. (1973). Relation of altruism to age, social class and ethnic identity. *Psychological Reports, 33,* 567–72.

McWilliams, N. (1976). *Helpers: A study in normal personality*. Unpublished doctoral dissertation, Rutgers University.

McWilliams, N. (1984). The psychology of the altruist. *Psychoanalytic Psychology, 1* (3), 193–213.

Midlarsky, E. (1971). Aiding under stress. *Journal of Personality, 39,* 132–49.

Midlarsky, E. (1984). Competence and helping: Notes toward a model. In E. Staub, D. Bar-Tal, J. Karylowski, & J. Reykowski (Eds.), *Development and maintenance of prosocial behavior* (pp. 291–308). New York: Plenum.

Midlarsky, E., & Baron, L. (Eds.) (1986). Altruism and prosocial behavior. *Humboldt Journal of Social Relations, 13* (1 & 2).

Milgram, S. (1974). *Obedience to authority: An experimental view*. New York: Harper & Row.

Monroe, K. R. (1991). John Donne's people: Explaining altruism through cognitive frameworks. *Journal of Politics, 53,* 394–433.

Monroe, K., Barton, M., & Klingemann, U. (1990, October). Altruism and the theory of rational action: Rescuers of Jews in Nazi Europe, *Ethics, 101,* 103–22.

Oliner, P., Oliner, S., Baron, L., Blum, L., Kress, D., & Smolenska, M. Z. (Eds.) (1992). *Embracing the other: Philosophical, psychological, and historical perspective on altruism.* New York: New York University Press.

Oliner, S., & Oliner, P. (1988). *The altruistic personality: Rescuers of Jews in Nazi Europe.* New York: Free Press.

Piaget, J. (1932). *The moral judgement of the child.* London: Routledge & Kegan Paul.

Piliavin, I. M., Piliavin, J. A., & Rodin, J. (1975). Good Samaritanism: An underground phenomenon? *Journal of Personality and Social Psychology, 35,* 429–38.

Poulos, R. W., & Liebert, R. M. (1972). Influence of modeling, exhortative verbalization, and surveillance on children's sharing. *Developmental Psychology, 6,* 402–8.

Radke-Yarrow, M., Scott, P. M., & Zahn-Waxler, C. (1973). Learning concern for others. *Developmental Psychology, 8* (2), 240–60.

Radke-Yarrow, M., & Zahn-Waxler, C. (1986). The role of familial factors in the development of prosocial behavior: Research findings and questions. In D. Olweus, J. Block, & M. Radke-Yarrow (Eds.), *Development of antisocial and prosocial behavior: Research, theories and issues* (pp. 207–33). New York: Academic Press.

Rest, J. R. (1976). New approaches in the assessment of moral judgment. In T. Lickona (Ed.), *Moral development and behavior.* New York: Holt, Rinehart and Winston.

Rosenhan, D. (1970). The natural socialization of altruistic autonomy (pp. 251–68). In J. Macauley & L. Berkowitz (Eds.), *Altruism and helping behavior.* New York: Academic Press.

Rosenhan, D. L. (1978). Toward resolving the altruism paradox. In L. Wispé (Ed.), *Altruism, sympathy and helping: Psychological and sociological principles* (pp. 101–13). New York: Academic Press.

Rosenhan, D. L., Moore, B. S., & Underwood, B. (1976). The social psychology of moral behavior. In T. Lickona (Ed.), *Moral development and behavior* (pp. 241–52). New York: Holt, Rinehart and Winston.

Rosenhan, D. L., Salovey, P., & Hargis, K. (1981). The joys of helping: Focus of attention mediated the impact of positive affect on altruism. *Journal of Personality and Social Psychology, 40* (5), 899–905.

Rosenhan, D. L., Underwood, B., & Moore, B. S. (1974). Affect moderates altruism and self gratification. *Journal of Personality and Social Psychology, 30,* 546–52.

Rosenhan, D., & White, G. M. (1967). Observation and rehearsal as determinants of prosocial behavior. *Journal of Personality and Social Psychology, 5,* 424–31.

Rotter, J. B. (1966). Generalized expectancies for internal vs. external locus of control of reinforcement. *Psychological Monograph, 80* (609).

Schulman, M., & Mekler, E. (1985). *Bringing up a moral child: A new approach for teaching your child to be kind, just, and responsible.* New York: Doubleday.

Schulweis, H. (1986, May). They were our brothers' keepers. *Moment,* pp. 47–50.

Schulweis, H. (1988). The bias against man. *Dimensions: A Journal of Holocaust Studies, 3* (3), 4–9.

Schulweis, H. (1990). The fear and suspicion of goodness. *Dimensions: A Journal of Holocaust Studies, 5* (3), 22–25.

Schulweis, H. (1993). The moral art of memory. *Dimensions: A Journal of Holocaust Studies, 7* (1), 3–7.

Schwartz, S. (1970). Elicitation of moral obligation and self-sacrificing behavior. *Journal of Personality and Social Psychology, 15,* 283–93.

Seligmann, A. (1992). An illegal way of life in Nazi Germany. *Leo Baeck Institute Year Book, XXXVII,* 327.

Staub, E. (1970). A child in distress: The effects of focusing responsibility on children on their attempts to help. *Developmental Psychology, 2,* 152–54.

Staub, E. (1978). *Positive social behavior and morality: Social and personal influences* (Vols. 1 & 2). New York: Academic Press.

Staub, E. (1978). *Positive social behavior and morality: Social and personal influences.* New York: Academic Press.

Staub, E., Bar-Tal, D., Karylowski, J., & Reykowski, J. (Eds.) (1984). *Development and maintenance of prosocial behavior: International perspectives on positive morality.* New York: Plenum.

Szonyi, D., & Fogelman, E. (Eds.) (1990). Moral courage during the Holocaust. *Dimensions: A Journal of Holocaust Studies, 5* (3).

Tec, N. (1985). The rescuer-rescued relationship: How did it begin? *Dimensions: A Journal of Holocaust Studies, 1* (2), 4–7.

Tec, N. (1986). *When light pierced the darkness: Christian rescue of Jews in Nazi-occupied Poland.* New York & Oxford: Oxford University Press.

Wiener, V. L., Fogelman, E., & Cohen, S. P. (1985). Why Righteous Gentiles risked their lives to save Jews. *Jewish Monthly: The B'nai B'rith International, 99* (5), 16–19.

Wolfson, M. (1970, April). *The subculture of freedom: Some people will not.* Paper presented to the regional meeting of the Western Political Science Association, Sacramento, CA.

Wundheiler, L. N. (1986). Oskar Schindler's moral development during the Holocaust. In E. Midlarsky and L. Baron (Eds.), Altruism and prosocial behavior. *Humboldt Journal of Social Relations, 13* (1 & 2), 333–56.

Wuthnow, R. (1991). *Acts of compassion.* Princeton: Princeton University Press.

Zahn-Waxler, C., & Radke-Yarrow, M. (1982). The development of altruism: Alternative research strategies. In N. Eisenberg (Ed.), *The development of prosocial behavior.* New York: Academic Press.

Zahn-Waxler, C., Radke-Yarrow, M., & King, R. (1979). Child rearing and children's prosocial initiations toward victims of distress. *Child Development, 50,* 319–30.

ACKNOWLEDGMENTS

MY SENSE OF HOPE in humanity was renewed by engaging in this study of conscience and courage amidst evil. For this opportunity, I am indebted to hundreds of people who have contributed to this book, particularly the rescuers and survivors, and to those who encouraged me in my personal and scientific search for the understanding of moral integrity in the face of inhumanity.

I would not have embarked upon becoming a social psychologist, or started this work, were it not for my inspirational mentor and friend Stephen P. Cohen. Steve's perseverance in his creative efforts to bring peace to the Middle East was a model for me in my own work. It was from Steve Cohen that I first learned the importance of integration of self with vocational choices which led to the journey that culminated in this book. I have valued his counsel and judgment at important junctures and crossroads.

I am sorry that John Slawson did not live to enjoy the fruits he planted in commissioning my original Rescuer Project at the Graduate Center of the City University of New York. His vision for social scientists to learn from altruistic behavior during the Holocaust (for present-day situations) as they did from the earlier authoritarian personality he supported is indeed becoming a reality.

My work has been tremendously enhanced by my association

with Judith Kestenberg and the late Milton Kestenberg of the International Study of Organized Persecution of Children, a project of Child Development Research. Milton's rare combination of legal and humane approaches and Judith's psychoanalytic perspective, passion, and dedication to related projects energized me. Not only did Milton and Judith Kestenberg's inquisitive natures inform, nurture, and enrich this work but they unhesitatingly interviewed rescuers and children who were rescued wherever they encountered them, translated material from Polish and German, and truly taught me the value of a collegial relationship.

Although Stanley Milgram did not live to see this book published, he brought a realism and vision to this work. Stanley Milgram understood the strengths and limitations of social psychology and human beings, and had the wonderful ability to elicit the most out of both his students and science. As a teacher-exemplar I cherished his guidance, altruistic nature, and the positive reinforcement I received from him.

I was fortunate to befriend Charles Kadushin at the Graduate Center and have benefited greatly from his facility and astuteness in quantitative analysis and in working with large data sets. He gave me the assurance I needed to identify the appropriate methodology for systematically analyzing my interviews. Most important, he gave me the courage to start this awesome task, to keep at it when other activities interfered, and to know when to stop. Charles Kadushin's ability to interpret detailed findings was most helpful in my own final interpretation of the findings. I will forever be indebted to him for helping me overcome my initial fears of computers.

Several times my path has crossed with that of Robert Jay Lifton. With my research on rescuers, Bob helped me appreciate the nuances of the narrative form and the value of the clinical interview which ultimately gave the work a more holistic form. Bob Lifton, a master at communicating ideas, helped me find a voice with which to express my perceptions and interpretations.

Rabbi Harold M. Schulweis's pioneering efforts in combining intellectual curiosity about good and evil and a pragmatic approach in assisting rescuers in their waning years have informed my work and given it new dimensions. Rabbi Schulweis's leadership in *hakarat hatov* (recognition of goodness) as a personal Jewish responsibility and a way to perpetuate goodness inspired me to work with him to set up the Foundation to Sustain Righteous Christians, which was later renamed the Jewish Foundation for Christian Rescuers, and given financial support and administrative assistance by the Anti-Defamation League at the urging of its national director, Abraham H. Foxman. I would like to thank the many people who have devoted themselves to the growth and development of this organization: E. Robert Goodkind, the indefatigable chairman for four years, and his devoted board members Harvey Schulweis (current chairman), Henry Ostberg, John Ruskay, Robert Goldman, Frank Morgens, Harvey Sarner, Roman Kent, Fanya Heller, Hadassa Rosensaft, Elaine Merians, Melvin Merians, Linda Bronfman, David Bellin, Melvin Salberg, Jack Salzberg, Jane Silverman, Cynthia Ozick, Leon Wieseltier, Morris Offit, Patricia Laskawy, Jeremy Mack, Judith Stern Peck, among others; tireless staff and volunteers Stanlee Stahl, Diana Stein, Ella Tracewicz, Dennis Klein, David Szonyi, Suzie Kaufman, Dick Adler, and Kathy Janowitz. Warmest gratitude to John Ruskay for sharing his administrative skills with me to start and maintain the foundation. Special thanks go to Abe Foxman and Charney Bromberg of the ADL for making it possible for me to continue this important project. I was pleased to be involved in the genesis of the photography-of-rescuers exhibition of Gay Block, which is now traveling worldwide.

This book would not have been possible without the initial financial support of the John Slawson Fund of the American Jewish Committee. I was subsequently fortunate to receive fellowships from the Memorial Foundation for Jewish Culture and the Rosenthal Institute for Holocaust Studies, CUNY. Warmest thanks to Jerry Hochbaum and Randolph Braham for their support throughout the years. Many thanks to Pamela Ween Bromberg, William Frost and the trustees of the Lucius N. Littauer Foundation, and Viola Bernard of the Tappanz Foundation for their grants. I would like to express appreciation to the University Seminars at Columbia University for assistance in the preparation of the manuscript for publication. The ideas presented also benefited from discussions in the University Seminar on Moral Education.

Thanks are also due to friends and family who contributed to this project: Judith and Milton Kestenberg of Child Development Research, Jeremy and Judith Mack of the Jeremy and Judith Mack Philanthropic Fund, Dr. Herman Pineas, Stanley Vine, Isaac Jesin, William Grossman, and Dorothy and Jay Fagelman.

This work required numerous volunteers to translate books, articles, correspondence, and, most important, interviews. For their arduous efforts in this regard I thank: Judith Kestenberg, Milton Kestenberg, Frank Morgens, Maria Morgens, Ella Tracewicz, Herman Pineas, Genia Malecki, Bella Tiberg, Jeremy Mack, Renee Lee, Nusia Shimrat, Dorothy Wallace, Andrea Fiano, Peter Jacobs, Pamela Oline, Kathy Janowitz, Leor Arian, Eva Rosenfeld, Valerie Lewis Wiener, Elizabeth Fuerst, Viola Wdowinsky, Ingrid Tauber, Aviva Kempner, Gila Fogelman, and interviewers of the Altruistic Personality Study.

For the arduous task of transcribing the interviews and support I thank Child Development Research, Beatrice Mosberg, and Barbara Jordan. Special thanks to Barbara Jordan for her continued support. Annette Insdorf and Aviva Kempner enriched the growing film bibliography.

This book benefited tremendously from Rachel Koenig as a second coder for the interviews and in assisting me in reinterviewing rescuers in order to increase the reliability of the data and fill gaps in missing data. But what I most cherished was Rachel's enthusiasm for the work and our stimulating discussions as we came to a similar image about each rescuer. I appreciate the many hours Kathleen Kelly and Harriet Arnone spent discussing hypotheses, methodology, and individual cases and helped me set realistic goals. For initially assisting me in transforming my academic language into a prose that is accessible to the general reader I would like to acknowledge the writer Bonnie Gordon.

This book benefited from many archival records at the Institut de Juive, Leo Baeck, the YIVO Institute for Jewish Research, the Wiener Library, but most important the Department of the Righteous at Yad Vashem. Special thanks to Mordecai Paldiel, Judge Moshe Bejski, Mina Yanco, Shalmi Barmor, and Yitzhak Maiz, who made my many trips to Yad Vashem inspiring and filled me with renewed enthusiasm and interesting ideas.

When I asked Charlotte Sheedy to be my agent I knew I picked the right person because of her immediate enthusiasm for the work. I can't thank her enough for being there during difficult moments. Much appreciation is due to Ellen Geiger for assisting Charlotte with this project.

Mary Bralove deserves recognition for her efforts in turning my words into prose and in providing a readable flow. But it was Harriet Arnone, my dear friend, who knew how to make order out of chaos, and Jerome Chanes, my beloved husband, who knows the English language as does no one else I know. I appreciate all the basketball games he had to miss in order to explore ideas with me and help edit this work, and to be my genuine fan.

This manuscript has benefited from friends who volunteered to read different drafts along the way and discuss theoretical points. For this I am especially grateful to Menachem Rosensaft for his historical knowledge, Otto Klineberg, John Darley, Harriet Arnone, Leo Goldberger, David Rosenhan, Ervin Staub, Helen Dermatis, Pamela Oline, Marion Pritchard, and Michael Schulman for their social-psychological expertise, and for writing style to Bill Novack, Nessa Rapoport, Helen Epstein, Daniel V. Allentuck, Kenneth Jacobson, Kathy Janowitz, and Sivan Baron.

Special thanks go to Sallye Leventhal, my first editor at Doubleday, who gave me consistent support, good sense about proceeding with each chapter, and proficient editing. Arabella Meyer skillfully took over as my editor and saw the book to a successful completion, with Martha Levin overseeing the production.

This book is dedicated to my loving parents, Simcha and Leah Fogelman. Despite everything they endured and lost, I profited immeasurably from their transmitting a sense of continuity and hope.

INDEX

ABOUT THE AUTHOR

EVA FOGELMAN, Ph.D., is a psychotherapist, social psychologist, and filmmaker. She is a founding director of the Jewish Foundation for Christian Rescuers (a project of the ADL), and is the codirector of psychotherapy with generations of the Holocaust and related traumas at the Training Institute for Mental Health. She is also a senior research fellow at the Center for Social Research at the Graduate Center of the City University of New York. Fogelman was a writer and co-producer of the PBS series *Breaking the Silence: The Generation After the Holocaust* (1984). She lives in New York City.